CIVIL WAR

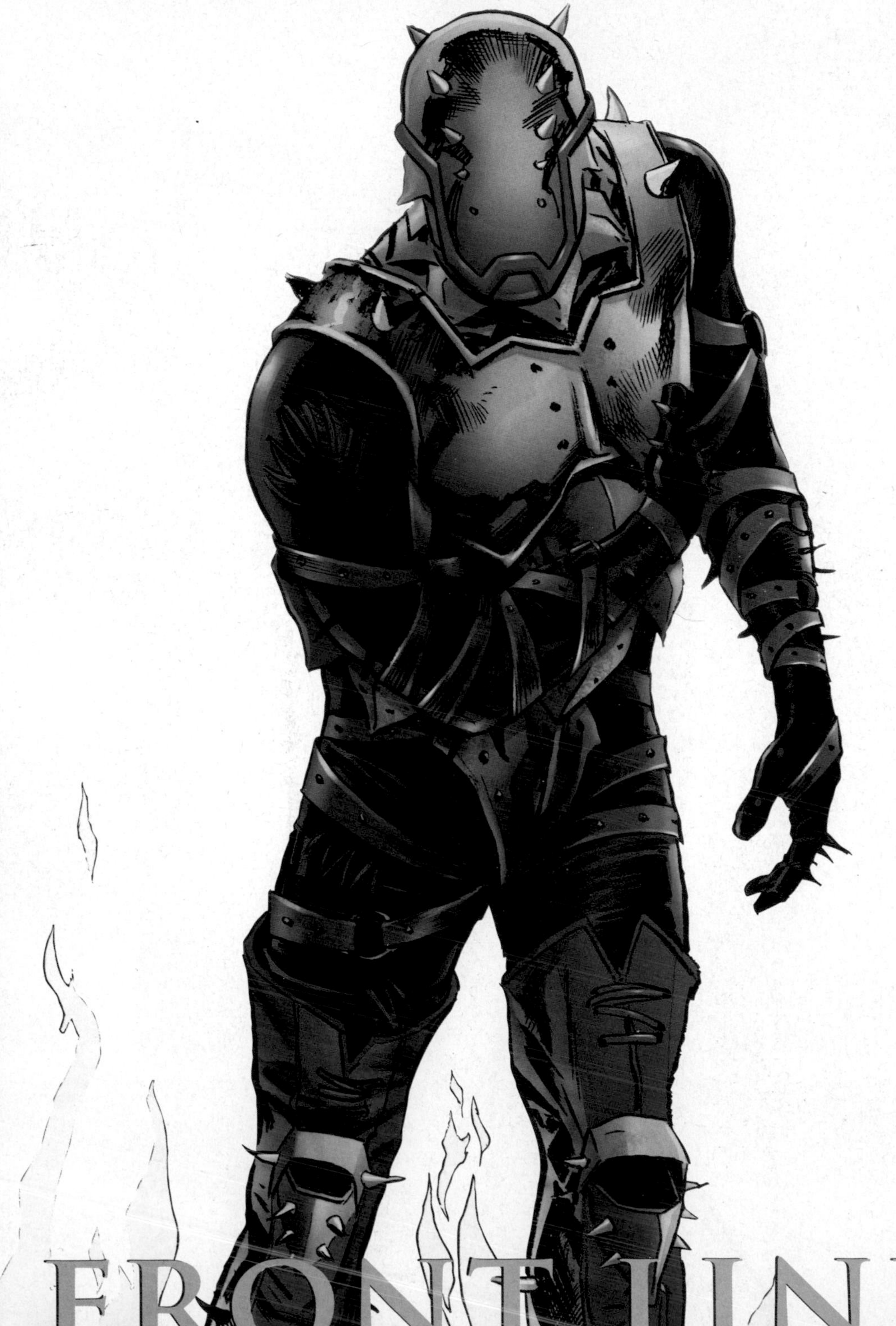

FRONT LINE

A

MARVEL COMICS

PRESENTATION

CIVIL

WRITER
PAUL JENKINS

"EMBEDDED"
PENCILER
RAMON BACHS

INKER
JOHN LUCAS

COLORIST
LAURA MARTIN
WITH LARRY MOLINAR (ISSUE #11)

"THE ACCUSED"
ARTIST
STEVE LIEBER

COLORIST
JUNE CHUNG

"WAR
CORRESPONDENCE"
ARTISTS
EDUARDO BARRETO,
FRAZER IRVING &
RAMON BACHS AND
JOHN LUCAS

COLOR ART
SOTOCOLOR'S A. CROSSLEY,
FRAZER IRVING & STUDIO F

"SLEEPER CELL"
PENCILER
LEE WEEKS

INKERS
LEE WEEKS & NELSON

COLORIST
SOTOCOLOR'S J. BROWN

LETTERER
VIRTUAL CALLIGRAPHY'S
RANDY GENTILE
WITH JOE CARAMAGNA

COVER ART
JOHN WATSON

ASSISTANT EDITORS
MOLLY LAZER &
AUBREY SITTERSON

EDITOR
TOM BREVOORT

COLLECTION EDITOR
JENNIFER GRÜNWALD

ASSISTANT EDITORS
MICHAEL SHORT &
CORY LEVINE

ASSOCIATE EDITOR
MARK D. BEAZLEY

SENIOR EDITOR,
SPECIAL PROJECTS
JEFF YOUNGQUIST

SENIOR VICE PRESIDENT
OF SALES
DAVID GABRIEL

PRODUCTION
JERRY KALINOWSKI

BOOK DESIGNER
DAYLE CHESLER

VICE PRESIDENT OF CREATIVE
TOM MARVELLI

EDITOR IN CHIEF
JOE QUESADA

PUBLISHER
DAN BUCKLEY

WAR
FRONT LINE

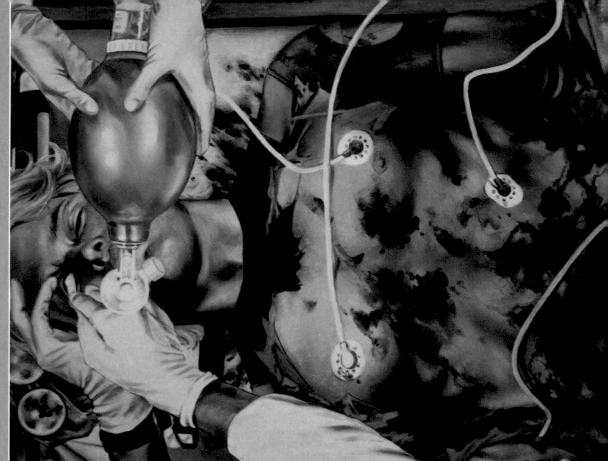

FRONT LINE
A MARVEL COMICS EVENT

CIVIL
WAR

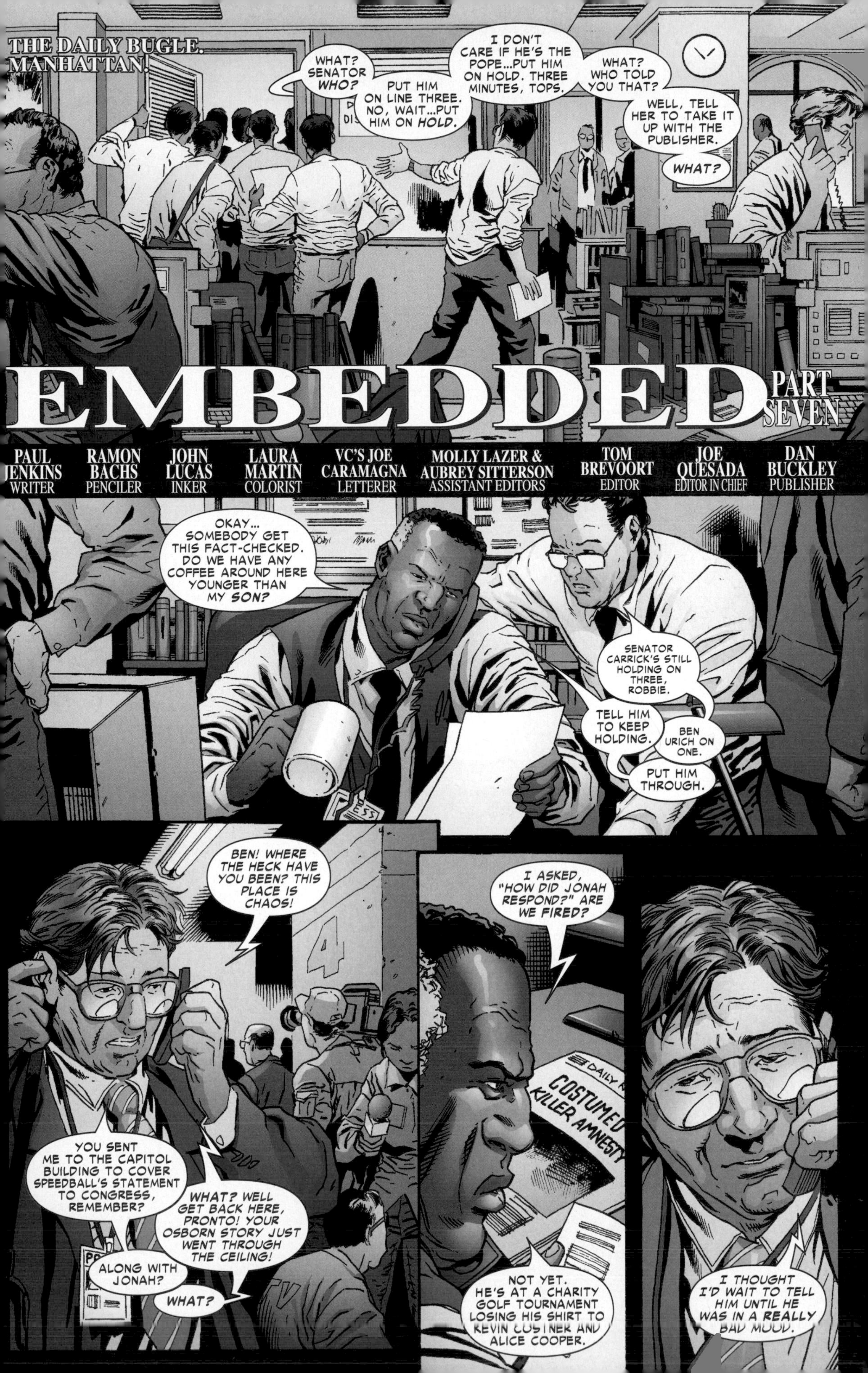
THE DAILY BUGLE. MANHATTAN!
WHAT? SENATOR WHO?
PUT HIM ON LINE THREE. NO, WAIT...PUT HIM ON HOLD.
I DON'T CARE IF HE'S THE POPE...PUT HIM ON HOLD. THREE MINUTES, TOPS.
WHAT? WHO TOLD YOU THAT?
WELL, TELL HER TO TAKE IT UP WITH THE PUBLISHER.
WHAT?
EMBEDDED PART SEVEN
PAUL JENKINS WRITER
RAMON BACHS PENCILER
JOHN LUCAS INKER
LAURA MARTIN COLORIST
VC'S JOE CARAMAGNA LETTERER
MOLLY LAZER & AUBREY SITTERSON ASSISTANT EDITORS
TOM BREVOORT EDITOR
JOE QUESADA EDITOR IN CHIEF
DAN BUCKLEY PUBLISHER
OKAY... SOMEBODY GET THIS FACT-CHECKED. DO WE HAVE ANY COFFEE AROUND HERE YOUNGER THAN MY SON?
SENATOR CARRICK'S STILL HOLDING ON THREE, ROBBIE.
TELL HIM TO KEEP HOLDING.
BEN URICH ON ONE.
PUT HIM THROUGH.
BEN! WHERE THE HECK HAVE YOU BEEN? THIS PLACE IS CHAOS!
YOU SENT ME TO THE CAPITOL BUILDING TO COVER SPEEDBALL'S STATEMENT TO CONGRESS, REMEMBER?
WHAT? WELL GET BACK HERE, PRONTO! YOUR OSBORN STORY JUST WENT THROUGH THE CEILING!
ALONG WITH JONAH?
WHAT?
I ASKED, "HOW DID JONAH RESPOND?" ARE WE FIRED?
COSTUMED KILLER AMNESTY
NOT YET. HE'S AT A CHARITY GOLF TOURNAMENT LOSING HIS SHIRT TO KEVIN COSTNER AND ALICE COOPER.
I THOUGHT I'D WAIT TO TELL HIM UNTIL HE WAS IN A REALLY BAD MOOD.

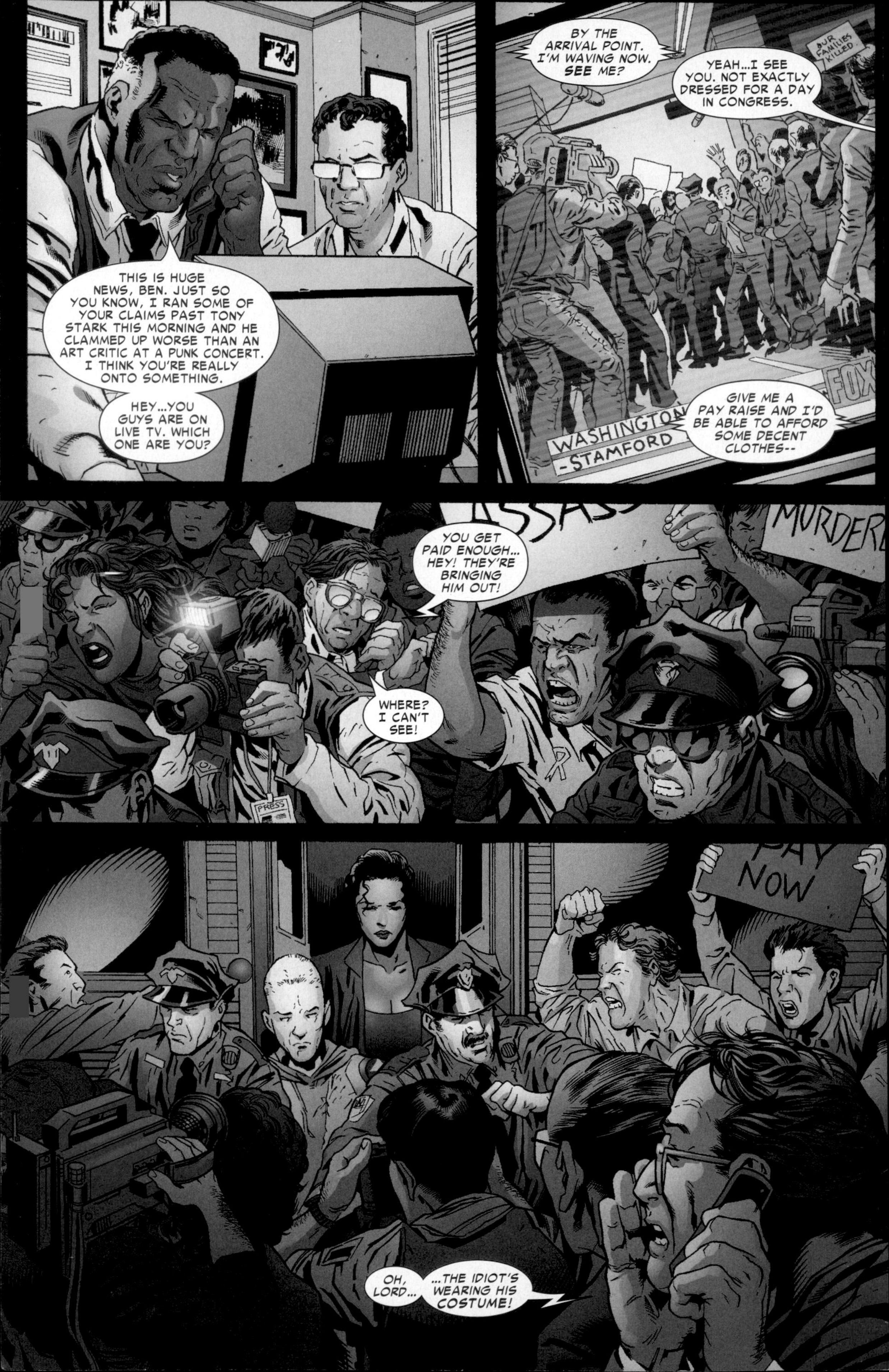
THIS IS HUGE NEWS, BEN. JUST SO YOU KNOW, I RAN SOME OF YOUR CLAIMS PAST TONY STARK THIS MORNING AND HE CLAMMED UP WORSE THAN AN ART CRITIC AT A PUNK CONCERT. I THINK YOU'RE REALLY ONTO SOMETHING.
HEY...YOU GUYS ARE ON LIVE TV. WHICH ONE ARE YOU?
BY THE ARRIVAL POINT. I'M WAVING NOW. SEE ME?
YEAH...I SEE YOU. NOT EXACTLY DRESSED FOR A DAY IN CONGRESS.
OUR FAMILIES KILLED
FOX
WASHINGTON
-STAMFORD
GIVE ME A PAY RAISE AND I'D BE ABLE TO AFFORD SOME DECENT CLOTHES--
YOU GET PAID ENOUGH... HEY! THEY'RE BRINGING HIM OUT!
WHERE? I CAN'T SEE!
PRESS
NOW
OH, LORD...
...THE IDIOT'S WEARING HIS COSTUME!

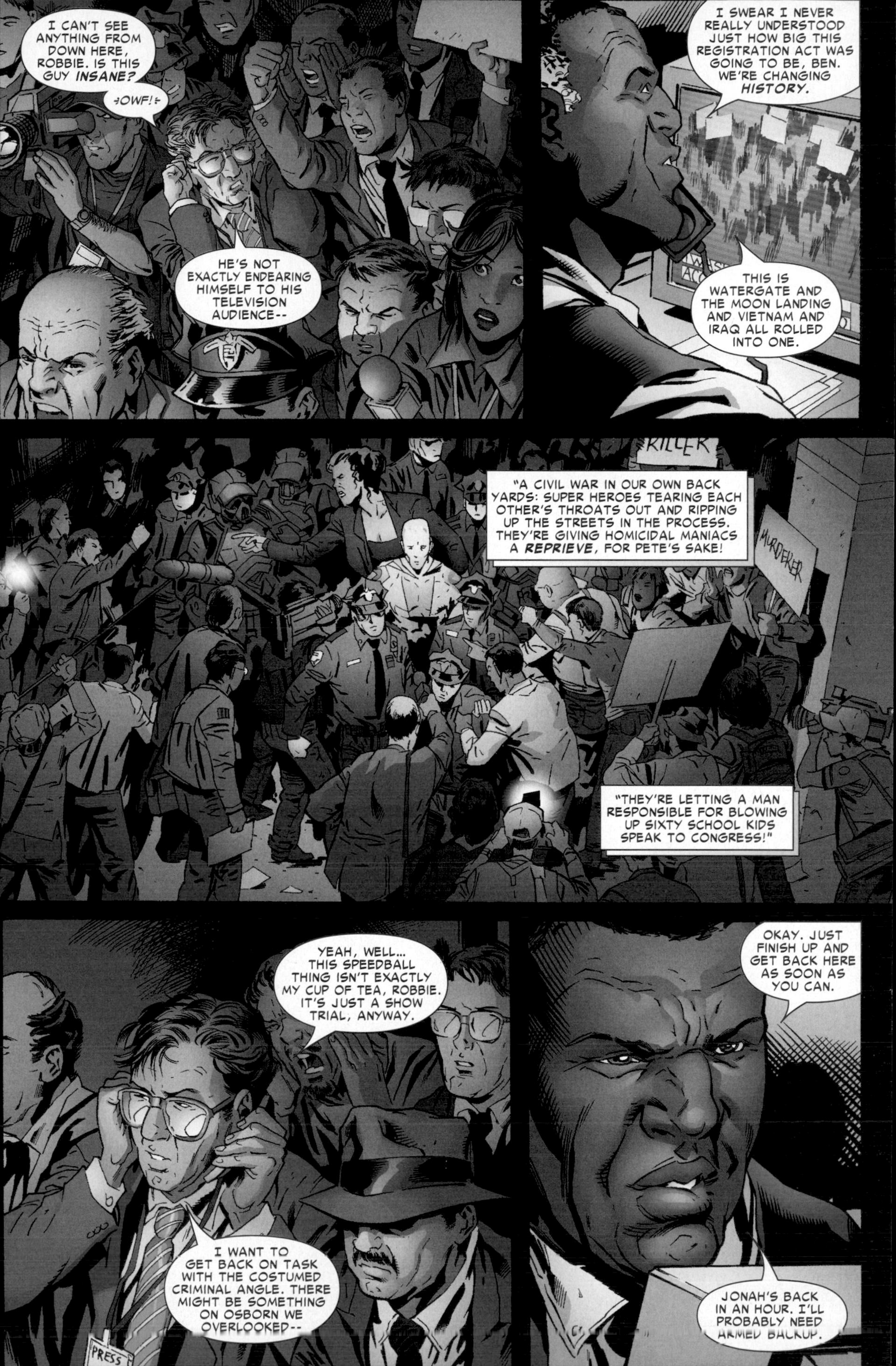

I CAN'T SEE ANYTHING FROM DOWN HERE, ROBBIE. IS THIS GUY *INSANE?*
OWF!
HE'S NOT EXACTLY ENDEARING HIMSELF TO HIS TELEVISION AUDIENCE--
I SWEAR I NEVER REALLY UNDERSTOOD JUST HOW BIG THIS REGISTRATION ACT WAS GOING TO BE, BEN. WE'RE CHANGING *HISTORY.*
THIS IS WATERGATE AND THE MOON LANDING AND VIETNAM AND IRAQ ALL ROLLED INTO ONE.
KILLER
"A CIVIL WAR IN OUR OWN BACK YARDS: SUPER HEROES TEARING EACH OTHER'S THROATS OUT AND RIPPING UP THE STREETS IN THE PROCESS. THEY'RE GIVING HOMICIDAL MANIACS A *REPRIEVE*, FOR PETE'S SAKE!
MURDERER
"THEY'RE LETTING A MAN RESPONSIBLE FOR BLOWING UP SIXTY SCHOOL KIDS SPEAK TO CONGRESS!"
YEAH, WELL... THIS SPEEDBALL THING ISN'T EXACTLY MY CUP OF TEA, ROBBIE. IT'S JUST A SHOW TRIAL, ANYWAY.
I WANT TO GET BACK ON TASK WITH THE COSTUMED CRIMINAL ANGLE. THERE MIGHT BE SOMETHING ON OSBORN WE OVERLOOKED--
PRESS
OKAY. JUST FINISH UP AND GET BACK HERE AS SOON AS YOU CAN.
JONAH'S BACK IN AN HOUR. I'LL PROBABLY NEED ARMED BACKUP.

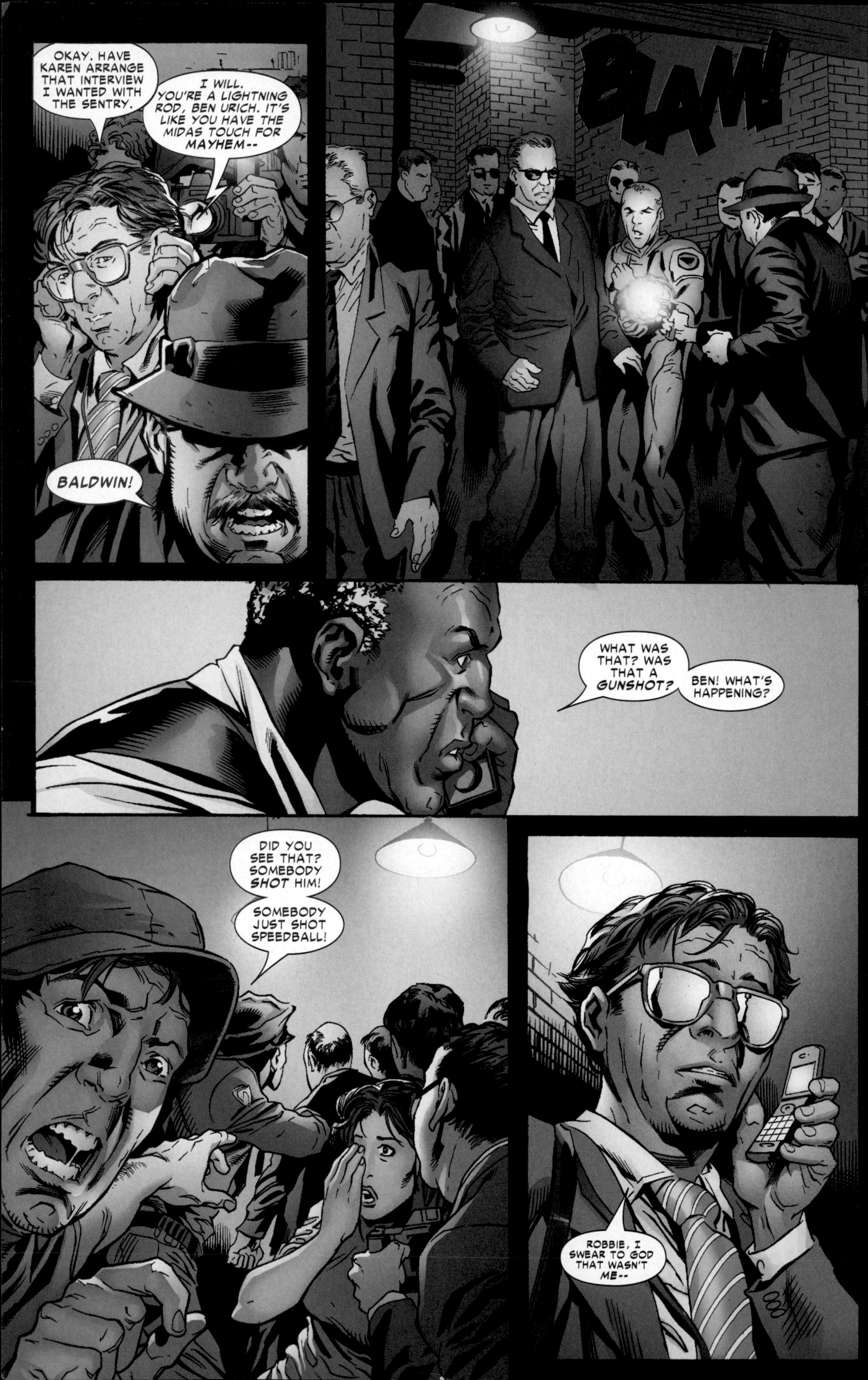

OKAY. HAVE KAREN ARRANGE THAT INTERVIEW I WANTED WITH THE SENTRY.
I WILL. YOU'RE A LIGHTNING ROD, BEN URICH. IT'S LIKE YOU HAVE THE MIDAS TOUCH FOR MAYHEM--
BALDWIN!
BLAM!
WHAT WAS THAT? WAS THAT A GUNSHOT?
BEN! WHAT'S HAPPENING?
DID YOU SEE THAT? SOMEBODY SHOT HIM!
SOMEBODY JUST SHOT SPEEDBALL!
ROBBIE, I SWEAR TO GOD THAT WASN'T ME--

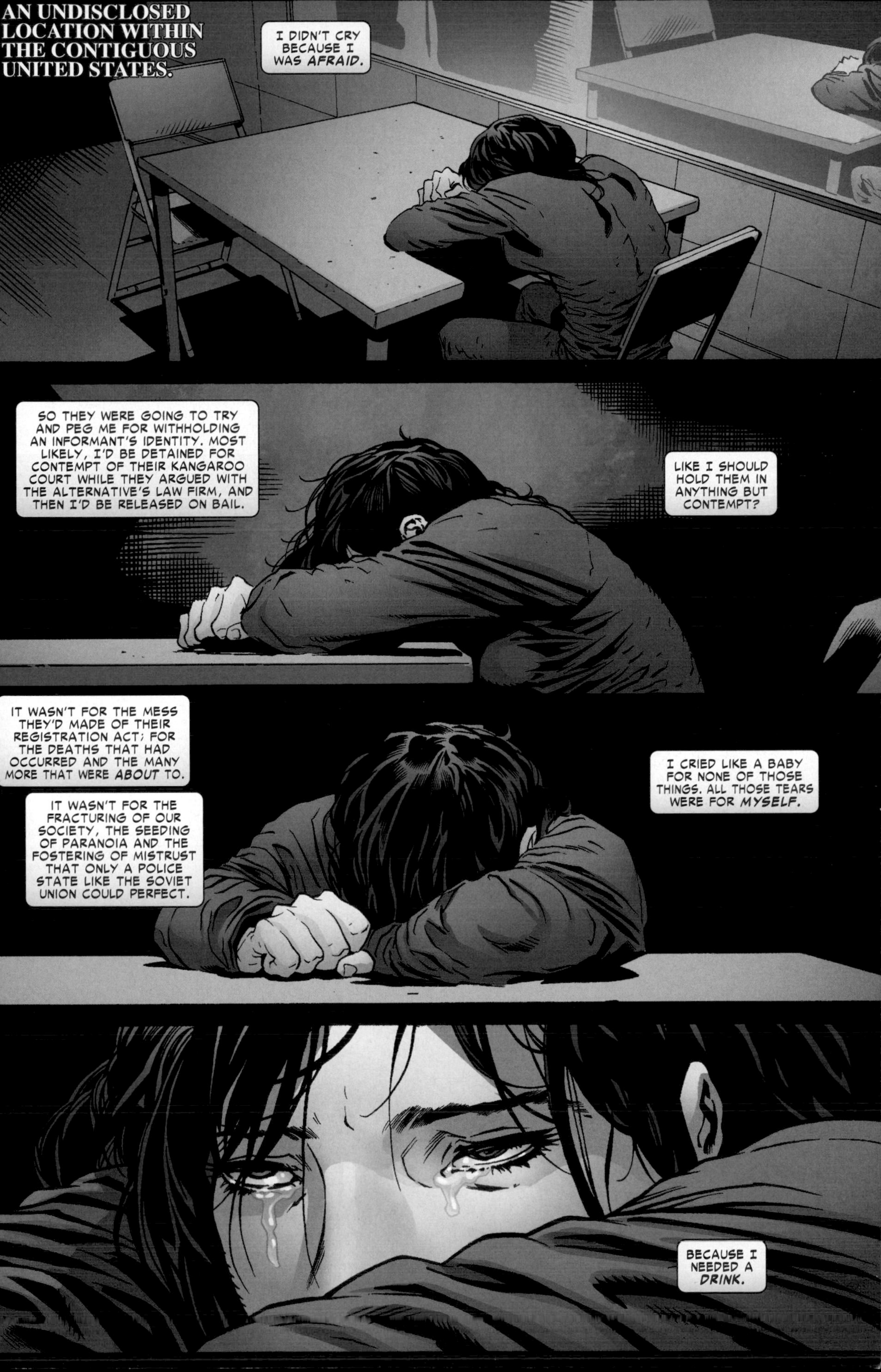
AN UNDISCLOSED LOCATION WITHIN THE CONTIGUOUS UNITED STATES.
I DIDN'T CRY BECAUSE I WAS AFRAID.
SO THEY WERE GOING TO TRY AND PEG ME FOR WITHHOLDING AN INFORMANT'S IDENTITY. MOST LIKELY, I'D BE DETAINED FOR CONTEMPT OF THEIR KANGAROO COURT WHILE THEY ARGUED WITH THE ALTERNATIVE'S LAW FIRM, AND THEN I'D BE RELEASED ON BAIL.
LIKE I SHOULD HOLD THEM IN ANYTHING BUT CONTEMPT?
IT WASN'T FOR THE MESS THEY'D MADE OF THEIR REGISTRATION ACT; FOR THE DEATHS THAT HAD OCCURRED AND THE MANY MORE THAT WERE ABOUT TO.
IT WASN'T FOR THE FRACTURING OF OUR SOCIETY, THE SEEDING OF PARANOIA AND THE FOSTERING OF MISTRUST THAT ONLY A POLICE STATE LIKE THE SOVIET UNION COULD PERFECT.
I CRIED LIKE A BABY FOR NONE OF THOSE THINGS. ALL THOSE TEARS WERE FOR MYSELF.
BECAUSE I NEEDED A DRINK.

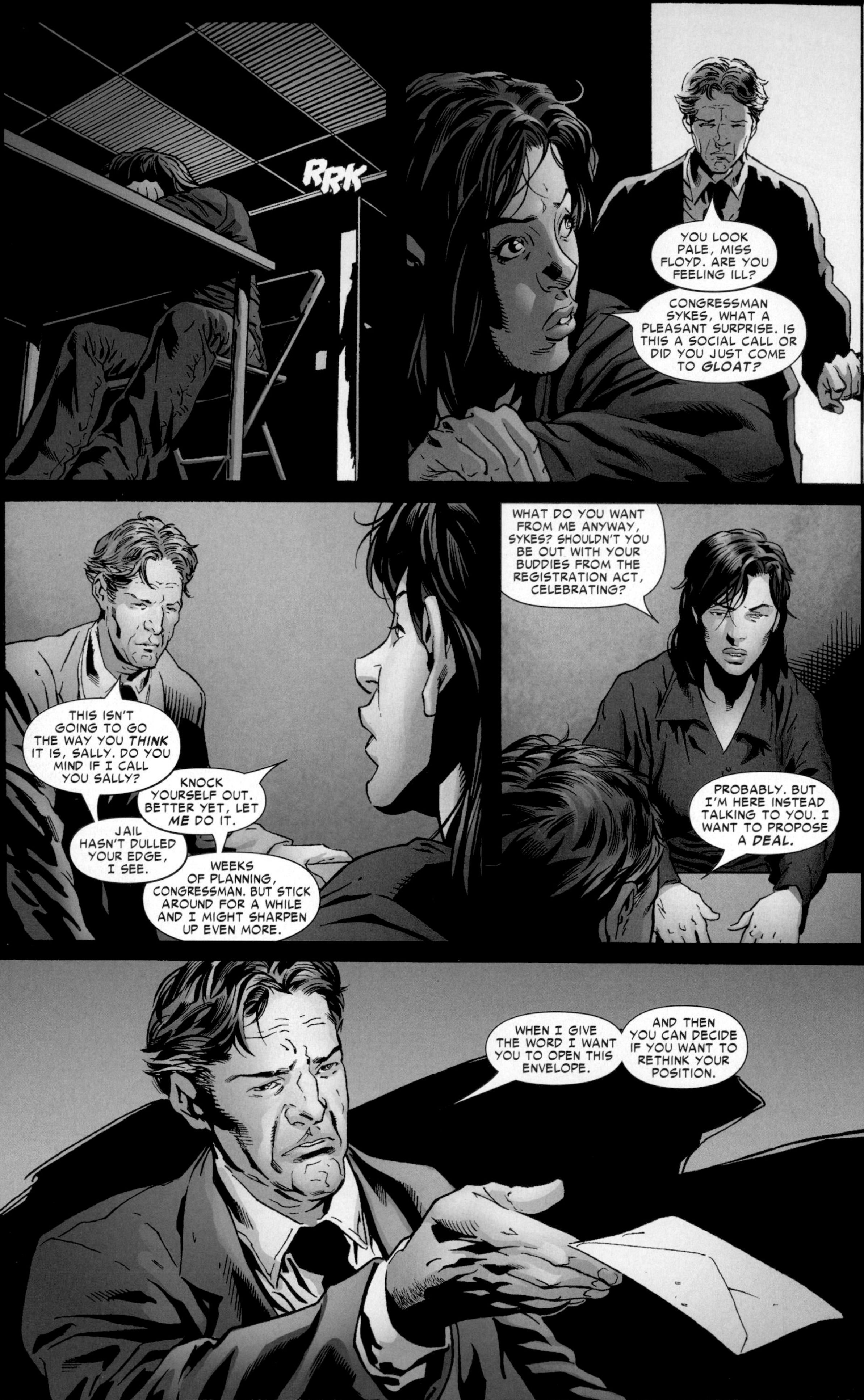
RRK
YOU LOOK PALE, MISS FLOYD. ARE YOU FEELING ILL?
CONGRESSMAN SYKES, WHAT A PLEASANT SURPRISE. IS THIS A SOCIAL CALL OR DID YOU JUST COME TO GLOAT?
THIS ISN'T GOING TO GO THE WAY YOU THINK IT IS, SALLY. DO YOU MIND IF I CALL YOU SALLY?
KNOCK YOURSELF OUT. BETTER YET, LET ME DO IT.
JAIL HASN'T DULLED YOUR EDGE, I SEE.
WEEKS OF PLANNING, CONGRESSMAN. BUT STICK AROUND FOR A WHILE AND I MIGHT SHARPEN UP EVEN MORE.
WHAT DO YOU WANT FROM ME ANYWAY, SYKES? SHOULDN'T YOU BE OUT WITH YOUR BUDDIES FROM THE REGISTRATION ACT, CELEBRATING?
PROBABLY. BUT I'M HERE INSTEAD TALKING TO YOU. I WANT TO PROPOSE A DEAL.
WHEN I GIVE THE WORD I WANT YOU TO OPEN THIS ENVELOPE.
AND THEN YOU CAN DECIDE IF YOU WANT TO RETHINK YOUR POSITION.

WHAT'S INSIDE?

JUST SOMETHING TO PROVE A *POINT*. THE DEAL INVOLVES YOU GIVING ME FIVE MINUTES OF YOUR TIME.

LIKE I HAVE A CHOICE?

YOU ALWAYS HAVE A CHOICE. TAKE TEN MINUTES. I'M GENEROUS LIKE THAT.

LIKE I SAID, THIS IS NOT GOING TO GO THE WAY YOU *EXPECT*. AS MUCH AS YOU CLAIM TO DESPISE ALL I STAND FOR, YOU'D BE SURPRISED WHAT YOU DON'T KNOW ABOUT ME.

WHOOP-DE-DOO. ENLIGHTEN THE CLASS, WHY DON'T YOU?

I AM A PATRIOT, WHETHER YOU LIKE IT OR NOT. LIKE YOU, I CARE ABOUT GETTING THINGS RIGHT.

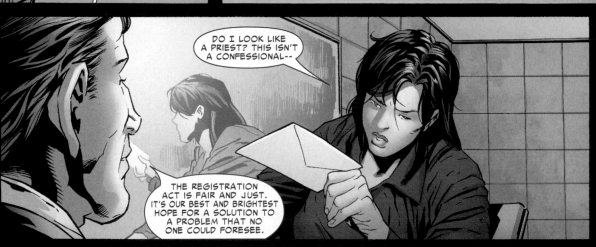

DO I LOOK LIKE A PRIEST? THIS ISN'T A CONFESSIONAL--

THE REGISTRATION ACT IS FAIR AND JUST. IT'S OUR BEST AND BRIGHTEST HOPE FOR A SOLUTION TO A PROBLEM THAT NO ONE COULD FORESEE.

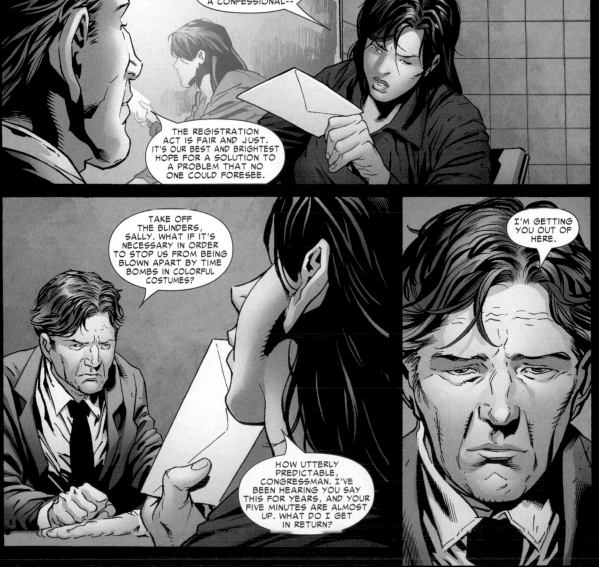

TAKE OFF THE BLINDERS, SALLY. WHAT IF IT'S NECESSARY IN ORDER TO STOP US FROM BEING BLOWN APART BY TIME BOMBS IN COLORFUL COSTUMES?

HOW UTTERLY PREDICTABLE, CONGRESSMAN. I'VE BEEN HEARING YOU SAY THIS FOR YEARS, AND YOUR FIVE MINUTES ARE ALMOST UP. WHAT DO I GET IN RETURN?

I'M GETTING YOU OUT OF HERE.

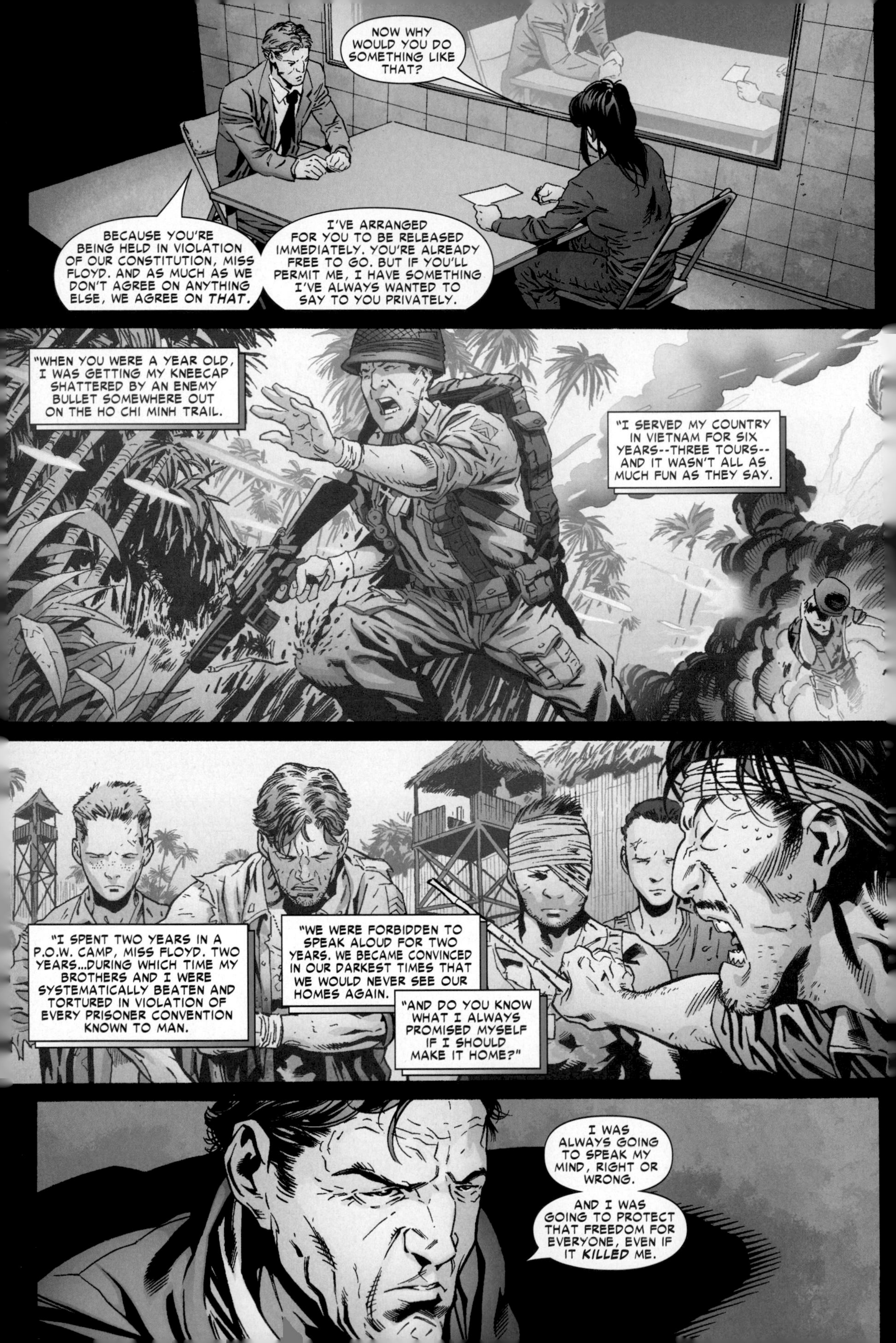
NOW WHY WOULD YOU DO SOMETHING LIKE THAT?
BECAUSE YOU'RE BEING HELD IN VIOLATION OF OUR CONSTITUTION, MISS FLOYD. AND AS MUCH AS WE DON'T AGREE ON ANYTHING ELSE, WE AGREE ON *THAT*.
I'VE ARRANGED FOR YOU TO BE RELEASED IMMEDIATELY. YOU'RE ALREADY FREE TO GO. BUT IF YOU'LL PERMIT ME, I HAVE SOMETHING I'VE ALWAYS WANTED TO SAY TO YOU PRIVATELY.
"WHEN YOU WERE A YEAR OLD, I WAS GETTING MY KNEECAP SHATTERED BY AN ENEMY BULLET SOMEWHERE OUT ON THE HO CHI MINH TRAIL.
"I SERVED MY COUNTRY IN VIETNAM FOR SIX YEARS--THREE TOURS--AND IT WASN'T ALL AS MUCH FUN AS THEY SAY.
"I SPENT TWO YEARS IN A P.O.W. CAMP, MISS FLOYD. TWO YEARS...DURING WHICH TIME MY BROTHERS AND I WERE SYSTEMATICALLY BEATEN AND TORTURED IN VIOLATION OF EVERY PRISONER CONVENTION KNOWN TO MAN.
"WE WERE FORBIDDEN TO SPEAK ALOUD FOR TWO YEARS. WE BECAME CONVINCED IN OUR DARKEST TIMES THAT WE WOULD NEVER SEE OUR HOMES AGAIN.
"AND DO YOU KNOW WHAT I ALWAYS PROMISED MYSELF IF I SHOULD MAKE IT HOME?"
I WAS ALWAYS GOING TO SPEAK MY MIND, RIGHT OR WRONG.
AND I WAS GOING TO PROTECT THAT FREEDOM FOR EVERYONE, EVEN IF IT *KILLED* ME.

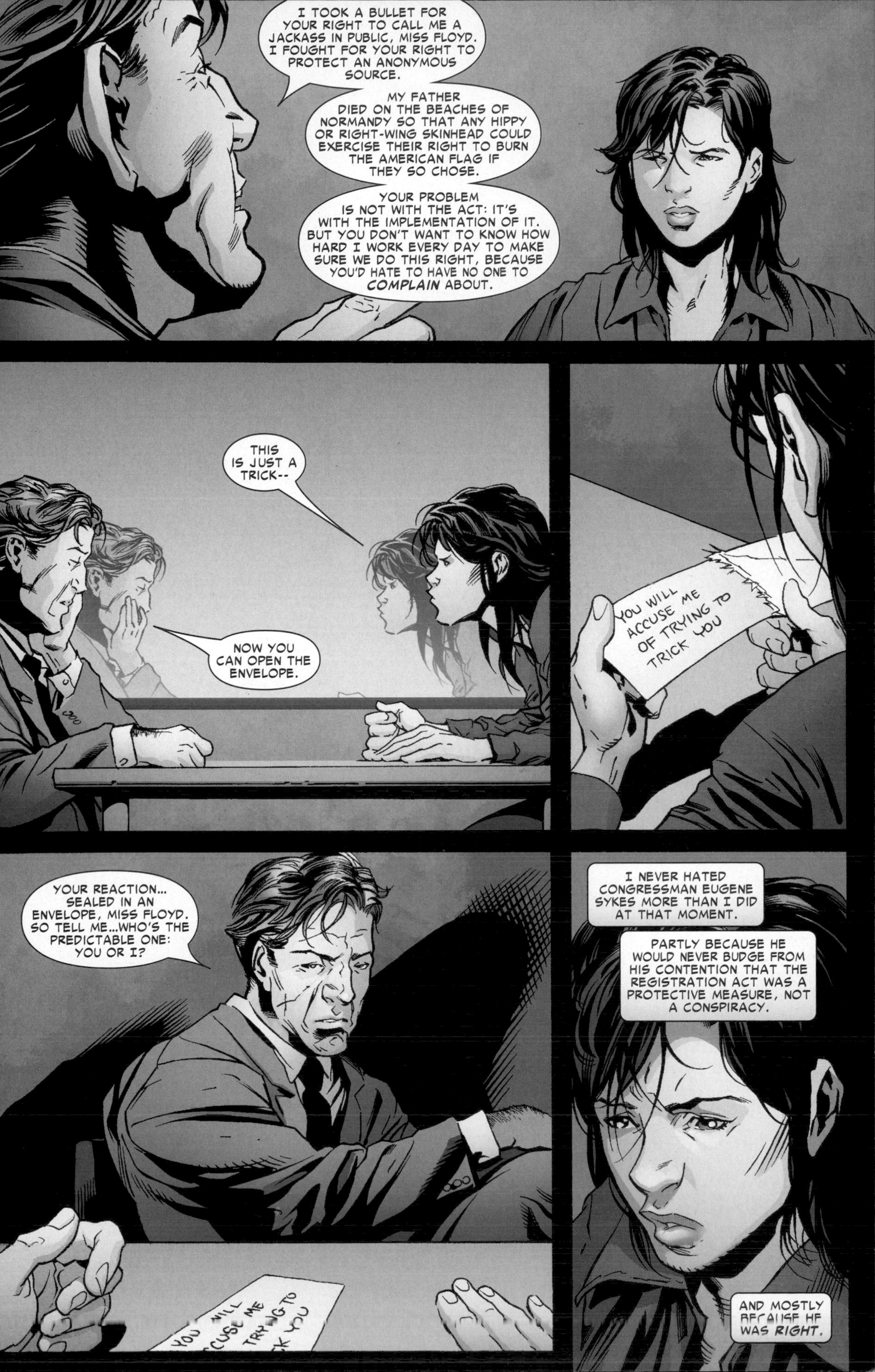
I TOOK A BULLET FOR YOUR RIGHT TO CALL ME A JACKASS IN PUBLIC, MISS FLOYD. I FOUGHT FOR YOUR RIGHT TO PROTECT AN ANONYMOUS SOURCE.
MY FATHER DIED ON THE BEACHES OF NORMANDY SO THAT ANY HIPPY OR RIGHT-WING SKINHEAD COULD EXERCISE THEIR RIGHT TO BURN THE AMERICAN FLAG IF THEY SO CHOSE.
YOUR PROBLEM IS NOT WITH THE ACT: IT'S WITH THE IMPLEMENTATION OF IT. BUT YOU DON'T WANT TO KNOW HOW HARD I WORK EVERY DAY TO MAKE SURE WE DO THIS RIGHT, BECAUSE YOU'D HATE TO HAVE NO ONE TO COMPLAIN ABOUT.
THIS IS JUST A TRICK--
NOW YOU CAN OPEN THE ENVELOPE.
YOU WILL ACCUSE ME OF TRYING TO TRICK YOU
YOUR REACTION... SEALED IN AN ENVELOPE, MISS FLOYD. SO TELL ME...WHO'S THE PREDICTABLE ONE: YOU OR I?
I NEVER HATED CONGRESSMAN EUGENE SYKES MORE THAN I DID AT THAT MOMENT.
PARTLY BECAUSE HE WOULD NEVER BUDGE FROM HIS CONTENTION THAT THE REGISTRATION ACT WAS A PROTECTIVE MEASURE, NOT A CONSPIRACY.
AND MOSTLY BECAUSE HE WAS RIGHT.

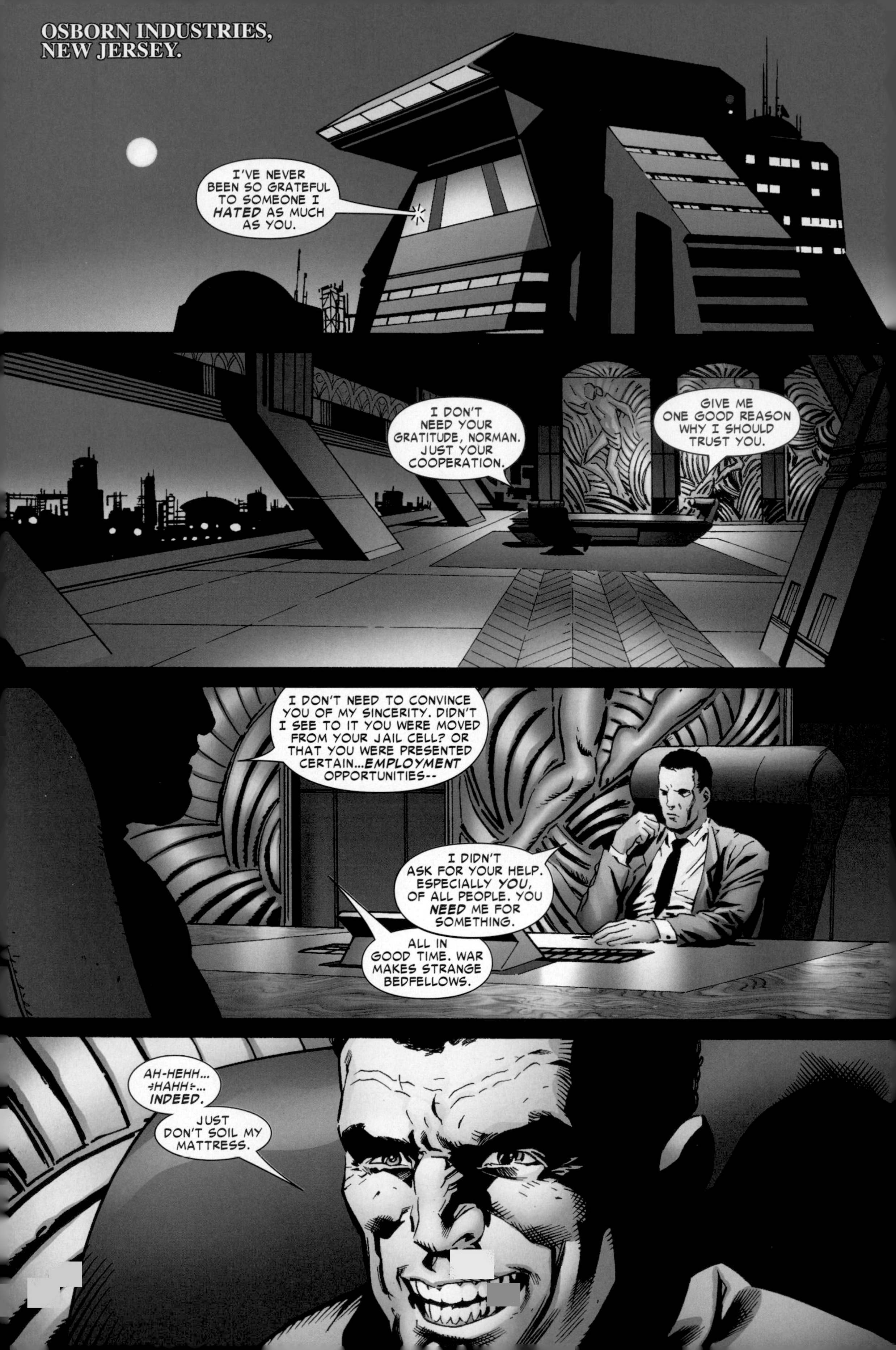
OSBORN INDUSTRIES, NEW JERSEY.
I'VE NEVER BEEN SO GRATEFUL TO SOMEONE I *HATED* AS MUCH AS YOU.
I DON'T NEED YOUR GRATITUDE, NORMAN. JUST YOUR COOPERATION.
GIVE ME ONE GOOD REASON WHY I SHOULD TRUST YOU.
I DON'T NEED TO CONVINCE YOU OF MY SINCERITY. DIDN'T I SEE TO IT YOU WERE MOVED FROM YOUR JAIL CELL? OR THAT YOU WERE PRESENTED CERTAIN...*EMPLOYMENT* OPPORTUNITIES--
I DIDN'T ASK FOR YOUR HELP. ESPECIALLY *YOU*, OF ALL PEOPLE. YOU *NEED* ME FOR SOMETHING.
ALL IN GOOD TIME. WAR MAKES STRANGE BEDFELLOWS.
AH-HEHH... ≑HAHH≑... *INDEED*.
JUST DON'T SOIL MY MATTRESS.

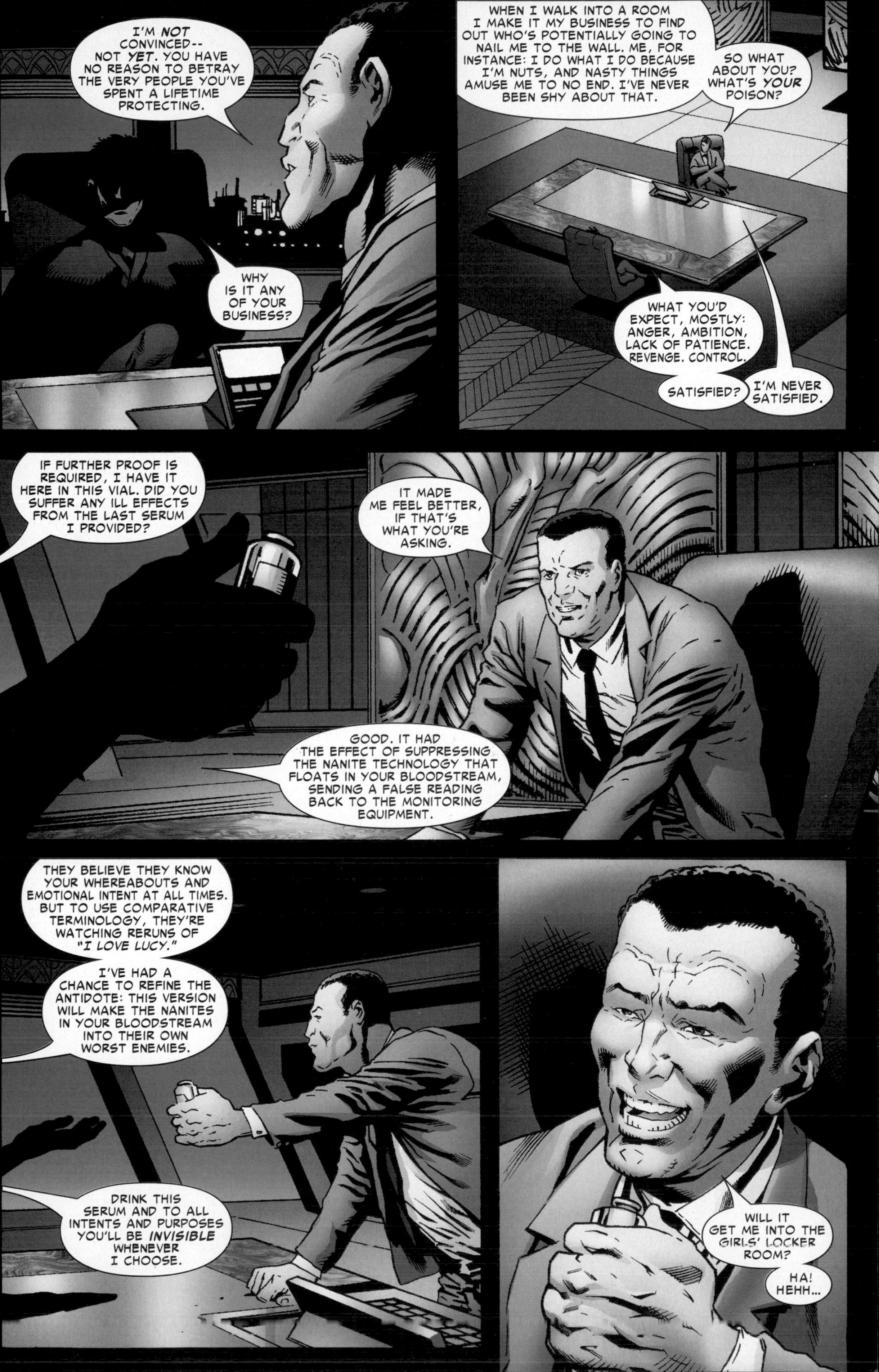
I'M NOT CONVINCED-- NOT YET. YOU HAVE NO REASON TO BETRAY THE VERY PEOPLE YOU'VE SPENT A LIFETIME PROTECTING.
WHY IS IT ANY OF YOUR BUSINESS?
WHEN I WALK INTO A ROOM I MAKE IT MY BUSINESS TO FIND OUT WHO'S POTENTIALLY GOING TO NAIL ME TO THE WALL. ME, FOR INSTANCE: I DO WHAT I DO BECAUSE I'M NUTS, AND NASTY THINGS AMUSE ME TO NO END. I'VE NEVER BEEN SHY ABOUT THAT.
SO WHAT ABOUT YOU? WHAT'S YOUR POISON?
WHAT YOU'D EXPECT, MOSTLY: ANGER, AMBITION, LACK OF PATIENCE. REVENGE. CONTROL.
SATISFIED?
I'M NEVER SATISFIED.
IF FURTHER PROOF IS REQUIRED, I HAVE IT HERE IN THIS VIAL. DID YOU SUFFER ANY ILL EFFECTS FROM THE LAST SERUM I PROVIDED?
IT MADE ME FEEL BETTER, IF THAT'S WHAT YOU'RE ASKING.
GOOD. IT HAD THE EFFECT OF SUPPRESSING THE NANITE TECHNOLOGY THAT FLOATS IN YOUR BLOODSTREAM, SENDING A FALSE READING BACK TO THE MONITORING EQUIPMENT.
THEY BELIEVE THEY KNOW YOUR WHEREABOUTS AND EMOTIONAL INTENT AT ALL TIMES. BUT TO USE COMPARATIVE TERMINOLOGY, THEY'RE WATCHING RERUNS OF "I LOVE LUCY."
I'VE HAD A CHANCE TO REFINE THE ANTIDOTE: THIS VERSION WILL MAKE THE NANITES IN YOUR BLOODSTREAM INTO THEIR OWN WORST ENEMIES.
DRINK THIS SERUM AND TO ALL INTENTS AND PURPOSES YOU'LL BE INVISIBLE WHENEVER I CHOOSE.
WILL IT GET ME INTO THE GIRLS' LOCKER ROOM?
HA! HEHH...

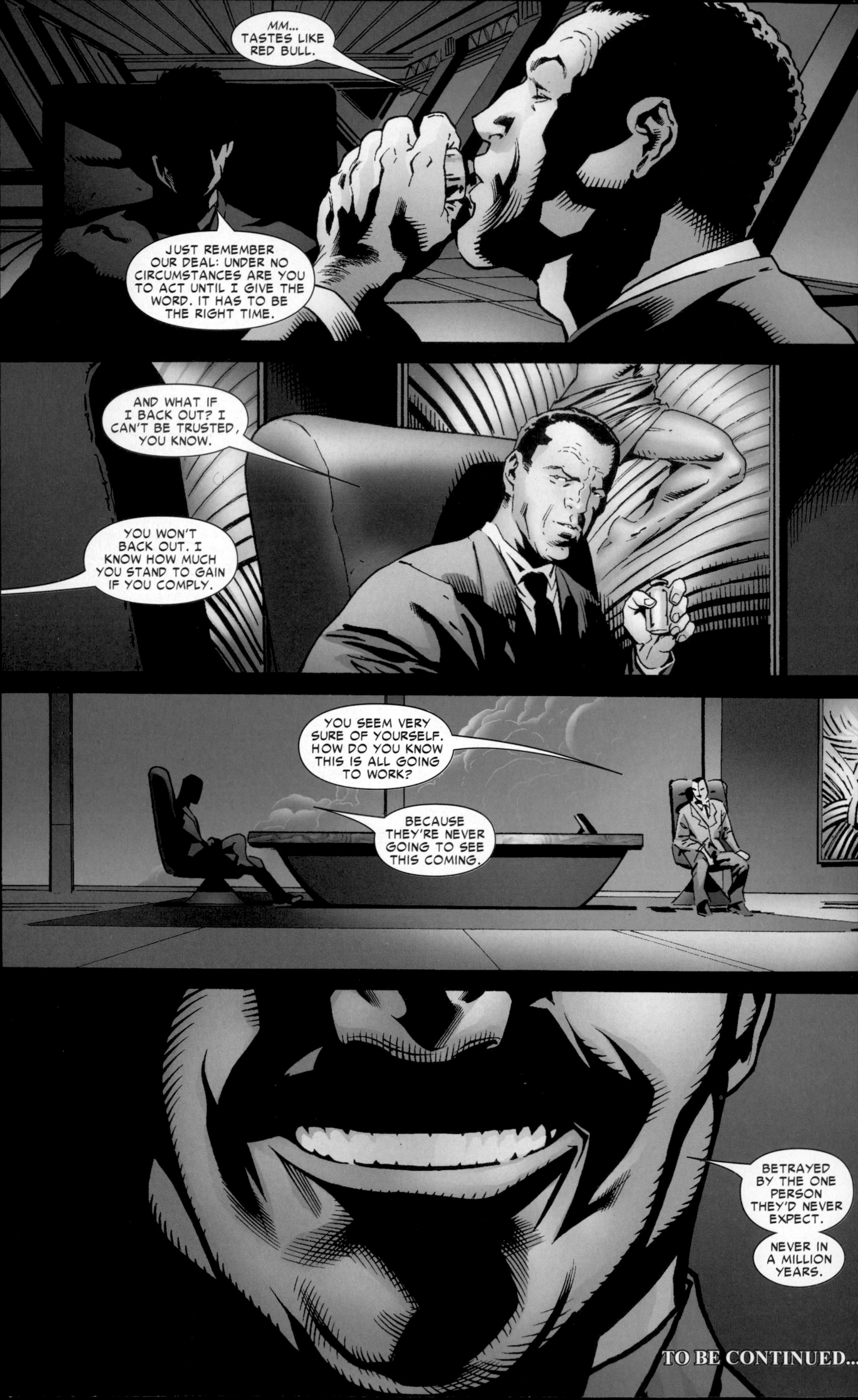
MM... TASTES LIKE RED BULL.
JUST REMEMBER OUR DEAL: UNDER NO CIRCUMSTANCES ARE YOU TO ACT UNTIL I GIVE THE WORD. IT HAS TO BE THE RIGHT TIME.
AND WHAT IF I BACK OUT? I CAN'T BE TRUSTED, YOU KNOW.
YOU WON'T BACK OUT. I KNOW HOW MUCH YOU STAND TO GAIN IF YOU COMPLY.
YOU SEEM VERY SURE OF YOURSELF. HOW DO YOU KNOW THIS IS ALL GOING TO WORK?
BECAUSE THEY'RE NEVER GOING TO SEE THIS COMING.
BETRAYED BY THE ONE PERSON THEY'D NEVER EXPECT.
NEVER IN A MILLION YEARS.
TO BE CONTINUED...

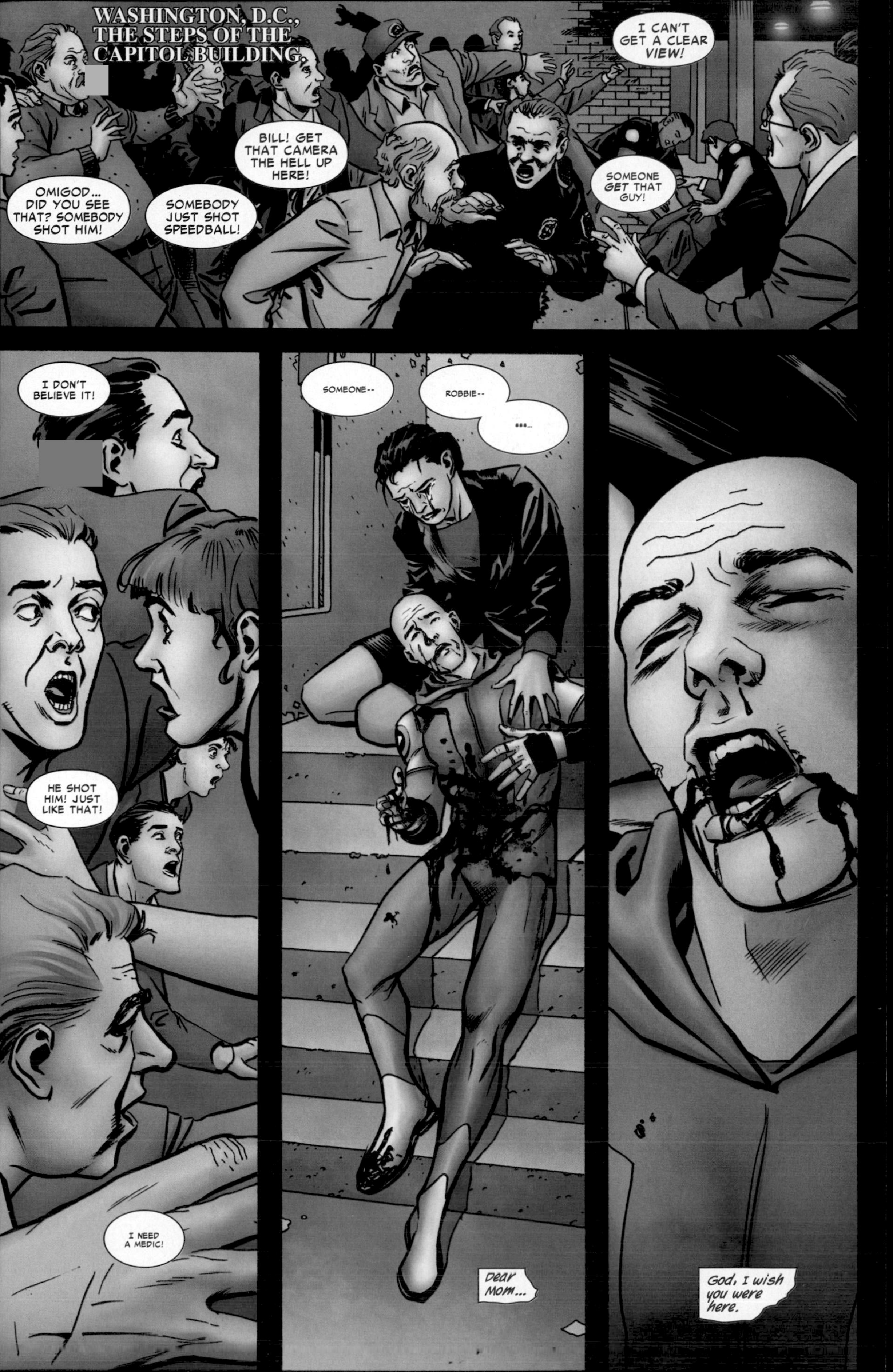
WASHINGTON, D.C., THE STEPS OF THE CAPITOL BUILDING.
OMIGOD... DID YOU SEE THAT? SOMEBODY SHOT HIM!
SOMEBODY JUST SHOT SPEEDBALL!
BILL! GET THAT CAMERA THE HELL UP HERE!
I CAN'T GET A CLEAR VIEW!
SOMEONE GET THAT GUY!
I DON'T BELIEVE IT!
HE SHOT HIM! JUST LIKE THAT!
I NEED A MEDIC!
SOMEONE--
ROBBIE--
Dear Mom...
God, I wish you were here.

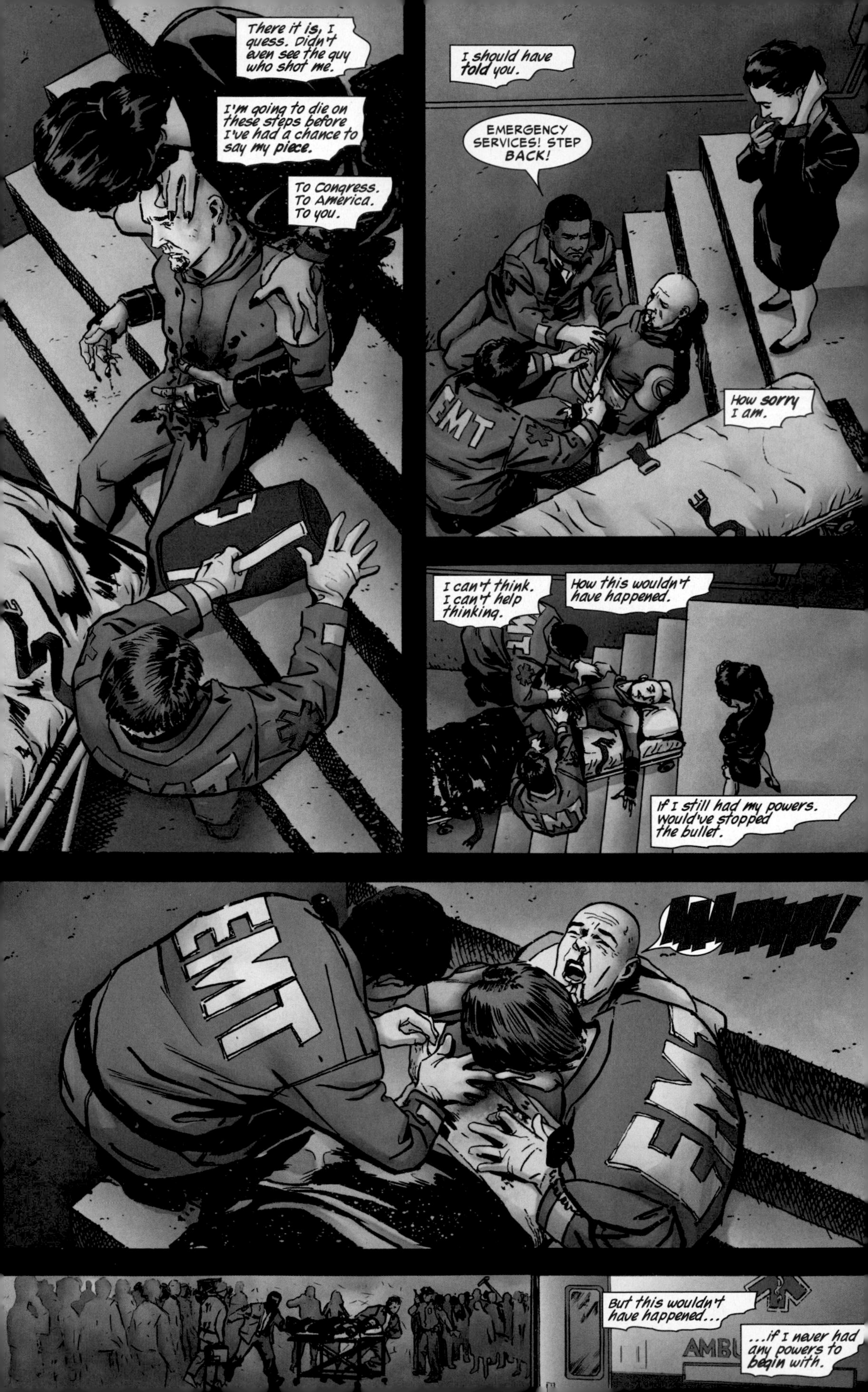
There it is, I guess. Didn't even see the guy who shot me.
I'm going to die on these steps before I've had a chance to say my piece.
To Congress. To America. To you.
I should have told you.
EMERGENCY SERVICES! STEP BACK!
EMT
How sorry I am.
I can't think. I can't help thinking.
How this wouldn't have happened.
If I still had my powers. Would've stopped the bullet.
EMT
HHAAHHH!
But this wouldn't have happened...
...if I never had any powers to begin with.

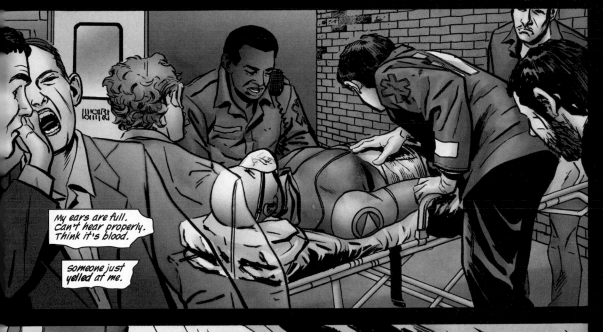

My ears are full. Can't hear properly. Think it's blood.

Someone just yelled at me.

I can't...

...think...

...is Rupert here?

I miss him.

He's licking my hand.

Loved that dog.

Remember how me an' him used to sit? Halfway up the stairs.

Waiting for Dad to come home.

We used to sit there a lot, Mom.

That was a lot of waiting.

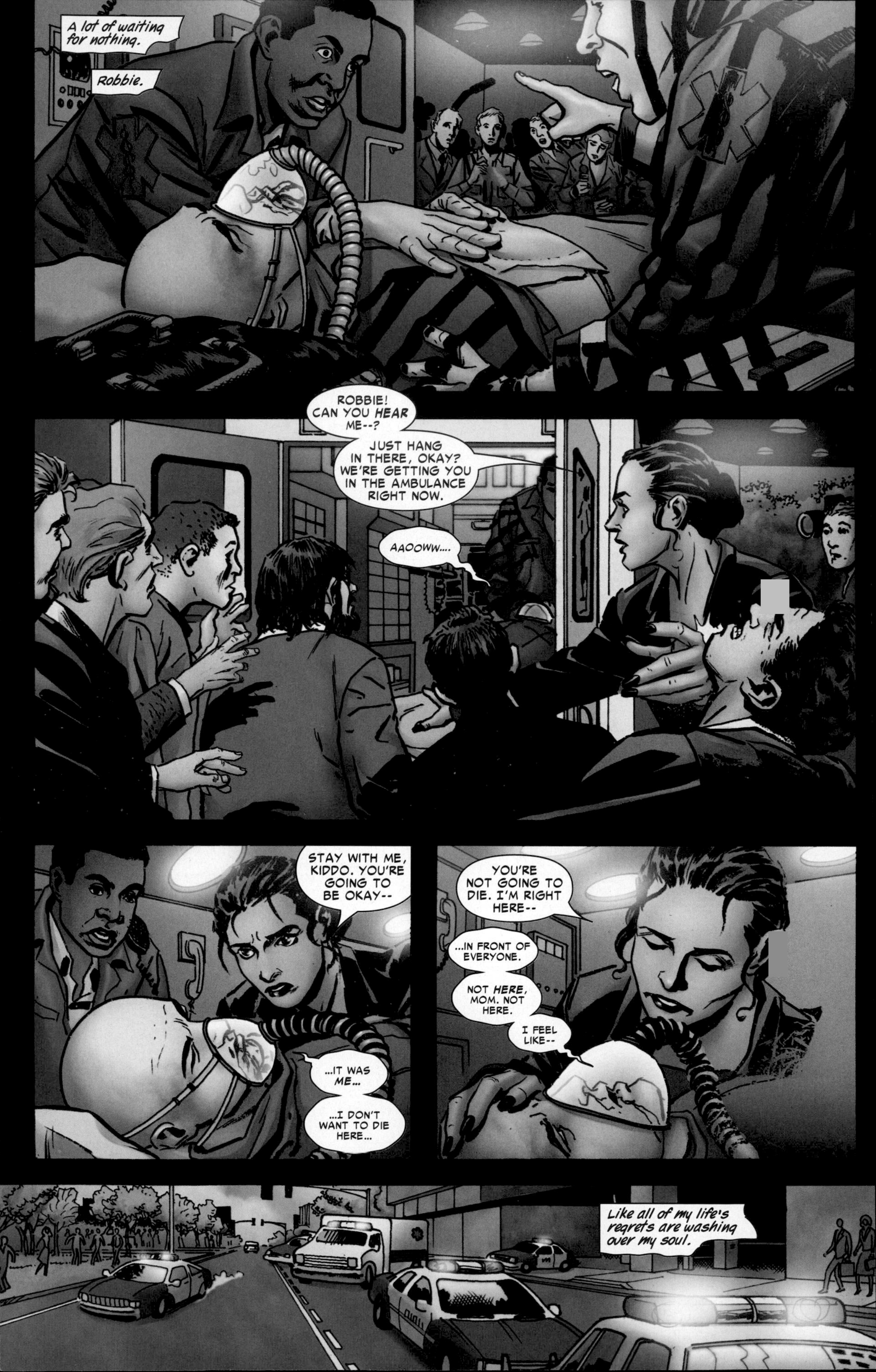
A lot of waiting for nothing.
Robbie.
ROBBIE! CAN YOU HEAR ME--?
JUST HANG IN THERE, OKAY? WE'RE GETTING YOU IN THE AMBULANCE RIGHT NOW.
AAOOWW....
STAY WITH ME, KIDDO. YOU'RE GOING TO BE OKAY--
...IT WAS ME...
...I DON'T WANT TO DIE HERE...
YOU'RE NOT GOING TO DIE. I'M RIGHT HERE--
...IN FRONT OF EVERYONE.
NOT HERE, MOM. NOT HERE.
I FEEL LIKE--
Like all of my life's regrets are washing over my soul.

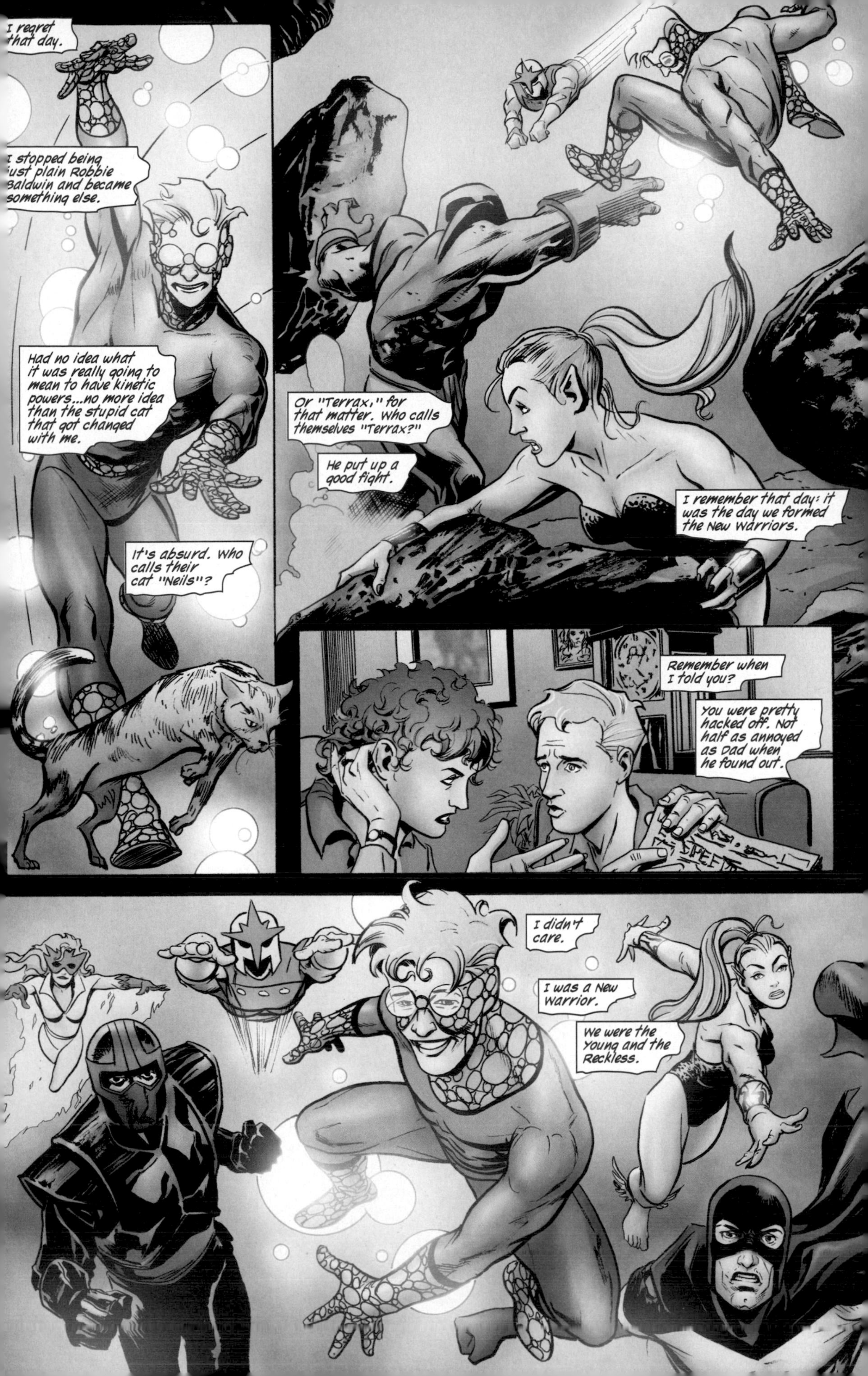

I regret that day.
I stopped being just plain Robbie Baldwin and became something else.
Had no idea what it was really going to mean to have kinetic powers...no more idea than the stupid cat that got changed with me.
It's absurd. Who calls their cat "Neils"?
Or "Terrax," for that matter. Who calls themselves "Terrax?"
He put up a good fight.
I remember that day: it was the day we formed the New Warriors.
Remember when I told you?
You were pretty hacked off. Not half as annoyed as Dad when he found out.
I didn't care.
I was a New Warrior.
We were the Young and the Reckless.

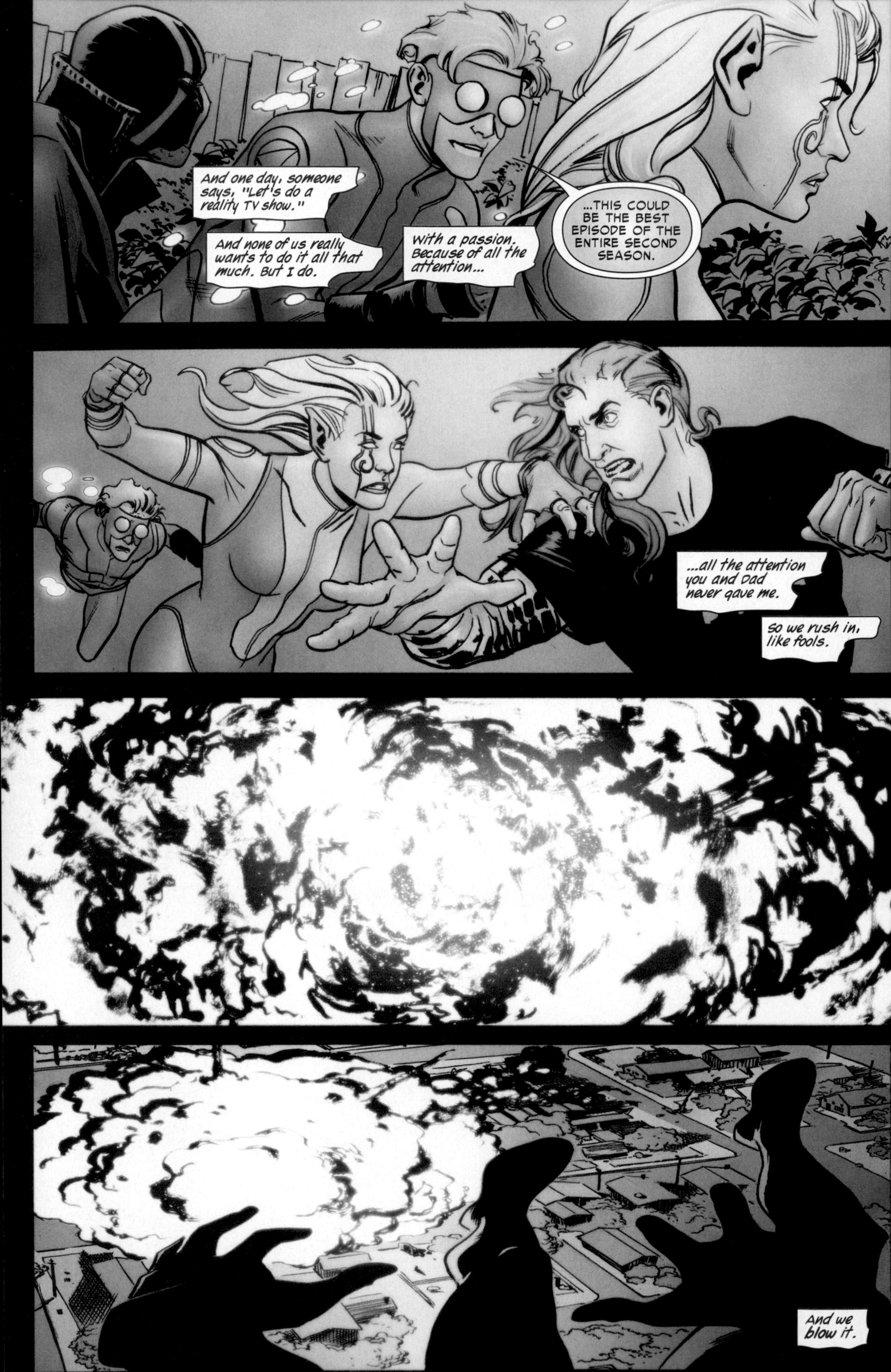

And one day, someone says, "Let's do a reality TV show."
And none of us really wants to do it all that much. But I do.
With a passion. Because of all the attention...
...THIS COULD BE THE BEST EPISODE OF THE ENTIRE SECOND SEASON.
...all the attention you and Dad never gave me.
So we rush in, like fools.
And we blow it.

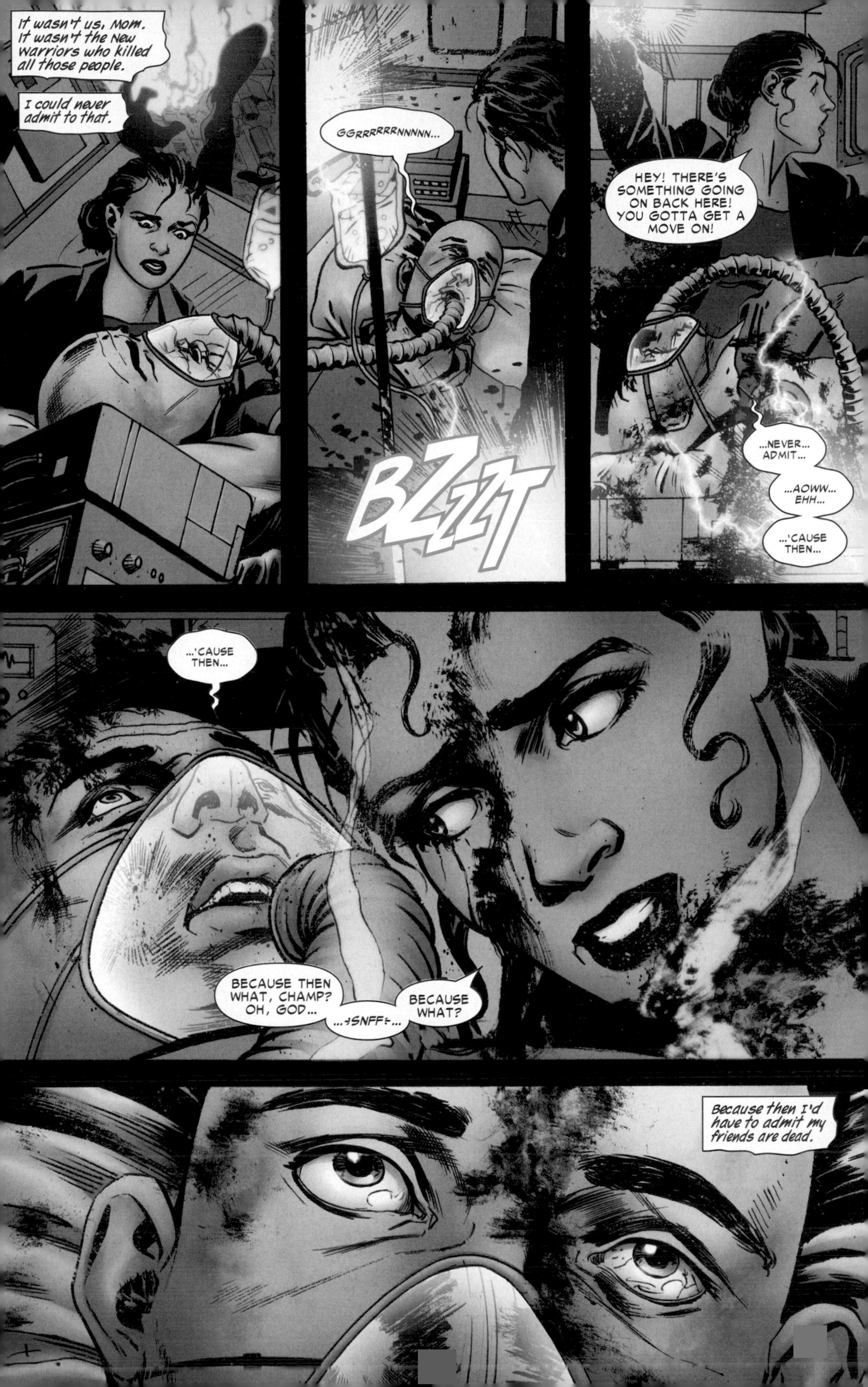
It wasn't us, Mom. It wasn't the New Warriors who killed all those people.
I could never admit to that.
GGRRRRRRNNNNN...
BZZZT
HEY! THERE'S SOMETHING GOING ON BACK HERE! YOU GOTTA GET A MOVE ON!
...NEVER... ADMIT...
...AOWW... EHH...
...'CAUSE THEN...
...'CAUSE THEN...
BECAUSE THEN WHAT, CHAMP? OH, GOD...
...SNFF...
BECAUSE WHAT?
Because then I'd have to admit my friends are dead.

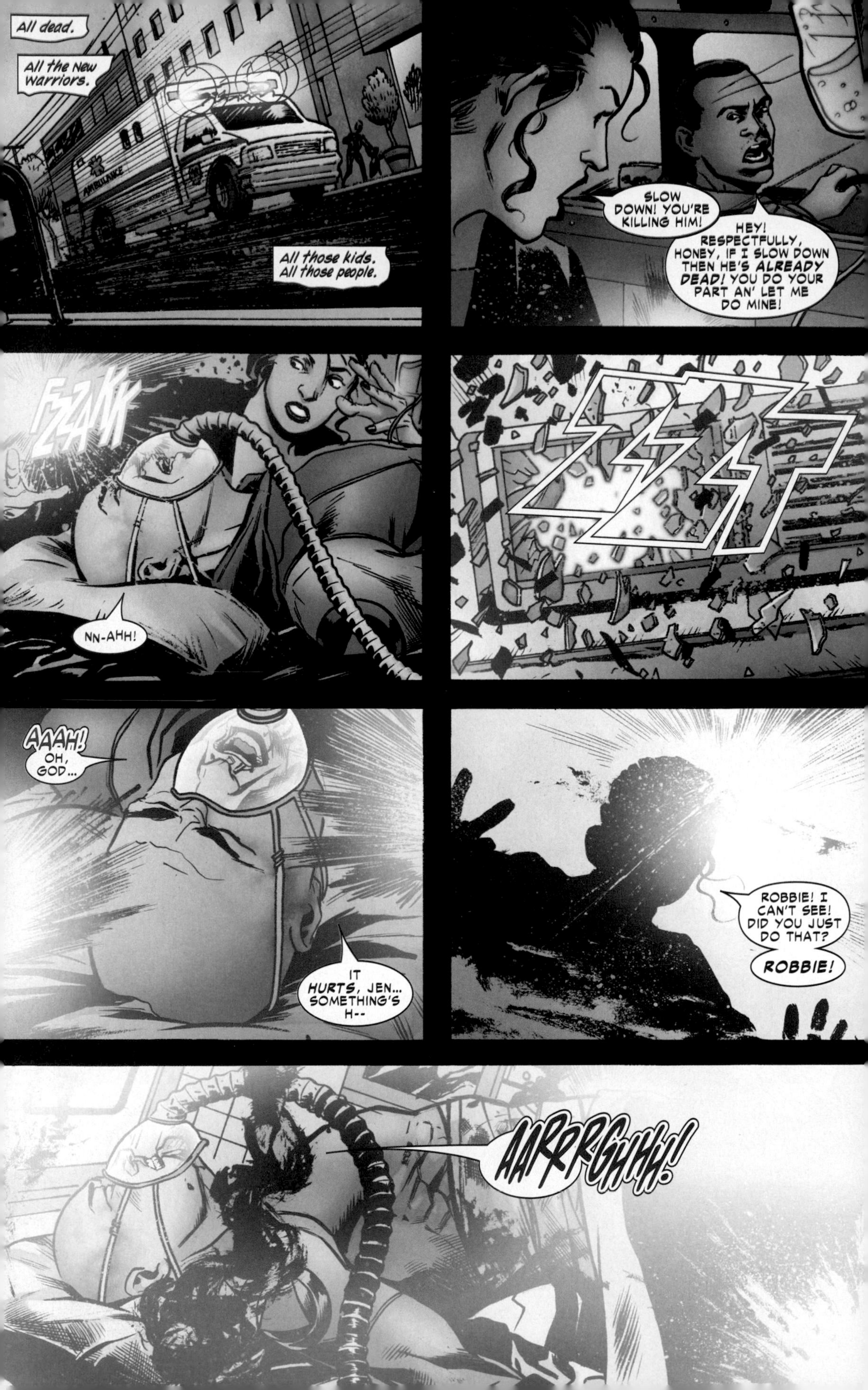
All dead.
All the New Warriors.
All those kids. All those people.
SLOW DOWN! YOU'RE KILLING HIM!
HEY! RESPECTFULLY, HONEY, IF I SLOW DOWN THEN HE'S *ALREADY DEAD!* YOU DO YOUR PART AN' LET ME DO MINE!
FZZAKK
NN-AHH!
AAAH! OH, GOD...
IT *HURTS*, JEN... SOMETHING'S H--
ROBBIE! I CAN'T SEE! DID YOU JUST DO THAT?
ROBBIE!
AARRRGHHH!

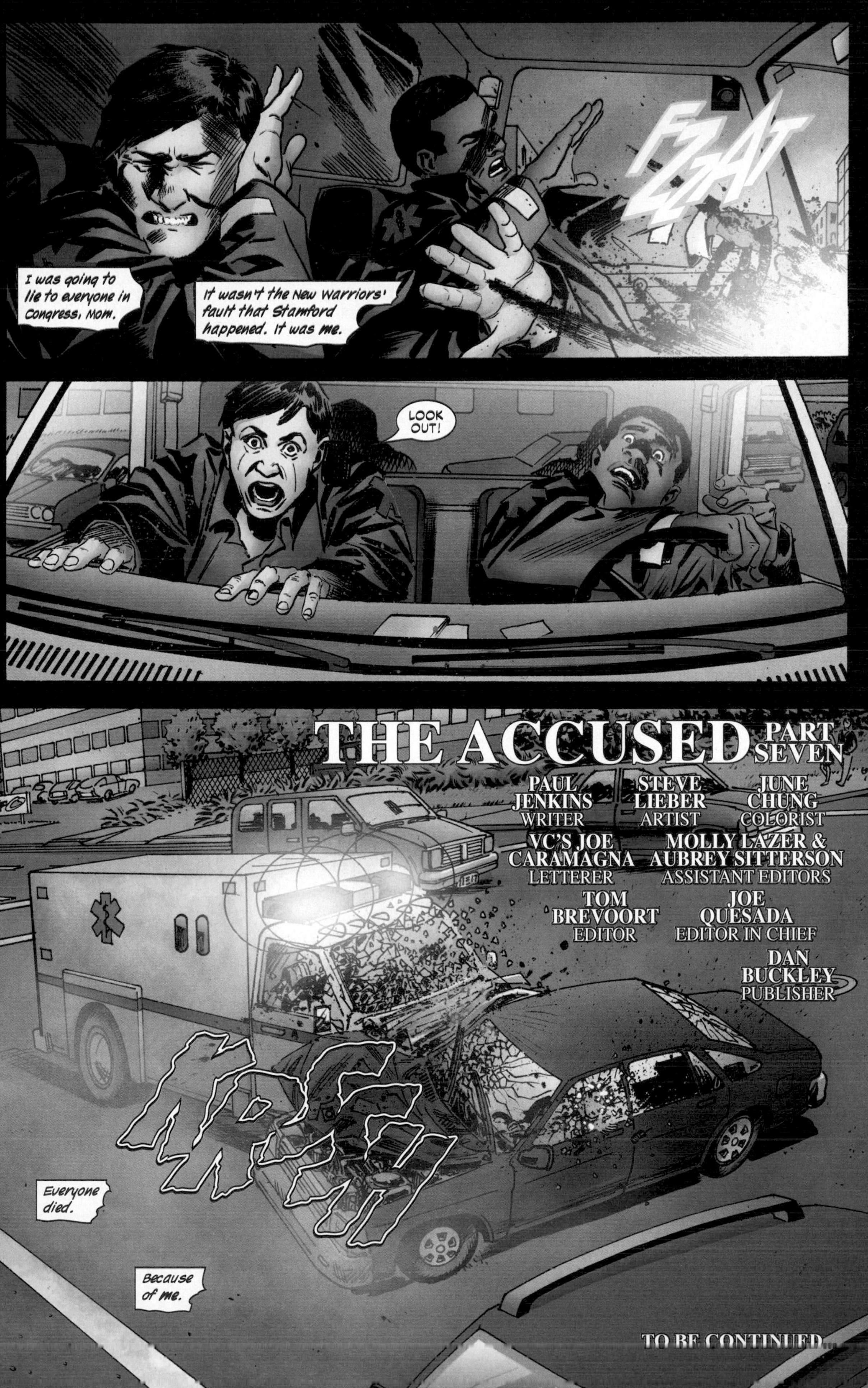

I was going to lie to everyone in Congress, Mom.
It wasn't the New Warriors' fault that Stamford happened. It was me.
FZZAT
LOOK OUT!
THE ACCUSED PART SEVEN
PAUL JENKINS WRITER
STEVE LIEBER ARTIST
JUNE CHUNG COLORIST
VC'S JOE CARAMAGNA LETTERER
MOLLY LAZER & AUBREY SITTERSON ASSISTANT EDITORS
TOM BREVOORT EDITOR
JOE QUESADA EDITOR IN CHIEF
DAN BUCKLEY PUBLISHER
Everyone died.
Because of me.
TO BE CONTINUED...

SLEEPER CELL

PART FIVE

PAUL JENKINS WRITER
LEE WEEKS ARTIST
SOTOCOLOR'S J. BROWN COLORS
VC'S JOE CARAMAGNA LETTERS
MOLLY LAZER & AUBREY SITTERSON ASSISTANT EDITORS
TOM BREVOORT EDITOR
JOE QUESADA EDITOR IN CHIEF
DAN BUCKLEY PUBLISHER

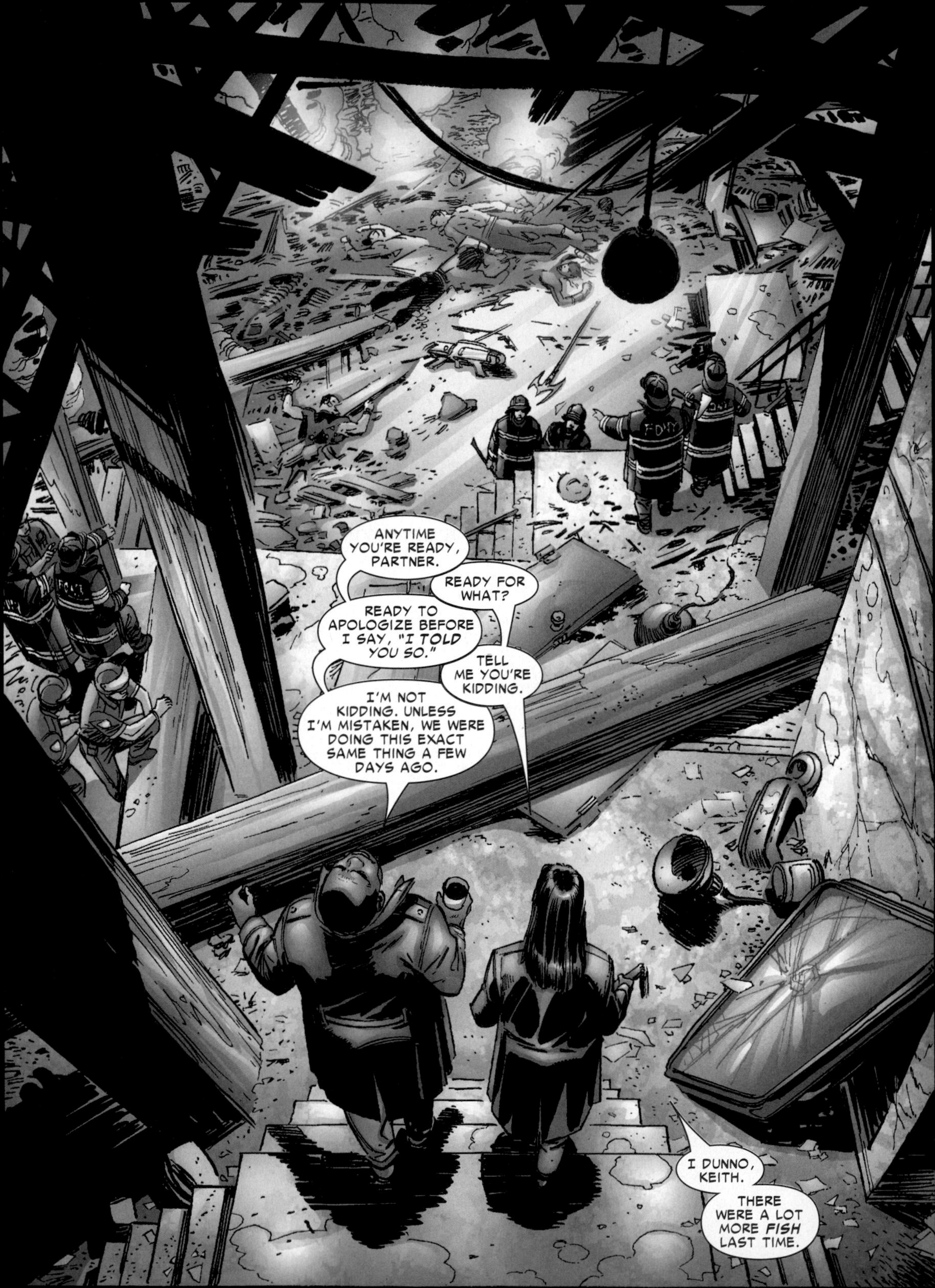

ANYTIME YOU'RE READY, PARTNER.
READY FOR WHAT?
READY TO APOLOGIZE BEFORE I SAY, "I *TOLD* YOU SO."
TELL ME YOU'RE KIDDING.
I'M NOT KIDDING. UNLESS I'M MISTAKEN, WE WERE DOING THIS EXACT SAME THING A FEW DAYS AGO.
I DUNNO, KEITH.
THERE WERE A LOT MORE *FISH* LAST TIME.

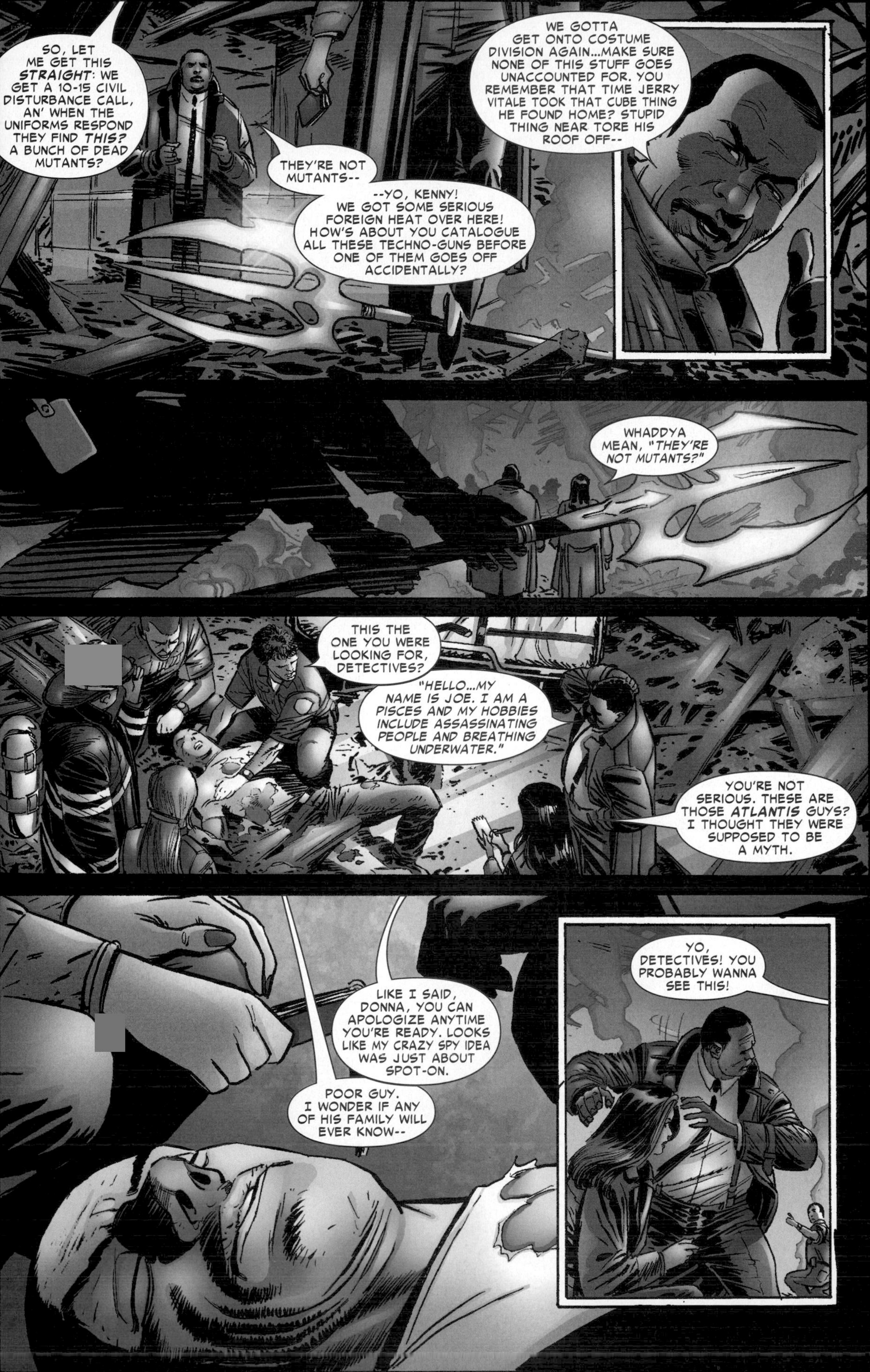
SO, LET ME GET THIS STRAIGHT: WE GET A 10-15 CIVIL DISTURBANCE CALL, AN' WHEN THE UNIFORMS RESPOND THEY FIND THIS? A BUNCH OF DEAD MUTANTS?
THEY'RE NOT MUTANTS--
--YO, KENNY! WE GOT SOME SERIOUS FOREIGN HEAT OVER HERE! HOW'S ABOUT YOU CATALOGUE ALL THESE TECHNO-GUNS BEFORE ONE OF THEM GOES OFF ACCIDENTALLY?
WE GOTTA GET ONTO COSTUME DIVISION AGAIN...MAKE SURE NONE OF THIS STUFF GOES UNACCOUNTED FOR. YOU REMEMBER THAT TIME JERRY VITALE TOOK THAT CUBE THING HE FOUND HOME? STUPID THING NEAR TORE HIS ROOF OFF--
WHADDYA MEAN, "THEY'RE NOT MUTANTS?"
THIS THE ONE YOU WERE LOOKING FOR, DETECTIVES?
"HELLO...MY NAME IS JOE. I AM A PISCES AND MY HOBBIES INCLUDE ASSASSINATING PEOPLE AND BREATHING UNDERWATER."
YOU'RE NOT SERIOUS. THESE ARE THOSE ATLANTIS GUYS? I THOUGHT THEY WERE SUPPOSED TO BE A MYTH.
LIKE I SAID, DONNA, YOU CAN APOLOGIZE ANYTIME YOU'RE READY. LOOKS LIKE MY CRAZY SPY IDEA WAS JUST ABOUT SPOT-ON.
POOR GUY. I WONDER IF ANY OF HIS FAMILY WILL EVER KNOW--
YO, DETECTIVES! YOU PROBABLY WANNA SEE THIS!

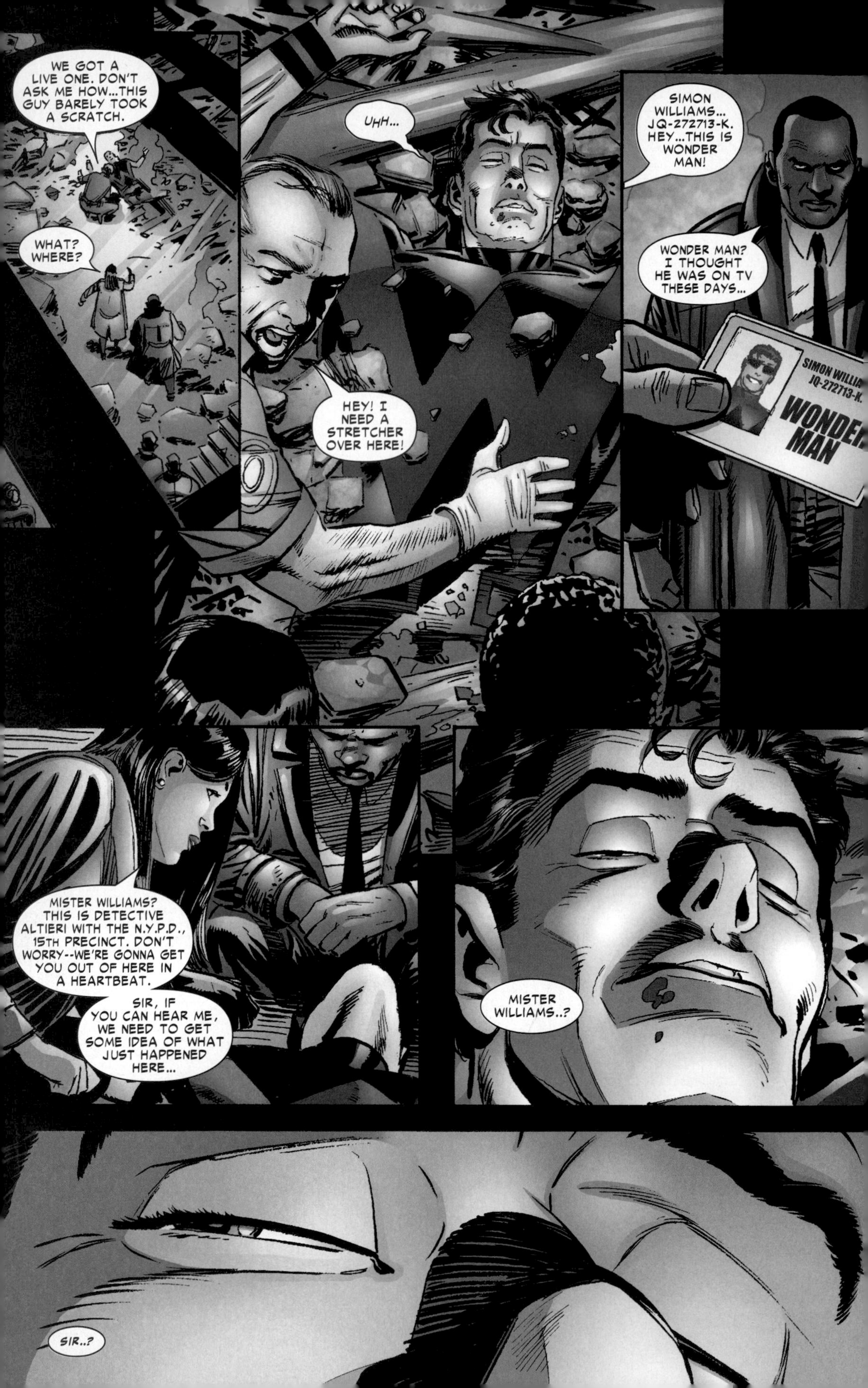
WE GOT A LIVE ONE. DON'T ASK ME HOW...THIS GUY BARELY TOOK A SCRATCH.
WHAT? WHERE?
UHH...
HEY! I NEED A STRETCHER OVER HERE!
SIMON WILLIAMS... JQ-272713-K. HEY...THIS IS WONDER MAN!
WONDER MAN? I THOUGHT HE WAS ON TV THESE DAYS...
SIMON WILLIA
JQ-272713-K.
WONDER MAN
MISTER WILLIAMS? THIS IS DETECTIVE ALTIERI WITH THE N.Y.P.D., 15TH PRECINCT. DON'T WORRY--WE'RE GONNA GET YOU OUT OF HERE IN A HEARTBEAT.
SIR, IF YOU CAN HEAR ME, WE NEED TO GET SOME IDEA OF WHAT JUST HAPPENED HERE...
MISTER WILLIAMS..?
SIR..?

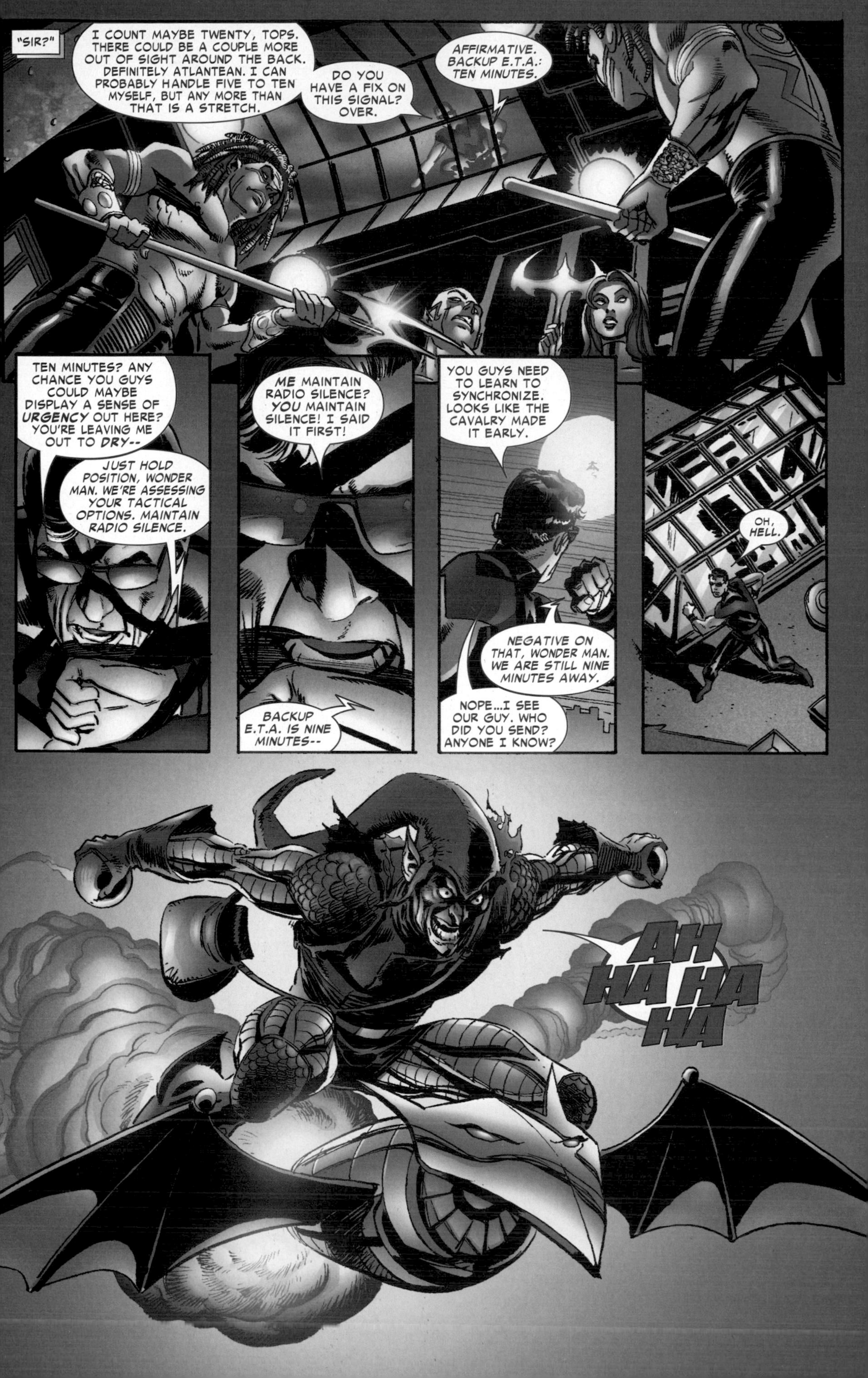
"SIR?"
I COUNT MAYBE TWENTY, TOPS. THERE COULD BE A COUPLE MORE OUT OF SIGHT AROUND THE BACK. DEFINITELY ATLANTEAN. I CAN PROBABLY HANDLE FIVE TO TEN MYSELF, BUT ANY MORE THAN THAT IS A STRETCH.
DO YOU HAVE A FIX ON THIS SIGNAL? OVER.
AFFIRMATIVE. BACKUP E.T.A.: TEN MINUTES.
TEN MINUTES? ANY CHANCE YOU GUYS COULD MAYBE DISPLAY A SENSE OF URGENCY OUT HERE? YOU'RE LEAVING ME OUT TO DRY--
JUST HOLD POSITION, WONDER MAN. WE'RE ASSESSING YOUR TACTICAL OPTIONS. MAINTAIN RADIO SILENCE.
ME MAINTAIN RADIO SILENCE? YOU MAINTAIN SILENCE! I SAID IT FIRST!
BACKUP E.T.A. IS NINE MINUTES--
YOU GUYS NEED TO LEARN TO SYNCHRONIZE. LOOKS LIKE THE CAVALRY MADE IT EARLY.
NEGATIVE ON THAT, WONDER MAN. WE ARE STILL NINE MINUTES AWAY.
NOPE...I SEE OUR GUY. WHO DID YOU SEND? ANYONE I KNOW?
OH, HELL.
AH HA HA HA HA

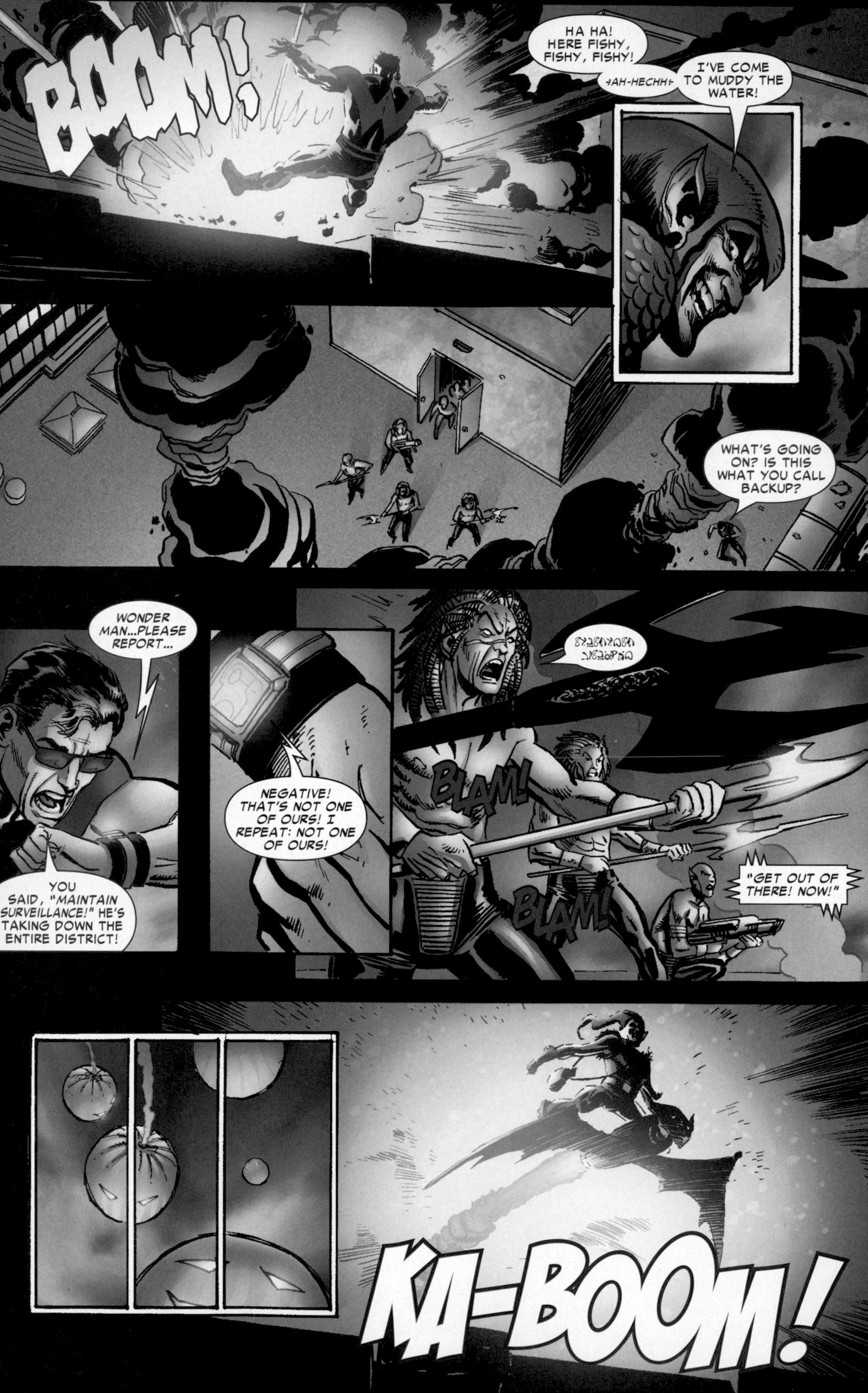
BOOM!
HA HA! HERE FISHY, FISHY, FISHY!
AH-HECHH
I'VE COME TO MUDDY THE WATER!
WHAT'S GOING ON? IS THIS WHAT YOU CALL BACKUP?
WONDER MAN...PLEASE REPORT...
YOU SAID, "MAINTAIN SURVEILLANCE!" HE'S TAKING DOWN THE ENTIRE DISTRICT!
NEGATIVE! THAT'S NOT ONE OF OURS! I REPEAT: NOT ONE OF OURS!
BLAM!
BLAM!
"GET OUT OF THERE! NOW!"
KA-BOOM!

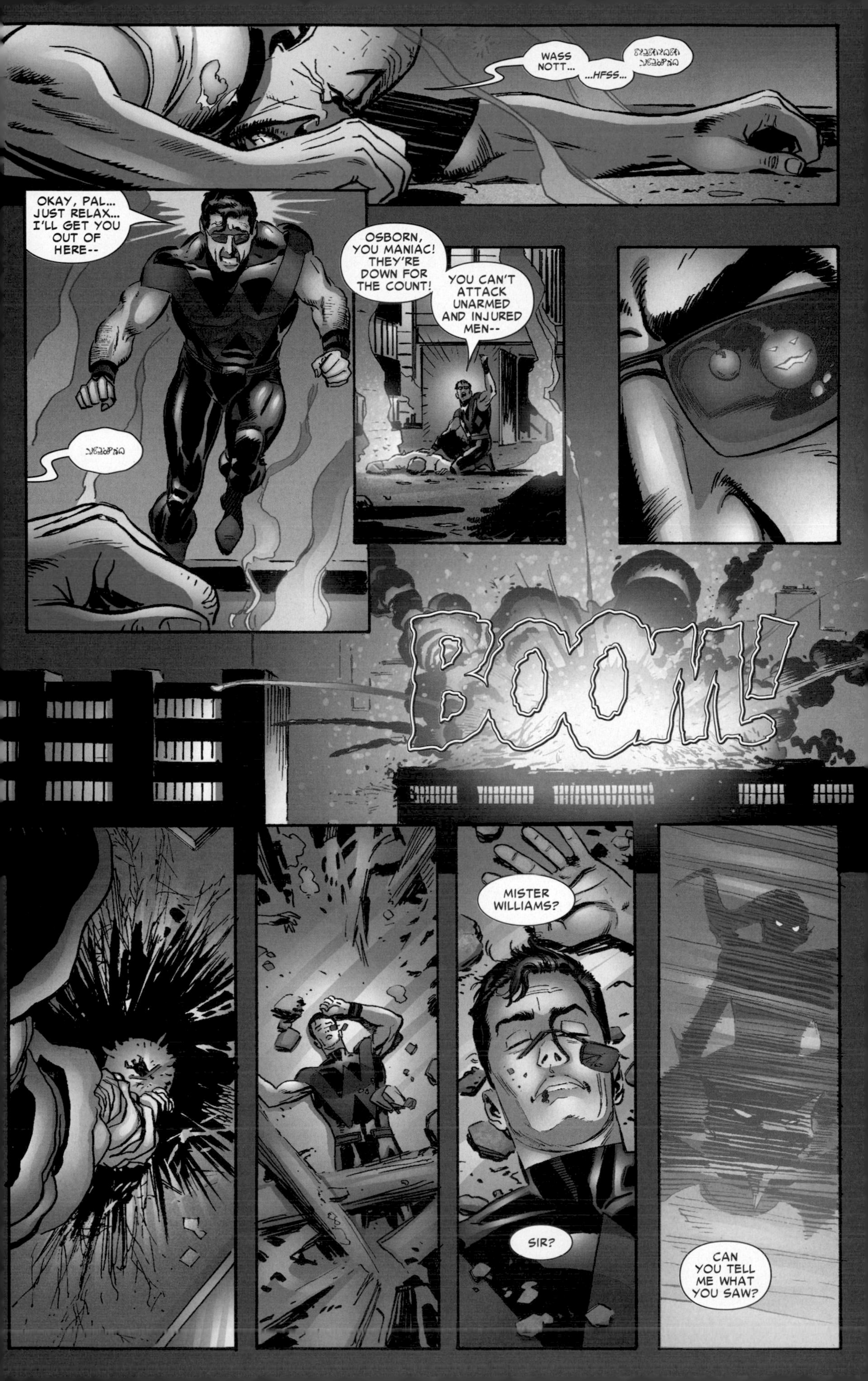
WASS NOTT...
...HFSS...
OKAY, PAL... JUST RELAX... I'LL GET YOU OUT OF HERE--
OSBORN, YOU MANIAC! THEY'RE DOWN FOR THE COUNT!
YOU CAN'T ATTACK UNARMED AND INJURED MEN--
BOOM!
MISTER WILLIAMS?
SIR?
CAN YOU TELL ME WHAT YOU SAW?

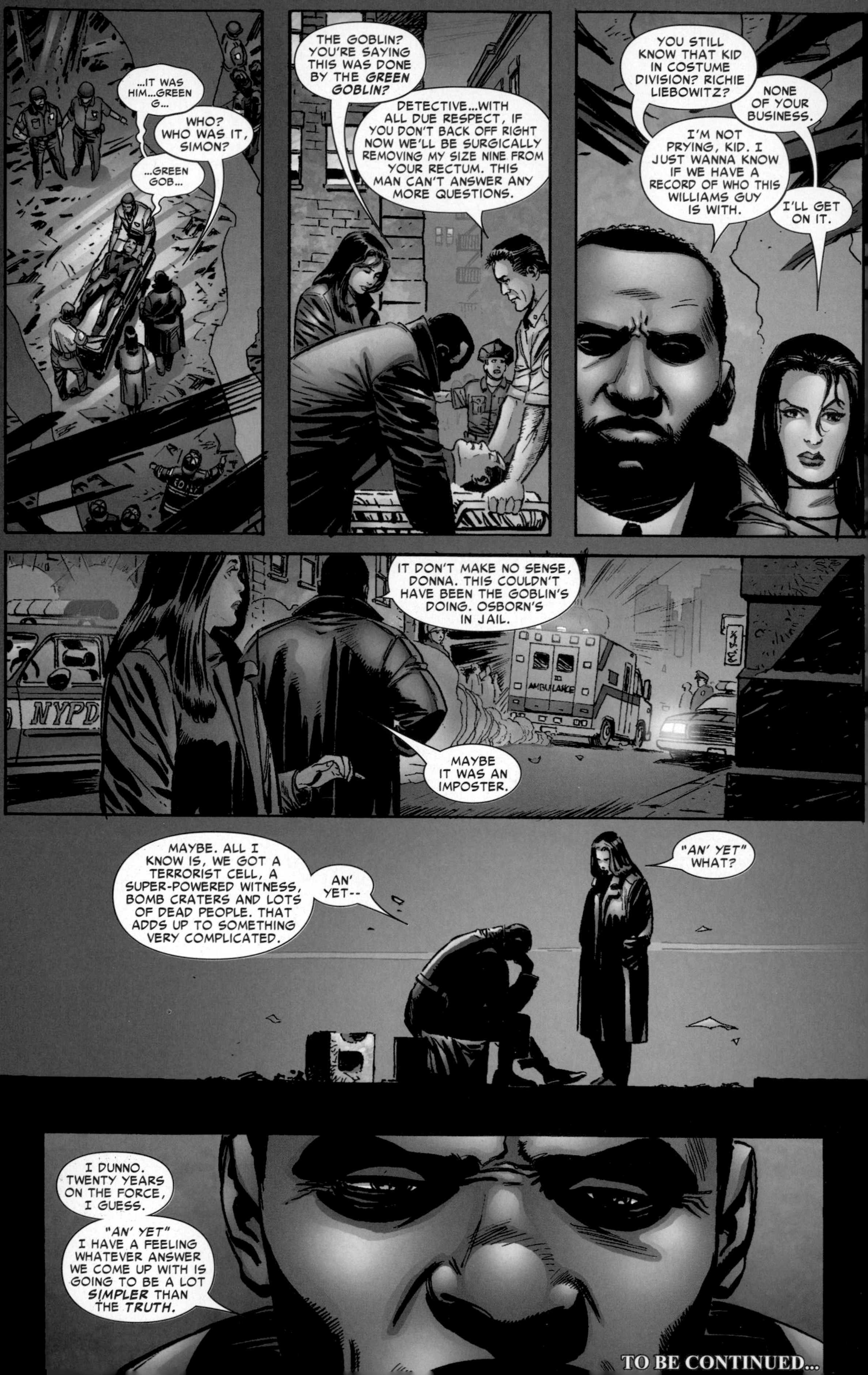
...IT WAS HIM...GREEN G...
WHO? WHO WAS IT, SIMON?
...GREEN GOB...
THE GOBLIN? YOU'RE SAYING THIS WAS DONE BY THE GREEN GOBLIN?
DETECTIVE...WITH ALL DUE RESPECT, IF YOU DON'T BACK OFF RIGHT NOW WE'LL BE SURGICALLY REMOVING MY SIZE NINE FROM YOUR RECTUM. THIS MAN CAN'T ANSWER ANY MORE QUESTIONS.
YOU STILL KNOW THAT KID IN COSTUME DIVISION? RICHIE LIEBOWITZ?
NONE OF YOUR BUSINESS.
I'M NOT PRYING, KID. I JUST WANNA KNOW IF WE HAVE A RECORD OF WHO THIS WILLIAMS GUY IS WITH.
I'LL GET ON IT.
NYPD
AMBULANCE
IT DON'T MAKE NO SENSE, DONNA. THIS COULDN'T HAVE BEEN THE GOBLIN'S DOING. OSBORN'S IN JAIL.
MAYBE IT WAS AN IMPOSTER.
MAYBE. ALL I KNOW IS, WE GOT A TERRORIST CELL, A SUPER-POWERED WITNESS, BOMB CRATERS AND LOTS OF DEAD PEOPLE. THAT ADDS UP TO SOMETHING VERY COMPLICATED.
AN' YET--
"AN' YET" WHAT?
I DUNNO. TWENTY YEARS ON THE FORCE, I GUESS.
"AN' YET" I HAVE A FEELING WHATEVER ANSWER WE COME UP WITH IS GOING TO BE A LOT SIMPLER THAN THE TRUTH.
TO BE CONTINUED...

On July 1st, 1916--as the larks sang across the devastation of no-man's land--British and French forces began the Somme Offensive.
Its intent: to divert German resources from the onslaught against the French at Verdun, and to achieve a significant territorial gain.
By day's end, over 58,000 British troops were dead, and there were an equal number of German casualties.
In many instances, the lines of trenches moved only a few hundred yards.
When the battle of the Somme came to a halt on November 18th, 1916, British casualties were estimated at over 450,000; German casualties at 500,000.
All for a few yards of mud.

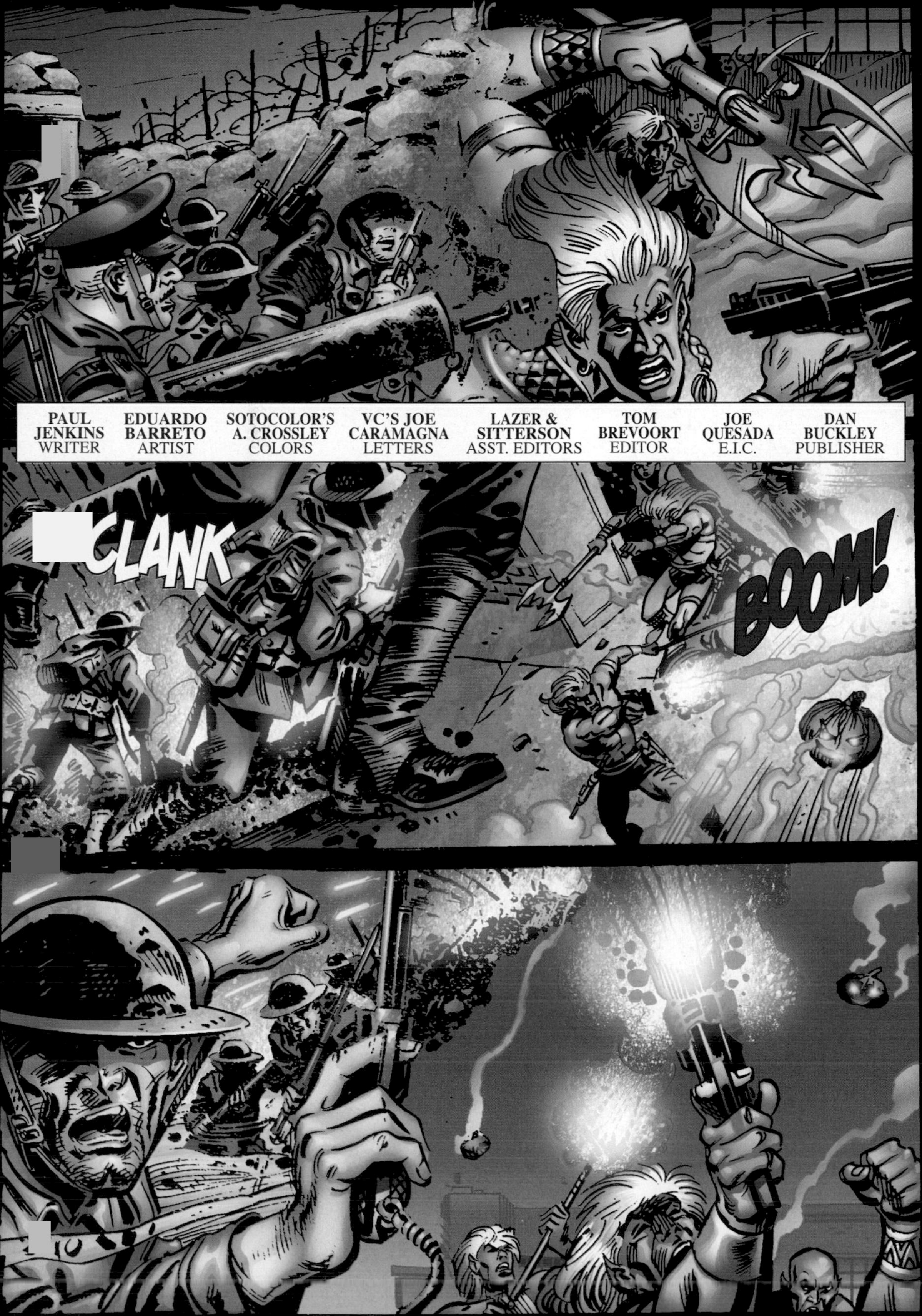
PAUL JENKINS WRITER
EDUARDO BARRETO ARTIST
SOTOCOLOR'S A. CROSSLEY COLORS
VC'S JOE CARAMAGNA LETTERS
LAZER & SITTERSON ASST. EDITORS
TOM BREVOORT EDITOR
JOE QUESADA E.I.C.
DAN BUCKLEY PUBLISHER
CLANK
BOOM!

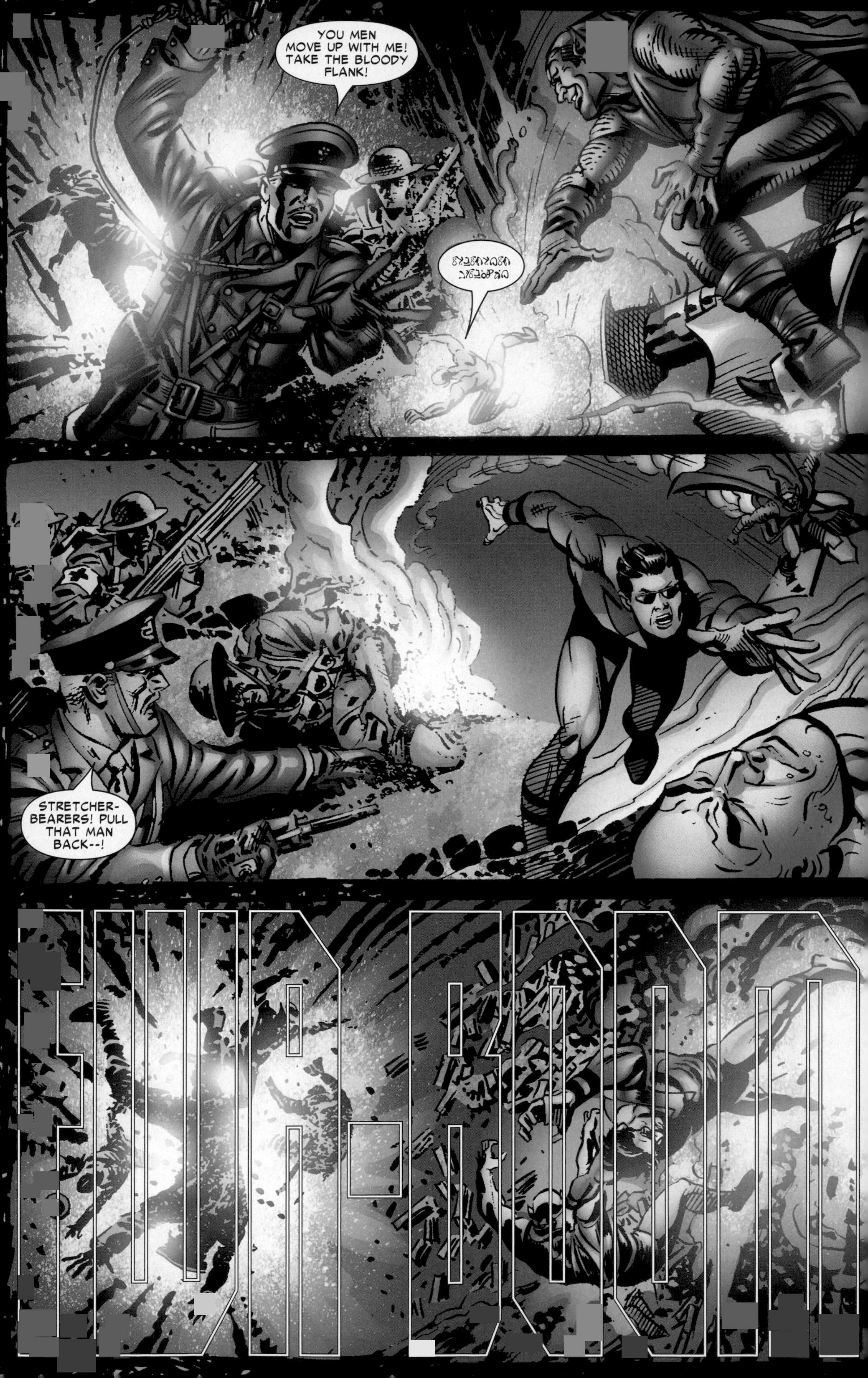
YOU MEN MOVE UP WITH ME! TAKE THE BLOODY FLANK!
STRETCHER-BEARERS! PULL THAT MAN BACK--!

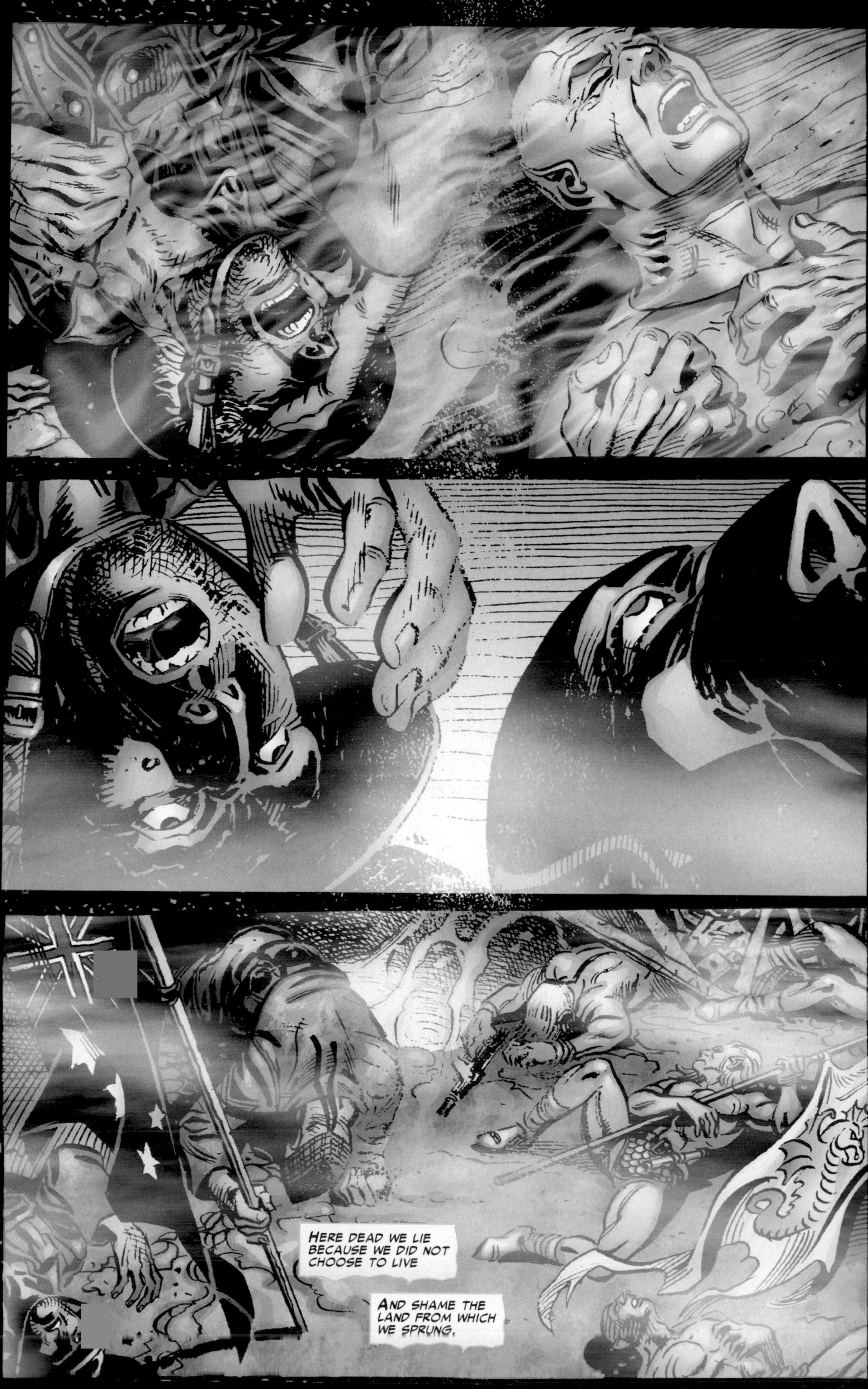
HERE DEAD WE LIE
BECAUSE WE DID NOT
CHOOSE TO LIVE
AND SHAME THE
LAND FROM WHICH
WE SPRUNG.

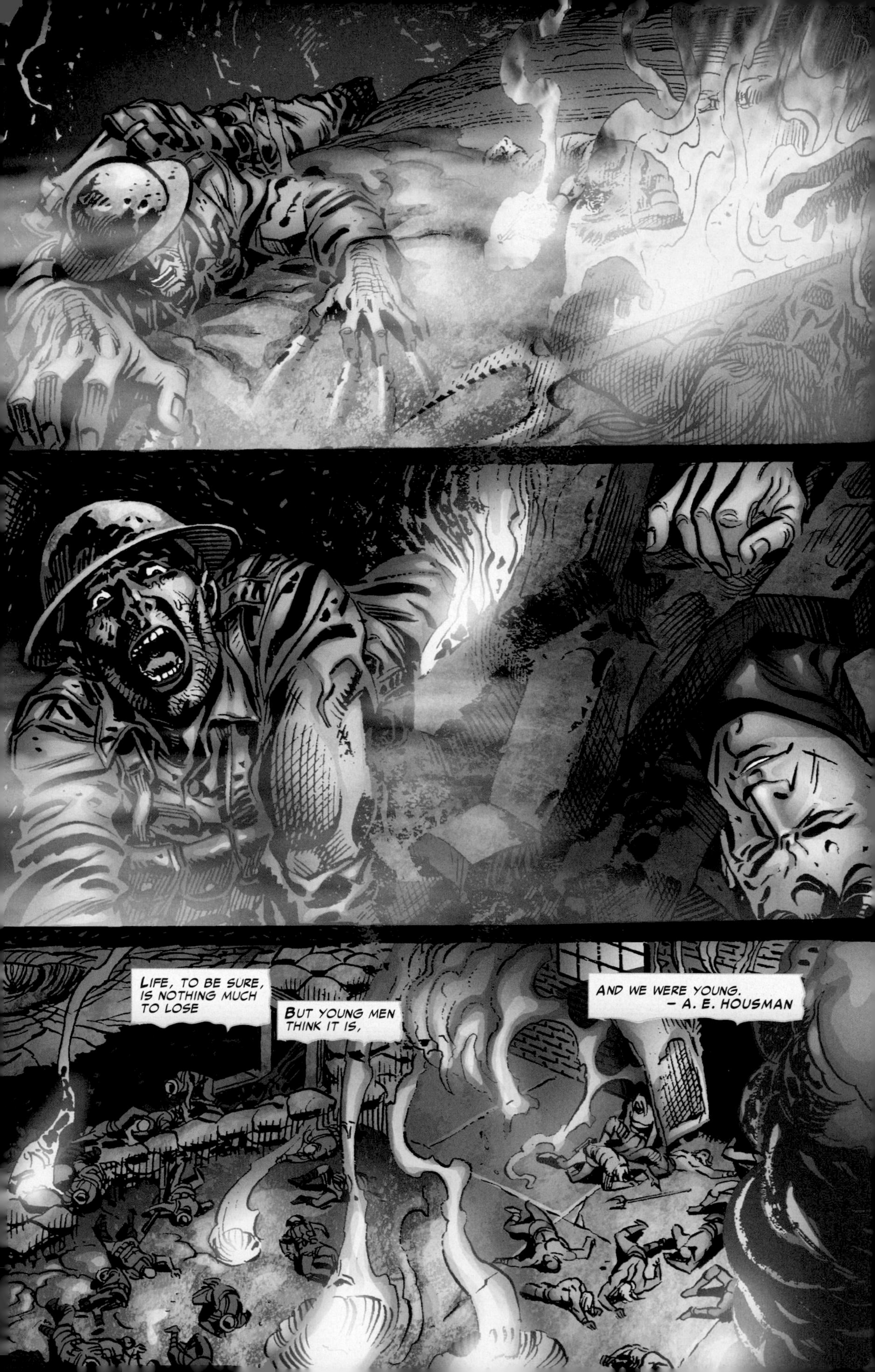
LIFE, TO BE SURE, IS NOTHING MUCH TO LOSE
BUT YOUNG MEN THINK IT IS,
AND WE WERE YOUNG.
– A. E. HOUSMAN

FRONT LINE
A MARVEL COMICS EVENT

CIVIL
WAR

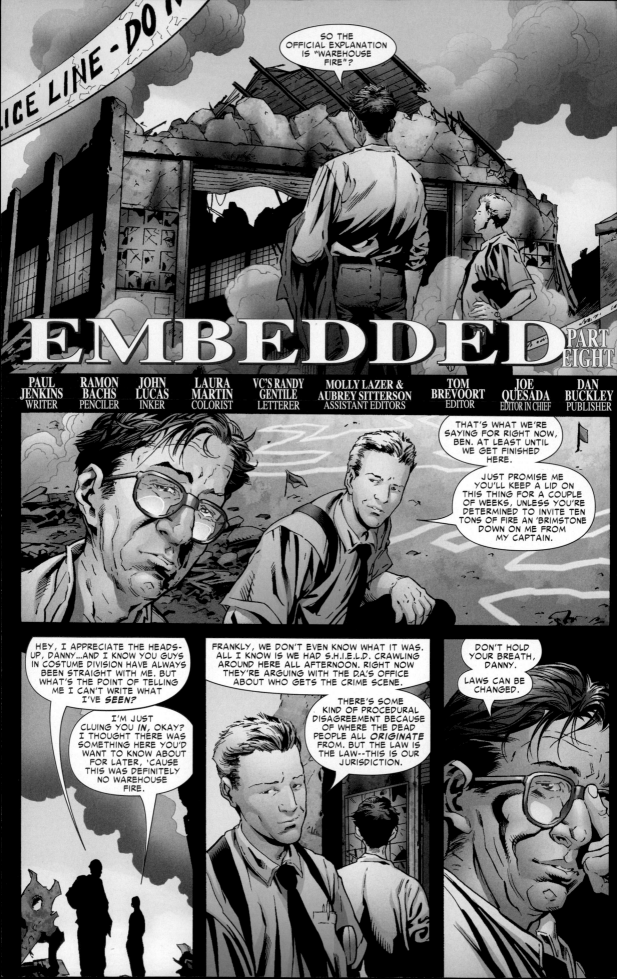

SO THE OFFICIAL EXPLANATION IS "WAREHOUSE FIRE"?

EMBEDDED PART EIGHT

| PAUL JENKINS WRITER | RAMON BACHS PENCILER | JOHN LUCAS INKER | LAURA MARTIN COLORIST | VC'S RANDY GENTILE LETTERER | MOLLY LAZER & AUBREY SITTERSON ASSISTANT EDITORS | TOM BREVOORT EDITOR | JOE QUESADA EDITOR IN CHIEF | DAN BUCKLEY PUBLISHER |

THAT'S WHAT WE'RE SAYING FOR RIGHT NOW, BEN. AT LEAST UNTIL WE GET FINISHED HERE.

JUST PROMISE ME YOU'LL KEEP A LID ON THIS THING FOR A COUPLE OF WEEKS, UNLESS YOU'RE DETERMINED TO INVITE TEN TONS OF FIRE AN 'BRIMSTONE DOWN ON ME FROM MY CAPTAIN.

HEY, I APPRECIATE THE HEADS-UP, DANNY...AND I KNOW YOU GUYS IN COSTUME DIVISION HAVE ALWAYS BEEN STRAIGHT WITH ME. BUT WHAT'S THE POINT OF TELLING ME I CAN'T WRITE WHAT I'VE SEEN?

I'M JUST CLUING YOU IN, OKAY? I THOUGHT THERE WAS SOMETHING HERE YOU'D WANT TO KNOW ABOUT FOR LATER, 'CAUSE THIS WAS DEFINITELY NO WAREHOUSE FIRE.

FRANKLY, WE DON'T EVEN KNOW WHAT IT WAS. ALL I KNOW IS WE HAD S.H.I.E.L.D. CRAWLING AROUND HERE ALL AFTERNOON. RIGHT NOW THEY'RE ARGUING WITH THE D.A.'S OFFICE ABOUT WHO GETS THE CRIME SCENE.

THERE'S SOME KIND OF PROCEDURAL DISAGREEMENT BECAUSE OF WHERE THE DEAD PEOPLE ALL ORIGINATE FROM. BUT THE LAW IS THE LAW--THIS IS OUR JURISDICTION.

DON'T HOLD YOUR BREATH, DANNY.

LAWS CAN BE CHANGED.

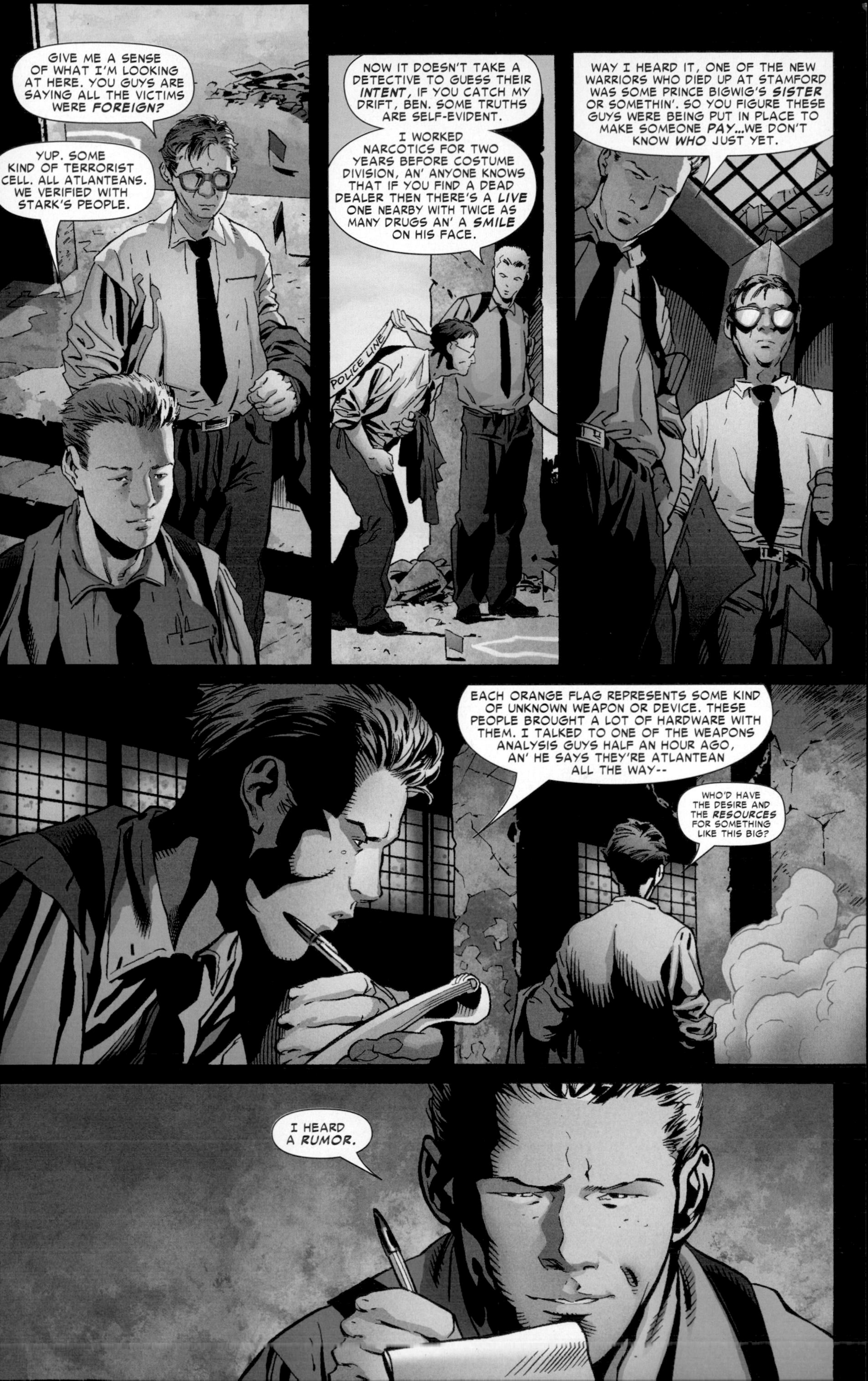
GIVE ME A SENSE OF WHAT I'M LOOKING AT HERE. YOU GUYS ARE SAYING ALL THE VICTIMS WERE FOREIGN?
YUP. SOME KIND OF TERRORIST CELL. ALL ATLANTEANS. WE VERIFIED WITH STARK'S PEOPLE.
NOW IT DOESN'T TAKE A DETECTIVE TO GUESS THEIR INTENT, IF YOU CATCH MY DRIFT, BEN. SOME TRUTHS ARE SELF-EVIDENT.
I WORKED NARCOTICS FOR TWO YEARS BEFORE COSTUME DIVISION, AN' ANYONE KNOWS THAT IF YOU FIND A DEAD DEALER THEN THERE'S A LIVE ONE NEARBY WITH TWICE AS MANY DRUGS AN' A SMILE ON HIS FACE.
POLICE LINE
WAY I HEARD IT, ONE OF THE NEW WARRIORS WHO DIED UP AT STAMFORD WAS SOME PRINCE BIGWIG'S SISTER OR SOMETHIN'. SO YOU FIGURE THESE GUYS WERE BEING PUT IN PLACE TO MAKE SOMEONE PAY...WE DON'T KNOW WHO JUST YET.
EACH ORANGE FLAG REPRESENTS SOME KIND OF UNKNOWN WEAPON OR DEVICE. THESE PEOPLE BROUGHT A LOT OF HARDWARE WITH THEM. I TALKED TO ONE OF THE WEAPONS ANALYSIS GUYS HALF AN HOUR AGO, AN' HE SAYS THEY'RE ATLANTEAN ALL THE WAY--
WHO'D HAVE THE DESIRE AND THE RESOURCES FOR SOMETHING LIKE THIS BIG?
I HEARD A RUMOR.

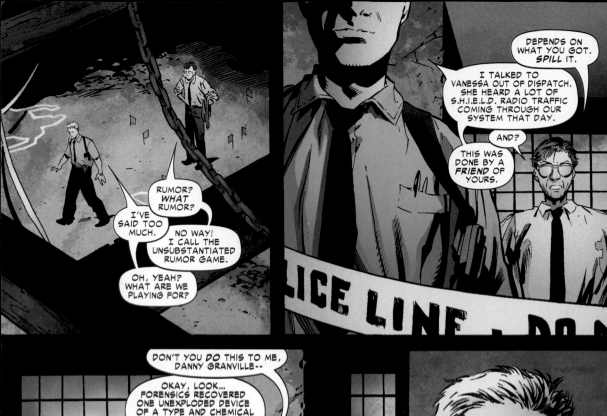

DEPENDS ON WHAT YOU GOT. *SPILL IT.*

I TALKED TO VANESSA OUT OF DISPATCH. SHE HEARD A LOT OF S.H.I.E.L.D. RADIO TRAFFIC COMING THROUGH OUR SYSTEM THAT DAY.

AND?

THIS WAS DONE BY A *FRIEND* OF YOURS.

RUMOR? *WHAT* RUMOR?

I'VE SAID TOO MUCH.

NO WAY! I CALL THE UNSUBSTANTIATED RUMOR GAME.

OH, YEAH? WHAT ARE WE PLAYING FOR?

DON'T YOU *DO* THIS TO ME, DANNY GRANVILLE--

OKAY, LOOK... FORENSICS RECOVERED ONE UNEXPLODED DEVICE OF A TYPE AND CHEMICAL CONSTITUENCY THAT CONNECTS IT TO SOMEONE WE KNOW.

WHO?

RHYMES WITH "GREEN GOBLIN."

WHAT DO I WIN?

OSBORN AGAIN? BUT WHY WOULD HE GO AFTER ATLANTEANS? HOW DID HE GET THE *INTELLIGENCE* ON THEM, FOR ONE THING--?

I GOT ONE MORE ITEM FOR YOU--A REAL KEEPER THIS TIME. BUT YOU GOTTA MAKE IT WORTH MY WHILE.

OKAY, ARE YOU STILL *SINGLE?*

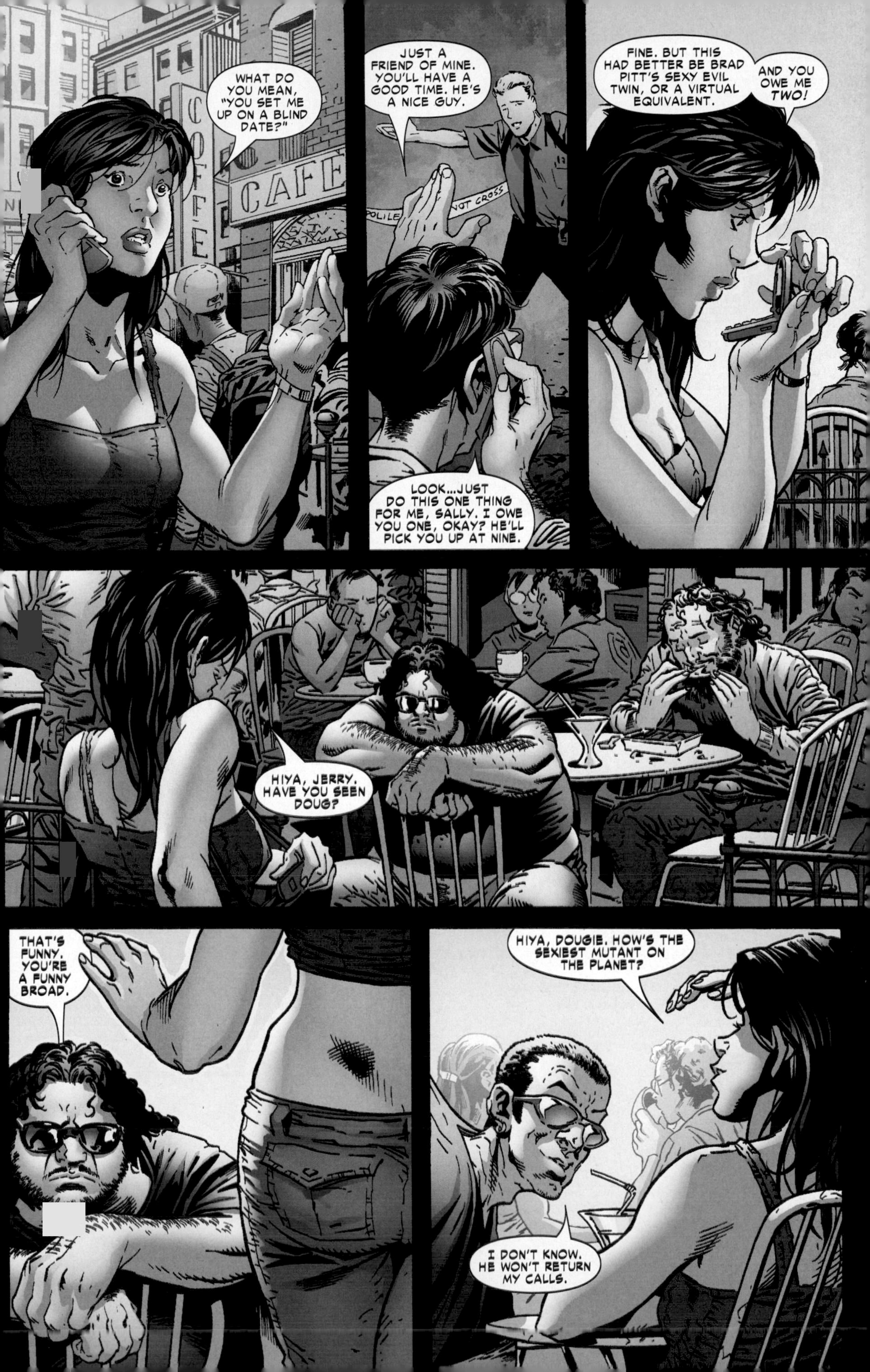
WHAT DO YOU MEAN, "YOU SET ME UP ON A BLIND DATE?"
CAFE
JUST A FRIEND OF MINE. YOU'LL HAVE A GOOD TIME. HE'S A NICE GUY.
LOOK...JUST DO THIS ONE THING FOR ME, SALLY. I OWE YOU ONE, OKAY? HE'LL PICK YOU UP AT NINE.
FINE. BUT THIS HAD BETTER BE BRAD PITT'S SEXY EVIL TWIN, OR A VIRTUAL EQUIVALENT.
AND YOU OWE ME TWO!
HIYA, JERRY. HAVE YOU SEEN DOUG?
THAT'S FUNNY. YOU'RE A FUNNY BROAD.
HIYA, DOUGIE. HOW'S THE SEXIEST MUTANT ON THE PLANET?
I DON'T KNOW. HE WON'T RETURN MY CALLS.

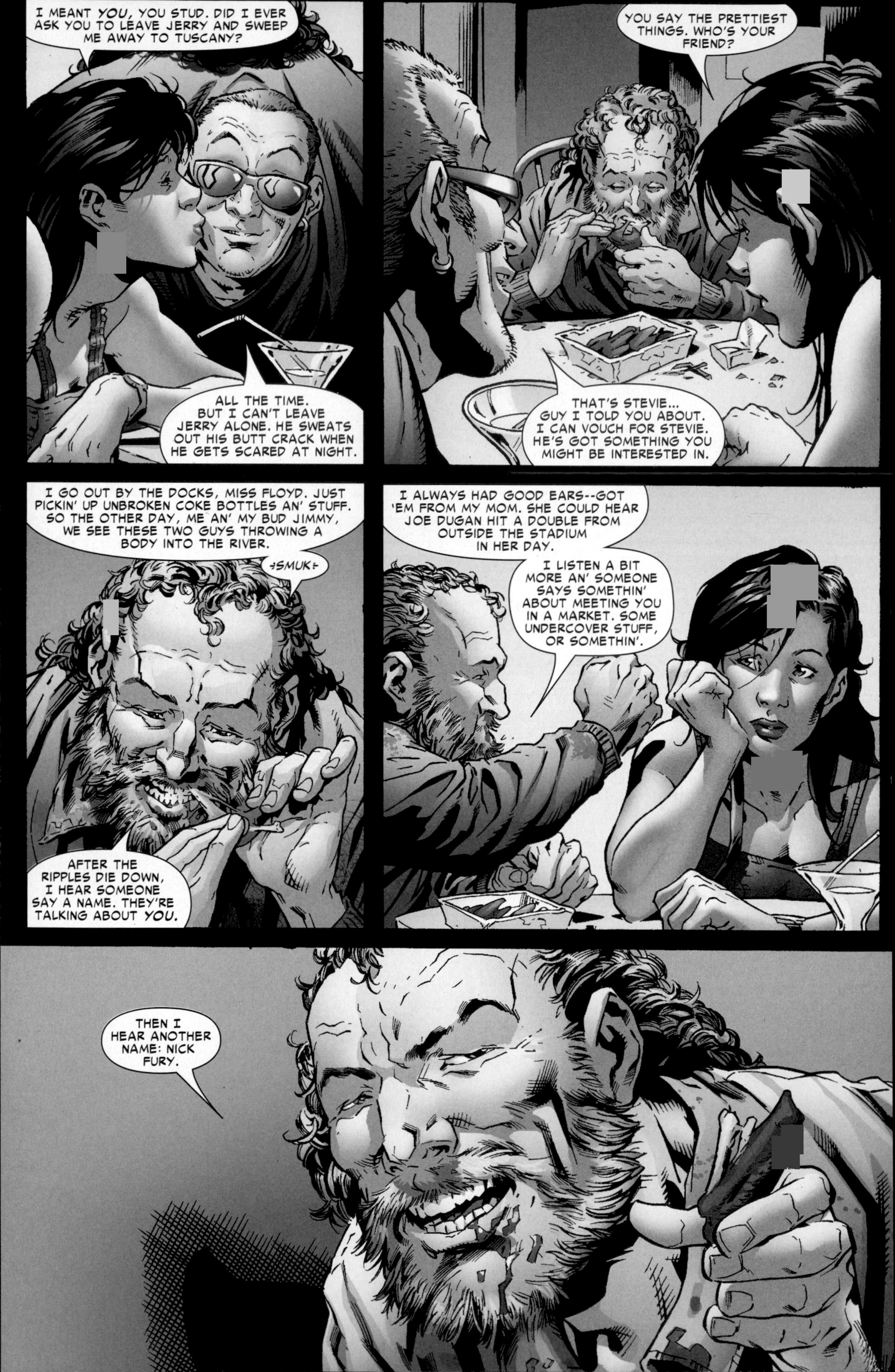
I MEANT YOU, YOU STUD. DID I EVER ASK YOU TO LEAVE JERRY AND SWEEP ME AWAY TO TUSCANY?
ALL THE TIME. BUT I CAN'T LEAVE JERRY ALONE. HE SWEATS OUT HIS BUTT CRACK WHEN HE GETS SCARED AT NIGHT.
YOU SAY THE PRETTIEST THINGS. WHO'S YOUR FRIEND?
THAT'S STEVIE... GUY I TOLD YOU ABOUT. I CAN VOUCH FOR STEVIE. HE'S GOT SOMETHING YOU MIGHT BE INTERESTED IN.
I GO OUT BY THE DOCKS, MISS FLOYD. JUST PICKIN' UP UNBROKEN COKE BOTTLES AN' STUFF. SO THE OTHER DAY, ME AN' MY BUD JIMMY, WE SEE THESE TWO GUYS THROWING A BODY INTO THE RIVER.
SMUK
AFTER THE RIPPLES DIE DOWN, I HEAR SOMEONE SAY A NAME. THEY'RE TALKING ABOUT YOU.
I ALWAYS HAD GOOD EARS--GOT 'EM FROM MY MOM. SHE COULD HEAR JOE DUGAN HIT A DOUBLE FROM OUTSIDE THE STADIUM IN HER DAY.
I LISTEN A BIT MORE AN' SOMEONE SAYS SOMETHIN' ABOUT MEETING YOU IN A MARKET. SOME UNDERCOVER STUFF, OR SOMETHIN'.
THEN I HEAR ANOTHER NAME: NICK FURY.

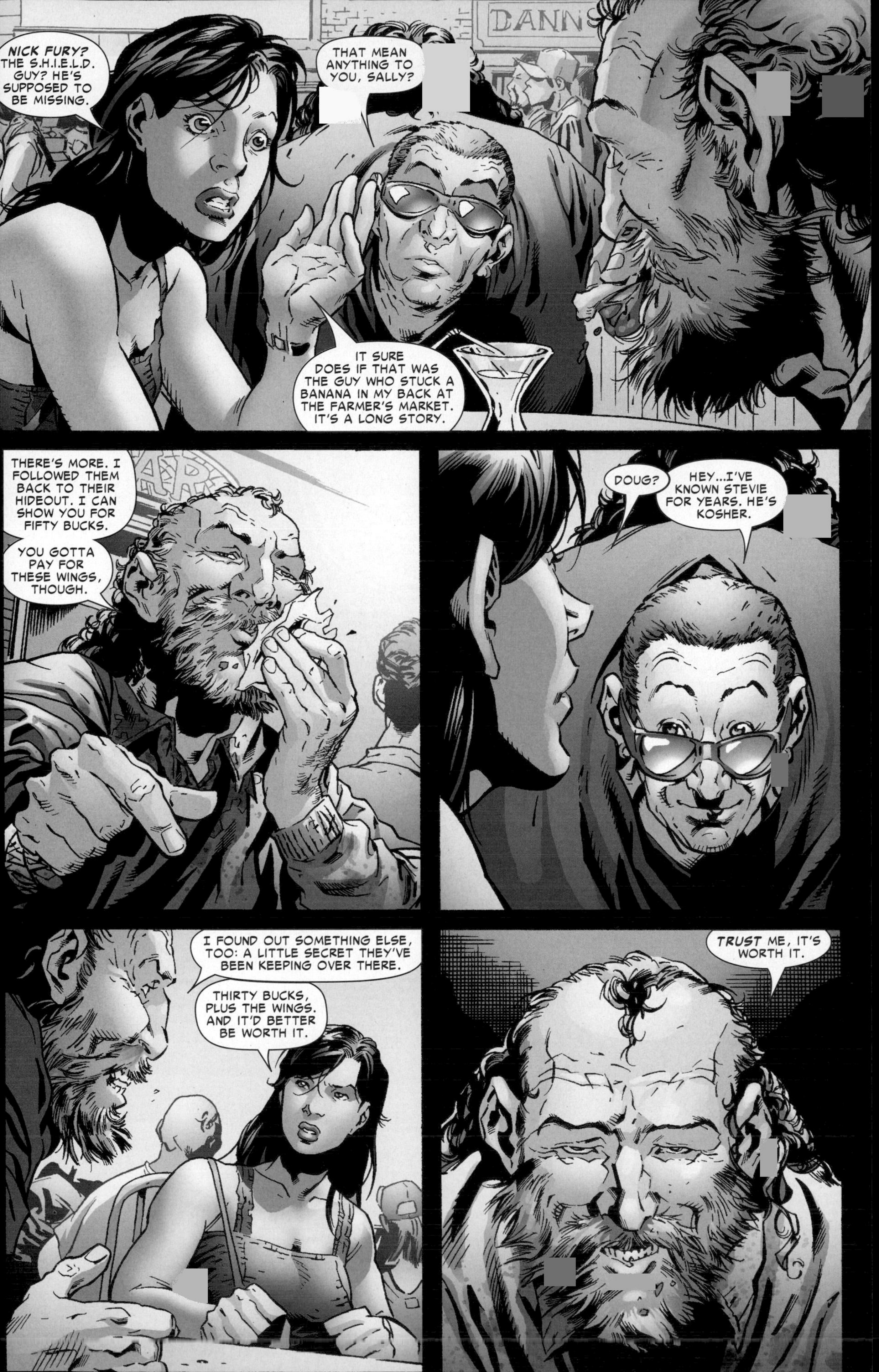
NICK FURY? THE S.H.I.E.L.D. GUY? HE'S SUPPOSED TO BE MISSING.
THAT MEAN ANYTHING TO YOU, SALLY?
IT SURE DOES IF THAT WAS THE GUY WHO STUCK A BANANA IN MY BACK AT THE FARMER'S MARKET. IT'S A LONG STORY.
THERE'S MORE. I FOLLOWED THEM BACK TO THEIR HIDEOUT. I CAN SHOW YOU FOR FIFTY BUCKS.
YOU GOTTA PAY FOR THESE WINGS, THOUGH.
DOUG?
HEY...I'VE KNOWN STEVIE FOR YEARS. HE'S KOSHER.
I FOUND OUT SOMETHING ELSE, TOO: A LITTLE SECRET THEY'VE BEEN KEEPING OVER THERE.
THIRTY BUCKS, PLUS THE WINGS. AND IT'D BETTER BE WORTH IT.
TRUST ME, IT'S WORTH IT.

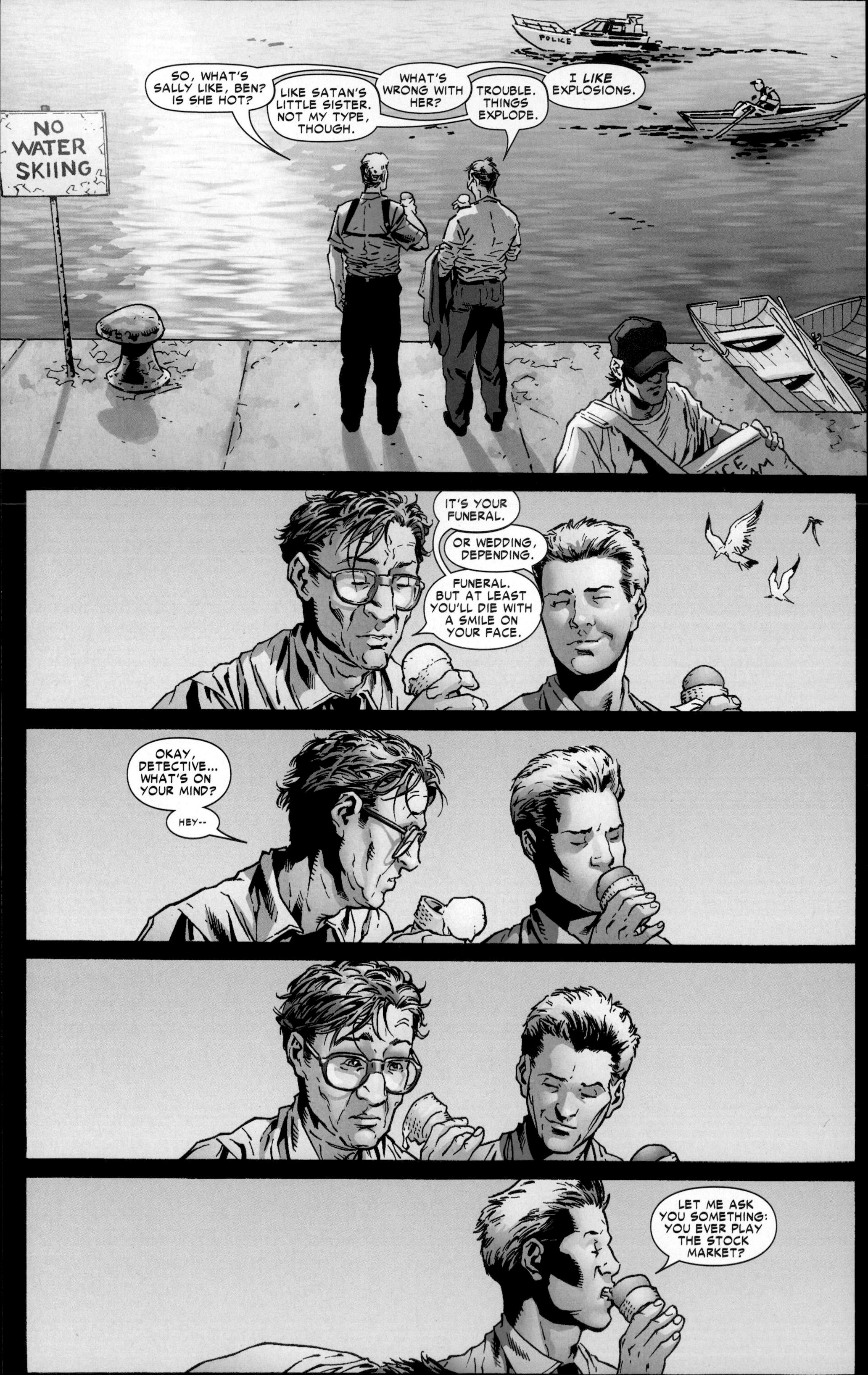

NO WATER SKIING
SO, WHAT'S SALLY LIKE, BEN? IS SHE HOT?
LIKE SATAN'S LITTLE SISTER. NOT MY TYPE, THOUGH.
WHAT'S WRONG WITH HER?
TROUBLE. THINGS EXPLODE.
I LIKE EXPLOSIONS.
POLICE
IT'S YOUR FUNERAL.
OR WEDDING, DEPENDING.
FUNERAL. BUT AT LEAST YOU'LL DIE WITH A SMILE ON YOUR FACE.
OKAY, DETECTIVE... WHAT'S ON YOUR MIND?
HEY--
LET ME ASK YOU SOMETHING: YOU EVER PLAY THE STOCK MARKET?

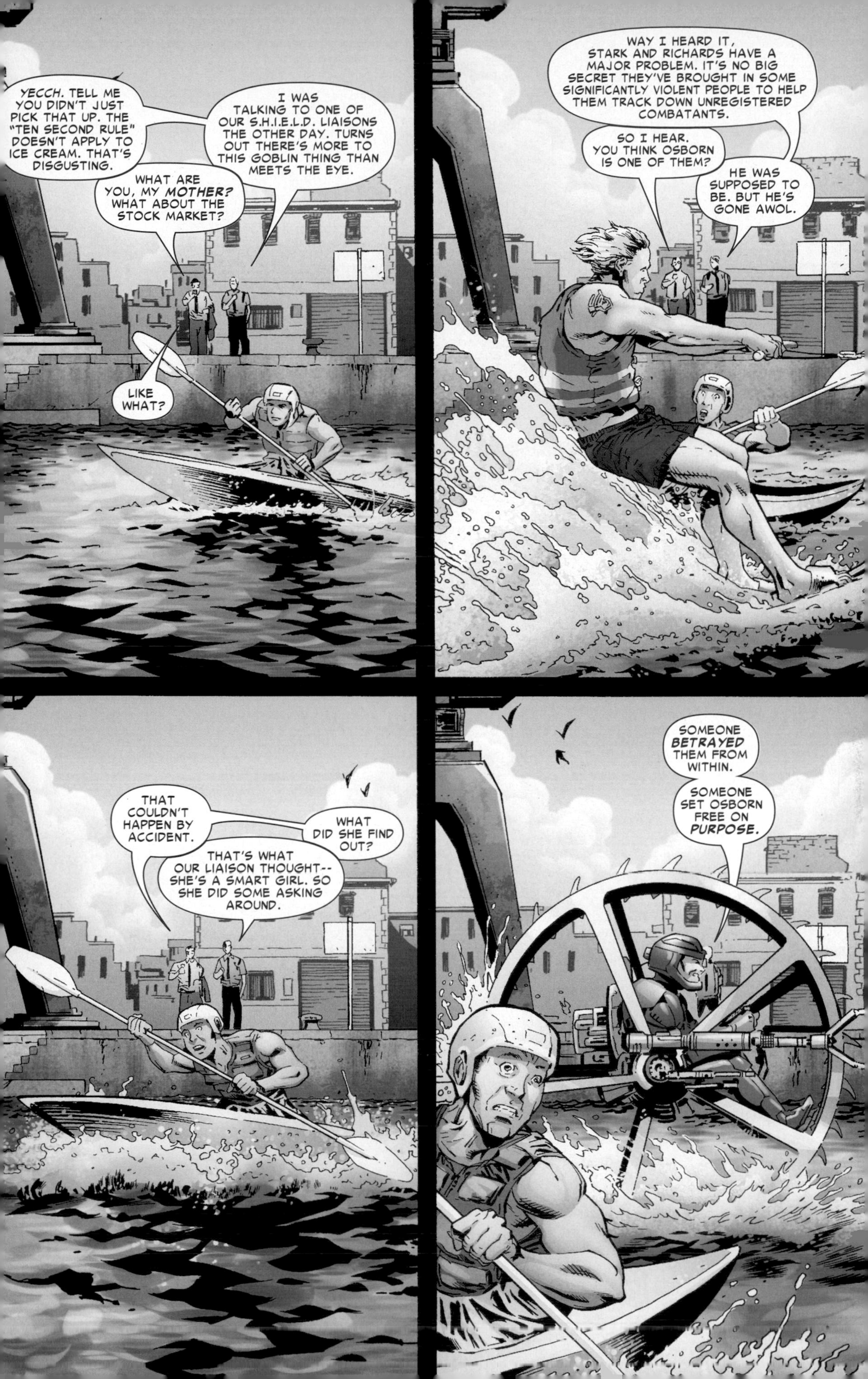
YECCH. TELL ME YOU DIDN'T JUST PICK THAT UP. THE "TEN SECOND RULE" DOESN'T APPLY TO ICE CREAM. THAT'S DISGUSTING.
WHAT ARE YOU, MY MOTHER? WHAT ABOUT THE STOCK MARKET?
I WAS TALKING TO ONE OF OUR S.H.I.E.L.D. LIAISONS THE OTHER DAY. TURNS OUT THERE'S MORE TO THIS GOBLIN THING THAN MEETS THE EYE.
LIKE WHAT?
WAY I HEARD IT, STARK AND RICHARDS HAVE A MAJOR PROBLEM. IT'S NO BIG SECRET THEY'VE BROUGHT IN SOME SIGNIFICANTLY VIOLENT PEOPLE TO HELP THEM TRACK DOWN UNREGISTERED COMBATANTS.
SO I HEAR. YOU THINK OSBORN IS ONE OF THEM?
HE WAS SUPPOSED TO BE. BUT HE'S GONE AWOL.
THAT COULDN'T HAPPEN BY ACCIDENT.
WHAT DID SHE FIND OUT?
THAT'S WHAT OUR LIAISON THOUGHT-- SHE'S A SMART GIRL. SO SHE DID SOME ASKING AROUND.
SOMEONE BETRAYED THEM FROM WITHIN.
SOMEONE SET OSBORN FREE ON PURPOSE.

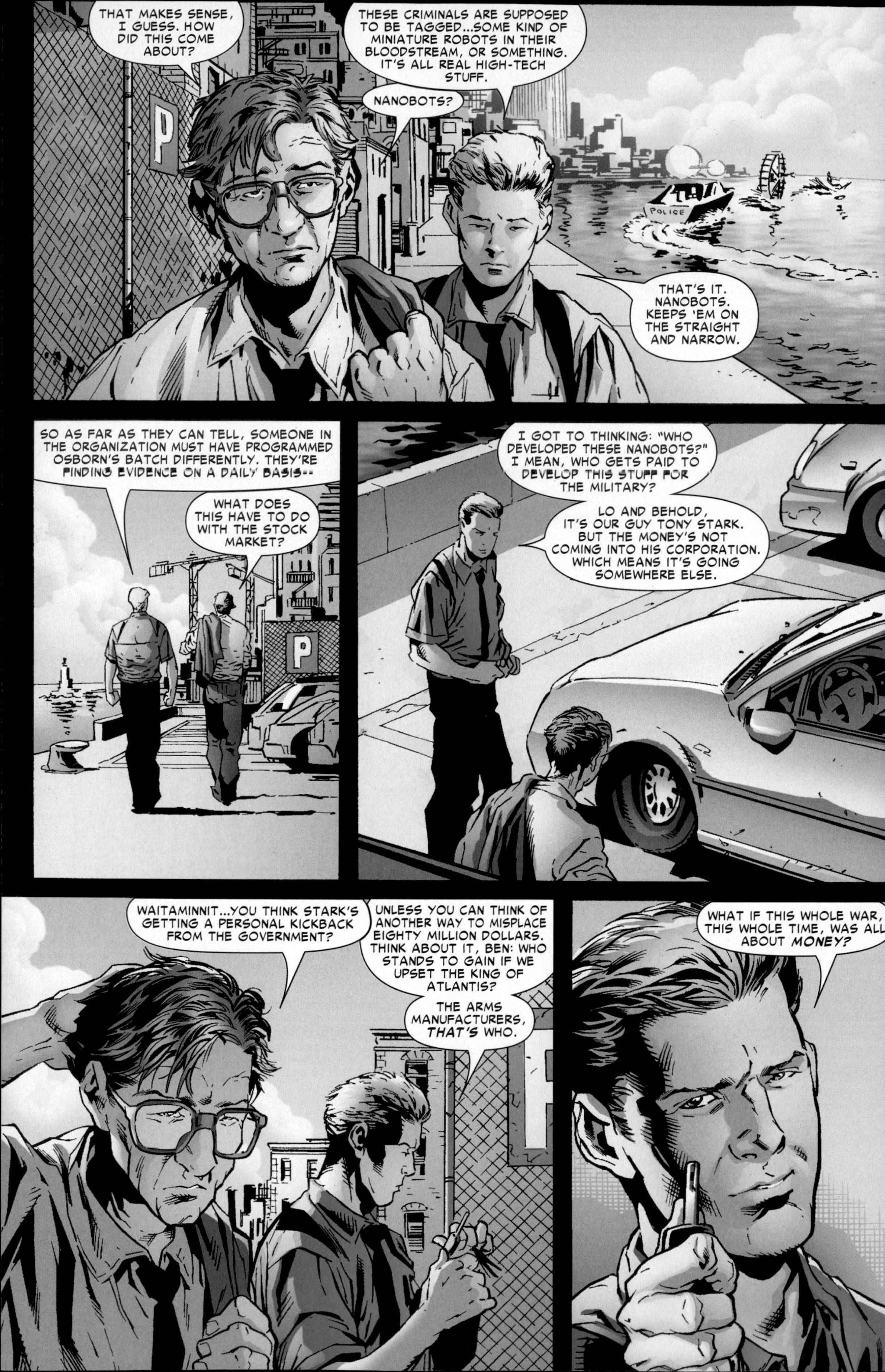

THAT MAKES SENSE, I GUESS. HOW DID THIS COME ABOUT?
THESE CRIMINALS ARE SUPPOSED TO BE TAGGED...SOME KIND OF MINIATURE ROBOTS IN THEIR BLOODSTREAM, OR SOMETHING. IT'S ALL REAL HIGH-TECH STUFF.
NANOBOTS?
THAT'S IT. NANOBOTS. KEEPS 'EM ON THE STRAIGHT AND NARROW.
P
POLICE
SO AS FAR AS THEY CAN TELL, SOMEONE IN THE ORGANIZATION MUST HAVE PROGRAMMED OSBORN'S BATCH DIFFERENTLY. THEY'RE FINDING EVIDENCE ON A DAILY BASIS--
WHAT DOES THIS HAVE TO DO WITH THE STOCK MARKET?
P
I GOT TO THINKING: "WHO DEVELOPED THESE NANOBOTS?" I MEAN, WHO GETS PAID TO DEVELOP THIS STUFF FOR THE MILITARY?
LO AND BEHOLD, IT'S OUR GUY TONY STARK. BUT THE MONEY'S NOT COMING INTO HIS CORPORATION. WHICH MEANS IT'S GOING SOMEWHERE ELSE.
WAITAMINNIT...YOU THINK STARK'S GETTING A PERSONAL KICKBACK FROM THE GOVERNMENT?
UNLESS YOU CAN THINK OF ANOTHER WAY TO MISPLACE EIGHTY MILLION DOLLARS. THINK ABOUT IT, BEN: WHO STANDS TO GAIN IF WE UPSET THE KING OF ATLANTIS?
THE ARMS MANUFACTURERS, *THAT'S* WHO.
WHAT IF THIS WHOLE WAR, THIS WHOLE TIME, WAS ALL ABOUT *MONEY?*

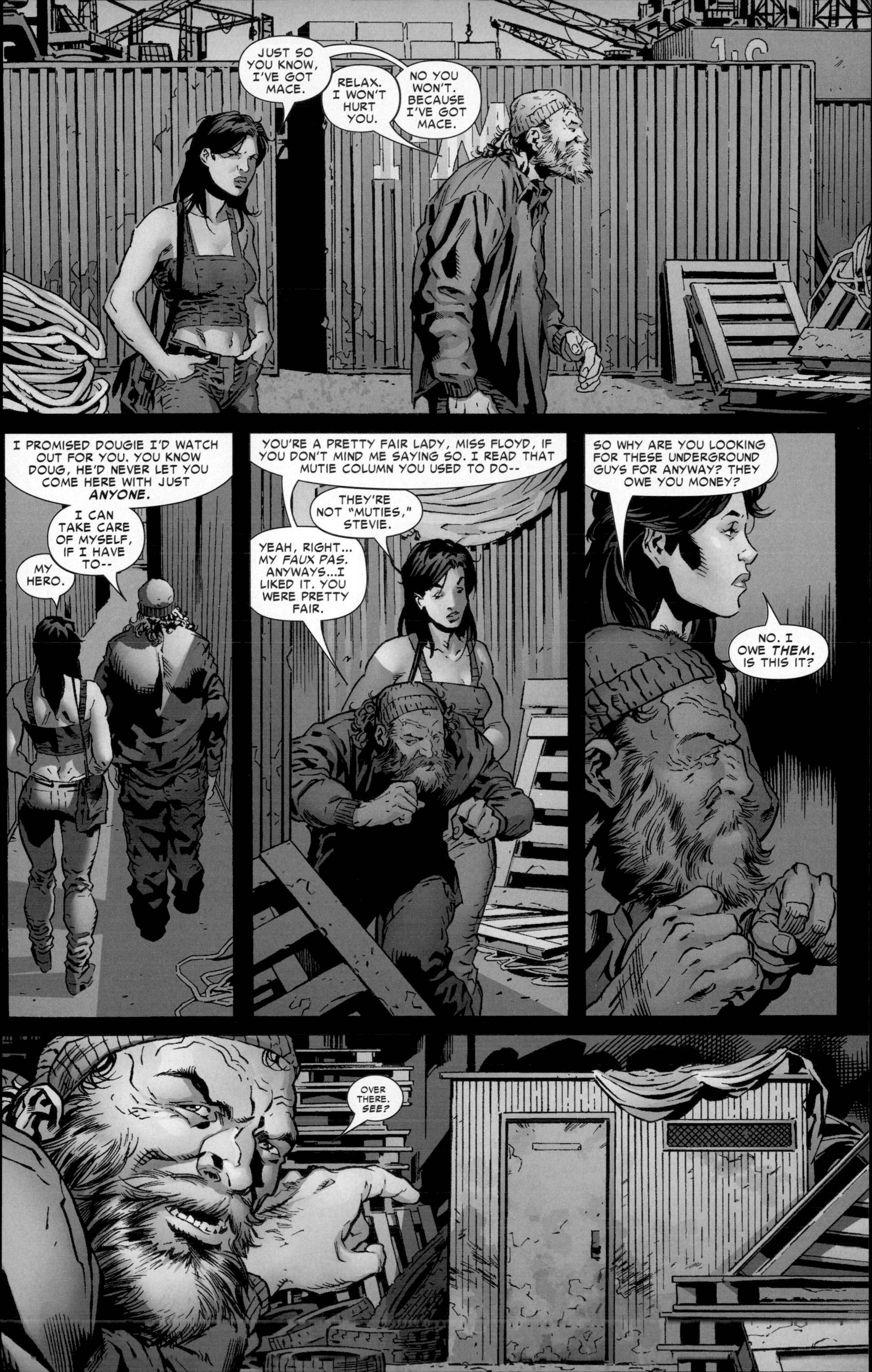

JUST SO YOU KNOW, I'VE GOT MACE.
RELAX. I WON'T HURT YOU.
NO YOU WON'T. BECAUSE I'VE GOT MACE.
I PROMISED DOUGIE I'D WATCH OUT FOR YOU. YOU KNOW DOUG, HE'D NEVER LET YOU COME HERE WITH JUST *ANYONE.*
I CAN TAKE CARE OF MYSELF, IF I HAVE TO--
MY HERO.
YOU'RE A PRETTY FAIR LADY, MISS FLOYD, IF YOU DON'T MIND ME SAYING SO. I READ THAT MUTIE COLUMN YOU USED TO DO--
THEY'RE NOT "MUTIES," STEVIE.
YEAH, RIGHT... MY *FAUX PAS.* ANYWAYS...I LIKED IT. YOU WERE PRETTY FAIR.
SO WHY ARE YOU LOOKING FOR THESE UNDERGROUND GUYS FOR ANYWAY? THEY OWE YOU MONEY?
NO. I OWE *THEM.* IS THIS IT?
OVER THERE. *SEE?*

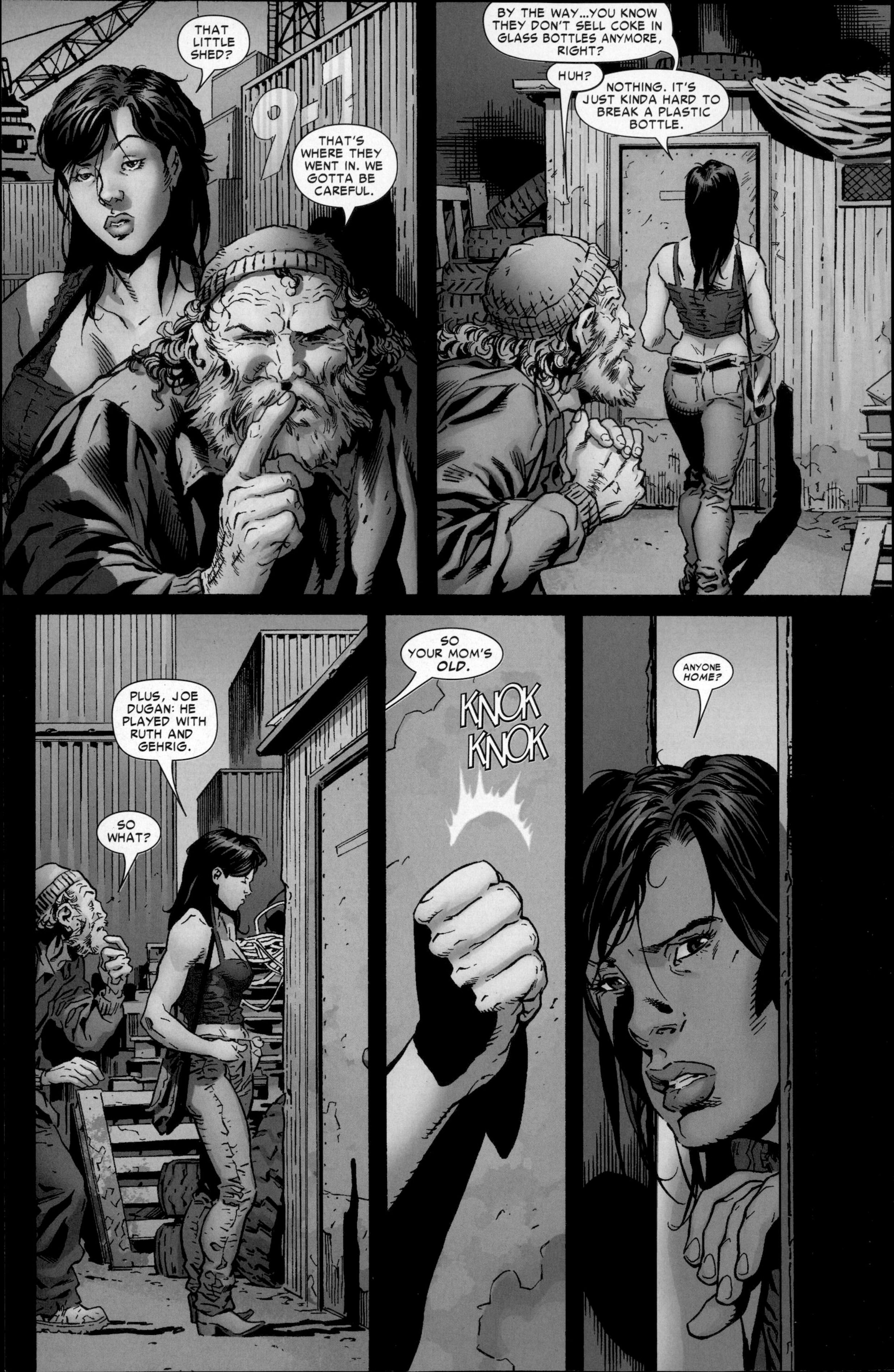
THAT LITTLE SHED?
THAT'S WHERE THEY WENT IN. WE GOTTA BE CAREFUL.
9-7
BY THE WAY...YOU KNOW THEY DON'T SELL COKE IN GLASS BOTTLES ANYMORE, RIGHT?
HUH?
NOTHING. IT'S JUST KINDA HARD TO BREAK A PLASTIC BOTTLE.
PLUS, JOE DUGAN: HE PLAYED WITH RUTH AND GEHRIG.
SO WHAT?
SO YOUR MOM'S OLD.
KNOK KNOK
ANYONE HOME?

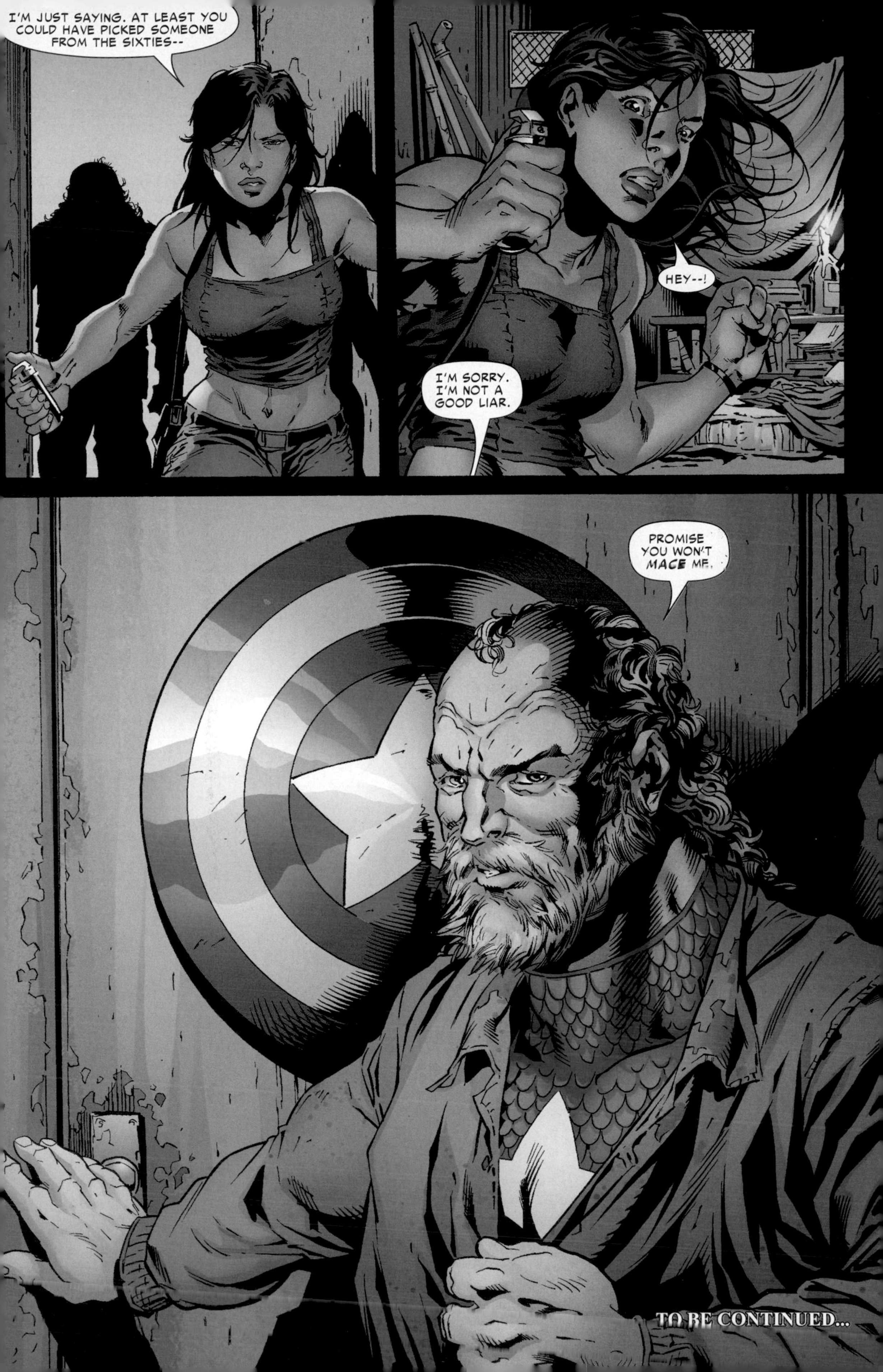
I'M JUST SAYING. AT LEAST YOU COULD HAVE PICKED SOMEONE FROM THE SIXTIES--
HEY--!
I'M SORRY. I'M NOT A GOOD LIAR.
PROMISE YOU WON'T MACE ME.
TO BE CONTINUED...

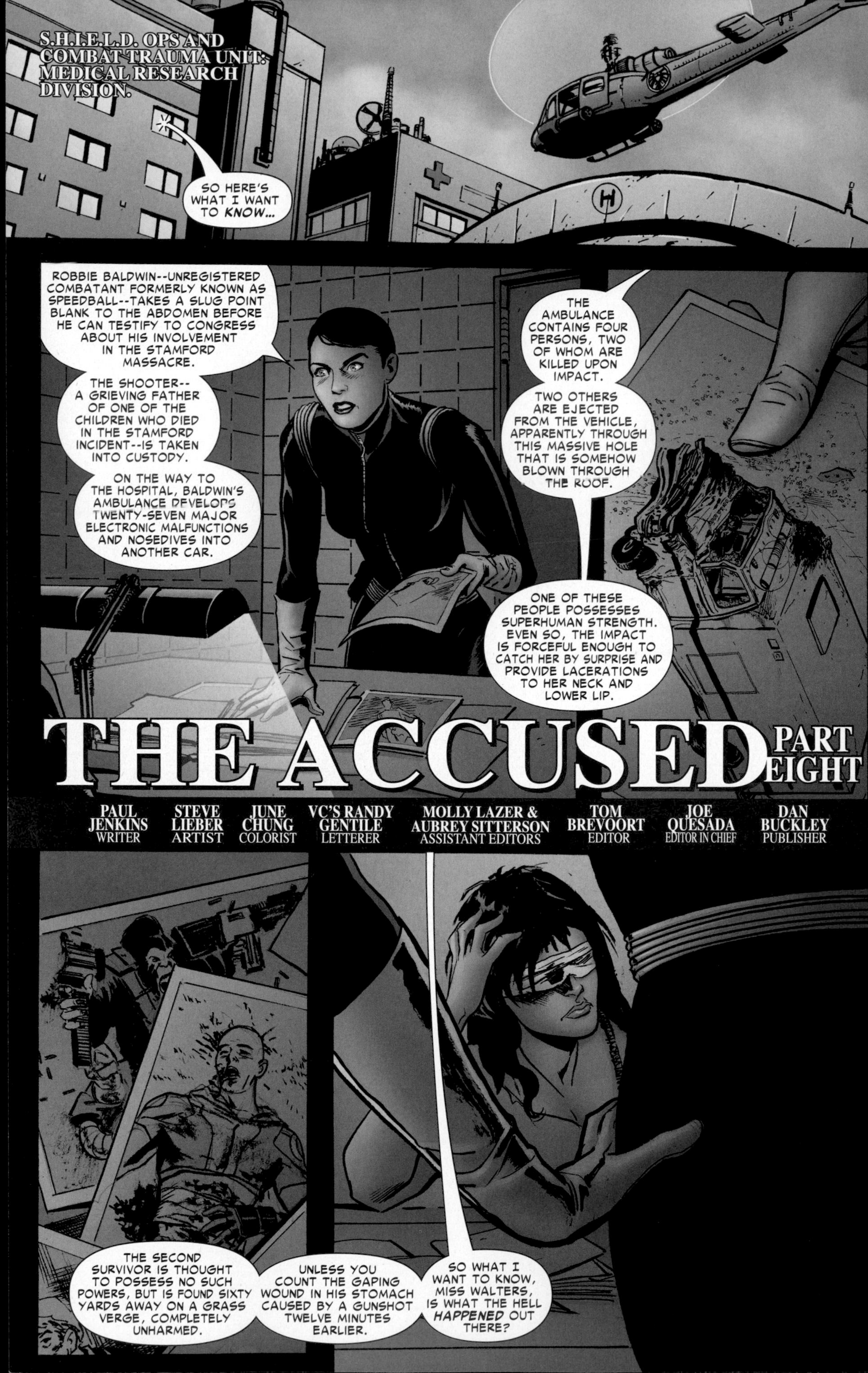

S.H.I.E.L.D. OPS AND COMBAT TRAUMA UNIT: MEDICAL RESEARCH DIVISION.
SO HERE'S WHAT I WANT TO *KNOW*...
ROBBIE BALDWIN--UNREGISTERED COMBATANT FORMERLY KNOWN AS SPEEDBALL--TAKES A SLUG POINT BLANK TO THE ABDOMEN BEFORE HE CAN TESTIFY TO CONGRESS ABOUT HIS INVOLVEMENT IN THE STAMFORD MASSACRE.
THE SHOOTER--A GRIEVING FATHER OF ONE OF THE CHILDREN WHO DIED IN THE STAMFORD INCIDENT--IS TAKEN INTO CUSTODY.
ON THE WAY TO THE HOSPITAL, BALDWIN'S AMBULANCE DEVELOPS TWENTY-SEVEN MAJOR ELECTRONIC MALFUNCTIONS AND NOSEDIVES INTO ANOTHER CAR.
THE AMBULANCE CONTAINS FOUR PERSONS, TWO OF WHOM ARE KILLED UPON IMPACT.
TWO OTHERS ARE EJECTED FROM THE VEHICLE, APPARENTLY THROUGH THIS MASSIVE HOLE THAT IS SOMEHOW BLOWN THROUGH THE ROOF.
ONE OF THESE PEOPLE POSSESSES SUPERHUMAN STRENGTH. EVEN SO, THE IMPACT IS FORCEFUL ENOUGH TO CATCH HER BY SURPRISE AND PROVIDE LACERATIONS TO HER NECK AND LOWER LIP.
THE ACCUSED PART EIGHT
PAUL JENKINS WRITER
STEVE LIEBER ARTIST
JUNE CHUNG COLORIST
VC'S RANDY GENTILE LETTERER
MOLLY LAZER & AUBREY SITTERSON ASSISTANT EDITORS
TOM BREVOORT EDITOR
JOE QUESADA EDITOR IN CHIEF
DAN BUCKLEY PUBLISHER
THE SECOND SURVIVOR IS THOUGHT TO POSSESS NO SUCH POWERS, BUT IS FOUND SIXTY YARDS AWAY ON A GRASS VERGE, COMPLETELY UNHARMED.
UNLESS YOU COUNT THE GAPING WOUND IN HIS STOMACH CAUSED BY A GUNSHOT TWELVE MINUTES EARLIER.
SO WHAT I WANT TO KNOW, MISS WALTERS, IS WHAT THE HELL *HAPPENED* OUT THERE?

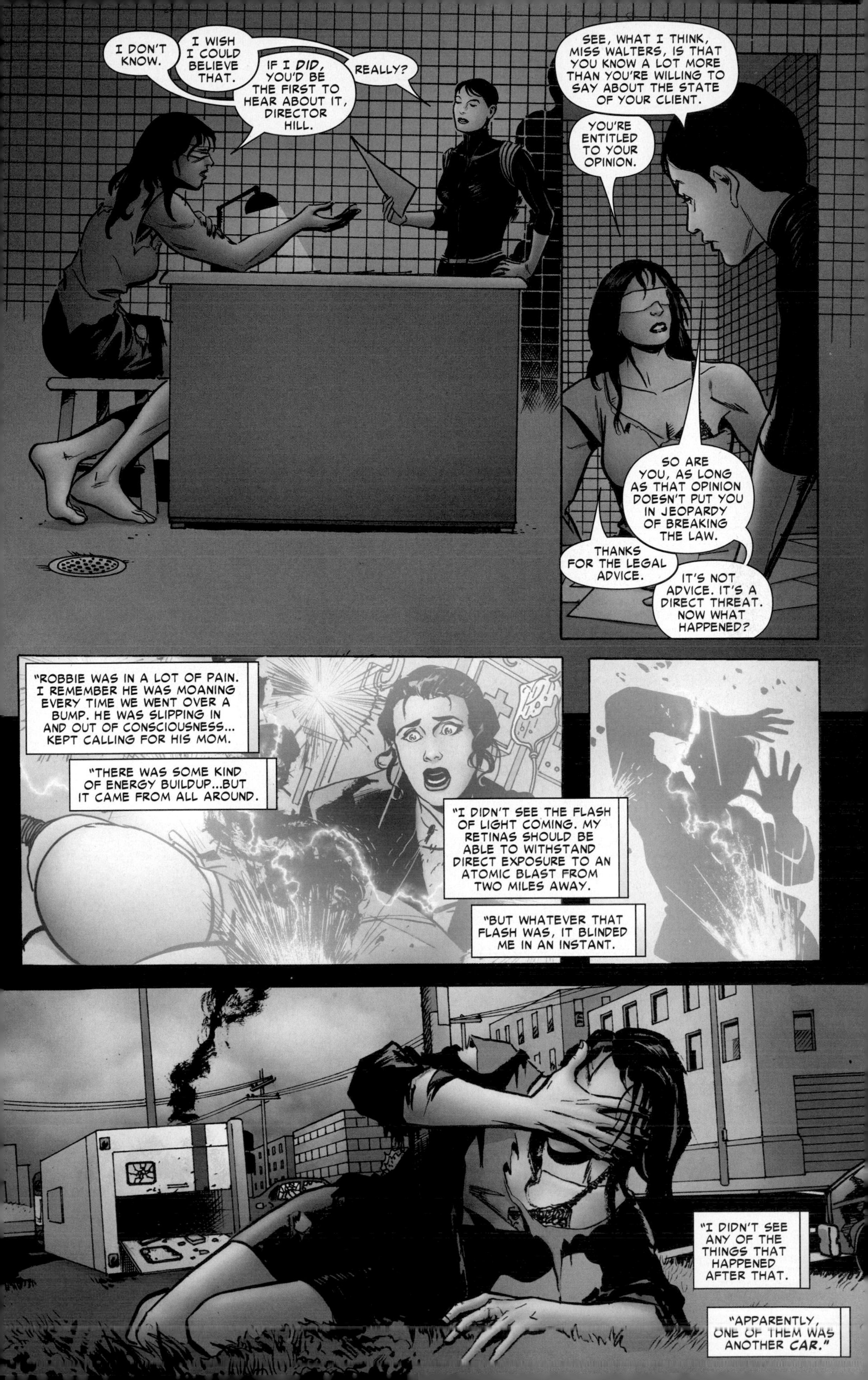
I DON'T KNOW.
REALLY?
IF I *DID*, YOU'D BE THE FIRST TO HEAR ABOUT IT, DIRECTOR HILL.
I WISH I COULD BELIEVE THAT.
SEE, WHAT I THINK, MISS WALTERS, IS THAT YOU KNOW A LOT MORE THAN YOU'RE WILLING TO SAY ABOUT THE STATE OF YOUR CLIENT.
YOU'RE ENTITLED TO YOUR OPINION.
SO ARE YOU, AS LONG AS THAT OPINION DOESN'T PUT YOU IN JEOPARDY OF BREAKING THE LAW.
THANKS FOR THE LEGAL ADVICE.
IT'S NOT ADVICE. IT'S A DIRECT THREAT. NOW WHAT HAPPENED?
"ROBBIE WAS IN A LOT OF PAIN. I REMEMBER HE WAS MOANING EVERY TIME WE WENT OVER A BUMP. HE WAS SLIPPING IN AND OUT OF CONSCIOUSNESS... KEPT CALLING FOR HIS MOM.
"THERE WAS SOME KIND OF ENERGY BUILDUP...BUT IT CAME FROM ALL AROUND.
"I DIDN'T SEE THE FLASH OF LIGHT COMING. MY RETINAS SHOULD BE ABLE TO WITHSTAND DIRECT EXPOSURE TO AN ATOMIC BLAST FROM TWO MILES AWAY.
"BUT WHATEVER THAT FLASH WAS, IT BLINDED ME IN AN INSTANT.
"I DIDN'T SEE ANY OF THE THINGS THAT HAPPENED AFTER THAT.
"APPARENTLY, ONE OF THEM WAS ANOTHER *CAR*."

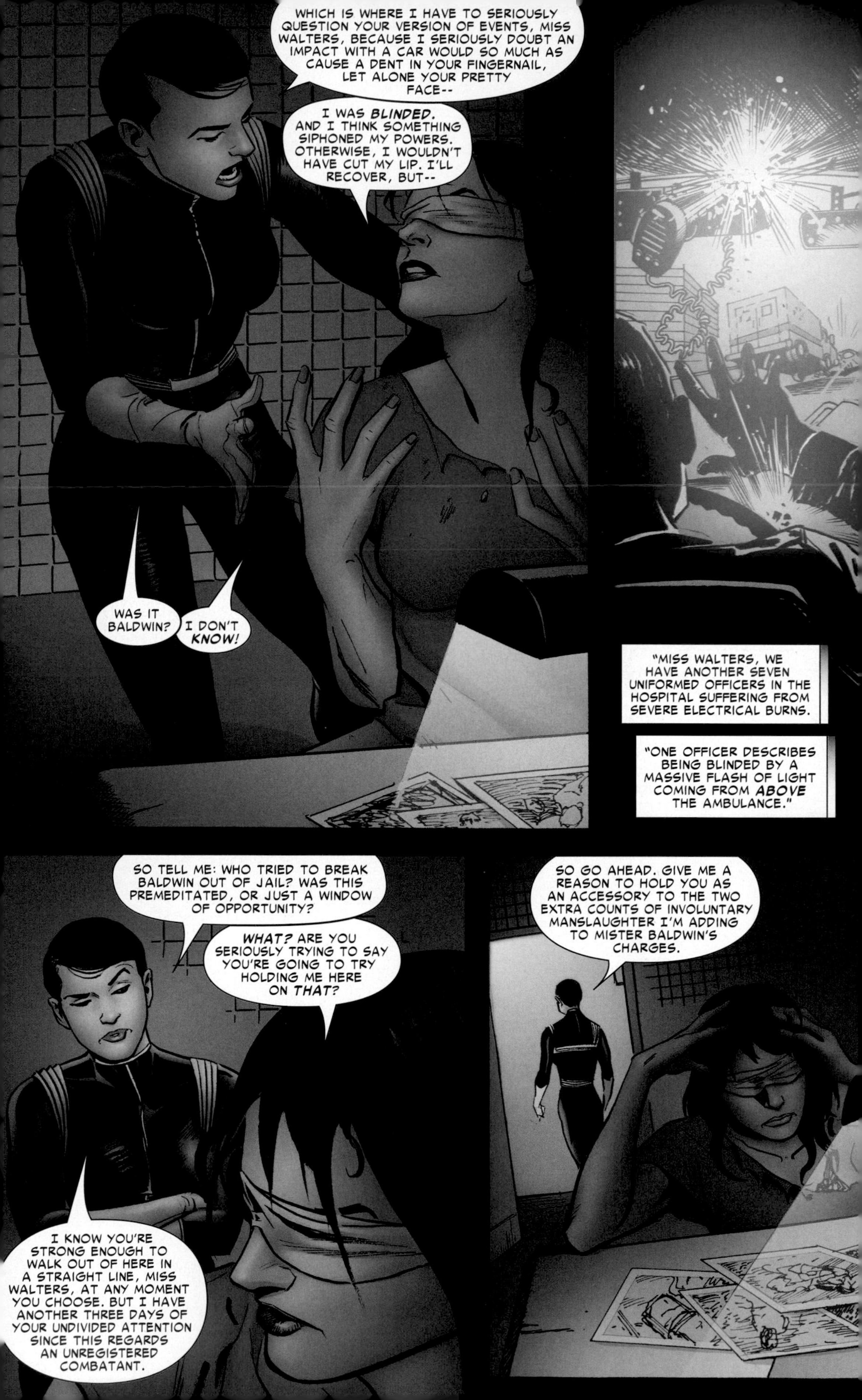
WHICH IS WHERE I HAVE TO SERIOUSLY QUESTION YOUR VERSION OF EVENTS, MISS WALTERS, BECAUSE I SERIOUSLY DOUBT AN IMPACT WITH A CAR WOULD SO MUCH AS CAUSE A DENT IN YOUR FINGERNAIL, LET ALONE YOUR PRETTY FACE--
I WAS BLINDED. AND I THINK SOMETHING SIPHONED MY POWERS. OTHERWISE, I WOULDN'T HAVE CUT MY LIP. I'LL RECOVER, BUT--
WAS IT BALDWIN?
I DON'T KNOW!
"MISS WALTERS, WE HAVE ANOTHER SEVEN UNIFORMED OFFICERS IN THE HOSPITAL SUFFERING FROM SEVERE ELECTRICAL BURNS.
"ONE OFFICER DESCRIBES BEING BLINDED BY A MASSIVE FLASH OF LIGHT COMING FROM ABOVE THE AMBULANCE."
SO TELL ME: WHO TRIED TO BREAK BALDWIN OUT OF JAIL? WAS THIS PREMEDITATED, OR JUST A WINDOW OF OPPORTUNITY?
WHAT? ARE YOU SERIOUSLY TRYING TO SAY YOU'RE GOING TO TRY HOLDING ME HERE ON THAT?
I KNOW YOU'RE STRONG ENOUGH TO WALK OUT OF HERE IN A STRAIGHT LINE, MISS WALTERS, AT ANY MOMENT YOU CHOOSE. BUT I HAVE ANOTHER THREE DAYS OF YOUR UNDIVIDED ATTENTION SINCE THIS REGARDS AN UNREGISTERED COMBATANT.
SO GO AHEAD. GIVE ME A REASON TO HOLD YOU AS AN ACCESSORY TO THE TWO EXTRA COUNTS OF INVOLUNTARY MANSLAUGHTER I'M ADDING TO MISTER BALDWIN'S CHARGES.

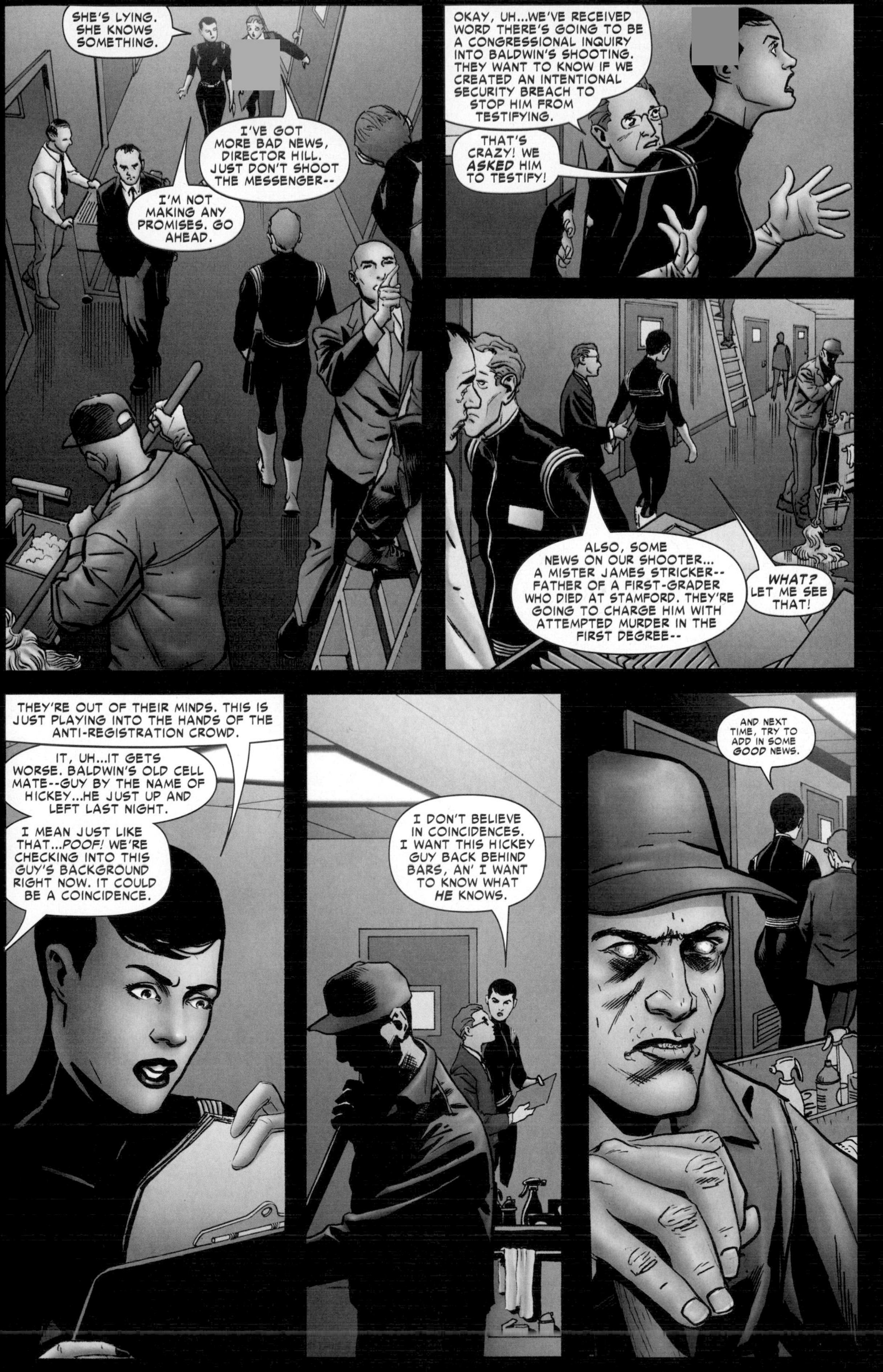
SHE'S LYING. SHE KNOWS SOMETHING.
I'VE GOT MORE BAD NEWS, DIRECTOR HILL. JUST DON'T SHOOT THE MESSENGER--
I'M NOT MAKING ANY PROMISES. GO AHEAD.
OKAY, UH...WE'VE RECEIVED WORD THERE'S GOING TO BE A CONGRESSIONAL INQUIRY INTO BALDWIN'S SHOOTING. THEY WANT TO KNOW IF WE CREATED AN INTENTIONAL SECURITY BREACH TO STOP HIM FROM TESTIFYING.
THAT'S CRAZY! WE ASKED HIM TO TESTIFY!
ALSO, SOME NEWS ON OUR SHOOTER... A MISTER JAMES STRICKER-- FATHER OF A FIRST-GRADER WHO DIED AT STAMFORD. THEY'RE GOING TO CHARGE HIM WITH ATTEMPTED MURDER IN THE FIRST DEGREE--
WHAT? LET ME SEE THAT!
THEY'RE OUT OF THEIR MINDS. THIS IS JUST PLAYING INTO THE HANDS OF THE ANTI-REGISTRATION CROWD.
IT, UH...IT GETS WORSE. BALDWIN'S OLD CELL MATE--GUY BY THE NAME OF HICKEY...HE JUST UP AND LEFT LAST NIGHT.
I MEAN JUST LIKE THAT...POOF! WE'RE CHECKING INTO THIS GUY'S BACKGROUND RIGHT NOW. IT COULD BE A COINCIDENCE.
I DON'T BELIEVE IN COINCIDENCES. I WANT THIS HICKEY GUY BACK BEHIND BARS, AN' I WANT TO KNOW WHAT HE KNOWS.
AND NEXT TIME, TRY TO ADD IN SOME GOOD NEWS.

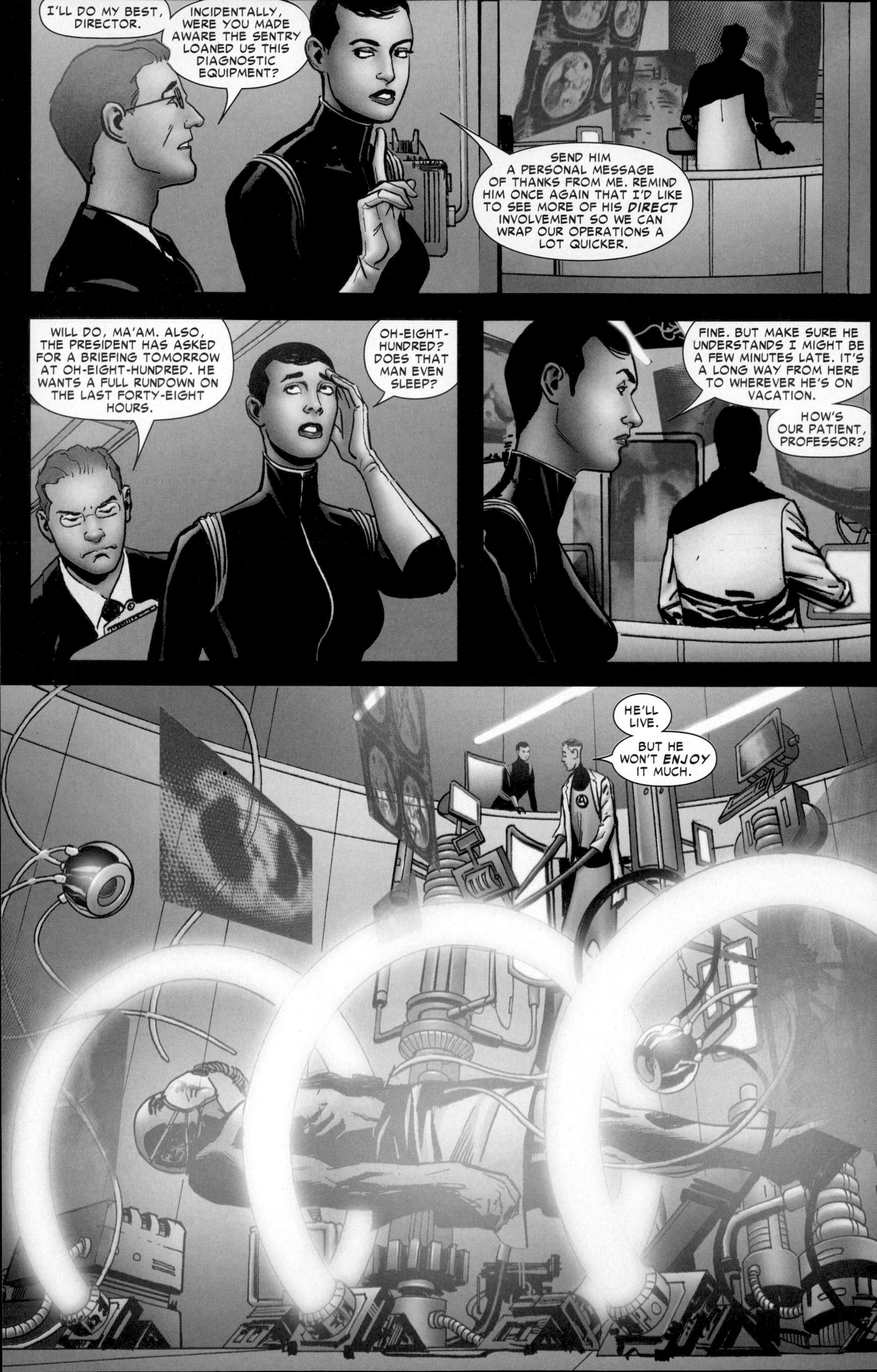
I'LL DO MY BEST, DIRECTOR.
INCIDENTALLY, WERE YOU MADE AWARE THE SENTRY LOANED US THIS DIAGNOSTIC EQUIPMENT?
SEND HIM A PERSONAL MESSAGE OF THANKS FROM ME. REMIND HIM ONCE AGAIN THAT I'D LIKE TO SEE MORE OF HIS *DIRECT* INVOLVEMENT SO WE CAN WRAP OUR OPERATIONS A LOT QUICKER.
WILL DO, MA'AM. ALSO, THE PRESIDENT HAS ASKED FOR A BRIEFING TOMORROW AT OH-EIGHT-HUNDRED. HE WANTS A FULL RUNDOWN ON THE LAST FORTY-EIGHT HOURS.
OH-EIGHT-HUNDRED? DOES THAT MAN EVEN SLEEP?
FINE. BUT MAKE SURE HE UNDERSTANDS I MIGHT BE A FEW MINUTES LATE. IT'S A LONG WAY FROM HERE TO WHEREVER HE'S ON VACATION.
HOW'S OUR PATIENT, PROFESSOR?
HE'LL LIVE.
BUT HE WON'T *ENJOY* IT MUCH.

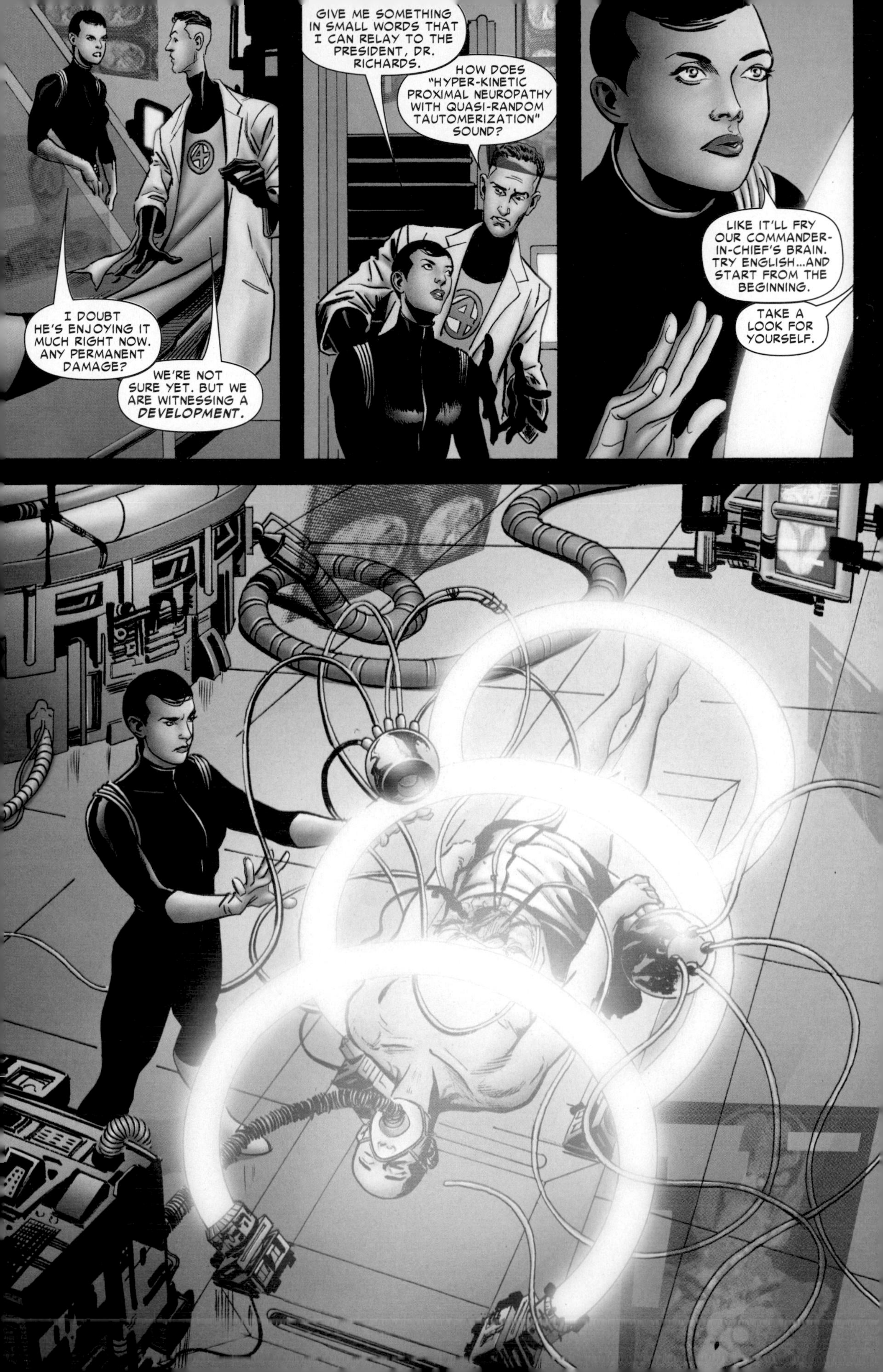
I DOUBT HE'S ENJOYING IT MUCH RIGHT NOW. ANY PERMANENT DAMAGE?
WE'RE NOT SURE YET. BUT WE ARE WITNESSING A *DEVELOPMENT*.
GIVE ME SOMETHING IN SMALL WORDS THAT I CAN RELAY TO THE PRESIDENT, DR. RICHARDS.
HOW DOES "HYPER-KINETIC PROXIMAL NEUROPATHY WITH QUASI-RANDOM TAUTOMERIZATION" SOUND?
LIKE IT'LL FRY OUR COMMANDER-IN-CHIEF'S BRAIN. TRY ENGLISH...AND START FROM THE BEGINNING.
TAKE A LOOK FOR YOURSELF.

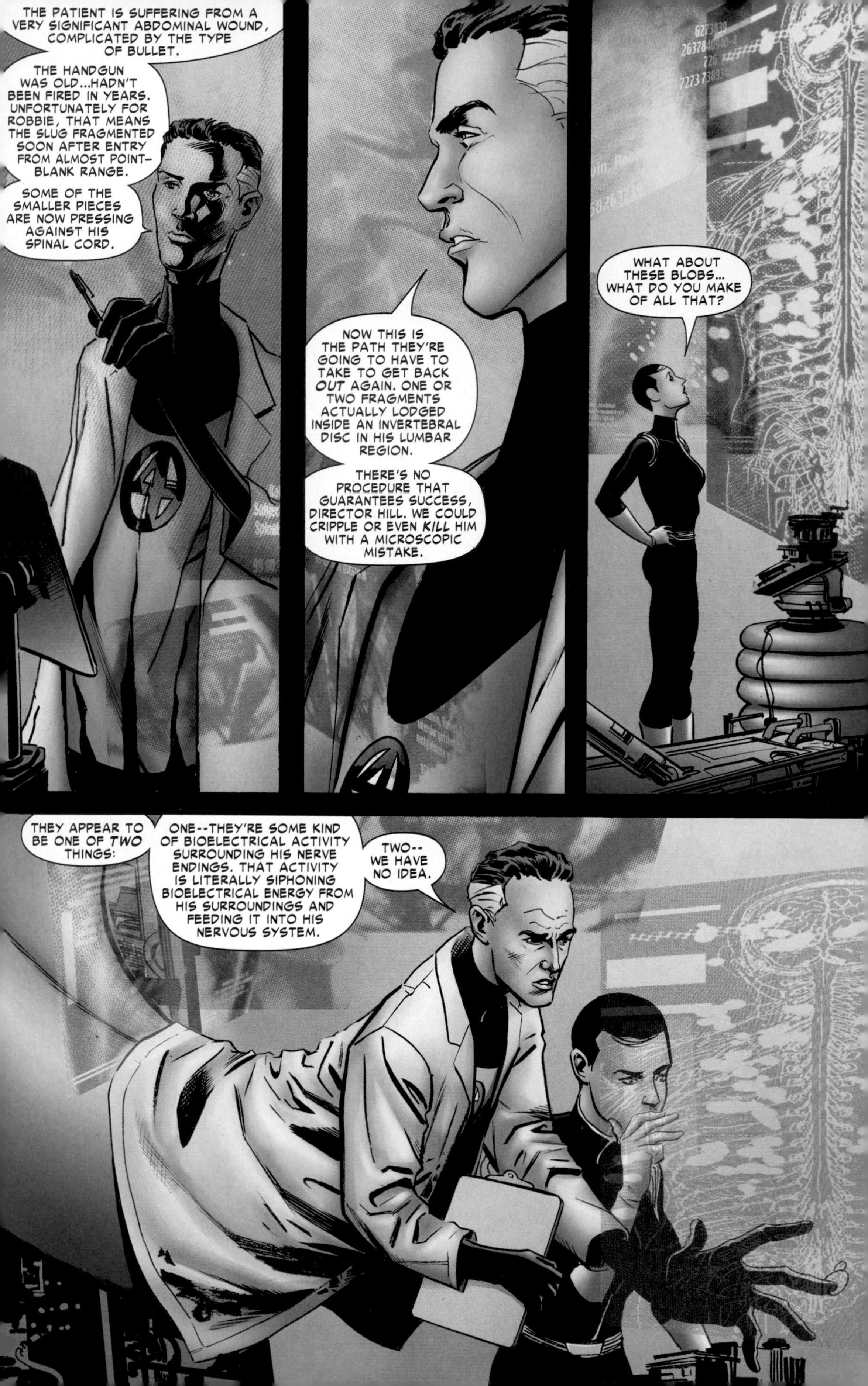
THE PATIENT IS SUFFERING FROM A VERY SIGNIFICANT ABDOMINAL WOUND, COMPLICATED BY THE TYPE OF BULLET.
THE HANDGUN WAS OLD...HADN'T BEEN FIRED IN YEARS. UNFORTUNATELY FOR ROBBIE, THAT MEANS THE SLUG FRAGMENTED SOON AFTER ENTRY FROM ALMOST POINT-BLANK RANGE.
SOME OF THE SMALLER PIECES ARE NOW PRESSING AGAINST HIS SPINAL CORD.
NOW THIS IS THE PATH THEY'RE GOING TO HAVE TO TAKE TO GET BACK *OUT* AGAIN. ONE OR TWO FRAGMENTS ACTUALLY LODGED INSIDE AN INVERTEBRAL DISC IN HIS LUMBAR REGION.
THERE'S NO PROCEDURE THAT GUARANTEES SUCCESS, DIRECTOR HILL. WE COULD CRIPPLE OR EVEN ***KILL*** HIM WITH A MICROSCOPIC MISTAKE.
WHAT ABOUT THESE BLOBS... WHAT DO YOU MAKE OF ALL THAT?
THEY APPEAR TO BE ONE OF *TWO* THINGS:
ONE--THEY'RE SOME KIND OF BIOELECTRICAL ACTIVITY SURROUNDING HIS NERVE ENDINGS. THAT ACTIVITY IS LITERALLY SIPHONING BIOELECTRICAL ENERGY FROM HIS SURROUNDINGS AND FEEDING IT INTO HIS NERVOUS SYSTEM.
TWO-- WE HAVE NO IDEA.

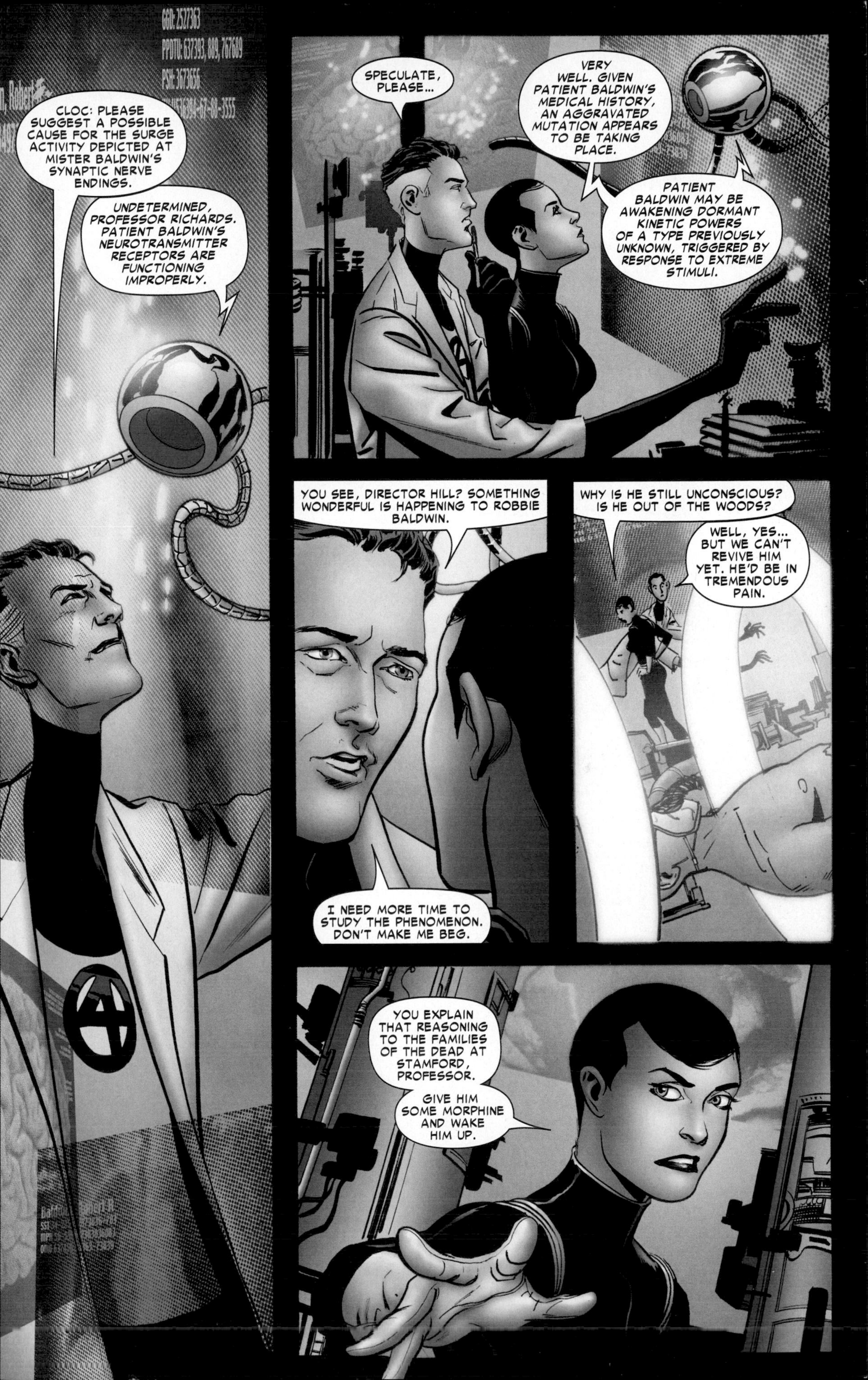
GBD: 2527363
PPDTU: 637393, 889, 767689
PSH: 3673656
CLOC: PLEASE SUGGEST A POSSIBLE CAUSE FOR THE SURGE ACTIVITY DEPICTED AT MISTER BALDWIN'S SYNAPTIC NERVE ENDINGS.
UNDETERMINED, PROFESSOR RICHARDS. PATIENT BALDWIN'S NEUROTRANSMITTER RECEPTORS ARE FUNCTIONING IMPROPERLY.
SPECULATE, PLEASE...
VERY WELL. GIVEN PATIENT BALDWIN'S MEDICAL HISTORY, AN AGGRAVATED MUTATION APPEARS TO BE TAKING PLACE.
PATIENT BALDWIN MAY BE AWAKENING DORMANT KINETIC POWERS OF A TYPE PREVIOUSLY UNKNOWN, TRIGGERED BY RESPONSE TO EXTREME STIMULI.
YOU SEE, DIRECTOR HILL? SOMETHING WONDERFUL IS HAPPENING TO ROBBIE BALDWIN.
I NEED MORE TIME TO STUDY THE PHENOMENON. DON'T MAKE ME BEG.
WHY IS HE STILL UNCONSCIOUS? IS HE OUT OF THE WOODS?
WELL, YES... BUT WE CAN'T REVIVE HIM YET. HE'D BE IN TREMENDOUS PAIN.
YOU EXPLAIN THAT REASONING TO THE FAMILIES OF THE DEAD AT STAMFORD, PROFESSOR.
GIVE HIM SOME MORPHINE AND WAKE HIM UP.

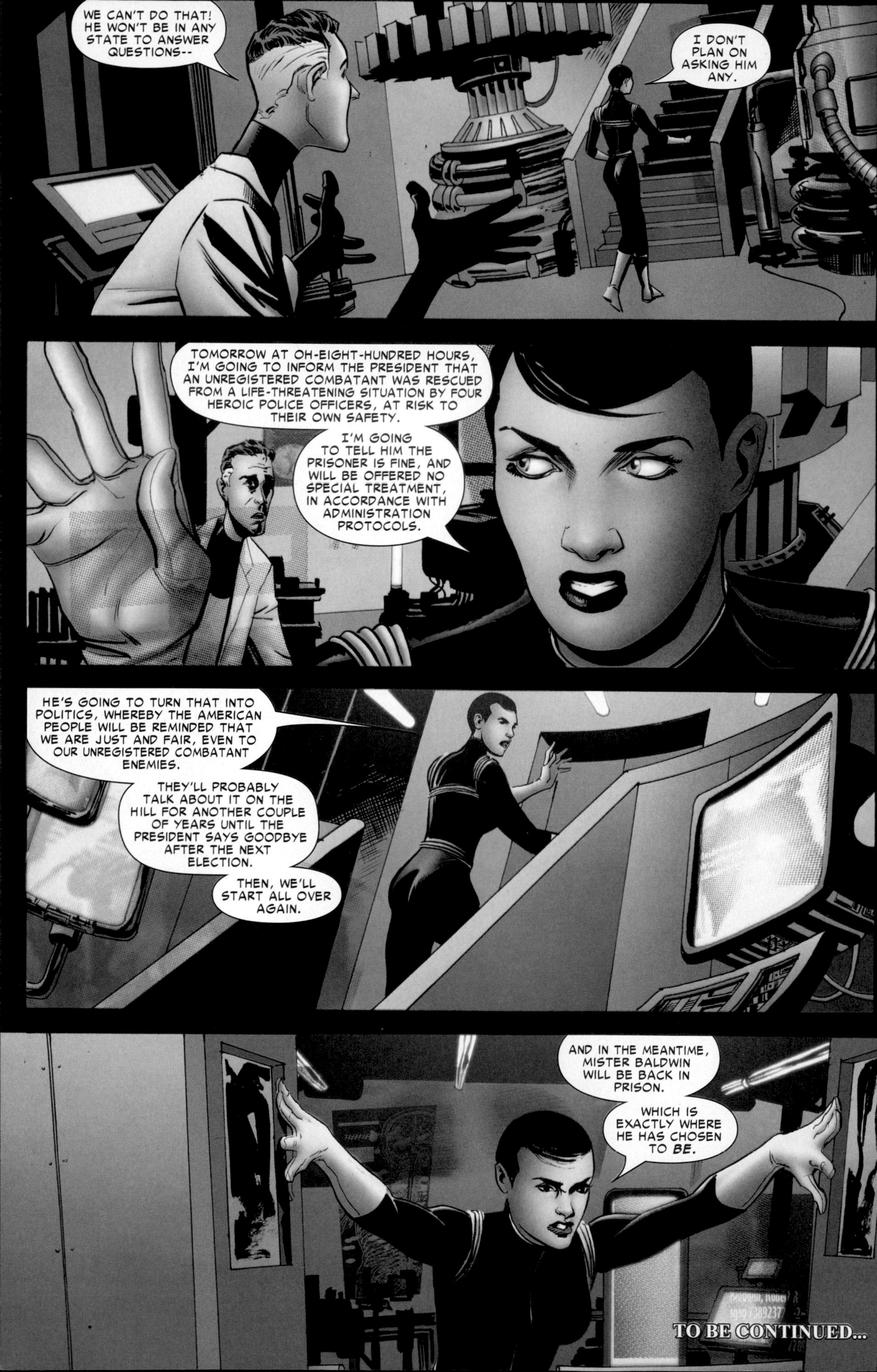
WE CAN'T DO THAT! HE WON'T BE IN ANY STATE TO ANSWER QUESTIONS--
I DON'T PLAN ON ASKING HIM ANY.
TOMORROW AT OH-EIGHT-HUNDRED HOURS, I'M GOING TO INFORM THE PRESIDENT THAT AN UNREGISTERED COMBATANT WAS RESCUED FROM A LIFE-THREATENING SITUATION BY FOUR HEROIC POLICE OFFICERS, AT RISK TO THEIR OWN SAFETY.
I'M GOING TO TELL HIM THE PRISONER IS FINE, AND WILL BE OFFERED NO SPECIAL TREATMENT, IN ACCORDANCE WITH ADMINISTRATION PROTOCOLS.
HE'S GOING TO TURN THAT INTO POLITICS, WHEREBY THE AMERICAN PEOPLE WILL BE REMINDED THAT WE ARE JUST AND FAIR, EVEN TO OUR UNREGISTERED COMBATANT ENEMIES.
THEY'LL PROBABLY TALK ABOUT IT ON THE HILL FOR ANOTHER COUPLE OF YEARS UNTIL THE PRESIDENT SAYS GOODBYE AFTER THE NEXT ELECTION.
THEN, WE'LL START ALL OVER AGAIN.
AND IN THE MEANTIME, MISTER BALDWIN WILL BE BACK IN PRISON.
WHICH IS EXACTLY WHERE HE HAS CHOSEN TO *BE*.
TO BE CONTINUED...

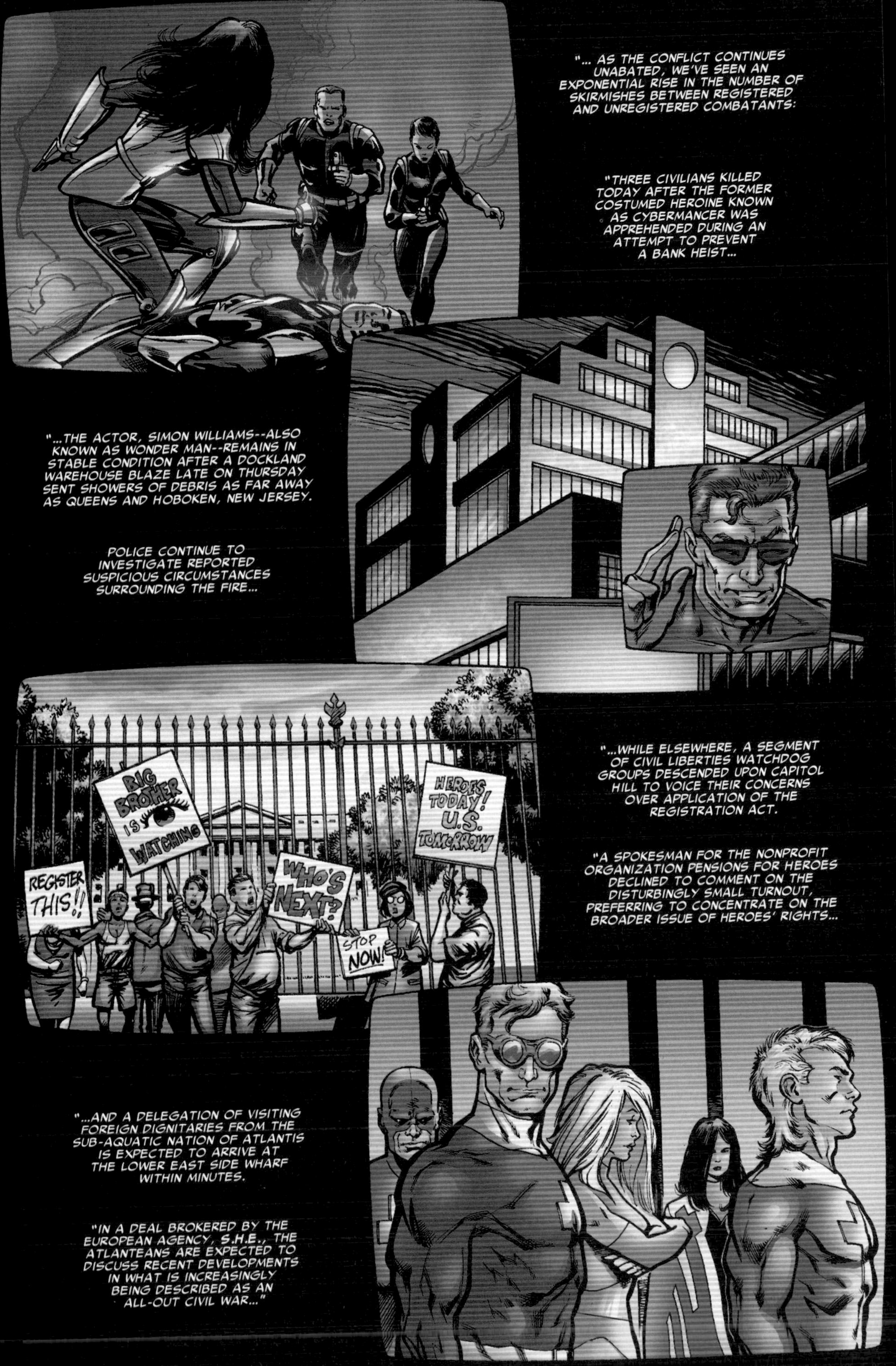
"... AS THE CONFLICT CONTINUES UNABATED, WE'VE SEEN AN EXPONENTIAL RISE IN THE NUMBER OF SKIRMISHES BETWEEN REGISTERED AND UNREGISTERED COMBATANTS:
"THREE CIVILIANS KILLED TODAY AFTER THE FORMER COSTUMED HEROINE KNOWN AS CYBERMANCER WAS APPREHENDED DURING AN ATTEMPT TO PREVENT A BANK HEIST...
"...THE ACTOR, SIMON WILLIAMS--ALSO KNOWN AS WONDER MAN--REMAINS IN STABLE CONDITION AFTER A DOCKLAND WAREHOUSE BLAZE LATE ON THURSDAY SENT SHOWERS OF DEBRIS AS FAR AWAY AS QUEENS AND HOBOKEN, NEW JERSEY.
POLICE CONTINUE TO INVESTIGATE REPORTED SUSPICIOUS CIRCUMSTANCES SURROUNDING THE FIRE...
BIG BROTHER IS WATCHING
REGISTER THIS!!
WHO'S NEXT?
HEROES TODAY! U.S. TOMORROW
STOP NOW!
"...WHILE ELSEWHERE, A SEGMENT OF CIVIL LIBERTIES WATCHDOG GROUPS DESCENDED UPON CAPITOL HILL TO VOICE THEIR CONCERNS OVER APPLICATION OF THE REGISTRATION ACT.
"A SPOKESMAN FOR THE NONPROFIT ORGANIZATION PENSIONS FOR HEROES DECLINED TO COMMENT ON THE DISTURBINGLY SMALL TURNOUT, PREFERRING TO CONCENTRATE ON THE BROADER ISSUE OF HEROES' RIGHTS...
"...AND A DELEGATION OF VISITING FOREIGN DIGNITARIES FROM THE SUB-AQUATIC NATION OF ATLANTIS IS EXPECTED TO ARRIVE AT THE LOWER EAST SIDE WHARF WITHIN MINUTES.
"IN A DEAL BROKERED BY THE EUROPEAN AGENCY, S.H.E., THE ATLANTEANS ARE EXPECTED TO DISCUSS RECENT DEVELOPMENTS IN WHAT IS INCREASINGLY BEING DESCRIBED AS AN ALL-OUT CIVIL WAR..."

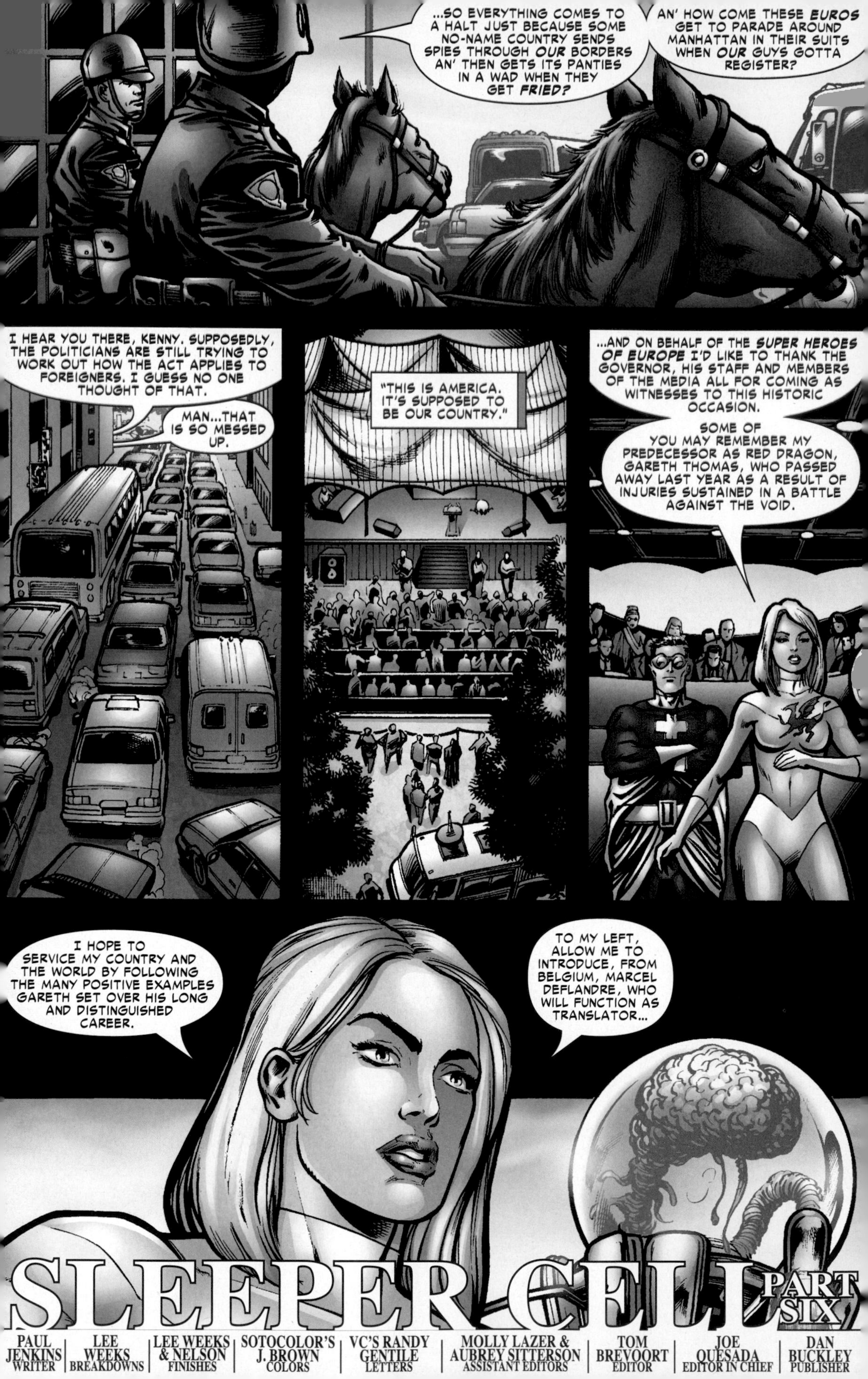
...SO EVERYTHING COMES TO A HALT JUST BECAUSE SOME NO-NAME COUNTRY SENDS SPIES THROUGH OUR BORDERS AN' THEN GETS ITS PANTIES IN A WAD WHEN THEY GET FRIED?
AN' HOW COME THESE EUROS GET TO PARADE AROUND MANHATTAN IN THEIR SUITS WHEN OUR GUYS GOTTA REGISTER?
I HEAR YOU THERE, KENNY. SUPPOSEDLY, THE POLITICIANS ARE STILL TRYING TO WORK OUT HOW THE ACT APPLIES TO FOREIGNERS. I GUESS NO ONE THOUGHT OF THAT.
MAN...THAT IS SO MESSED UP.
"THIS IS AMERICA. IT'S SUPPOSED TO BE OUR COUNTRY."
...AND ON BEHALF OF THE SUPER HEROES OF EUROPE I'D LIKE TO THANK THE GOVERNOR, HIS STAFF AND MEMBERS OF THE MEDIA ALL FOR COMING AS WITNESSES TO THIS HISTORIC OCCASION.
SOME OF YOU MAY REMEMBER MY PREDECESSOR AS RED DRAGON, GARETH THOMAS, WHO PASSED AWAY LAST YEAR AS A RESULT OF INJURIES SUSTAINED IN A BATTLE AGAINST THE VOID.
I HOPE TO SERVICE MY COUNTRY AND THE WORLD BY FOLLOWING THE MANY POSITIVE EXAMPLES GARETH SET OVER HIS LONG AND DISTINGUISHED CAREER.
TO MY LEFT, ALLOW ME TO INTRODUCE, FROM BELGIUM, MARCEL DEFLANDRE, WHO WILL FUNCTION AS TRANSLATOR...
SLEEPER CELL PART SIX
PAUL JENKINS WRITER
LEE WEEKS BREAKDOWNS
LEE WEEKS & NELSON FINISHES
SOTOCOLOR'S J. BROWN COLORS
VC'S RANDY GENTILE LETTERS
MOLLY LAZER & AUBREY SITTERSON ASSISTANT EDITORS
TOM BREVOORT EDITOR
JOE QUESADA EDITOR IN CHIEF
DAN BUCKLEY PUBLISHER

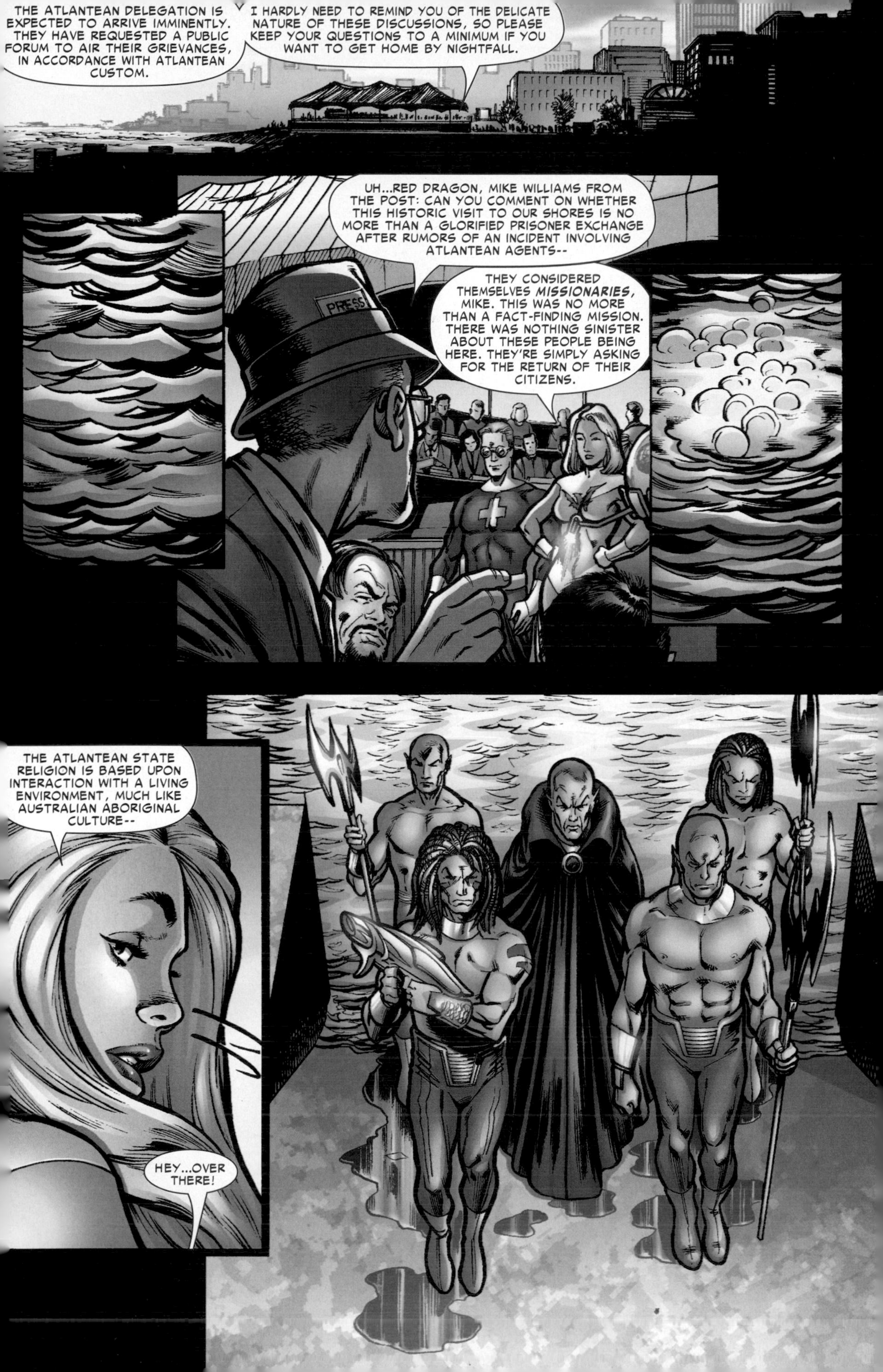
THE ATLANTEAN DELEGATION IS EXPECTED TO ARRIVE IMMINENTLY. THEY HAVE REQUESTED A PUBLIC FORUM TO AIR THEIR GRIEVANCES, IN ACCORDANCE WITH ATLANTEAN CUSTOM.
I HARDLY NEED TO REMIND YOU OF THE DELICATE NATURE OF THESE DISCUSSIONS, SO PLEASE KEEP YOUR QUESTIONS TO A MINIMUM IF YOU WANT TO GET HOME BY NIGHTFALL.
UH...RED DRAGON, MIKE WILLIAMS FROM THE POST: CAN YOU COMMENT ON WHETHER THIS HISTORIC VISIT TO OUR SHORES IS NO MORE THAN A GLORIFIED PRISONER EXCHANGE AFTER RUMORS OF AN INCIDENT INVOLVING ATLANTEAN AGENTS--
PRESS
THEY CONSIDERED THEMSELVES *MISSIONARIES*, MIKE. THIS WAS NO MORE THAN A FACT-FINDING MISSION. THERE WAS NOTHING SINISTER ABOUT THESE PEOPLE BEING HERE. THEY'RE SIMPLY ASKING FOR THE RETURN OF THEIR CITIZENS.
THE ATLANTEAN STATE RELIGION IS BASED UPON INTERACTION WITH A LIVING ENVIRONMENT, MUCH LIKE AUSTRALIAN ABORIGINAL CULTURE--
HEY...OVER THERE!

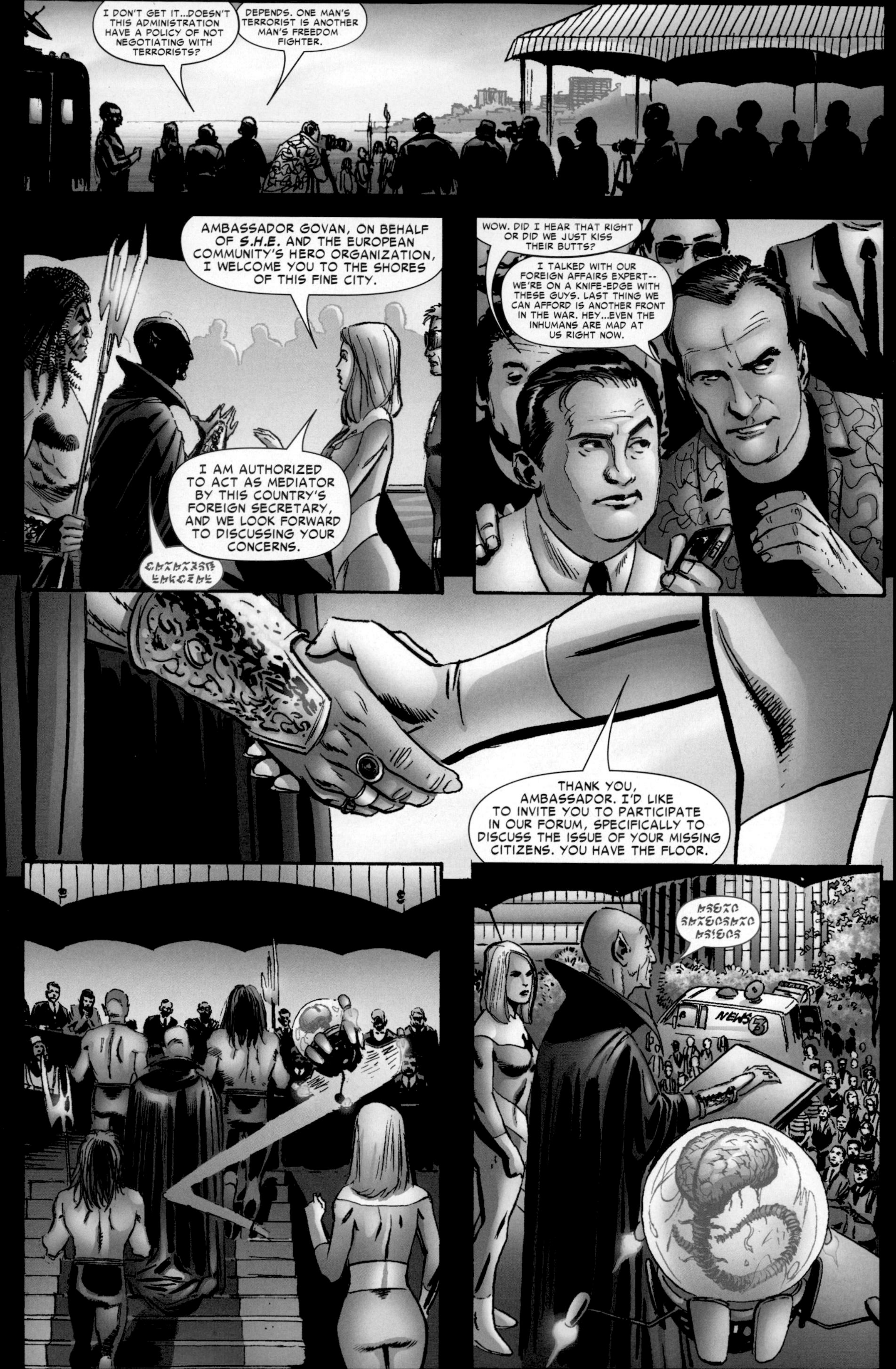
I DON'T GET IT...DOESN'T THIS ADMINISTRATION HAVE A POLICY OF NOT NEGOTIATING WITH TERRORISTS?
DEPENDS. ONE MAN'S TERRORIST IS ANOTHER MAN'S FREEDOM FIGHTER.
AMBASSADOR GOVAN, ON BEHALF OF S.H.E. AND THE EUROPEAN COMMUNITY'S HERO ORGANIZATION, I WELCOME YOU TO THE SHORES OF THIS FINE CITY.
I AM AUTHORIZED TO ACT AS MEDIATOR BY THIS COUNTRY'S FOREIGN SECRETARY, AND WE LOOK FORWARD TO DISCUSSING YOUR CONCERNS.
WOW. DID I HEAR THAT RIGHT OR DID WE JUST KISS THEIR BUTTS?
I TALKED WITH OUR FOREIGN AFFAIRS EXPERT-- WE'RE ON A KNIFE-EDGE WITH THESE GUYS. LAST THING WE CAN AFFORD IS ANOTHER FRONT IN THE WAR. HEY...EVEN THE INHUMANS ARE MAD AT US RIGHT NOW.
THANK YOU, AMBASSADOR. I'D LIKE TO INVITE YOU TO PARTICIPATE IN OUR FORUM, SPECIFICALLY TO DISCUSS THE ISSUE OF YOUR MISSING CITIZENS. YOU HAVE THE FLOOR.
NEWS 3

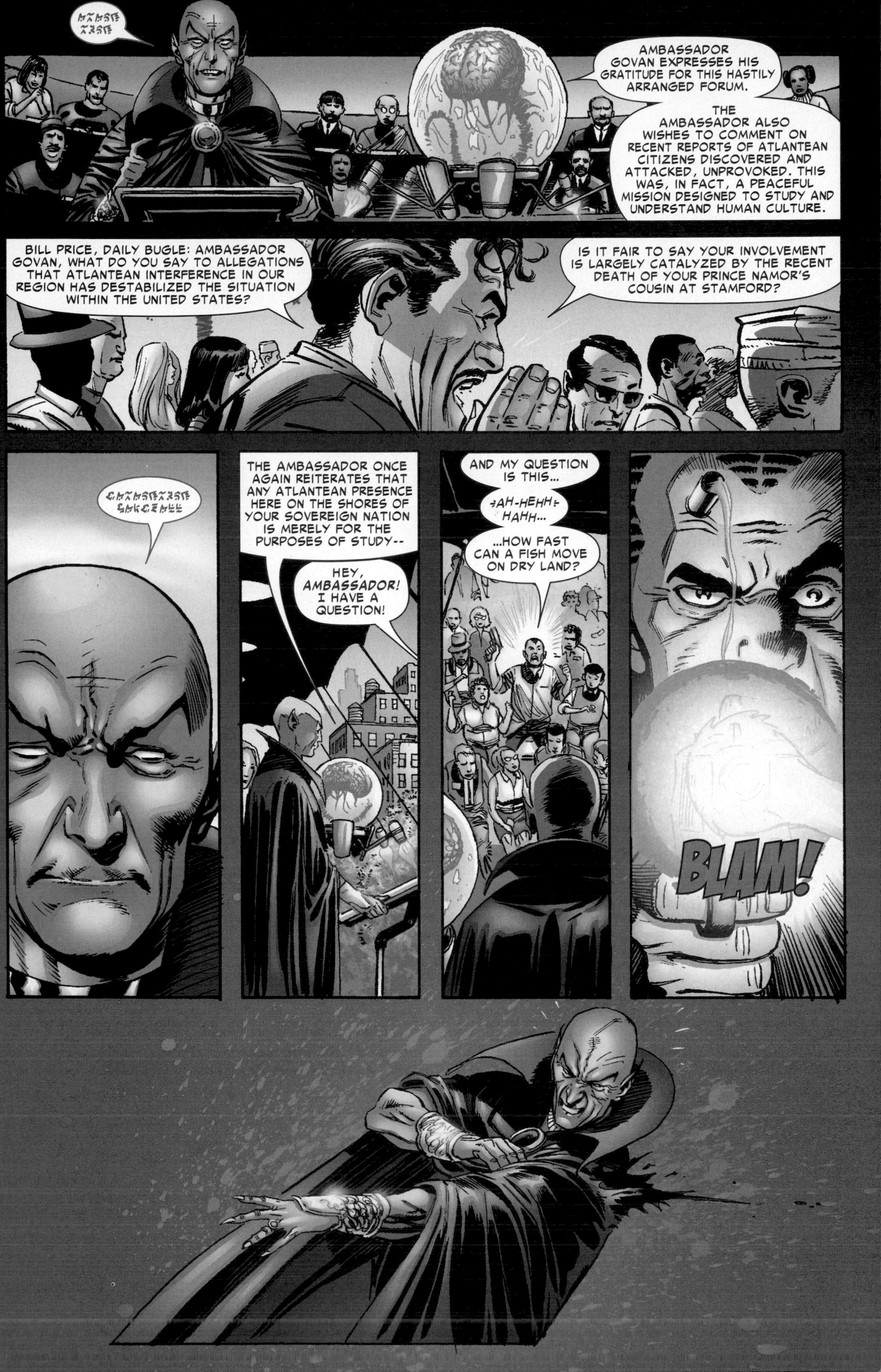
AMBASSADOR GOVAN EXPRESSES HIS GRATITUDE FOR THIS HASTILY ARRANGED FORUM.
THE AMBASSADOR ALSO WISHES TO COMMENT ON RECENT REPORTS OF ATLANTEAN CITIZENS DISCOVERED AND ATTACKED, UNPROVOKED. THIS WAS, IN FACT, A PEACEFUL MISSION DESIGNED TO STUDY AND UNDERSTAND HUMAN CULTURE.
BILL PRICE, DAILY BUGLE: AMBASSADOR GOVAN, WHAT DO YOU SAY TO ALLEGATIONS THAT ATLANTEAN INTERFERENCE IN OUR REGION HAS DESTABILIZED THE SITUATION WITHIN THE UNITED STATES?
IS IT FAIR TO SAY YOUR INVOLVEMENT IS LARGELY CATALYZED BY THE RECENT DEATH OF YOUR PRINCE NAMOR'S COUSIN AT STAMFORD?
THE AMBASSADOR ONCE AGAIN REITERATES THAT ANY ATLANTEAN PRESENCE HERE ON THE SHORES OF YOUR SOVEREIGN NATION IS MERELY FOR THE PURPOSES OF STUDY--
HEY, AMBASSADOR! I HAVE A QUESTION!
AND MY QUESTION IS THIS...
AH-HEHH HAHH...
...HOW FAST CAN A FISH MOVE ON DRY LAND?
BLAM!

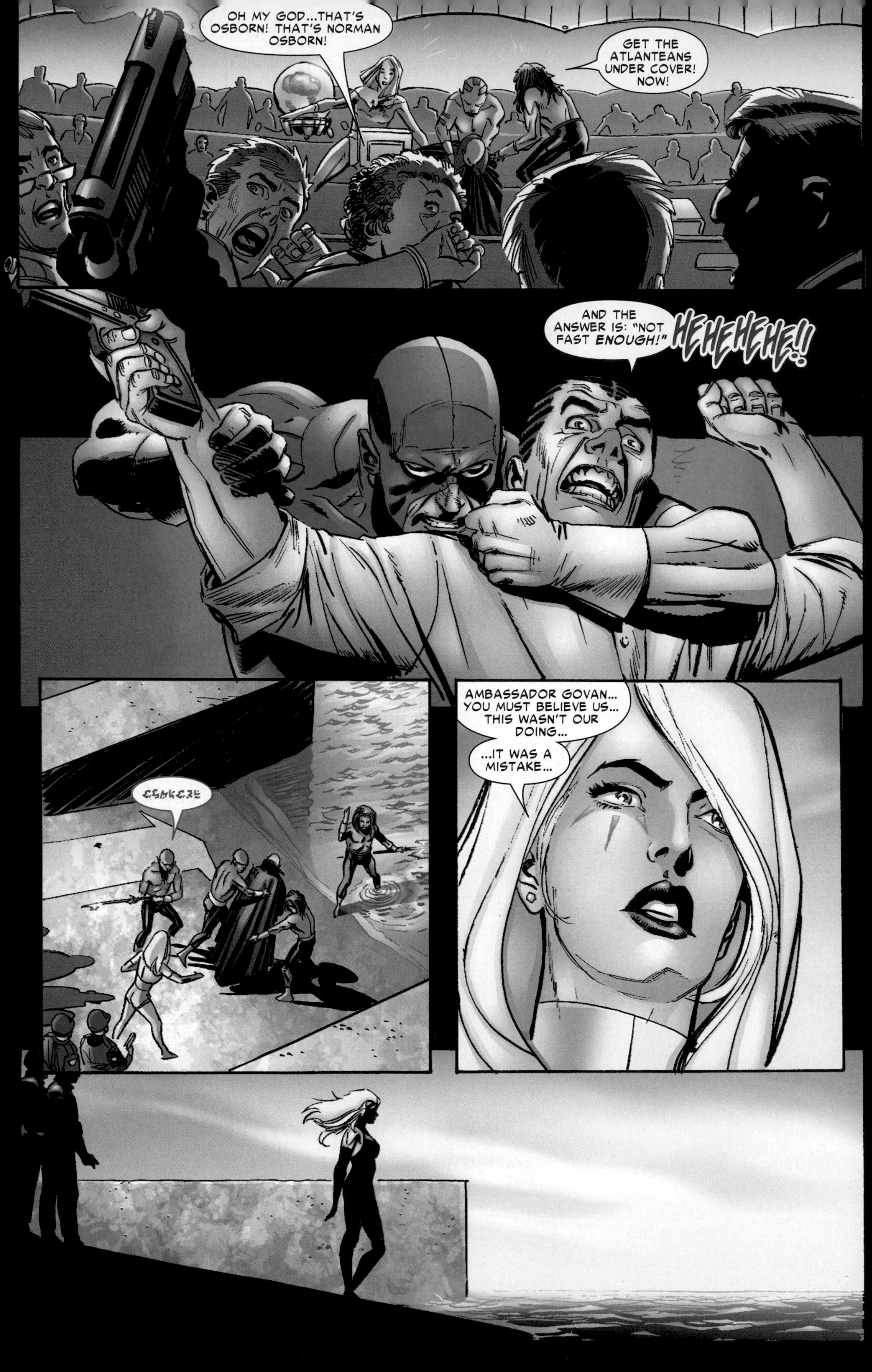
OH MY GOD...THAT'S OSBORN! THAT'S NORMAN OSBORN!
GET THE ATLANTEANS UNDER COVER! NOW!
AND THE ANSWER IS: "NOT FAST ENOUGH!"
HEHEHEHE!!
AMBASSADOR GOVAN... YOU MUST BELIEVE US... THIS WASN'T OUR DOING...
...IT WAS A MISTAKE...

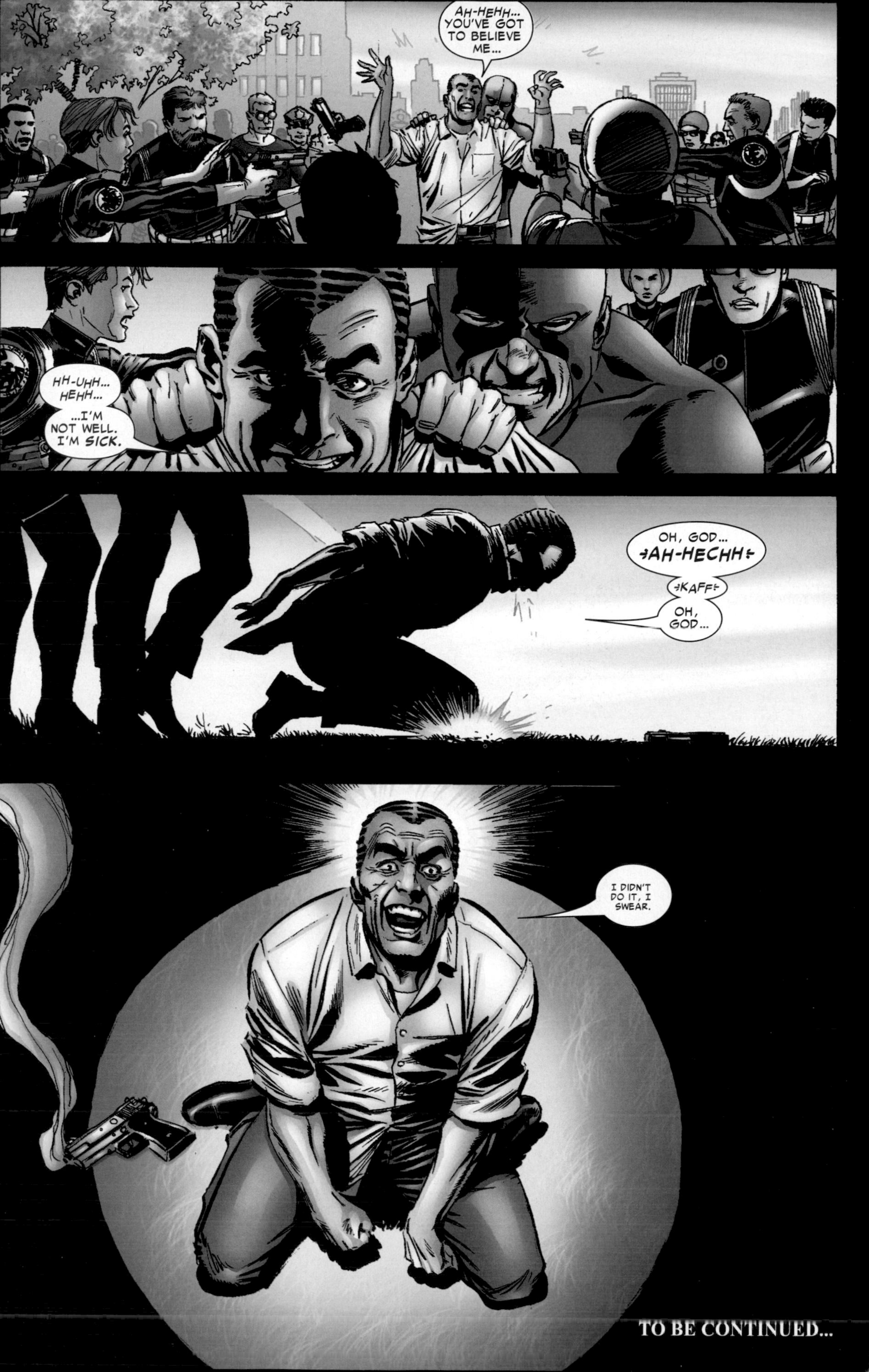
AH-HEHH... YOU'VE GOT TO BELIEVE ME...
HH-UHH... HEHH...
...I'M NOT WELL. I'M SICK.
OH, GOD...
AH-HECHH
KAFF
OH, GOD...
I DIDN'T DO IT, I SWEAR.
TO BE CONTINUED...

The battle of Edgehill, which began on October 16th, 1642, was the first--and some say the bloodiest--of the English Civil War.

The Royalist and Parliamentarian armies met in a massive skirmish on an open field near Kineton, Warwickshire. Most combatants were armed on[redacted]th pitch forks or cudgels. By day's end, huge swathes of troops lay dead and badly wounded. The bodies were looted for clothes and mone[redacted]d left on the field.

So bloody was the carnage that stories began to surface of the battle being replayed again and again in the skies above Kineton. King Charles the First became intrigued by these tales: weeks after the fight he sent some of his senior officers to investigate and interrogate witnesses.

To his alarm, his men returned, ashen-faced, to confirm that they themselves had seen the grisly battle still raging in the sky. In fact, they had even witnessed the deaths of former friends and colleagues as the battle raged in the clouds.

According to local legend, the Battle of Edgehill continues to replay in the sky each year on the anniversary of the conflict.

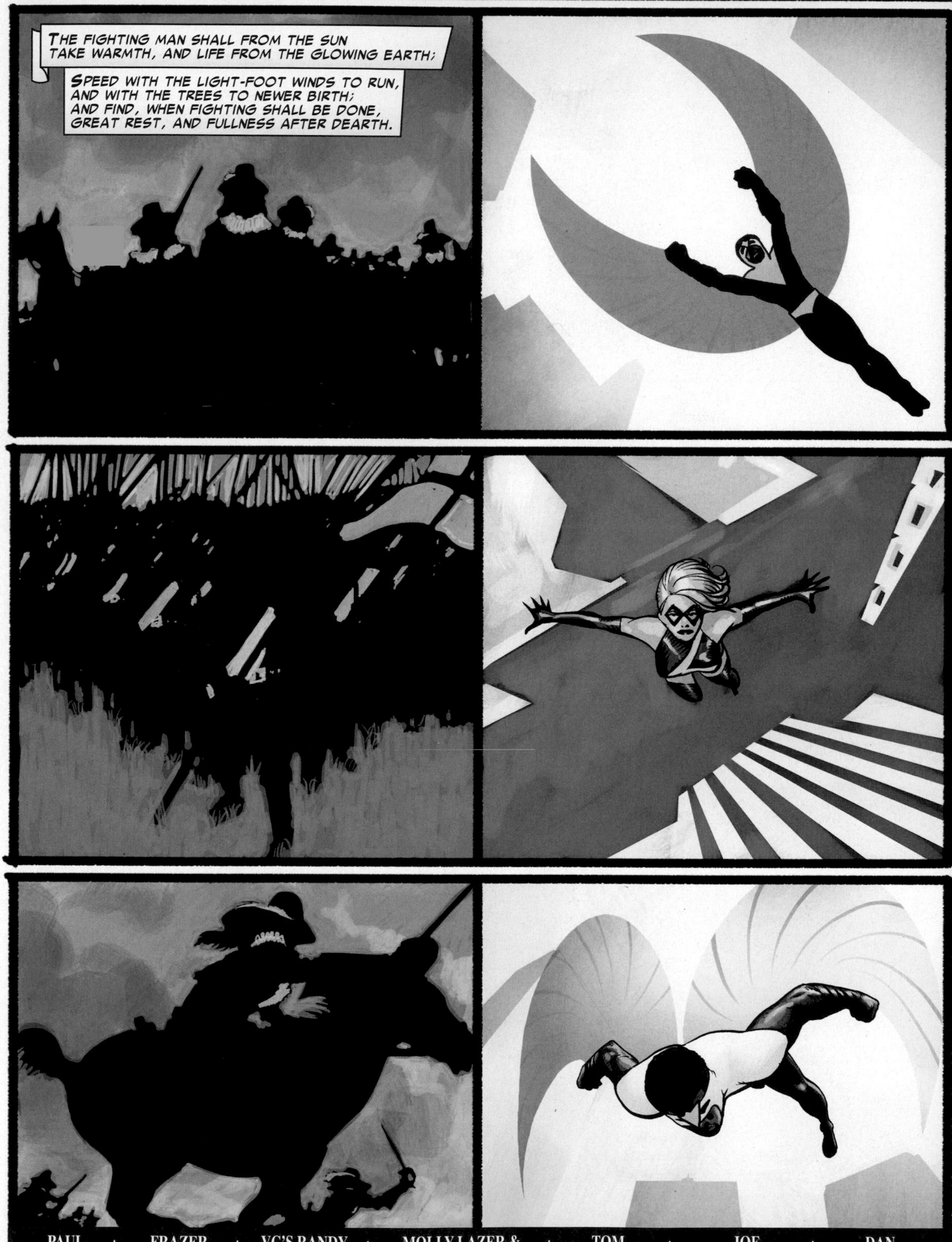
THE FIGHTING MAN SHALL FROM THE SUN
TAKE WARMTH, AND LIFE FROM THE GLOWING EARTH;
SPEED WITH THE LIGHT-FOOT WINDS TO RUN,
AND WITH THE TREES TO NEWER BIRTH;
AND FIND, WHEN FIGHTING SHALL BE DONE,
GREAT REST, AND FULLNESS AFTER DEARTH.

PAUL JENKINS WRITER | FRAZER IRVING ARTIST | VC'S RANDY GENTILE LETTERS | MOLLY LAZER & AUBREY SITTERSON ASSISTANT EDITORS | TOM BREVOORT EDITOR | JOE QUESADA EDITOR IN CHIEF | DAN BUCKLEY PUBLISHER

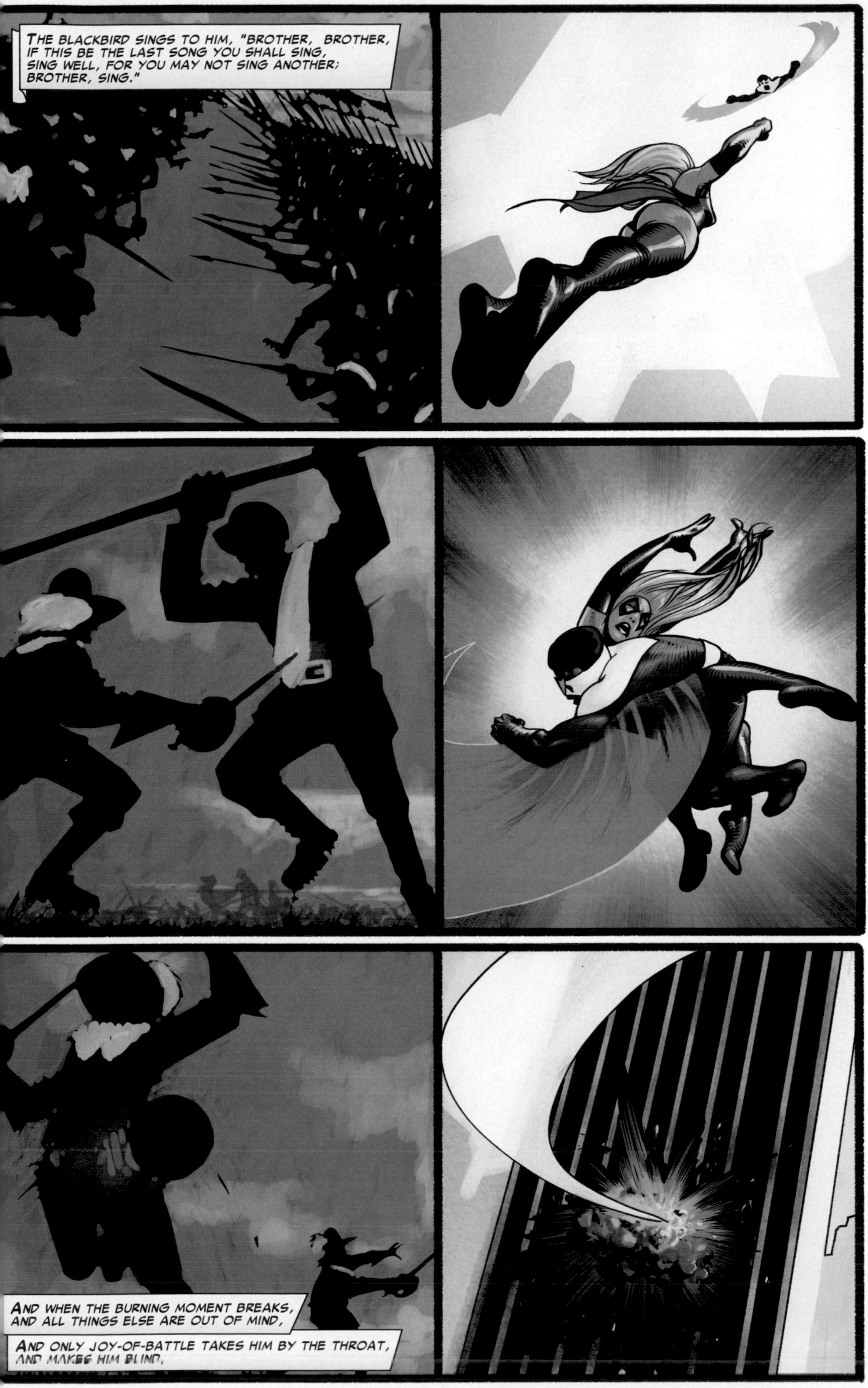
THE BLACKBIRD SINGS TO HIM, "BROTHER, BROTHER, IF THIS BE THE LAST SONG YOU SHALL SING, SING WELL, FOR YOU MAY NOT SING ANOTHER; BROTHER, SING."
AND WHEN THE BURNING MOMENT BREAKS, AND ALL THINGS ELSE ARE OUT OF MIND,
AND ONLY JOY-OF-BATTLE TAKES HIM BY THE THROAT, AND MAKES HIM BLIND.

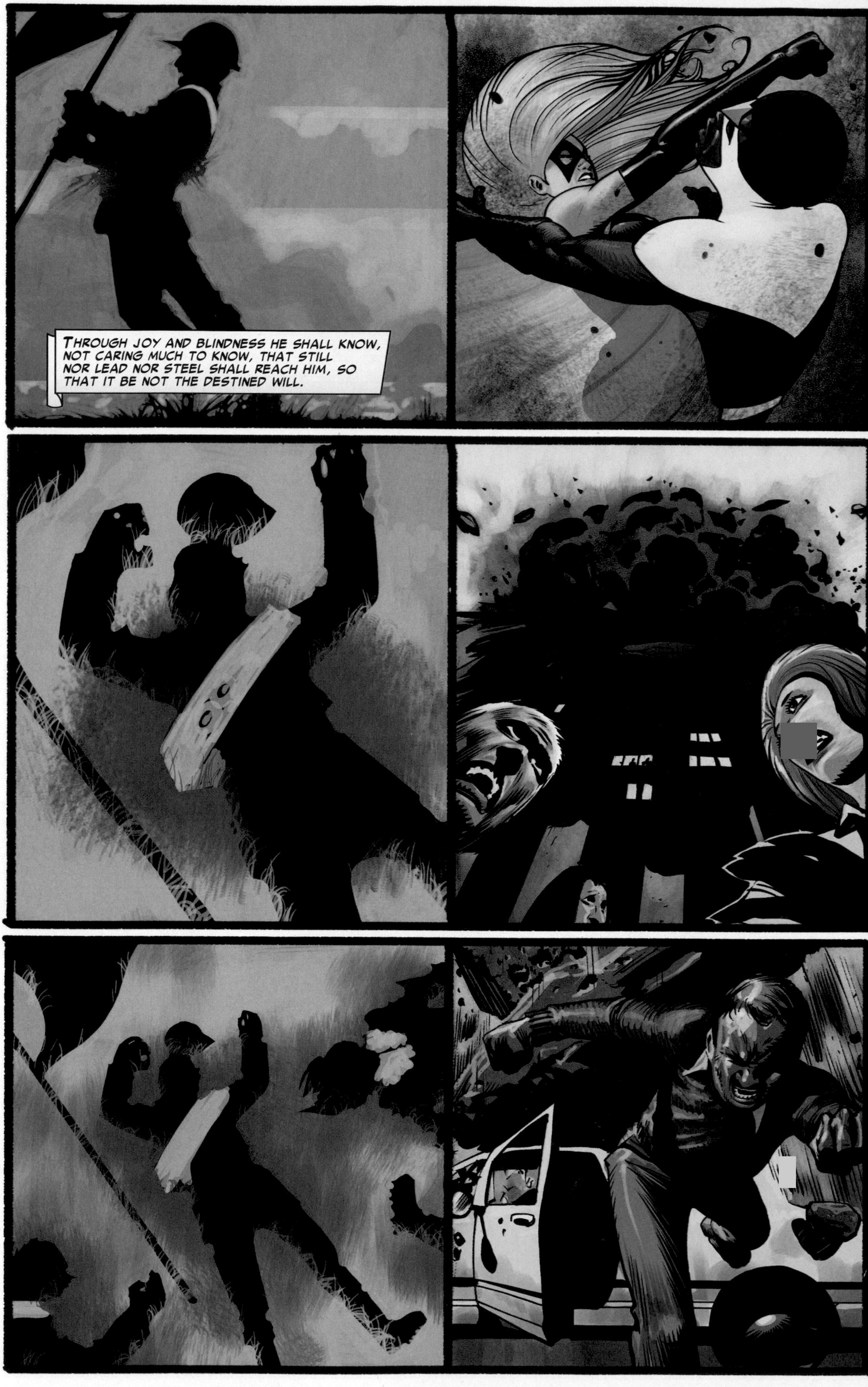
THROUGH JOY AND BLINDNESS HE SHALL KNOW, NOT CARING MUCH TO KNOW, THAT STILL NOR LEAD NOR STEEL SHALL REACH HIM, SO THAT IT BE NOT THE DESTINED WILL.

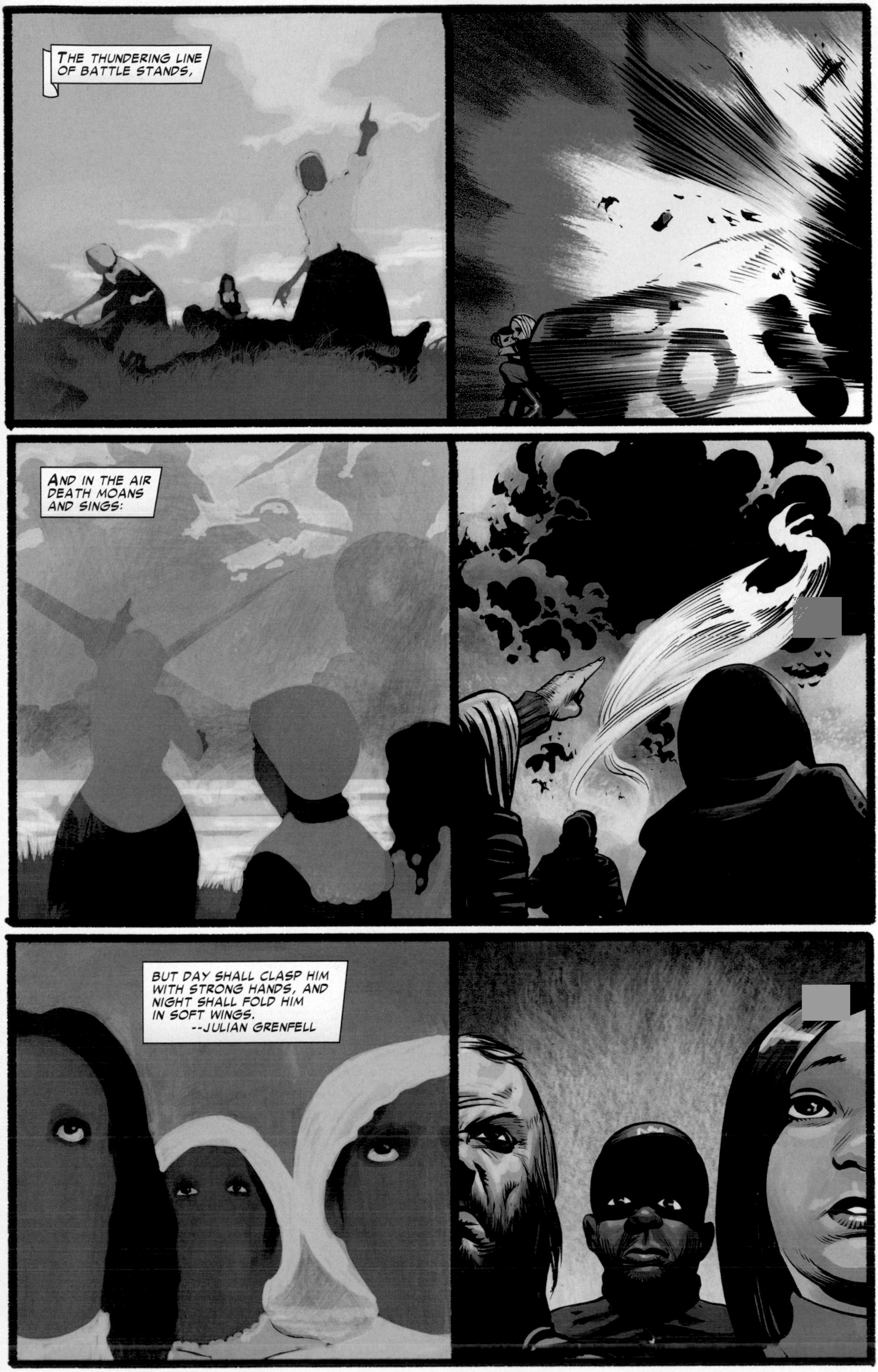
THE THUNDERING LINE OF BATTLE STANDS,
AND IN THE AIR DEATH MOANS AND SINGS:
BUT DAY SHALL CLASP HIM WITH STRONG HANDS, AND NIGHT SHALL FOLD HIM IN SOFT WINGS.
--JULIAN GRENFELL

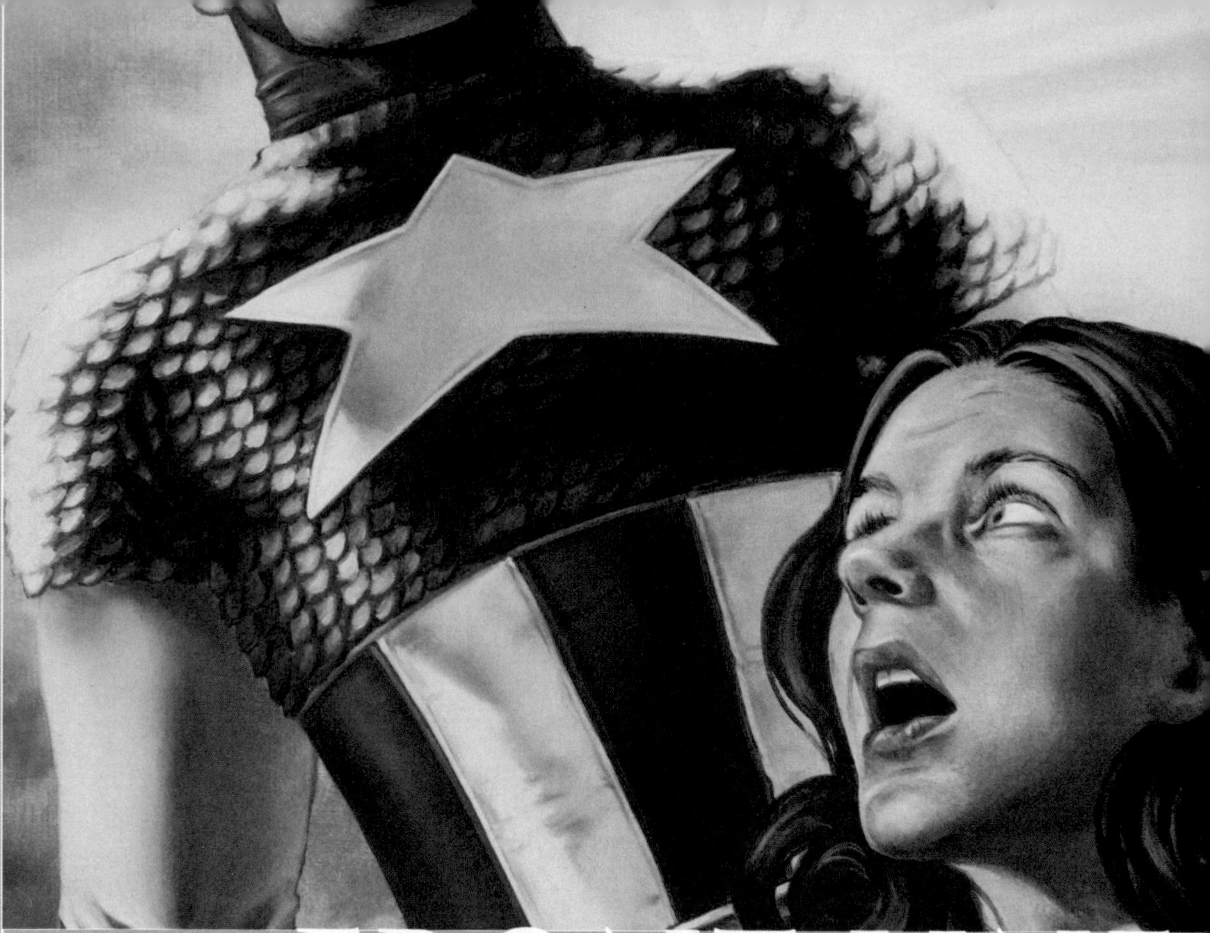

FRONT LINE

A MARVEL COMICS EVENT

CIVIL WAR

CIVIL WAR: FRONT LINE #9

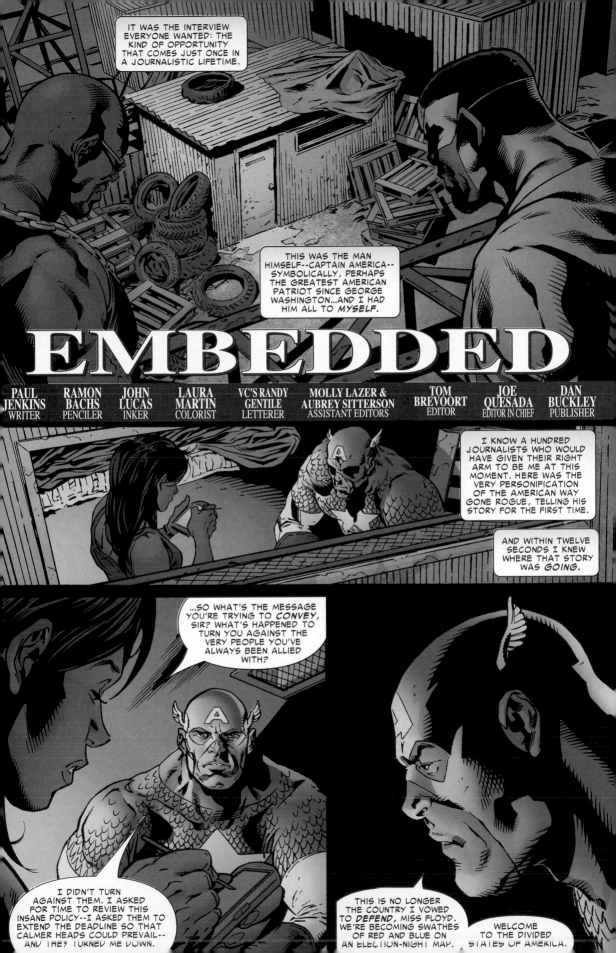

IT WAS THE INTERVIEW EVERYONE WANTED: THE KIND OF OPPORTUNITY THAT COMES JUST ONCE IN A JOURNALISTIC LIFETIME.

THIS WAS THE MAN HIMSELF--CAPTAIN AMERICA--SYMBOLICALLY, PERHAPS THE GREATEST AMERICAN PATRIOT SINCE GEORGE WASHINGTON...AND I HAD HIM ALL TO *MYSELF*.

EMBEDDED

PAUL JENKINS
WRITER

RAMON BACHS
PENCILER

JOHN LUCAS
INKER

LAURA MARTIN
COLORIST

VC'S RANDY GENTILE
LETTERER

MOLLY LAZER & AUBREY SITTERSON
ASSISTANT EDITORS

TOM BREVOORT
EDITOR

JOE QUESADA
EDITOR IN CHIEF

DAN BUCKLEY
PUBLISHER

I KNOW A HUNDRED JOURNALISTS WHO WOULD HAVE GIVEN THEIR RIGHT ARM TO BE ME AT THIS MOMENT. HERE WAS THE VERY PERSONIFICATION OF THE AMERICAN WAY GONE ROGUE, TELLING HIS STORY FOR THE FIRST TIME.

AND WITHIN TWELVE SECONDS I KNEW WHERE THAT STORY WAS *GOING*.

...SO WHAT'S THE MESSAGE YOU'RE TRYING TO *CONVEY*, SIR? WHAT'S HAPPENED TO TURN YOU AGAINST THE VERY PEOPLE YOU'VE ALWAYS BEEN ALLIED WITH?

I DIDN'T TURN AGAINST THEM. I ASKED FOR TIME TO REVIEW THIS INSANE POLICY--I ASKED THEM TO EXTEND THE DEADLINE SO THAT CALMER HEADS COULD PREVAIL--AND THEY TURNED ME DOWN.

THIS IS NO LONGER THE COUNTRY I VOWED TO *DEFEND*, MISS FLOYD. WE'RE BECOMING SWATHES OF RED AND BLUE ON AN ELECTION-NIGHT MAP.

WELCOME TO THE DIVIDED STATES OF AMERICA.

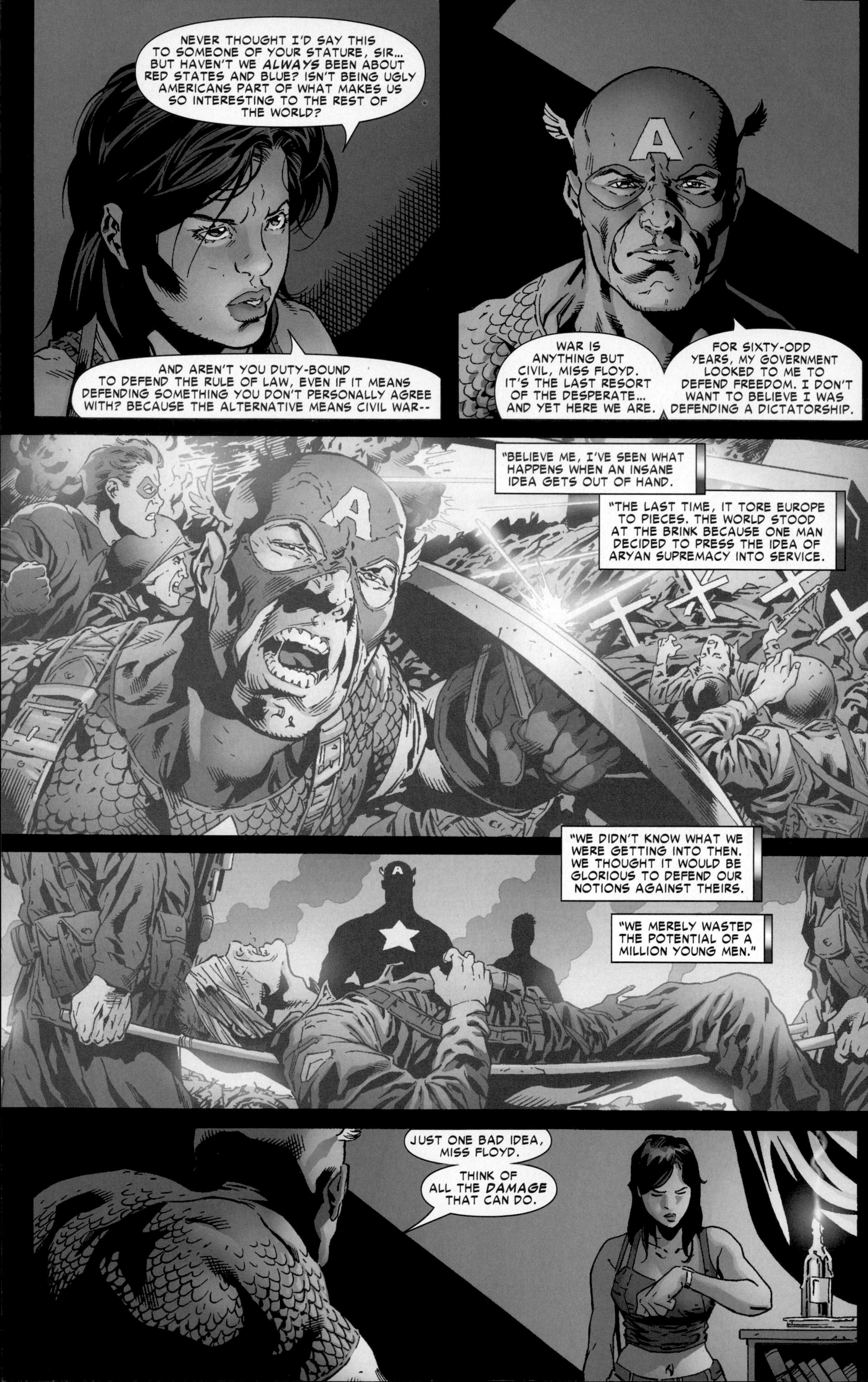
NEVER THOUGHT I'D SAY THIS TO SOMEONE OF YOUR STATURE, SIR... BUT HAVEN'T WE *ALWAYS* BEEN ABOUT RED STATES AND BLUE? ISN'T BEING UGLY AMERICANS PART OF WHAT MAKES US SO INTERESTING TO THE REST OF THE WORLD?
AND AREN'T YOU DUTY-BOUND TO DEFEND THE RULE OF LAW, EVEN IF IT MEANS DEFENDING SOMETHING YOU DON'T PERSONALLY AGREE WITH? BECAUSE THE ALTERNATIVE MEANS CIVIL WAR--
WAR IS ANYTHING BUT CIVIL, MISS FLOYD. IT'S THE LAST RESORT OF THE DESPERATE... AND YET HERE WE ARE.
FOR SIXTY-ODD YEARS, MY GOVERNMENT LOOKED TO ME TO DEFEND FREEDOM. I DON'T WANT TO BELIEVE I WAS DEFENDING A DICTATORSHIP.
"BELIEVE ME, I'VE SEEN WHAT HAPPENS WHEN AN INSANE IDEA GETS OUT OF HAND.
"THE LAST TIME, IT TORE EUROPE TO PIECES. THE WORLD STOOD AT THE BRINK BECAUSE ONE MAN DECIDED TO PRESS THE IDEA OF ARYAN SUPREMACY INTO SERVICE.
"WE DIDN'T KNOW WHAT WE WERE GETTING INTO THEN. WE THOUGHT IT WOULD BE GLORIOUS TO DEFEND OUR NOTIONS AGAINST THEIRS.
"WE MERELY WASTED THE POTENTIAL OF A MILLION YOUNG MEN."
JUST ONE BAD IDEA, MISS FLOYD.
THINK OF ALL THE *DAMAGE* THAT CAN DO.

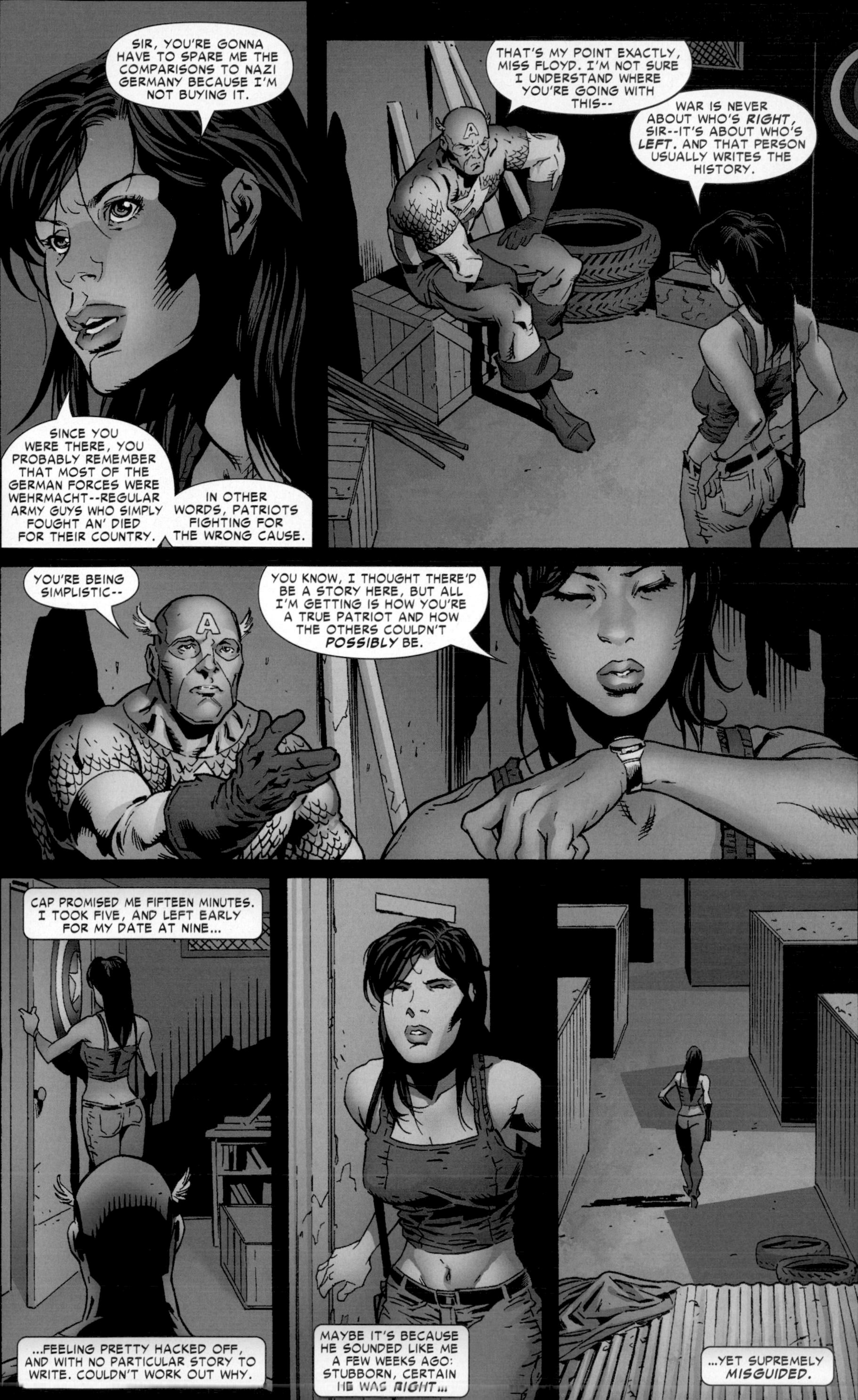
SIR, YOU'RE GONNA HAVE TO SPARE ME THE COMPARISONS TO NAZI GERMANY BECAUSE I'M NOT BUYING IT.
SINCE YOU WERE THERE, YOU PROBABLY REMEMBER THAT MOST OF THE GERMAN FORCES WERE WEHRMACHT--REGULAR ARMY GUYS WHO SIMPLY FOUGHT AN' DIED FOR THEIR COUNTRY.
IN OTHER WORDS, PATRIOTS FIGHTING FOR THE WRONG CAUSE.
THAT'S MY POINT EXACTLY, MISS FLOYD. I'M NOT SURE I UNDERSTAND WHERE YOU'RE GOING WITH THIS--
WAR IS NEVER ABOUT WHO'S *RIGHT*, SIR--IT'S ABOUT WHO'S *LEFT*. AND THAT PERSON USUALLY WRITES THE HISTORY.
YOU'RE BEING SIMPLISTIC--
YOU KNOW, I THOUGHT THERE'D BE A STORY HERE, BUT ALL I'M GETTING IS HOW YOU'RE A TRUE PATRIOT AND HOW THE OTHERS COULDN'T *POSSIBLY* BE.
CAP PROMISED ME FIFTEEN MINUTES. I TOOK FIVE, AND LEFT EARLY FOR MY DATE AT NINE...
...FEELING PRETTY HACKED OFF, AND WITH NO PARTICULAR STORY TO WRITE. COULDN'T WORK OUT WHY.
MAYBE IT'S BECAUSE HE SOUNDED LIKE ME A FEW WEEKS AGO: STUBBORN, CERTAIN HE WAS *RIGHT*...
...YET SUPREMELY *MISGUIDED*.

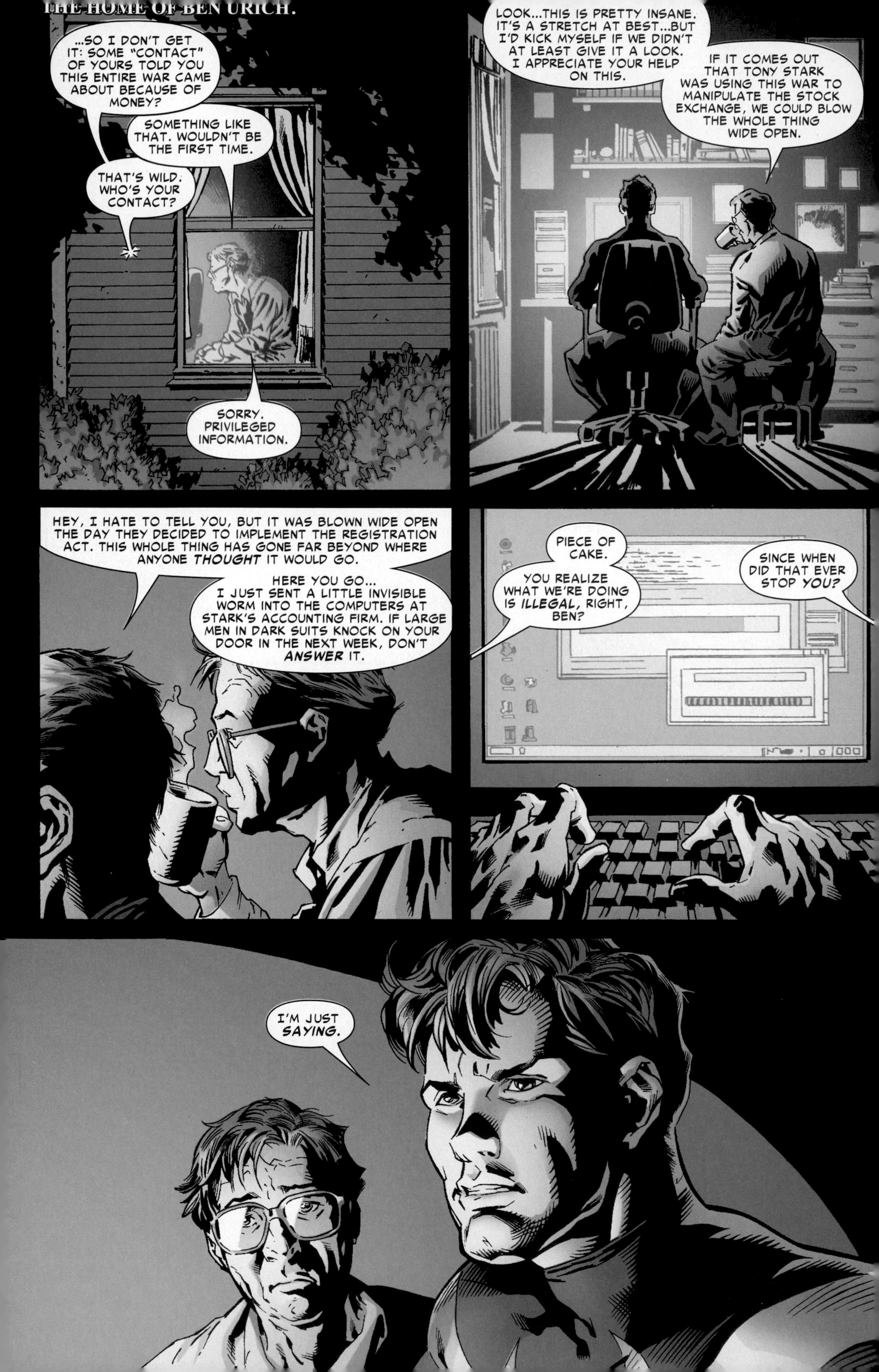
THE HOME OF BEN URICH.
...SO I DON'T GET IT: SOME "CONTACT" OF YOURS TOLD YOU THIS ENTIRE WAR CAME ABOUT BECAUSE OF MONEY?
SOMETHING LIKE THAT. WOULDN'T BE THE FIRST TIME.
THAT'S WILD. WHO'S YOUR CONTACT?
SORRY. PRIVILEGED INFORMATION.
LOOK...THIS IS PRETTY INSANE. IT'S A STRETCH AT BEST...BUT I'D KICK MYSELF IF WE DIDN'T AT LEAST GIVE IT A LOOK. I APPRECIATE YOUR HELP ON THIS.
IF IT COMES OUT THAT TONY STARK WAS USING THIS WAR TO MANIPULATE THE STOCK EXCHANGE, WE COULD BLOW THE WHOLE THING WIDE OPEN.
HEY, I HATE TO TELL YOU, BUT IT WAS BLOWN WIDE OPEN THE DAY THEY DECIDED TO IMPLEMENT THE REGISTRATION ACT. THIS WHOLE THING HAS GONE FAR BEYOND WHERE ANYONE *THOUGHT* IT WOULD GO.
HERE YOU GO... I JUST SENT A LITTLE INVISIBLE WORM INTO THE COMPUTERS AT STARK'S ACCOUNTING FIRM. IF LARGE MEN IN DARK SUITS KNOCK ON YOUR DOOR IN THE NEXT WEEK, DON'T ***ANSWER*** IT.
PIECE OF CAKE.
YOU REALIZE WHAT WE'RE DOING IS *ILLEGAL*, RIGHT, BEN?
SINCE WHEN DID THAT EVER STOP *YOU?*
I'M JUST *SAYING.*

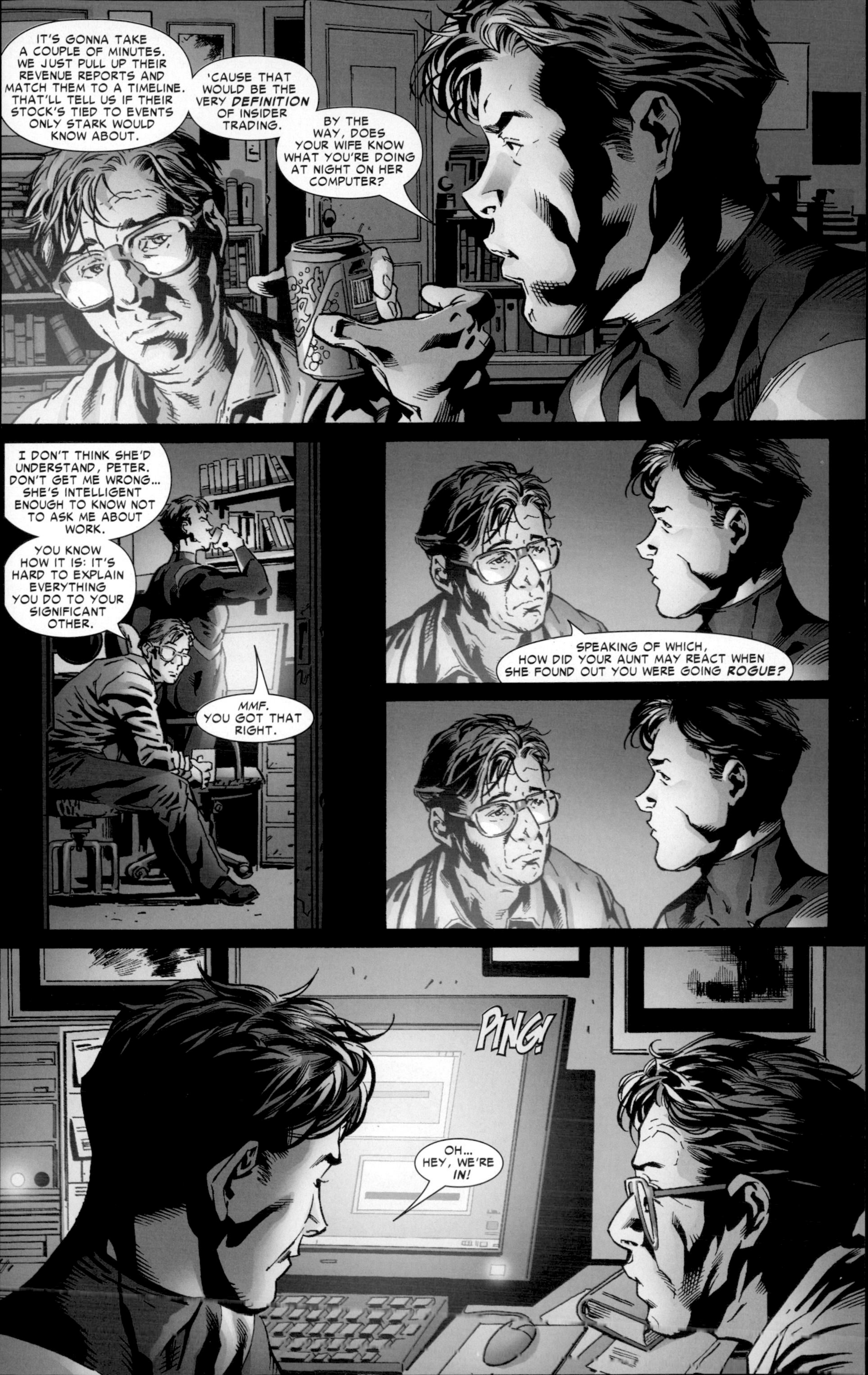

IT'S GONNA TAKE A COUPLE OF MINUTES. WE JUST PULL UP THEIR REVENUE REPORTS AND MATCH THEM TO A TIMELINE. THAT'LL TELL US IF THEIR STOCK'S TIED TO EVENTS ONLY STARK WOULD KNOW ABOUT.
'CAUSE THAT WOULD BE THE VERY *DEFINITION* OF INSIDER TRADING.
BY THE WAY, DOES YOUR WIFE KNOW WHAT YOU'RE DOING AT NIGHT ON HER COMPUTER?
I DON'T THINK SHE'D UNDERSTAND, PETER. DON'T GET ME WRONG... SHE'S INTELLIGENT ENOUGH TO KNOW NOT TO ASK ME ABOUT WORK.
YOU KNOW HOW IT IS: IT'S HARD TO EXPLAIN EVERYTHING YOU DO TO YOUR SIGNIFICANT OTHER.
MMF. YOU GOT THAT RIGHT.
SPEAKING OF WHICH, HOW DID YOUR AUNT MAY REACT WHEN SHE FOUND OUT YOU WERE GOING *ROGUE?*
PING!
OH... HEY, WE'RE *IN!*

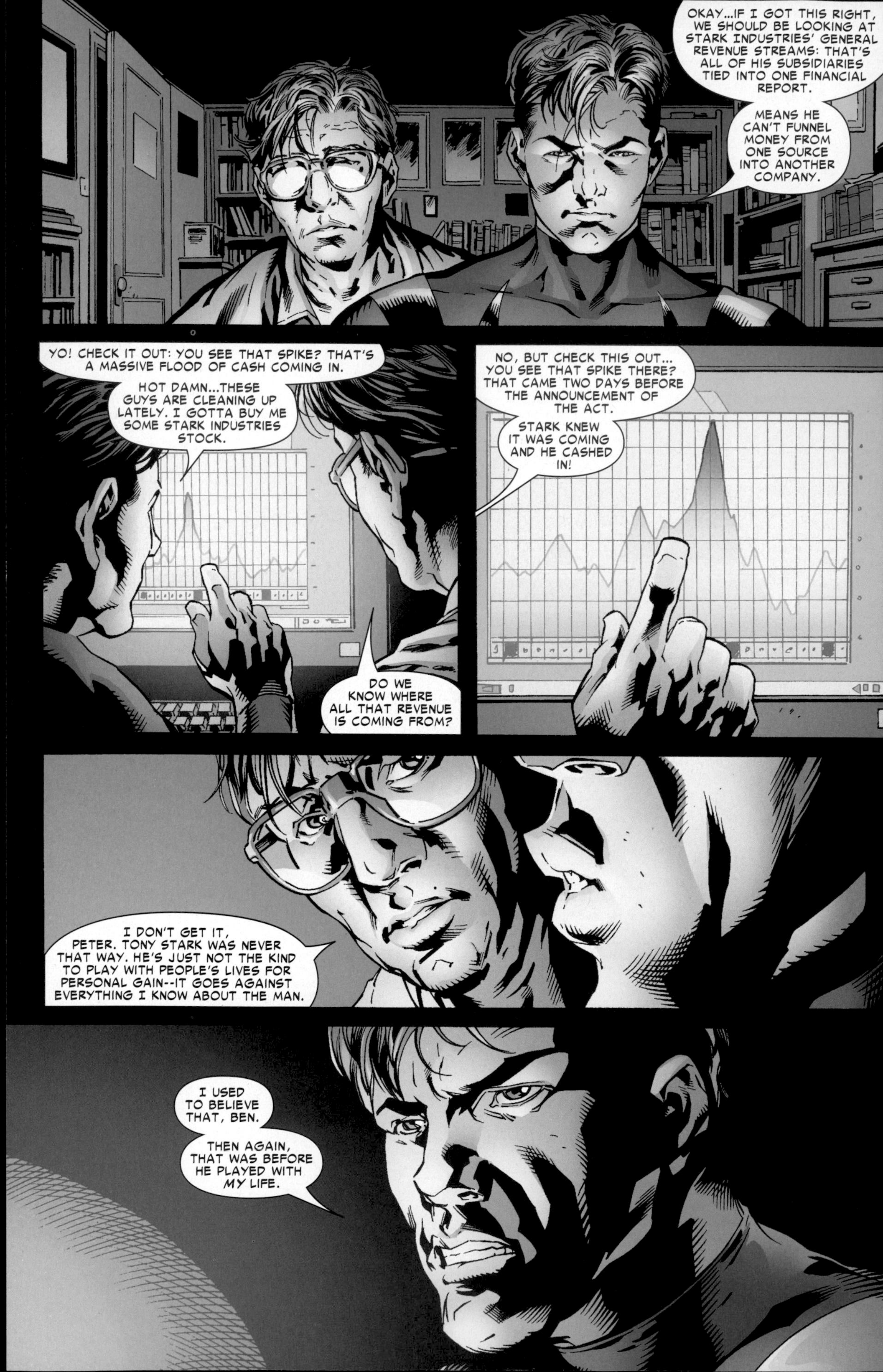
OKAY...IF I GOT THIS RIGHT, WE SHOULD BE LOOKING AT STARK INDUSTRIES' GENERAL REVENUE STREAMS: THAT'S ALL OF HIS SUBSIDIARIES TIED INTO ONE FINANCIAL REPORT.
MEANS HE CAN'T FUNNEL MONEY FROM ONE SOURCE INTO ANOTHER COMPANY.
YO! CHECK IT OUT: YOU SEE THAT SPIKE? THAT'S A MASSIVE FLOOD OF CASH COMING IN.
HOT DAMN...THESE GUYS ARE CLEANING UP LATELY. I GOTTA BUY ME SOME STARK INDUSTRIES STOCK.
DO WE KNOW WHERE ALL THAT REVENUE IS COMING FROM?
NO, BUT CHECK THIS OUT... YOU SEE THAT SPIKE THERE? THAT CAME TWO DAYS BEFORE THE ANNOUNCEMENT OF THE ACT.
STARK KNEW IT WAS COMING AND HE CASHED IN!
I DON'T GET IT, PETER. TONY STARK WAS NEVER THAT WAY. HE'S JUST NOT THE KIND TO PLAY WITH PEOPLE'S LIVES FOR PERSONAL GAIN--IT GOES AGAINST EVERYTHING I KNOW ABOUT THE MAN.
I USED TO BELIEVE THAT, BEN.
THEN AGAIN, THAT WAS BEFORE HE PLAYED WITH *MY* LIFE.

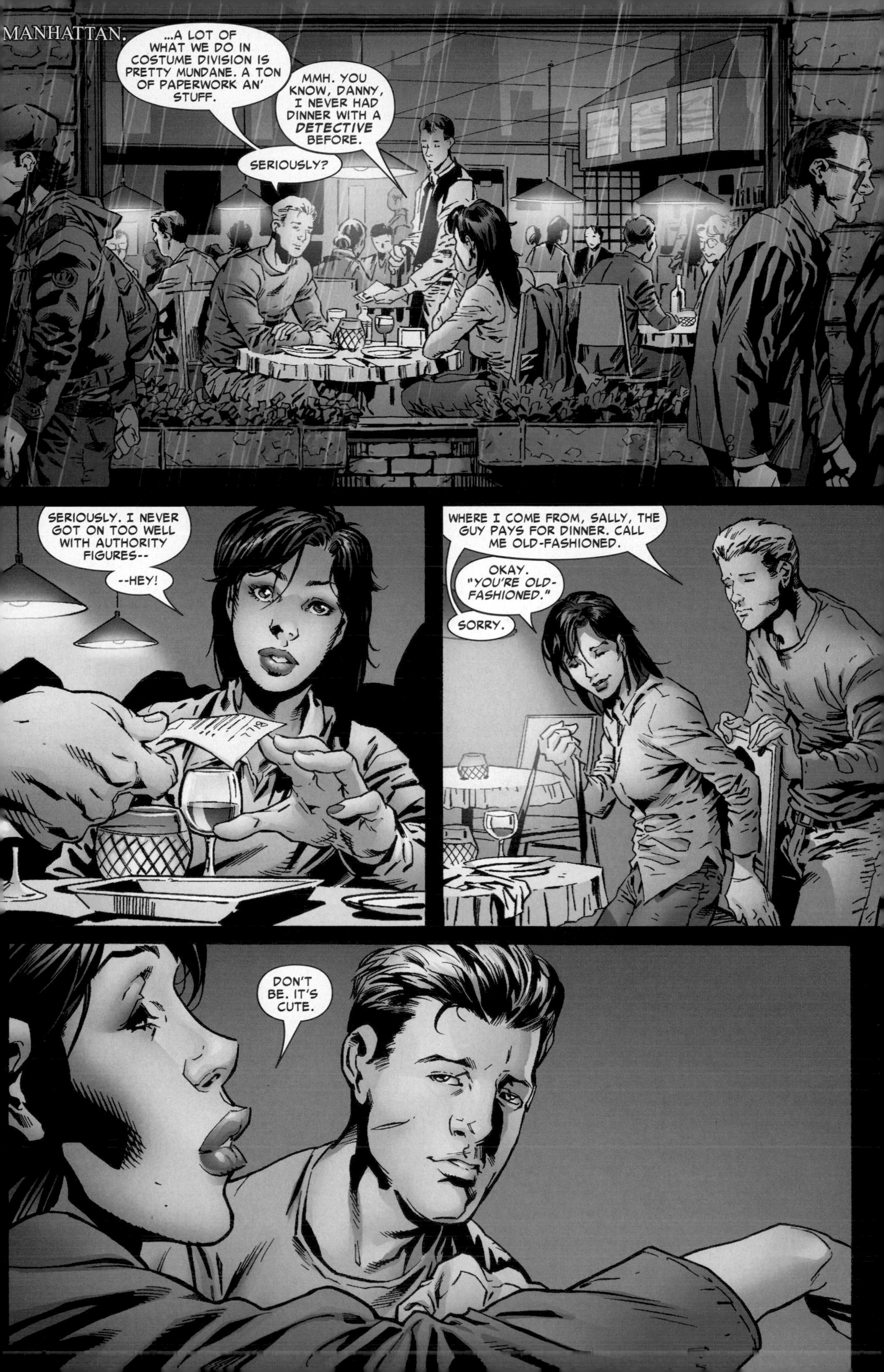
MANHATTAN.
...A LOT OF WHAT WE DO IN COSTUME DIVISION IS PRETTY MUNDANE. A TON OF PAPERWORK AN' STUFF.
MMH. YOU KNOW, DANNY, I NEVER HAD DINNER WITH A *DETECTIVE* BEFORE.
SERIOUSLY?
SERIOUSLY. I NEVER GOT ON TOO WELL WITH AUTHORITY FIGURES--
--HEY!
BILL
WHERE I COME FROM, SALLY, THE GUY PAYS FOR DINNER. CALL ME OLD-FASHIONED.
OKAY. *"YOU'RE OLD-FASHIONED."*
SORRY.
DON'T BE. IT'S CUTE.

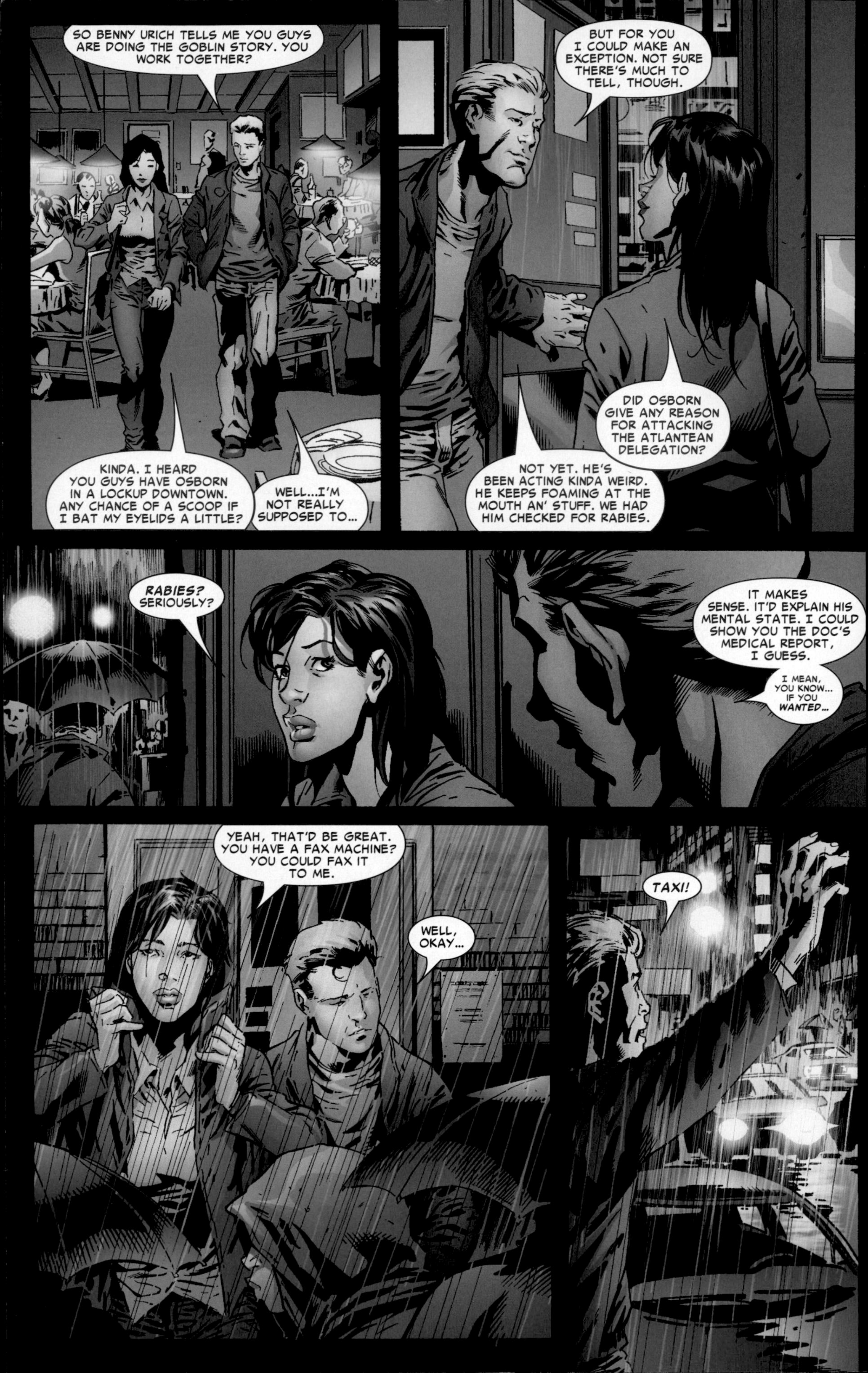
SO BENNY URICH TELLS ME YOU GUYS ARE DOING THE GOBLIN STORY. YOU WORK TOGETHER?
KINDA. I HEARD YOU GUYS HAVE OSBORN IN A LOCKUP DOWNTOWN. ANY CHANCE OF A SCOOP IF I BAT MY EYELIDS A LITTLE?
WELL...I'M NOT REALLY SUPPOSED TO...
BUT FOR YOU I COULD MAKE AN EXCEPTION. NOT SURE THERE'S MUCH TO TELL, THOUGH.
DID OSBORN GIVE ANY REASON FOR ATTACKING THE ATLANTEAN DELEGATION?
NOT YET. HE'S BEEN ACTING KINDA WEIRD. HE KEEPS FOAMING AT THE MOUTH AN' STUFF. WE HAD HIM CHECKED FOR RABIES.
RABIES? SERIOUSLY?
IT MAKES SENSE. IT'D EXPLAIN HIS MENTAL STATE. I COULD SHOW YOU THE DOC'S MEDICAL REPORT, I GUESS.
I MEAN, YOU KNOW... IF YOU **WANTED**...
YEAH, THAT'D BE GREAT. YOU HAVE A FAX MACHINE? YOU COULD FAX IT TO ME.
WELL, OKAY...
TAXI!

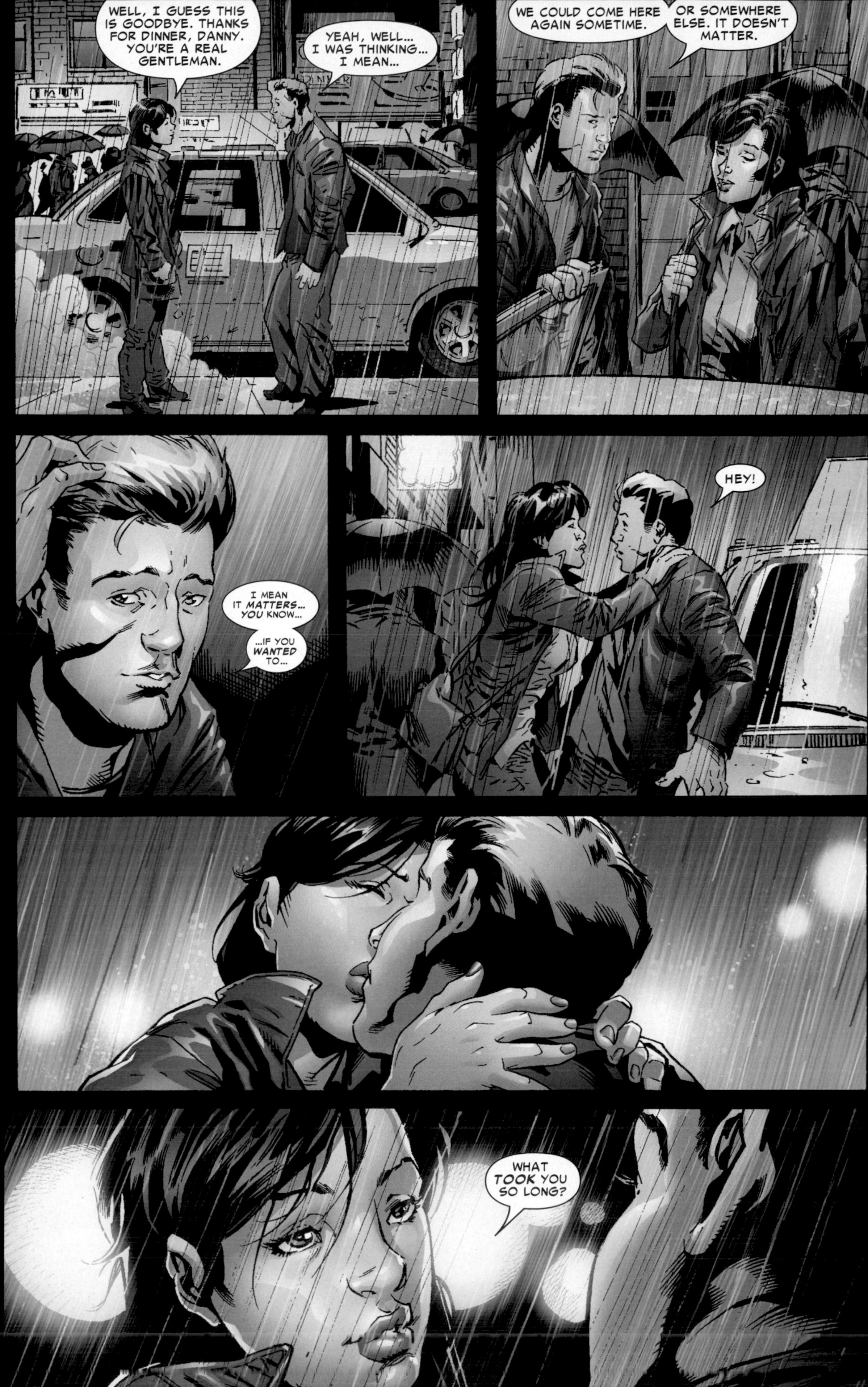
WELL, I GUESS THIS IS GOODBYE. THANKS FOR DINNER, DANNY. YOU'RE A REAL GENTLEMAN.
YEAH, WELL... I WAS THINKING... I MEAN...
WE COULD COME HERE AGAIN SOMETIME.
OR SOMEWHERE ELSE. IT DOESN'T MATTER.
I MEAN IT MATTERS... YOU KNOW...
...IF YOU WANTED TO...
HEY!
WHAT TOOK YOU SO LONG?

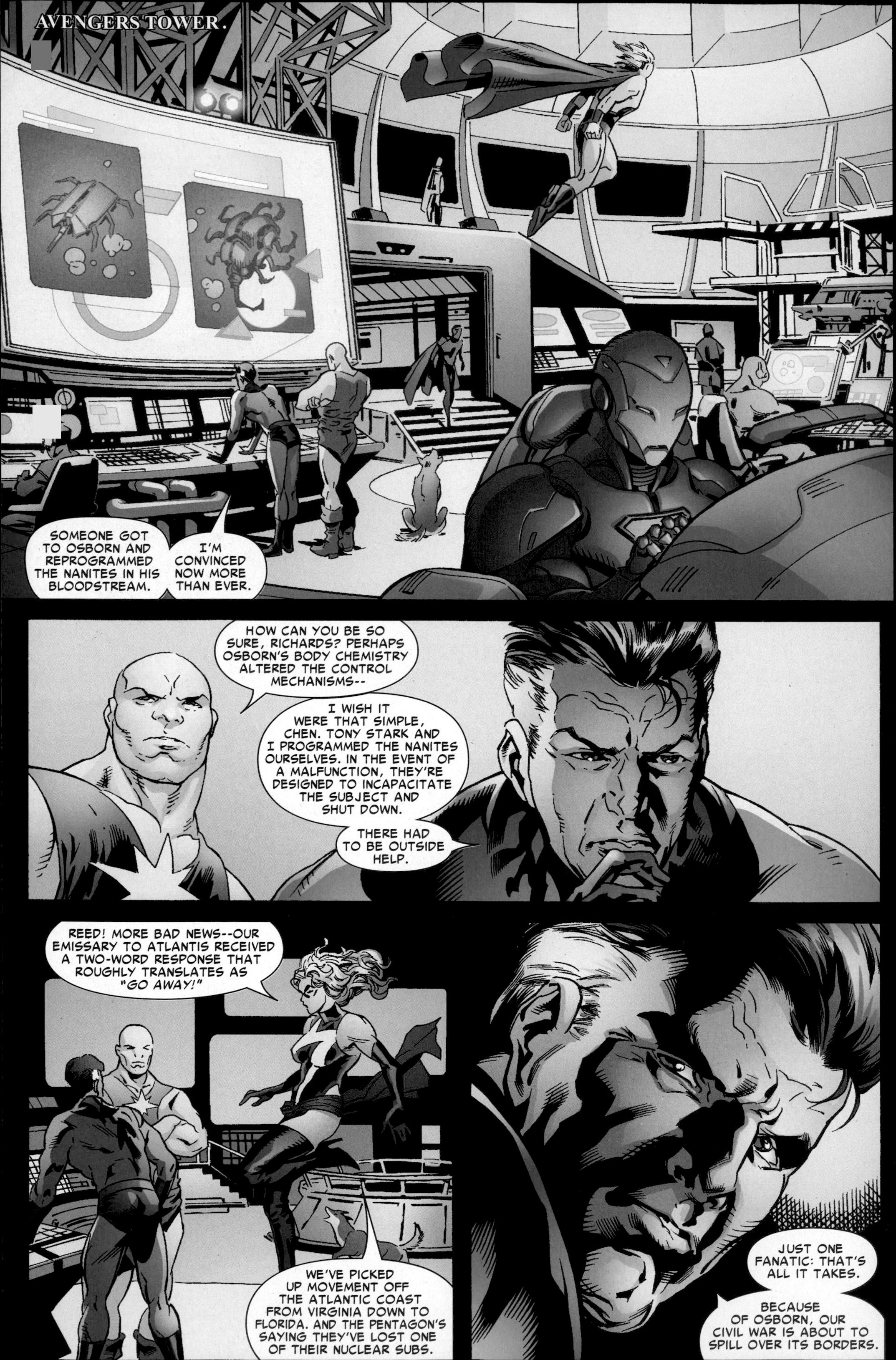
AVENGERS TOWER.
SOMEONE GOT TO OSBORN AND REPROGRAMMED THE NANITES IN HIS BLOODSTREAM.
I'M CONVINCED NOW MORE THAN EVER.
HOW CAN YOU BE SO SURE, RICHARDS? PERHAPS OSBORN'S BODY CHEMISTRY ALTERED THE CONTROL MECHANISMS--
I WISH IT WERE THAT SIMPLE, CHEN. TONY STARK AND I PROGRAMMED THE NANITES OURSELVES. IN THE EVENT OF A MALFUNCTION, THEY'RE DESIGNED TO INCAPACITATE THE SUBJECT AND SHUT DOWN.
THERE HAD TO BE OUTSIDE HELP.
REED! MORE BAD NEWS--OUR EMISSARY TO ATLANTIS RECEIVED A TWO-WORD RESPONSE THAT ROUGHLY TRANSLATES AS "GO AWAY!"
WE'VE PICKED UP MOVEMENT OFF THE ATLANTIC COAST FROM VIRGINIA DOWN TO FLORIDA. AND THE PENTAGON'S SAYING THEY'VE LOST ONE OF THEIR NUCLEAR SUBS.
JUST ONE FANATIC: THAT'S ALL IT TAKES.
BECAUSE OF OSBORN, OUR CIVIL WAR IS ABOUT TO SPILL OVER ITS BORDERS.

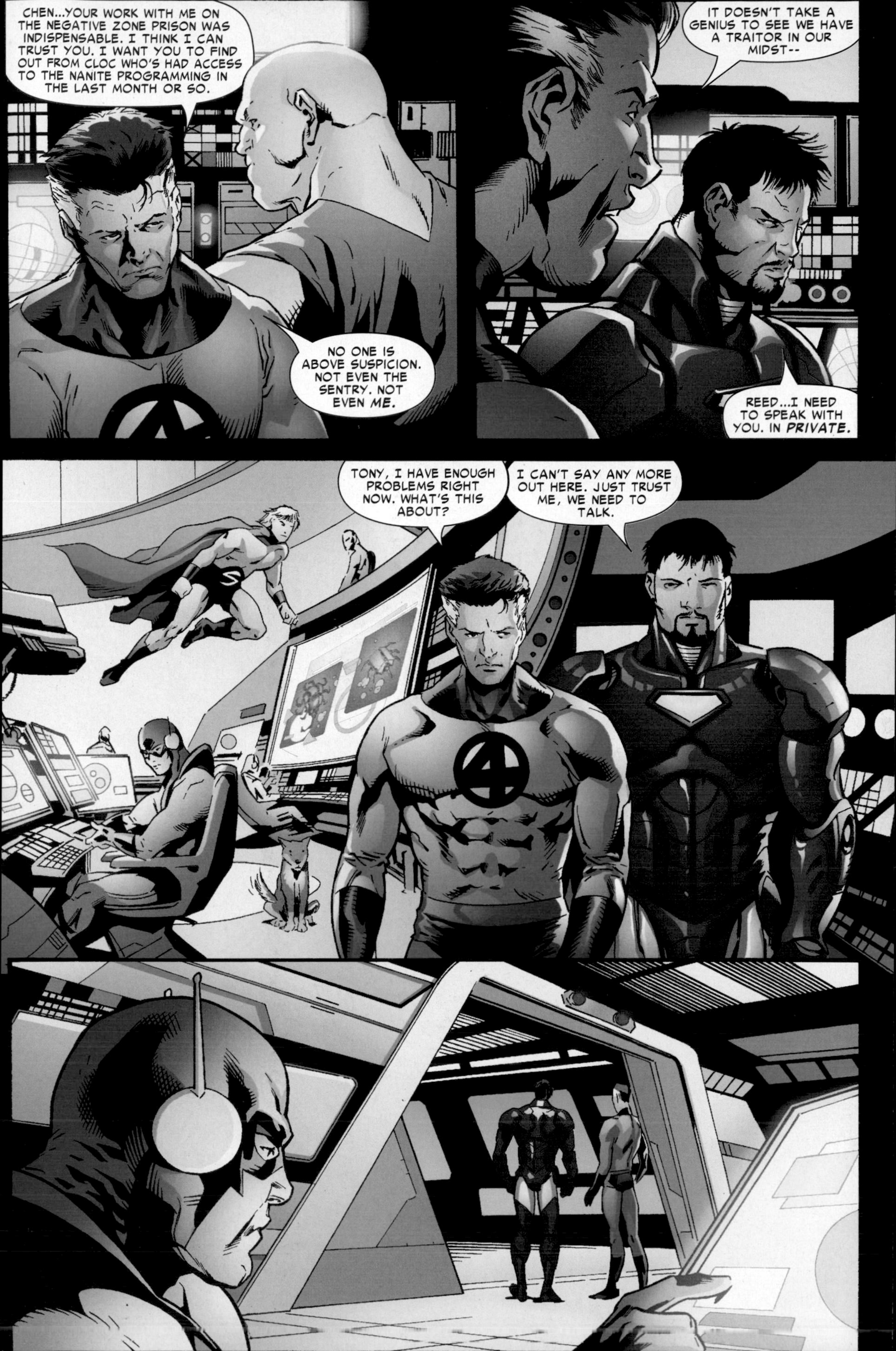
CHEN...YOUR WORK WITH ME ON THE NEGATIVE ZONE PRISON WAS INDISPENSABLE. I THINK I CAN TRUST YOU. I WANT YOU TO FIND OUT FROM CLOC WHO'S HAD ACCESS TO THE NANITE PROGRAMMING IN THE LAST MONTH OR SO.
NO ONE IS ABOVE SUSPICION. NOT EVEN THE SENTRY. NOT EVEN *ME*.
IT DOESN'T TAKE A GENIUS TO SEE WE HAVE A TRAITOR IN OUR MIDST--
REED...I NEED TO SPEAK WITH YOU. IN *PRIVATE*.
TONY, I HAVE ENOUGH PROBLEMS RIGHT NOW. WHAT'S THIS ABOUT?
I CAN'T SAY ANY MORE OUT HERE. JUST TRUST ME, WE NEED TO TALK.

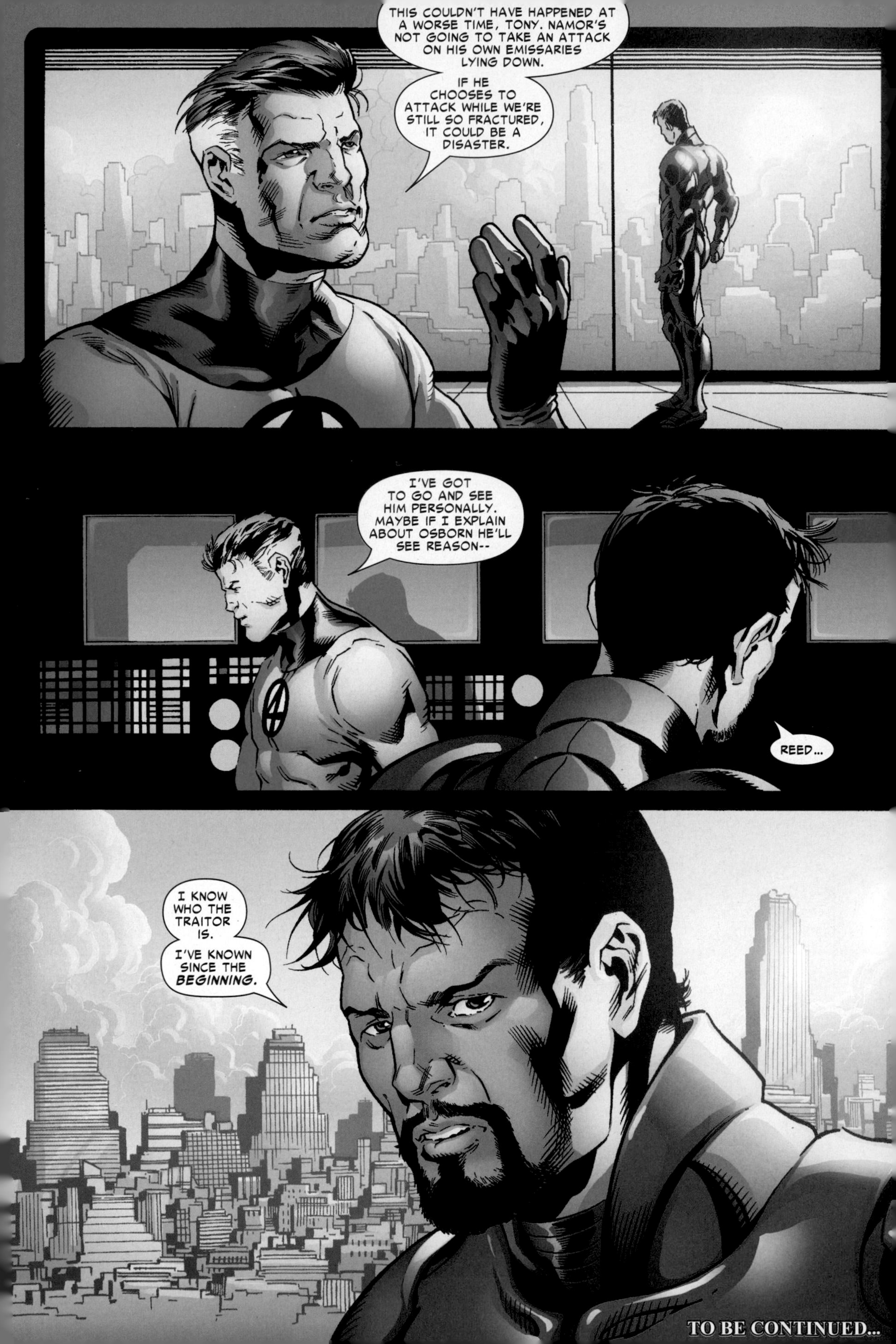
THIS COULDN'T HAVE HAPPENED AT A WORSE TIME, TONY. NAMOR'S NOT GOING TO TAKE AN ATTACK ON HIS OWN EMISSARIES LYING DOWN.
IF HE CHOOSES TO ATTACK WHILE WE'RE STILL SO FRACTURED, IT COULD BE A DISASTER.
I'VE GOT TO GO AND SEE HIM PERSONALLY. MAYBE IF I EXPLAIN ABOUT OSBORN HE'LL SEE REASON--
REED...
I KNOW WHO THE TRAITOR IS.
I'VE KNOWN SINCE THE *BEGINNING*.
TO BE CONTINUED...

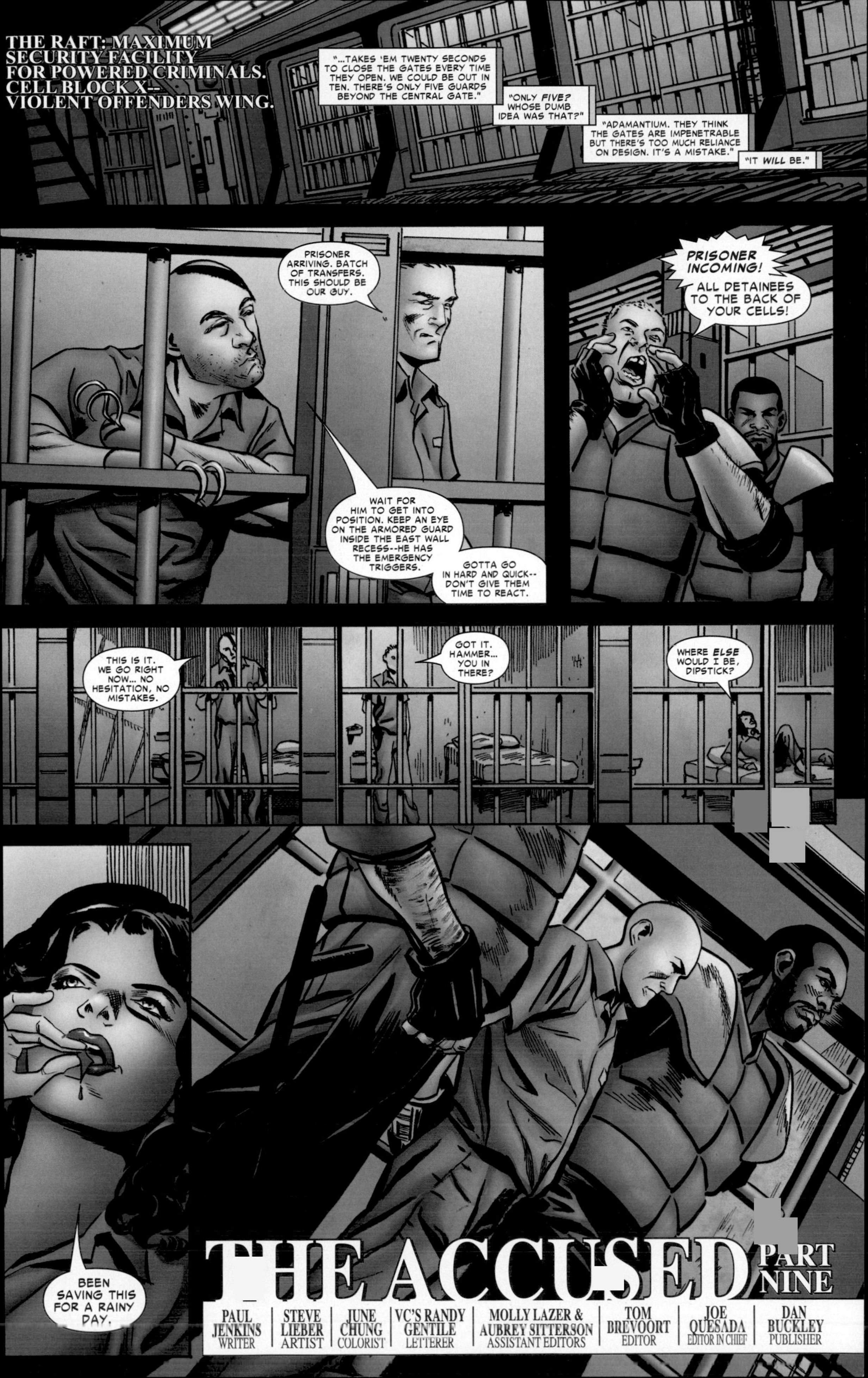
THE RAFT: MAXIMUM SECURITY FACILITY FOR POWERED CRIMINALS. CELL BLOCK X-- VIOLENT OFFENDERS WING.
"...TAKES 'EM TWENTY SECONDS TO CLOSE THE GATES EVERY TIME THEY OPEN. WE COULD BE OUT IN TEN. THERE'S ONLY FIVE GUARDS BEYOND THE CENTRAL GATE."
"ONLY FIVE? WHOSE DUMB IDEA WAS THAT?"
"ADAMANTIUM. THEY THINK THE GATES ARE IMPENETRABLE BUT THERE'S TOO MUCH RELIANCE ON DESIGN. IT'S A MISTAKE."
"IT WILL BE."
PRISONER ARRIVING. BATCH OF TRANSFERS. THIS SHOULD BE OUR GUY.
WAIT FOR HIM TO GET INTO POSITION. KEEP AN EYE ON THE ARMORED GUARD INSIDE THE EAST WALL RECESS--HE HAS THE EMERGENCY TRIGGERS.
GOTTA GO IN HARD AND QUICK--DON'T GIVE THEM TIME TO REACT.
PRISONER INCOMING!
ALL DETAINEES TO THE BACK OF YOUR CELLS!
THIS IS IT. WE GO RIGHT NOW... NO HESITATION, NO MISTAKES.
GOT IT. HAMMER... YOU IN THERE?
WHERE ELSE WOULD I BE, DIPSTICK?
BEEN SAVING THIS FOR A RAINY DAY.
THE ACCUSED PART NINE
PAUL JENKINS WRITER
STEVE LIEBER ARTIST
JUNE CHUNG COLORIST
VC'S RANDY GENTILE LETTERER
MOLLY LAZER & AUBREY SITTERSON ASSISTANT EDITORS
TOM BREVOORT EDITOR
JOE QUESADA EDITOR IN CHIEF
DAN BUCKLEY PUBLISHER

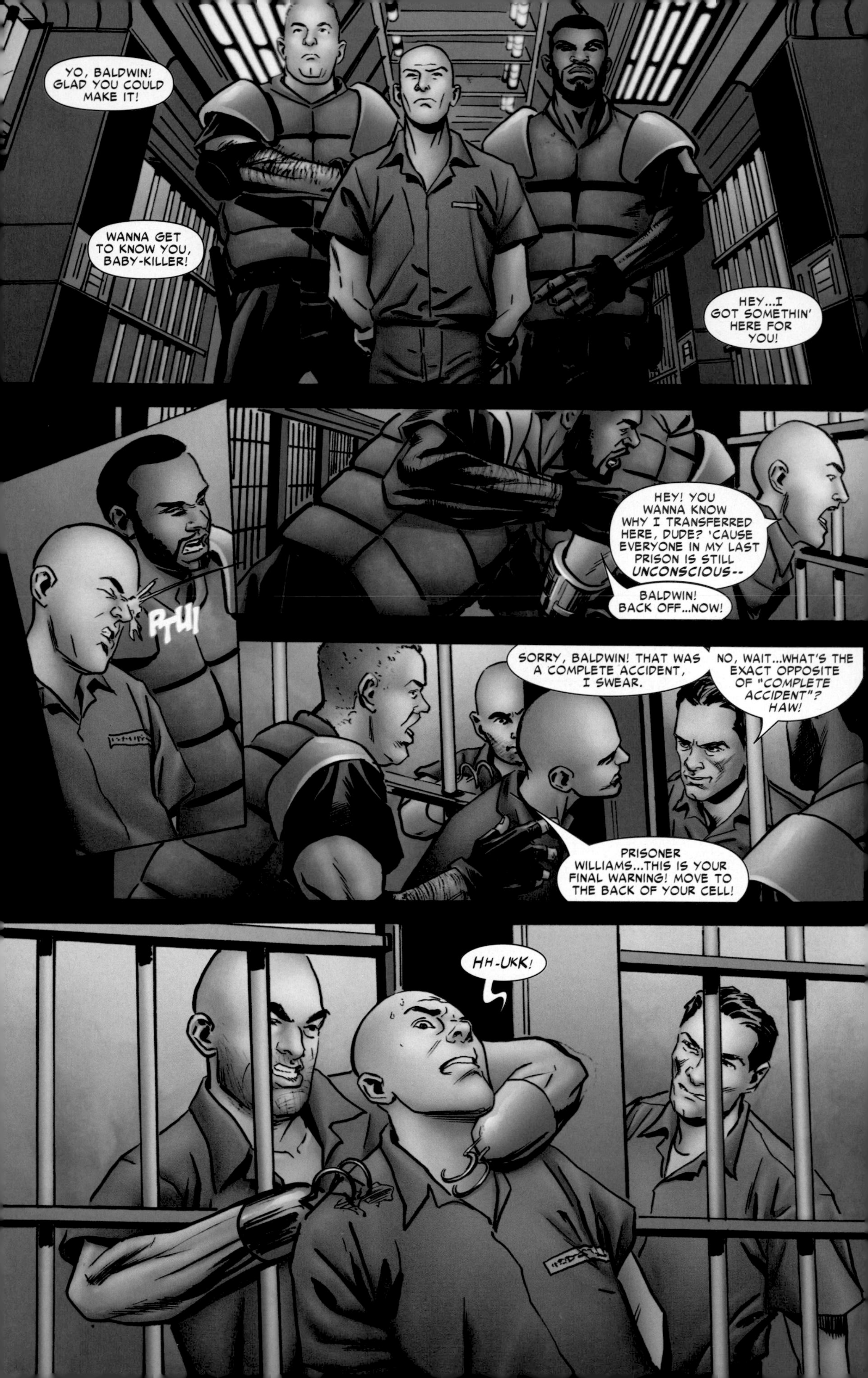
YO, BALDWIN! GLAD YOU COULD MAKE IT!
WANNA GET TO KNOW YOU, BABY-KILLER!
HEY...I GOT SOMETHIN' HERE FOR YOU!
PTUI
HEY! YOU WANNA KNOW WHY I TRANSFERRED HERE, DUDE? 'CAUSE EVERYONE IN MY LAST PRISON IS STILL UNCONSCIOUS--
BALDWIN! BACK OFF...NOW!
SORRY, BALDWIN! THAT WAS A COMPLETE ACCIDENT, I SWEAR.
NO, WAIT...WHAT'S THE EXACT OPPOSITE OF "COMPLETE ACCIDENT"? HAW!
PRISONER WILLIAMS...THIS IS YOUR FINAL WARNING! MOVE TO THE BACK OF YOUR CELL!
HH-UKK!

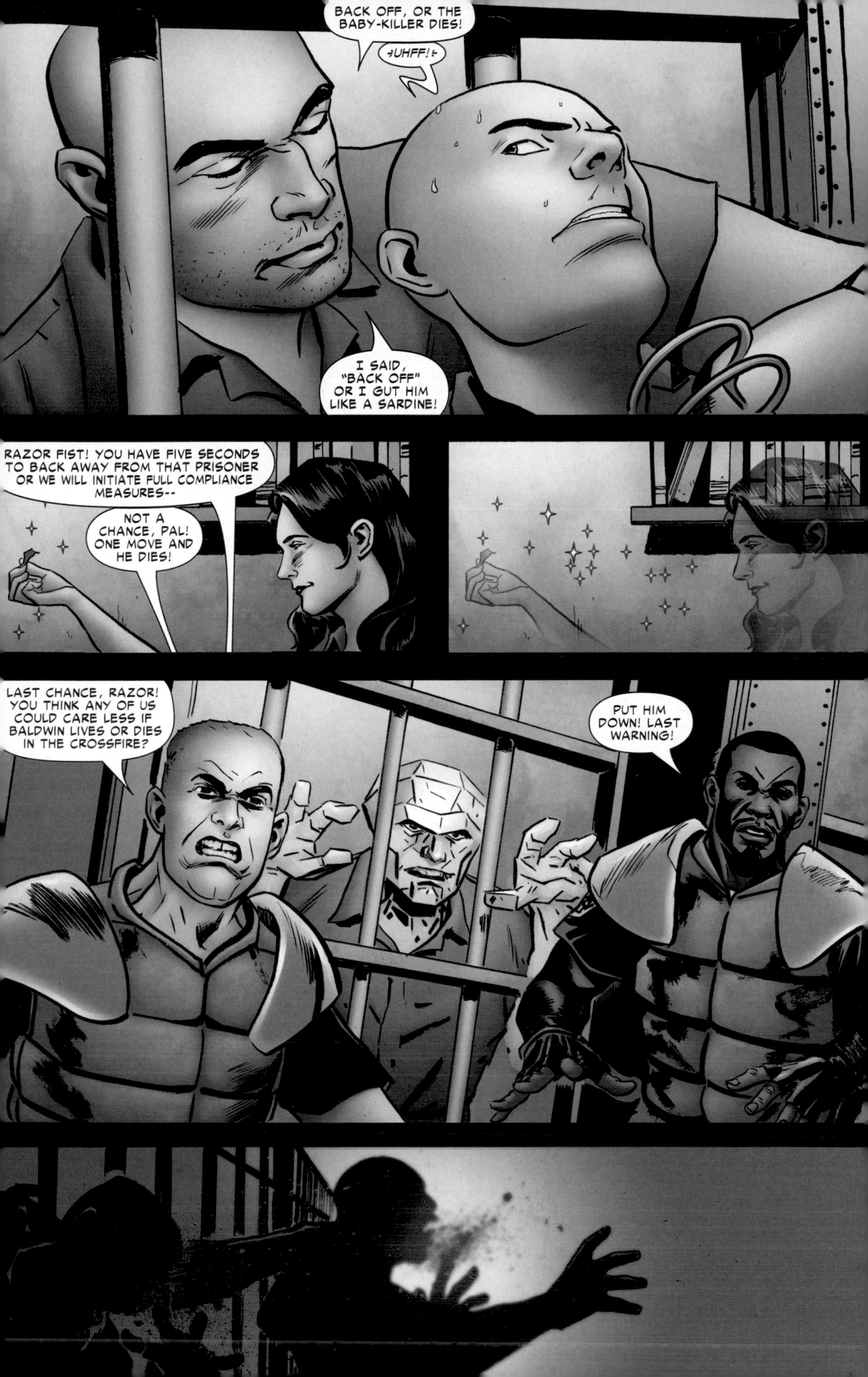
BACK OFF, OR THE BABY-KILLER DIES!
UHFF!
I SAID, "BACK OFF" OR I GUT HIM LIKE A SARDINE!
RAZOR FIST! YOU HAVE FIVE SECONDS TO BACK AWAY FROM THAT PRISONER OR WE WILL INITIATE FULL COMPLIANCE MEASURES--
NOT A CHANCE, PAL! ONE MOVE AND HE DIES!
LAST CHANCE, RAZOR! YOU THINK ANY OF US COULD CARE LESS IF BALDWIN LIVES OR DIES IN THE CROSSFIRE?
PUT HIM DOWN! LAST WARNING!

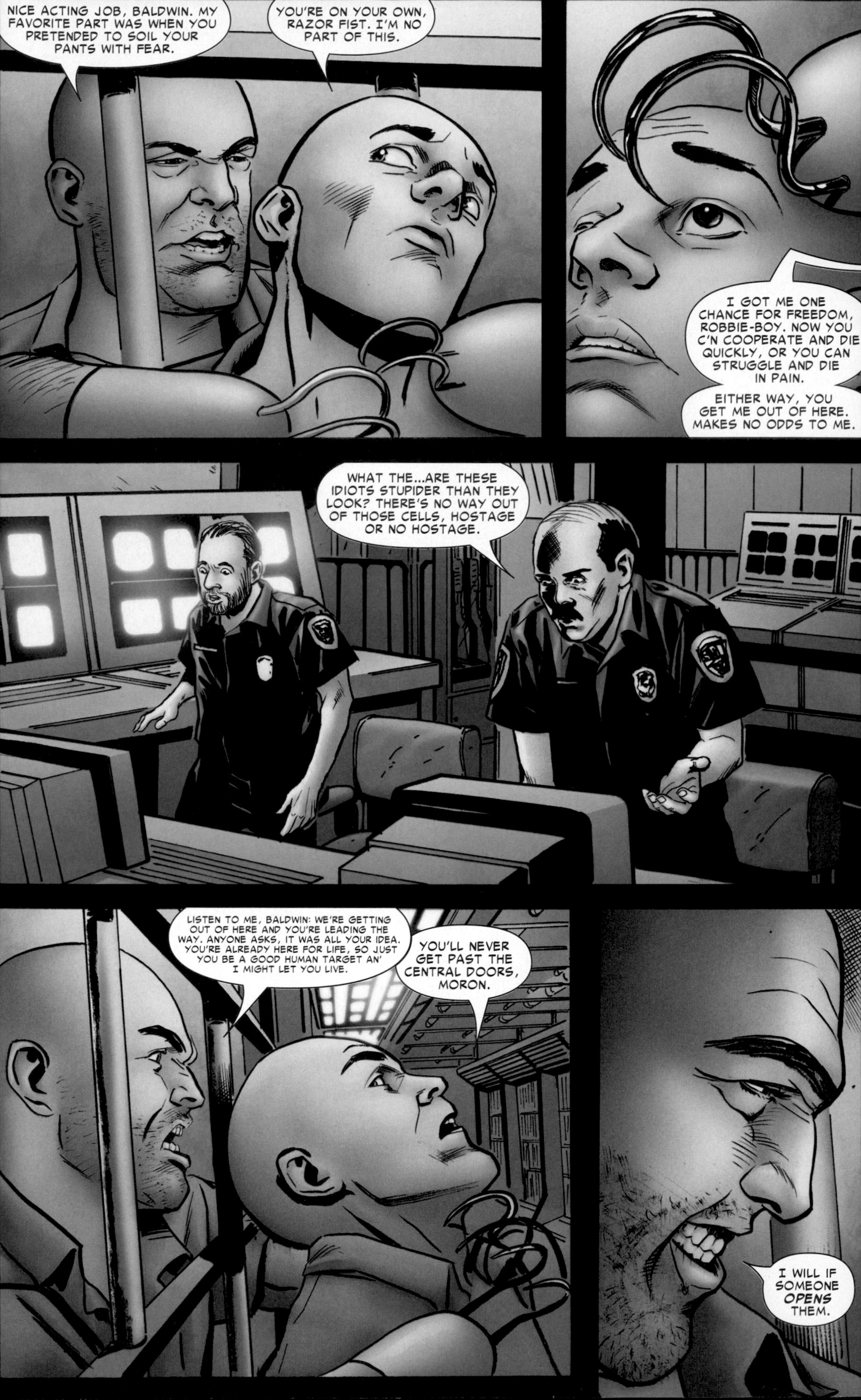
NICE ACTING JOB, BALDWIN. MY FAVORITE PART WAS WHEN YOU PRETENDED TO SOIL YOUR PANTS WITH FEAR.
YOU'RE ON YOUR OWN, RAZOR FIST. I'M NO PART OF THIS.
I GOT ME ONE CHANCE FOR FREEDOM, ROBBIE-BOY. NOW YOU C'N COOPERATE AND DIE QUICKLY, OR YOU CAN STRUGGLE AND DIE IN PAIN.
EITHER WAY, YOU GET ME OUT OF HERE. MAKES NO ODDS TO ME.
WHAT THE...ARE THESE IDIOTS STUPIDER THAN THEY LOOK? THERE'S NO WAY OUT OF THOSE CELLS, HOSTAGE OR NO HOSTAGE.
LISTEN TO ME, BALDWIN: WE'RE GETTING OUT OF HERE AND YOU'RE LEADING THE WAY. ANYONE ASKS, IT WAS ALL YOUR IDEA. YOU'RE ALREADY HERE FOR LIFE, SO JUST YOU BE A GOOD HUMAN TARGET AN' I MIGHT LET YOU LIVE.
YOU'LL NEVER GET PAST THE CENTRAL DOORS, MORON.
I WILL IF SOMEONE OPENS THEM.

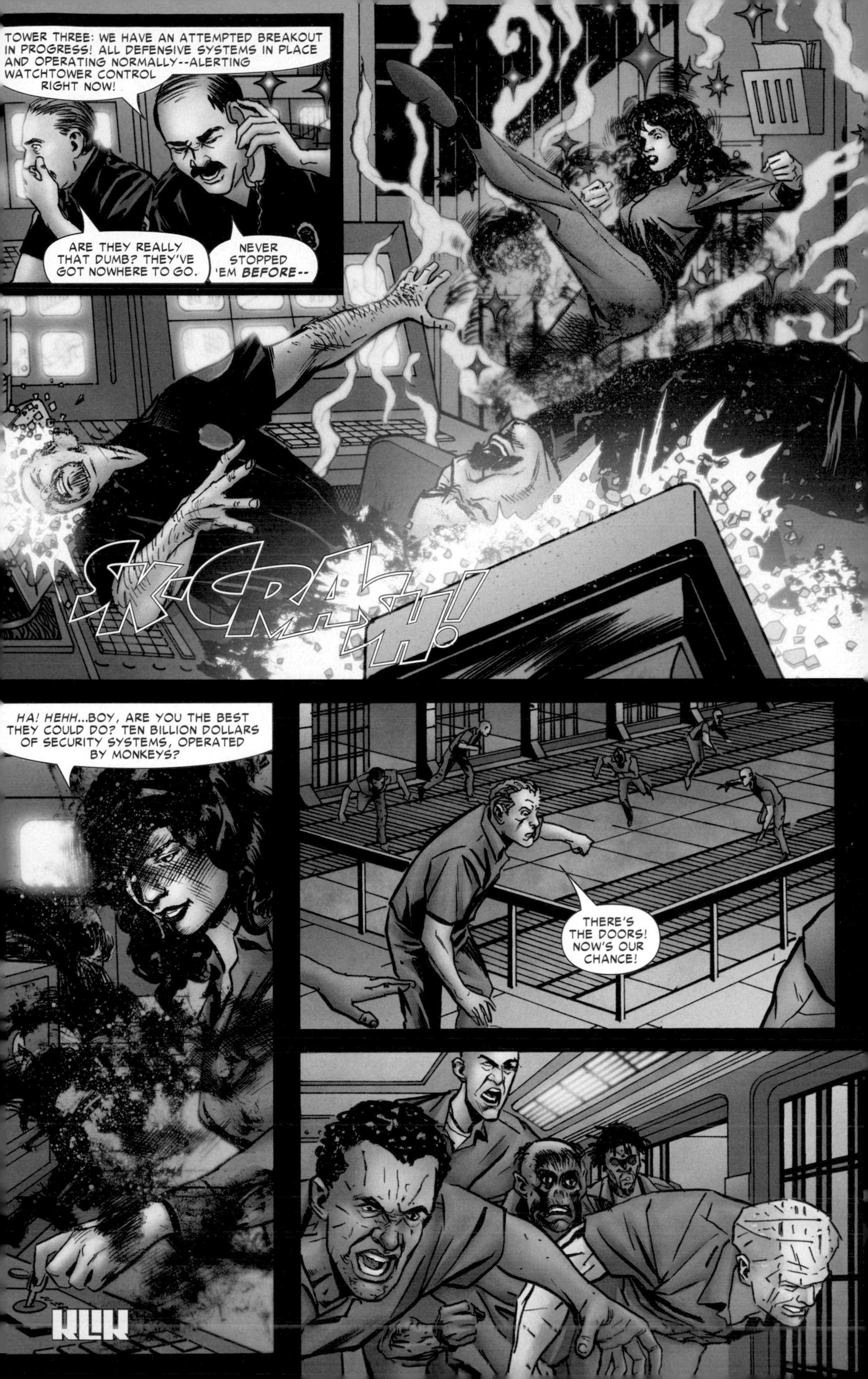

TOWER THREE: WE HAVE AN ATTEMPTED BREAKOUT IN PROGRESS! ALL DEFENSIVE SYSTEMS IN PLACE AND OPERATING NORMALLY--ALERTING WATCHTOWER CONTROL RIGHT NOW!
ARE THEY REALLY THAT DUMB? THEY'VE GOT NOWHERE TO GO.
NEVER STOPPED 'EM BEFORE--
SK-CRASH!
HA! HEHH...BOY, ARE YOU THE BEST THEY COULD DO? TEN BILLION DOLLARS OF SECURITY SYSTEMS, OPERATED BY MONKEYS?
KLIK
THERE'S THE DOORS! NOW'S OUR CHANCE!

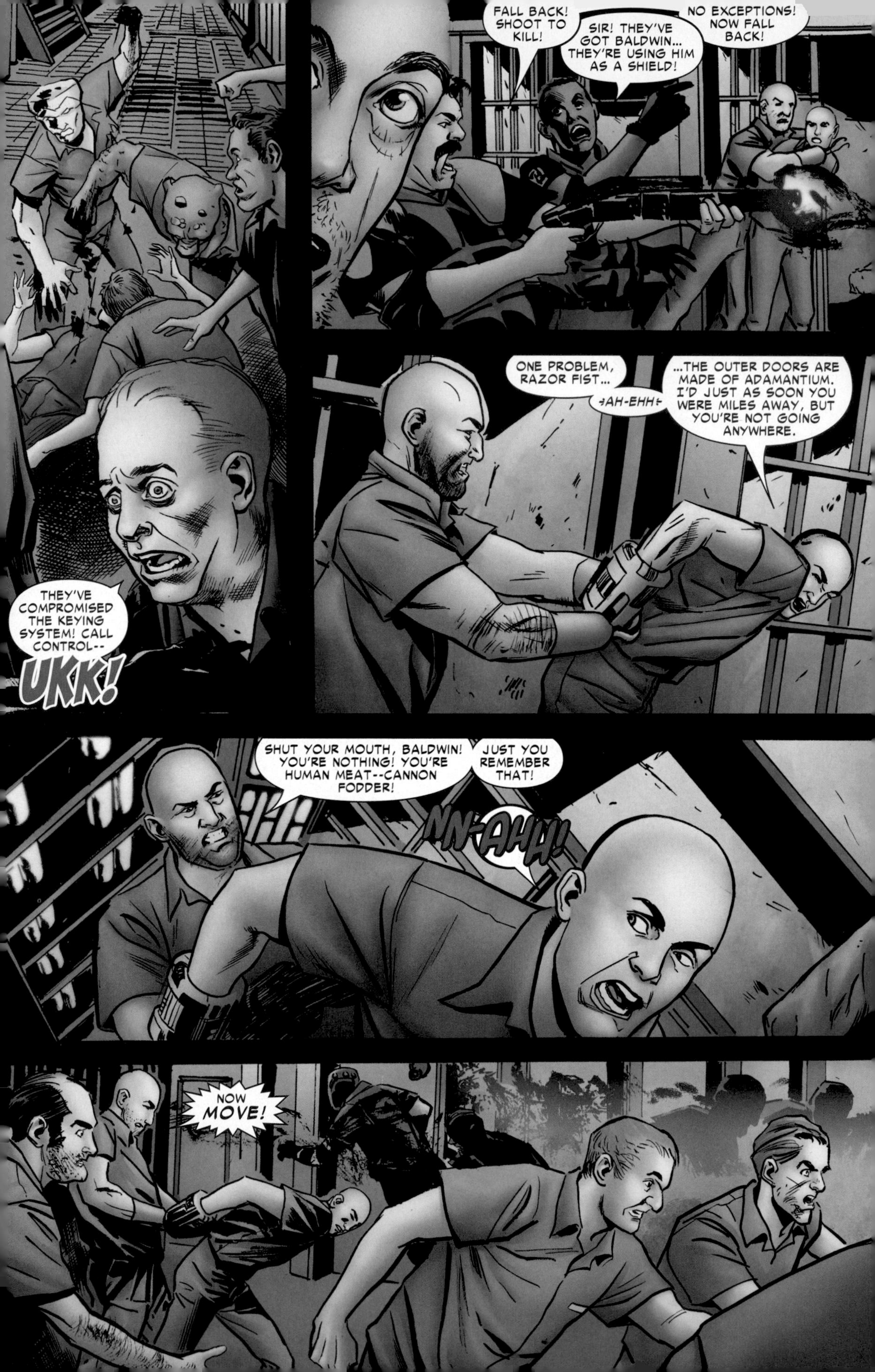

THEY'VE COMPROMISED THE KEYING SYSTEM! CALL CONTROL--
UKK!
FALL BACK! SHOOT TO KILL!
SIR! THEY'VE GOT BALDWIN... THEY'RE USING HIM AS A SHIELD!
NO EXCEPTIONS! NOW FALL BACK!
ONE PROBLEM, RAZOR FIST...
AH-EHH
...THE OUTER DOORS ARE MADE OF ADAMANTIUM. I'D JUST AS SOON YOU WERE MILES AWAY, BUT YOU'RE NOT GOING ANYWHERE.
SHUT YOUR MOUTH, BALDWIN! YOU'RE NOTHING! YOU'RE HUMAN MEAT--CANNON FODDER!
JUST YOU REMEMBER THAT!
NN-AHH!
NOW MOVE!

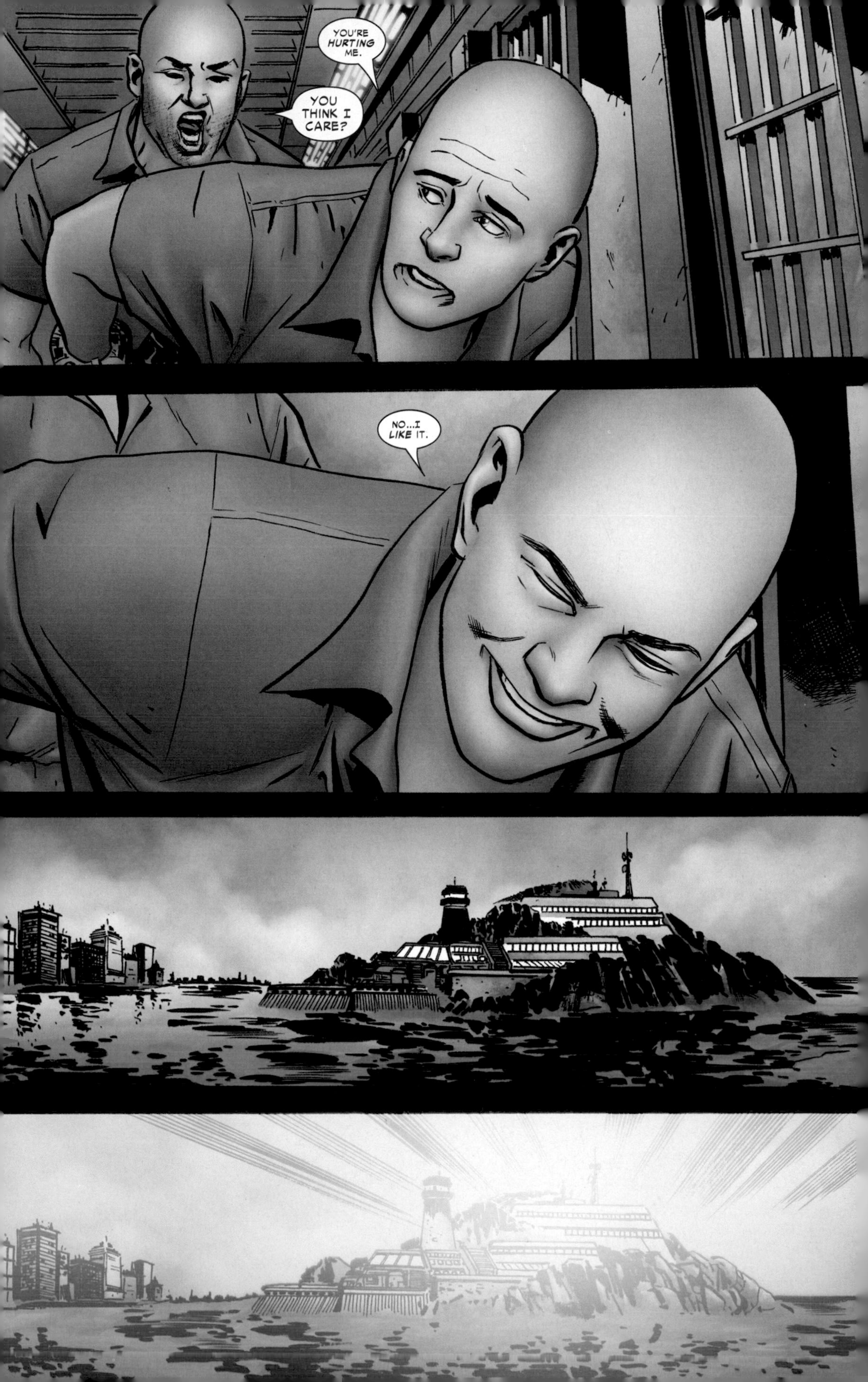
YOU'RE HURTING ME.
YOU THINK I CARE?
NO...I LIKE IT.

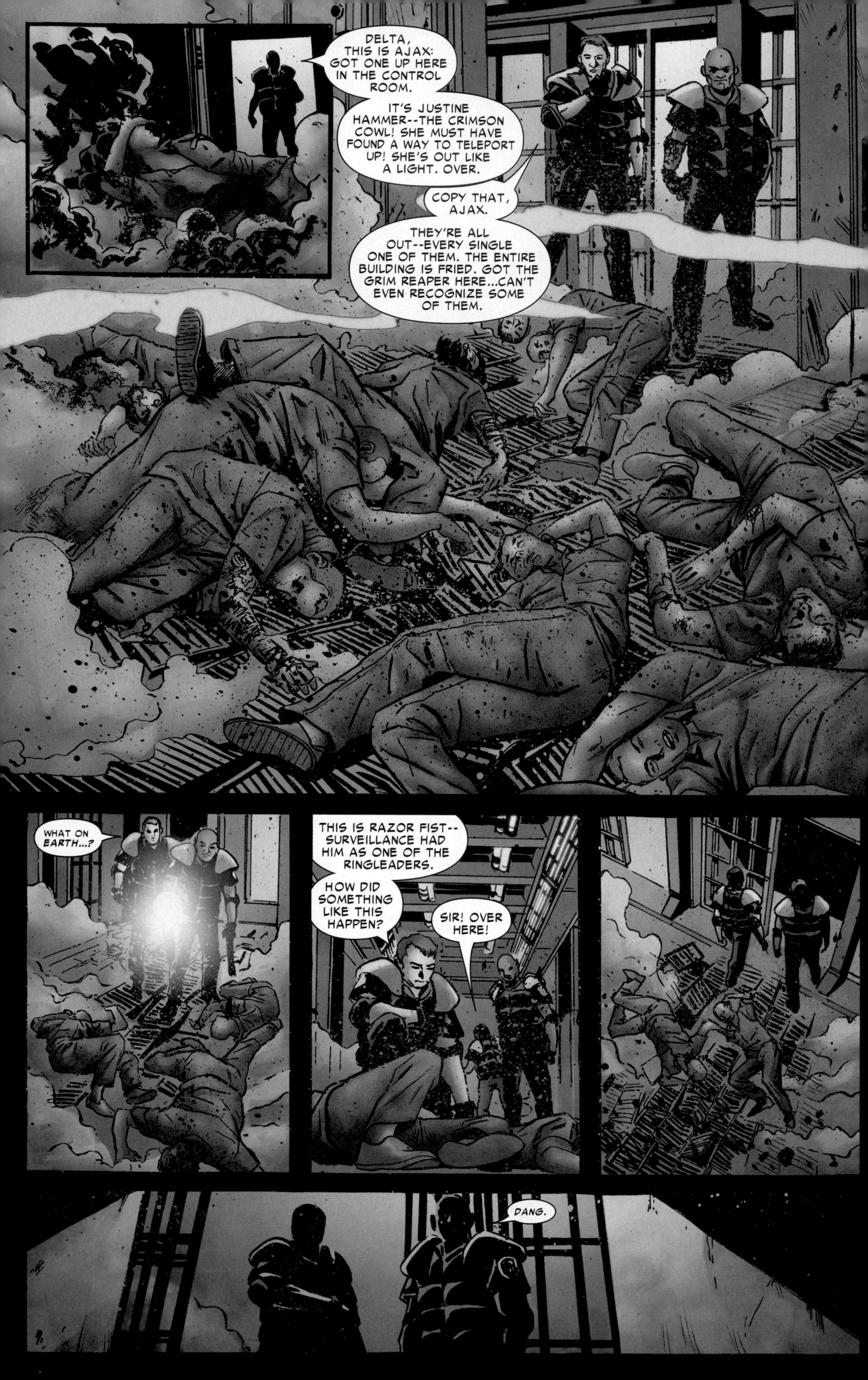
DELTA, THIS IS AJAX: GOT ONE UP HERE IN THE CONTROL ROOM.
IT'S JUSTINE HAMMER--THE CRIMSON COWL! SHE MUST HAVE FOUND A WAY TO TELEPORT UP! SHE'S OUT LIKE A LIGHT. OVER.
COPY THAT, AJAX.
THEY'RE ALL OUT--EVERY SINGLE ONE OF THEM. THE ENTIRE BUILDING IS FRIED. GOT THE GRIM REAPER HERE...CAN'T EVEN RECOGNIZE SOME OF THEM.
WHAT ON *EARTH*...?
THIS IS RAZOR FIST--SURVEILLANCE HAD HIM AS ONE OF THE RINGLEADERS.
HOW DID SOMETHING LIKE THIS HAPPEN?
SIR! OVER HERE!
DANG.

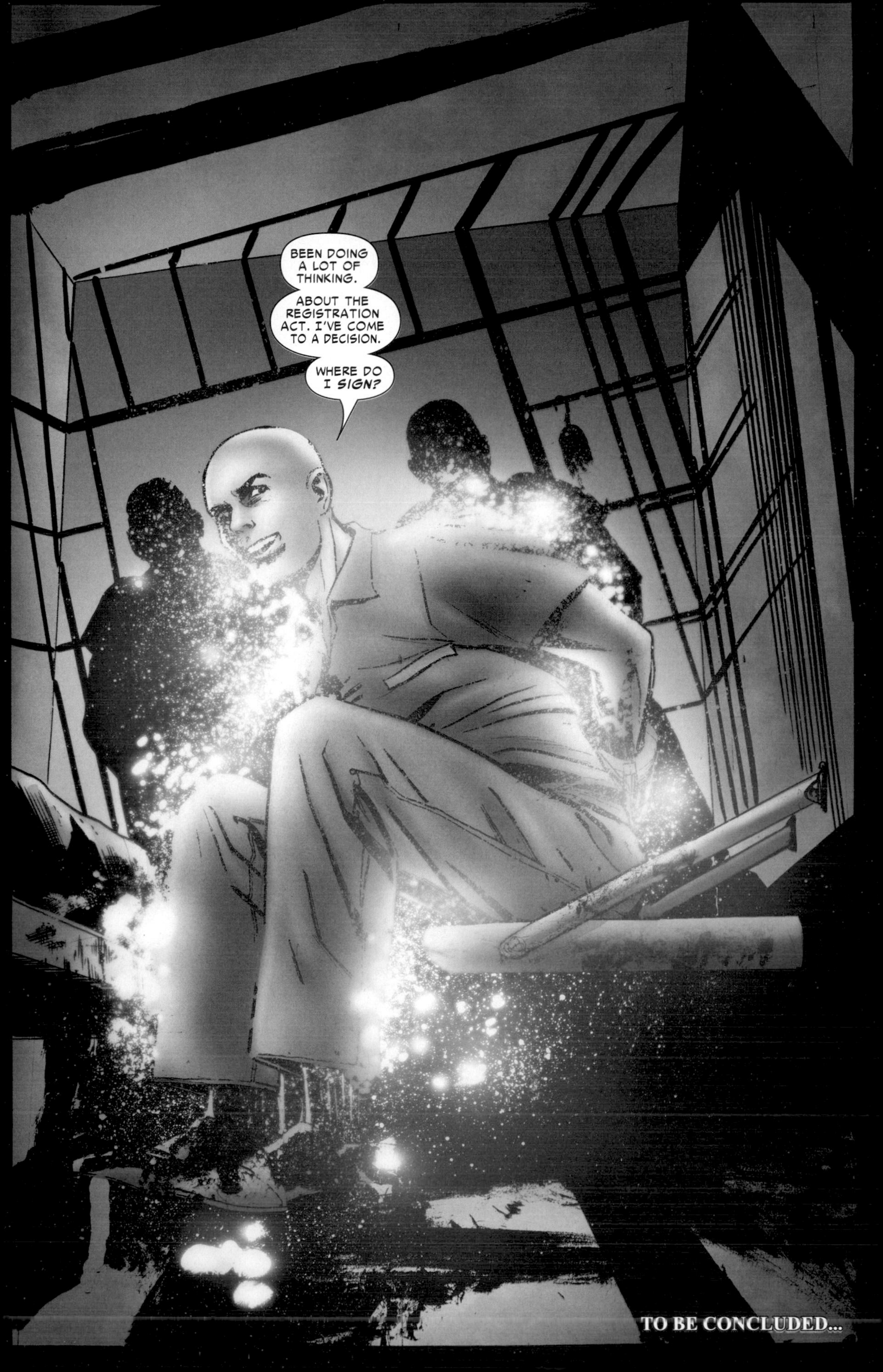
BEEN DOING A LOT OF THINKING.
ABOUT THE REGISTRATION ACT. I'VE COME TO A DECISION.
WHERE DO I SIGN?
TO BE CONCLUDED...

HE'S NOT TALKING.

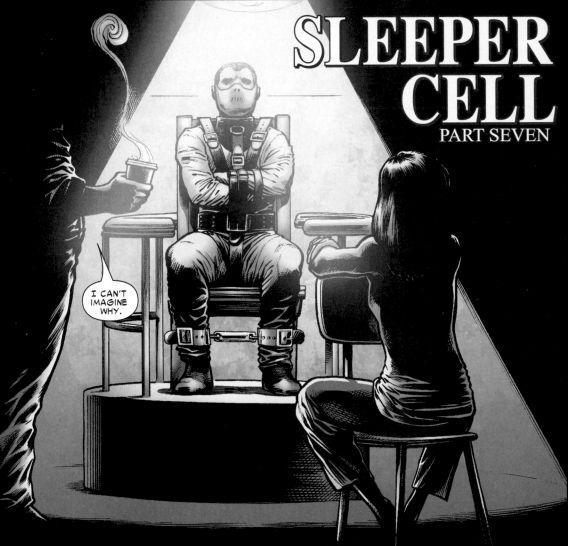

SLEEPER CELL
PART SEVEN

I CAN'T IMAGINE WHY.

PAUL JENKINS WRITER | LEE WEEKS BREAKDOWNS | NELSON FINISHES | VC'S RANDY GENTILE LETTERS | MOLLY LAZER & AUBREY SITTERSON ASSISTANT EDITORS | TOM BREVOORT EDITOR | JOE QUESADA EDITOR IN CHIEF | DAN BUCKLEY PUBLISHER

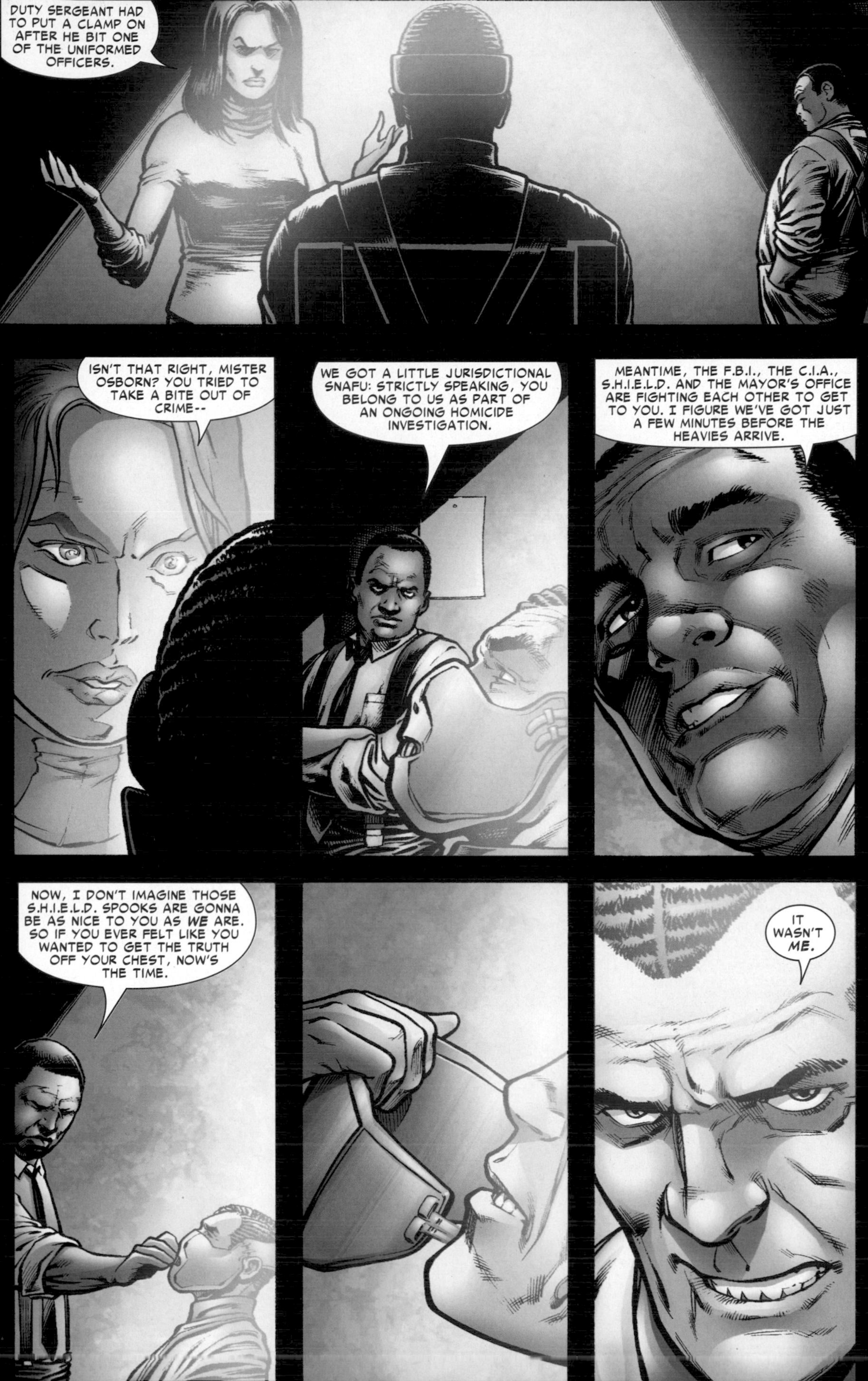
DUTY SERGEANT HAD TO PUT A CLAMP ON AFTER HE BIT ONE OF THE UNIFORMED OFFICERS.
ISN'T THAT RIGHT, MISTER OSBORN? YOU TRIED TO TAKE A BITE OUT OF CRIME--
WE GOT A LITTLE JURISDICTIONAL SNAFU: STRICTLY SPEAKING, YOU BELONG TO US AS PART OF AN ONGOING HOMICIDE INVESTIGATION.
MEANTIME, THE F.B.I., THE C.I.A., S.H.I.E.L.D. AND THE MAYOR'S OFFICE ARE FIGHTING EACH OTHER TO GET TO YOU. I FIGURE WE'VE GOT JUST A FEW MINUTES BEFORE THE HEAVIES ARRIVE.
NOW, I DON'T IMAGINE THOSE S.H.I.E.L.D. SPOOKS ARE GONNA BE AS NICE TO YOU AS *WE* ARE. SO IF YOU EVER FELT LIKE YOU WANTED TO GET THE TRUTH OFF YOUR CHEST, NOW'S THE TIME.
IT WASN'T *ME.*

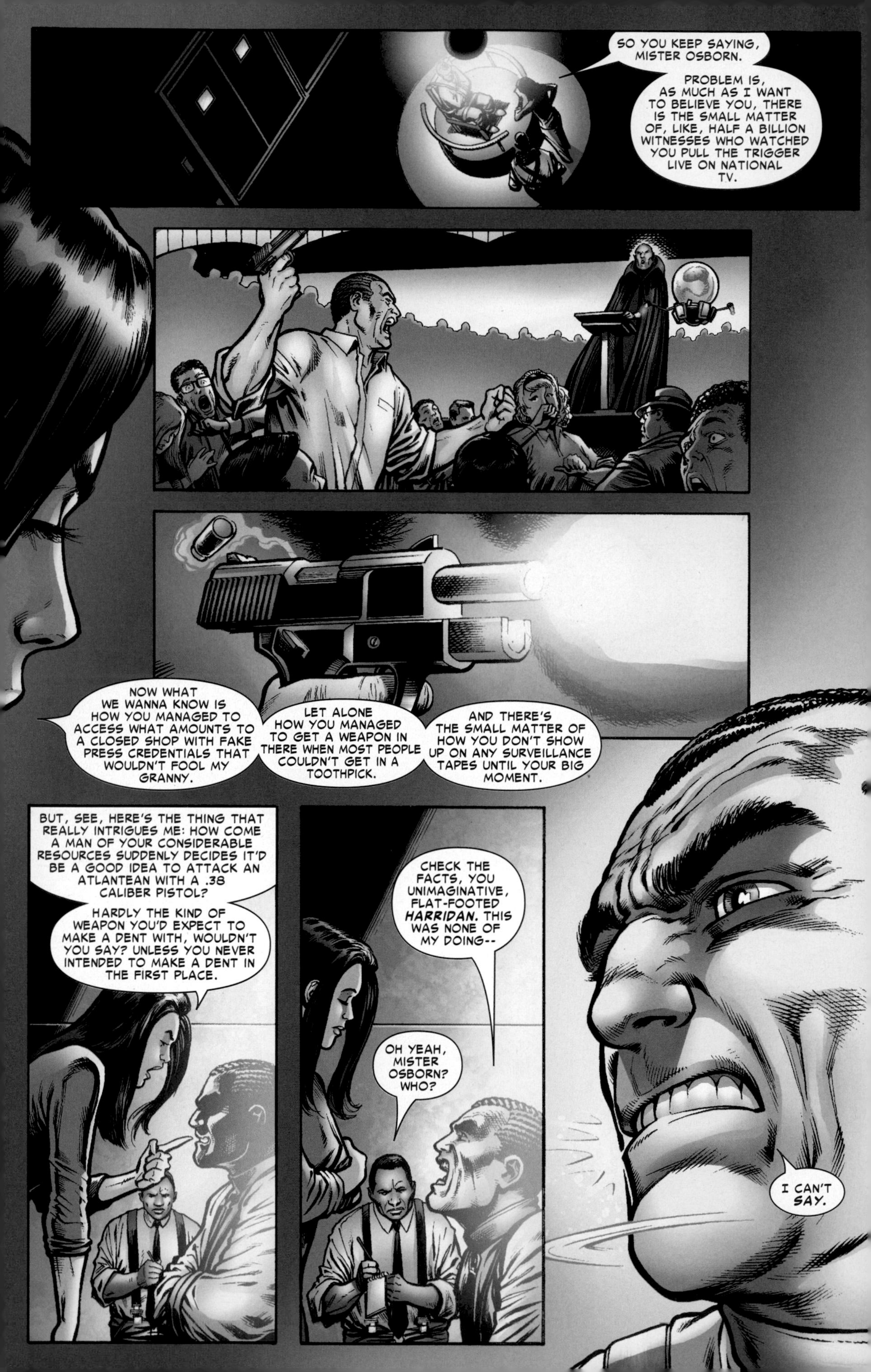
SO YOU KEEP SAYING, MISTER OSBORN.
PROBLEM IS, AS MUCH AS I WANT TO BELIEVE YOU, THERE IS THE SMALL MATTER OF, LIKE, HALF A BILLION WITNESSES WHO WATCHED YOU PULL THE TRIGGER LIVE ON NATIONAL TV.
NOW WHAT WE WANNA KNOW IS HOW YOU MANAGED TO ACCESS WHAT AMOUNTS TO A CLOSED SHOP WITH FAKE PRESS CREDENTIALS THAT WOULDN'T FOOL MY GRANNY.
LET ALONE HOW YOU MANAGED TO GET A WEAPON IN THERE WHEN MOST PEOPLE COULDN'T GET IN A TOOTHPICK.
AND THERE'S THE SMALL MATTER OF HOW YOU DON'T SHOW UP ON ANY SURVEILLANCE TAPES UNTIL YOUR BIG MOMENT.
BUT, SEE, HERE'S THE THING THAT REALLY INTRIGUES ME: HOW COME A MAN OF YOUR CONSIDERABLE RESOURCES SUDDENLY DECIDES IT'D BE A GOOD IDEA TO ATTACK AN ATLANTEAN WITH A .38 CALIBER PISTOL?
HARDLY THE KIND OF WEAPON YOU'D EXPECT TO MAKE A DENT WITH, WOULDN'T YOU SAY? UNLESS YOU NEVER INTENDED TO MAKE A DENT IN THE FIRST PLACE.
CHECK THE FACTS, YOU UNIMAGINATIVE, FLAT-FOOTED *HARRIDAN.* THIS WAS NONE OF MY DOING--
OH YEAH, MISTER OSBORN? WHO?
I CAN'T *SAY.*

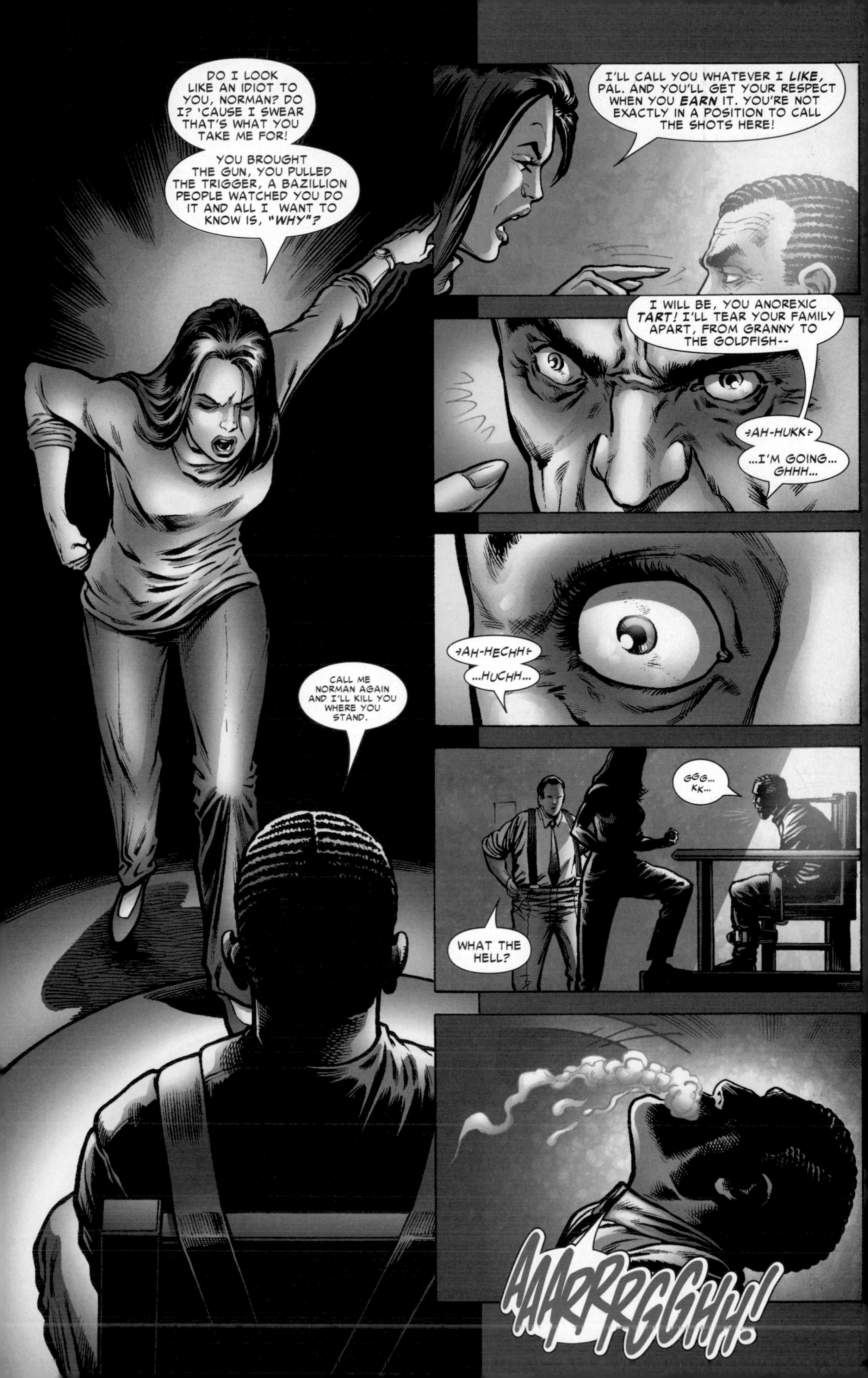
DO I LOOK LIKE AN IDIOT TO YOU, NORMAN? DO I? 'CAUSE I SWEAR THAT'S WHAT YOU TAKE ME FOR!
YOU BROUGHT THE GUN, YOU PULLED THE TRIGGER, A BAZILLION PEOPLE WATCHED YOU DO IT AND ALL I WANT TO KNOW IS, "WHY"?
CALL ME NORMAN AGAIN AND I'LL KILL YOU WHERE YOU STAND.
I'LL CALL YOU WHATEVER I LIKE, PAL. AND YOU'LL GET YOUR RESPECT WHEN YOU EARN IT. YOU'RE NOT EXACTLY IN A POSITION TO CALL THE SHOTS HERE!
I WILL BE, YOU ANOREXIC TART! I'LL TEAR YOUR FAMILY APART, FROM GRANNY TO THE GOLDFISH--
AH-HUKK
...I'M GOING... GHHH...
AH-HECHH
...HUCHH...
GGG... KK...
WHAT THE HELL?
AAARRRGGHH!

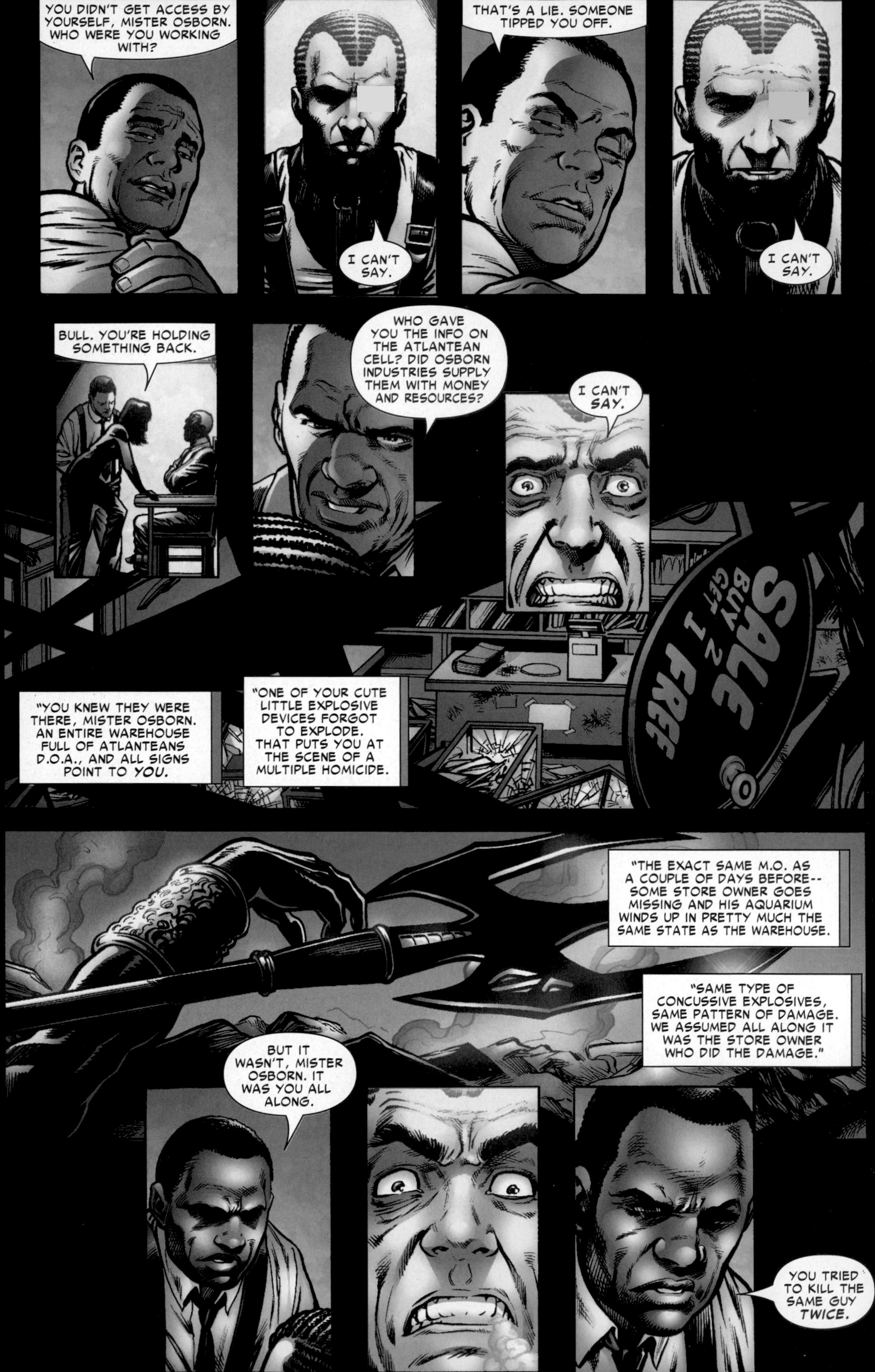
YOU DIDN'T GET ACCESS BY YOURSELF, MISTER OSBORN. WHO WERE YOU WORKING WITH?
I CAN'T SAY.
THAT'S A LIE. SOMEONE TIPPED YOU OFF.
I CAN'T SAY.
BULL. YOU'RE HOLDING SOMETHING BACK.
WHO GAVE YOU THE INFO ON THE ATLANTEAN CELL? DID OSBORN INDUSTRIES SUPPLY THEM WITH MONEY AND RESOURCES?
I CAN'T SAY.
SALE
BUY 2
GET 1 FREE
"YOU KNEW THEY WERE THERE, MISTER OSBORN. AN ENTIRE WAREHOUSE FULL OF ATLANTEANS D.O.A., AND ALL SIGNS POINT TO YOU.
"ONE OF YOUR CUTE LITTLE EXPLOSIVE DEVICES FORGOT TO EXPLODE. THAT PUTS YOU AT THE SCENE OF A MULTIPLE HOMICIDE.
"THE EXACT SAME M.O. AS A COUPLE OF DAYS BEFORE-- SOME STORE OWNER GOES MISSING AND HIS AQUARIUM WINDS UP IN PRETTY MUCH THE SAME STATE AS THE WAREHOUSE.
"SAME TYPE OF CONCUSSIVE EXPLOSIVES, SAME PATTERN OF DAMAGE. WE ASSUMED ALL ALONG IT WAS THE STORE OWNER WHO DID THE DAMAGE."
BUT IT WASN'T, MISTER OSBORN. IT WAS YOU ALL ALONG.
YOU TRIED TO KILL THE SAME GUY TWICE.

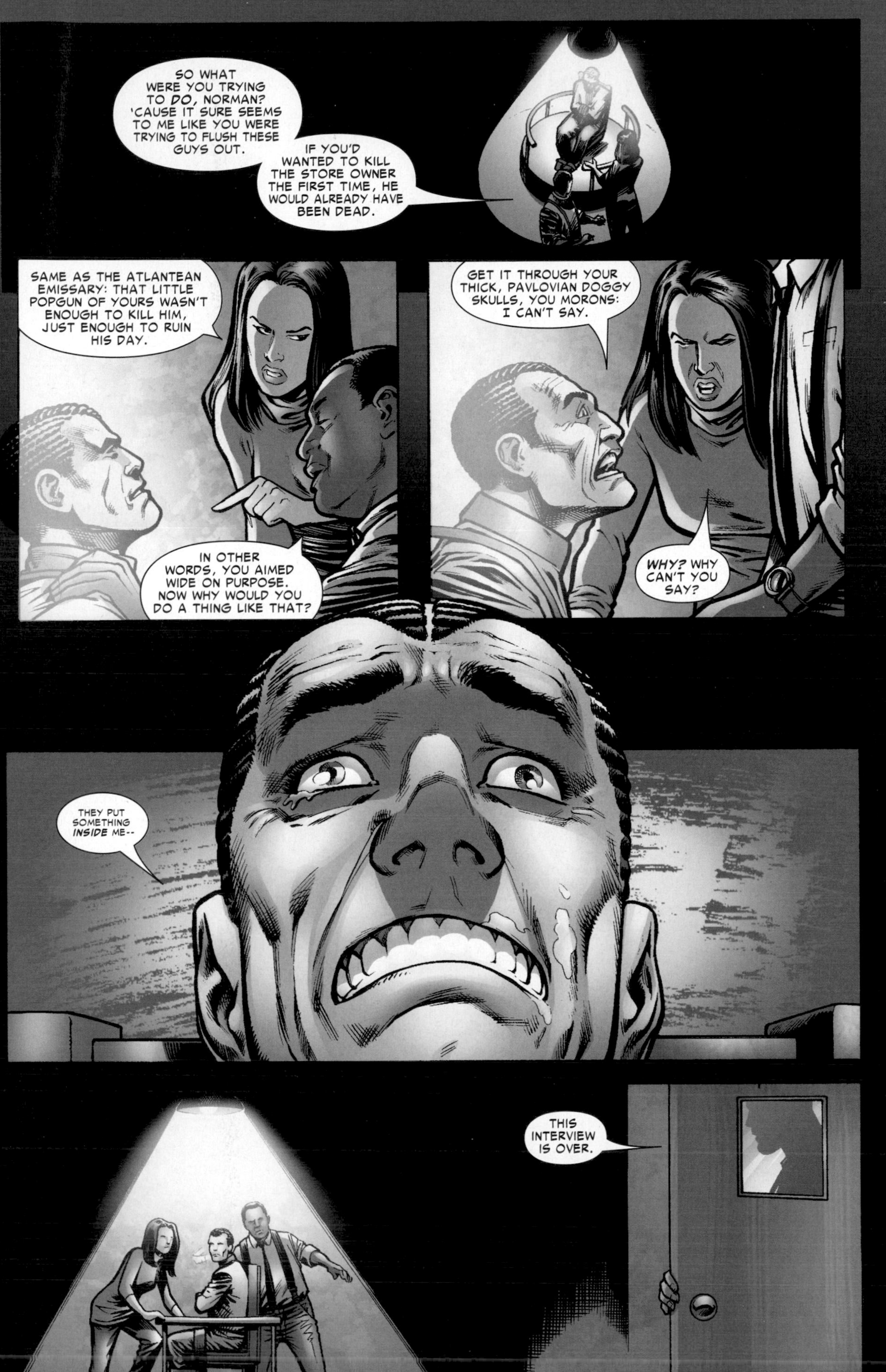
SO WHAT WERE YOU TRYING TO DO, NORMAN? 'CAUSE IT SURE SEEMS TO ME LIKE YOU WERE TRYING TO FLUSH THESE GUYS OUT.
IF YOU'D WANTED TO KILL THE STORE OWNER THE FIRST TIME, HE WOULD ALREADY HAVE BEEN DEAD.
SAME AS THE ATLANTEAN EMISSARY: THAT LITTLE POPGUN OF YOURS WASN'T ENOUGH TO KILL HIM, JUST ENOUGH TO RUIN HIS DAY.
IN OTHER WORDS, YOU AIMED WIDE ON PURPOSE. NOW WHY WOULD YOU DO A THING LIKE THAT?
GET IT THROUGH YOUR THICK, PAVLOVIAN DOGGY SKULLS, YOU MORONS: I CAN'T SAY.
WHY? WHY CAN'T YOU SAY?
THEY PUT SOMETHING INSIDE ME--
THIS INTERVIEW IS OVER.

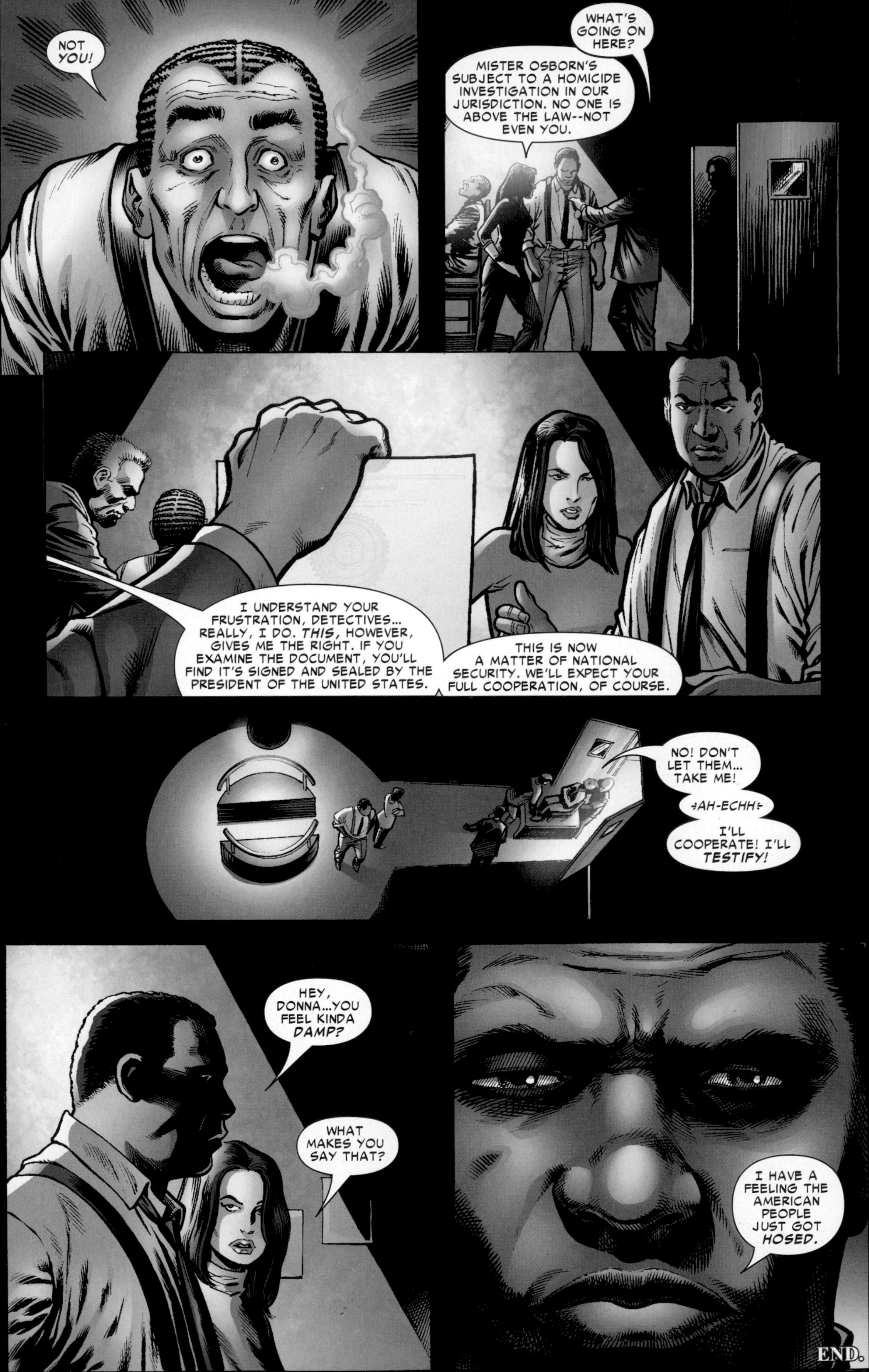
NOT YOU!
WHAT'S GOING ON HERE?
MISTER OSBORN'S SUBJECT TO A HOMICIDE INVESTIGATION IN OUR JURISDICTION. NO ONE IS ABOVE THE LAW--NOT EVEN YOU.
I UNDERSTAND YOUR FRUSTRATION, DETECTIVES... REALLY, I DO. THIS, HOWEVER, GIVES ME THE RIGHT. IF YOU EXAMINE THE DOCUMENT, YOU'LL FIND IT'S SIGNED AND SEALED BY THE PRESIDENT OF THE UNITED STATES.
THIS IS NOW A MATTER OF NATIONAL SECURITY. WE'LL EXPECT YOUR FULL COOPERATION, OF COURSE.
NO! DON'T LET THEM... TAKE ME!
AH-ECHH
I'LL COOPERATE! I'LL TESTIFY!
HEY, DONNA...YOU FEEL KINDA DAMP?
WHAT MAKES YOU SAY THAT?
I HAVE A FEELING THE AMERICAN PEOPLE JUST GOT HOSED.
END.

Private William Eldridge of Battersea, London, enlisted in the 13th Battalion of the Royal Fusiliers just a few short months after his wedding day. He fought at Arras, France, and was wounded in battle in the early days of November, 1917.

William was taken to a clearing station on the outskirts of Thiepval, France, where he died as a result of his wounds on November 4th.

His body was laid to rest in the Duisans British Cemetery, Etrun. He lies in Section 1, Row O, Grave Number 22.

William Eldridge was my great grandfather.

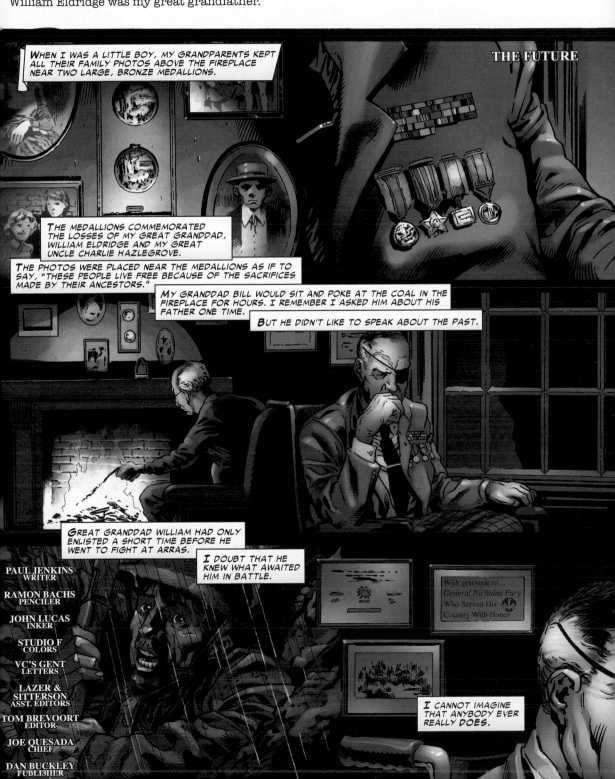

WHEN I WAS A LITTLE BOY, MY GRANDPARENTS KEPT ALL THEIR FAMILY PHOTOS ABOVE THE FIREPLACE NEAR TWO LARGE, BRONZE MEDALLIONS.

THE FUTURE

THE MEDALLIONS COMMEMORATED THE LOSSES OF MY GREAT GRANDDAD, WILLIAM ELDRIDGE AND MY GREAT UNCLE CHARLIE HAZLEGROVE.

THE PHOTOS WERE PLACED NEAR THE MEDALLIONS AS IF TO SAY, "THESE PEOPLE LIVE FREE BECAUSE OF THE SACRIFICES MADE BY THEIR ANCESTORS."

MY GRANDDAD BILL WOULD SIT AND POKE AT THE COAL IN THE FIREPLACE FOR HOURS. I REMEMBER I ASKED HIM ABOUT HIS FATHER ONE TIME.

BUT HE DIDN'T LIKE TO SPEAK ABOUT THE PAST.

GREAT GRANDDAD WILLIAM HAD ONLY ENLISTED A SHORT TIME BEFORE HE WENT TO FIGHT AT ARRAS.

I DOUBT THAT HE KNEW WHAT AWAITED HIM IN BATTLE.

With gratitude to...
General Nicholas Fury
Who Served His
Country With Honor

I CANNOT IMAGINE THAT ANYBODY EVER REALLY DOES.

PAUL JENKINS
WRITER

RAMON BACHS
PENCILER

JOHN LUCAS
INKER

STUDIO F
COLORS

VC'S GENT
LETTERS

LAZER &
SITTERSON
ASST. EDITORS

TOM BREVOORT
EDITOR

JOE QUESADA
CHIEF

DAN BUCKLEY
PUBLISHER

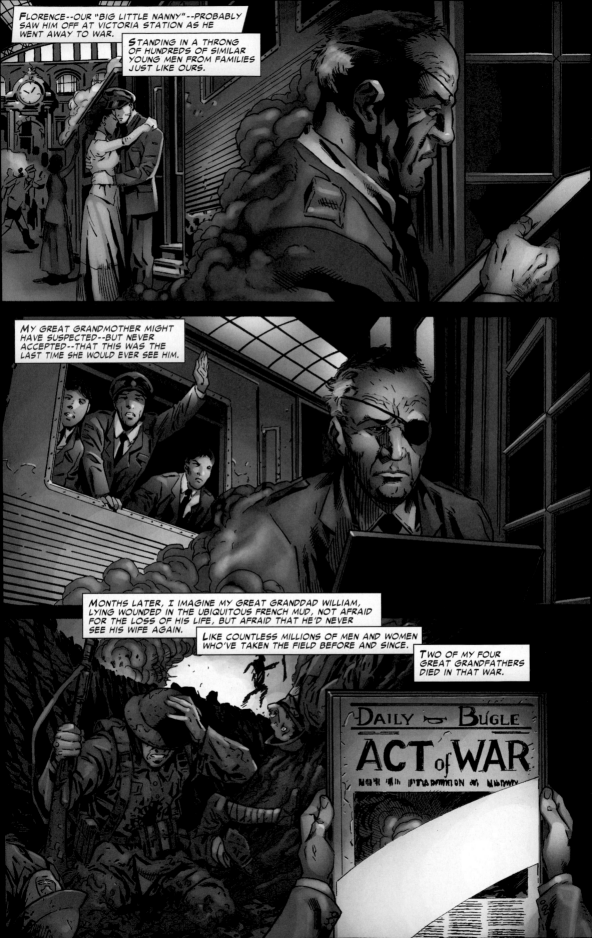

FLORENCE--OUR "BIG LITTLE NANNY"--PROBABLY SAW HIM OFF AT VICTORIA STATION AS HE WENT AWAY TO WAR.

STANDING IN A THRONG OF HUNDREDS OF SIMILAR YOUNG MEN FROM FAMILIES JUST LIKE OURS.

MY GREAT GRANDMOTHER MIGHT HAVE SUSPECTED--BUT NEVER ACCEPTED--THAT THIS WAS THE LAST TIME SHE WOULD EVER SEE HIM.

MONTHS LATER, I IMAGINE MY GREAT GRANDDAD WILLIAM, LYING WOUNDED IN THE UBIQUITOUS FRENCH MUD, NOT AFRAID FOR THE LOSS OF HIS LIFE, BUT AFRAID THAT HE'D NEVER SEE HIS WIFE AGAIN.

LIKE COUNTLESS MILLIONS OF MEN AND WOMEN WHO'VE TAKEN THE FIELD BEFORE AND SINCE.

TWO OF MY FOUR GREAT GRANDFATHERS DIED IN THAT WAR.

DAILY BUGLE
ACT of WAR

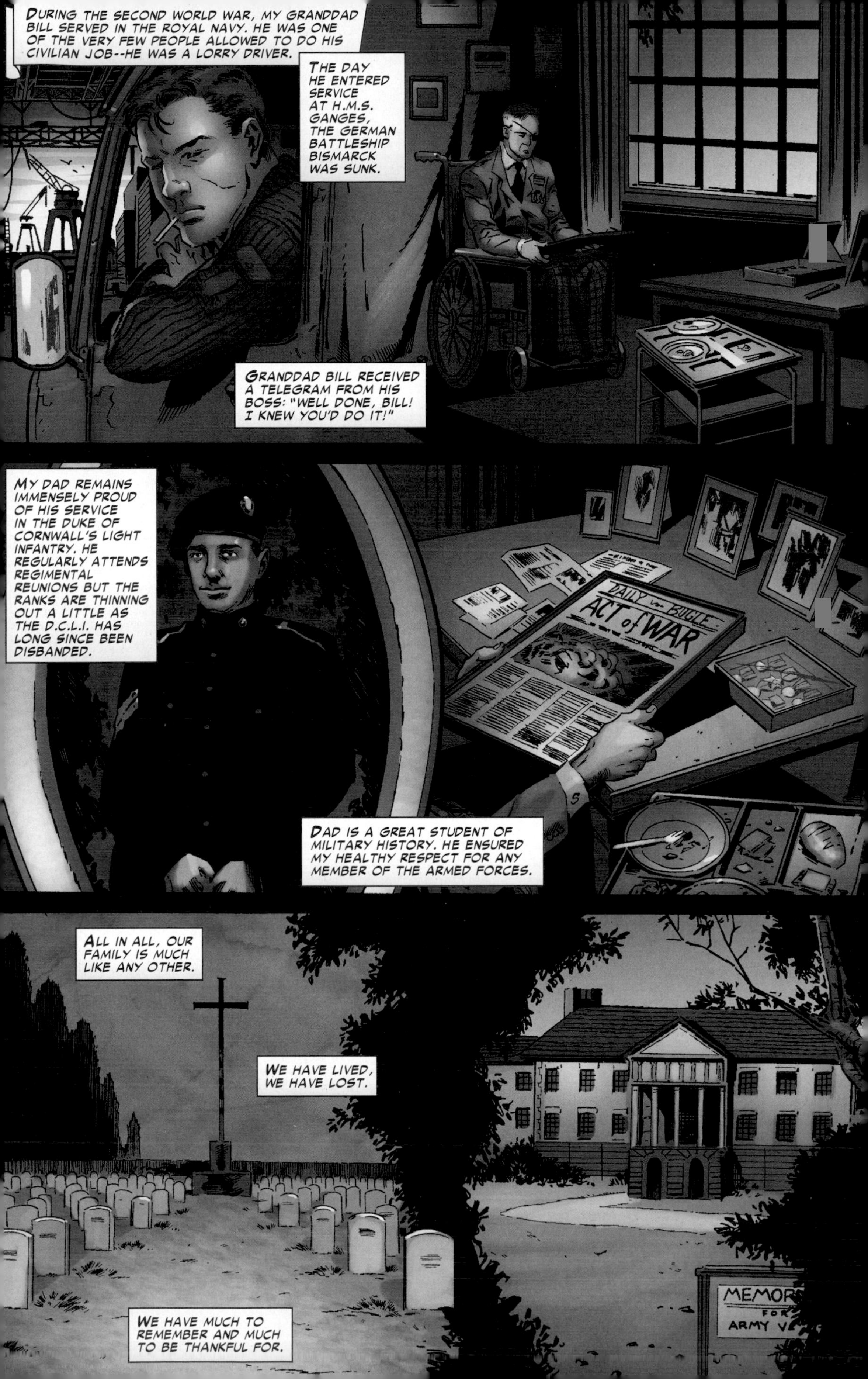
During the Second World War, my granddad Bill served in the Royal Navy. He was one of the very few people allowed to do his civilian job--he was a lorry driver.
The day he entered service at H.M.S. Ganges, the German battleship Bismarck was sunk.
Granddad Bill received a telegram from his boss: "Well done, Bill! I knew you'd do it!"
My dad remains immensely proud of his service in the Duke of Cornwall's Light Infantry. He regularly attends regimental reunions but the ranks are thinning out a little as the D.C.L.I. has long since been disbanded.
DAILY BUGLE
ACT of WAR
Dad is a great student of military history. He ensured my healthy respect for any member of the armed forces.
All in all, our family is much like any other.
We have lived, we have lost.
We have much to remember and much to be thankful for.
MEMOR
FOR
ARMY V

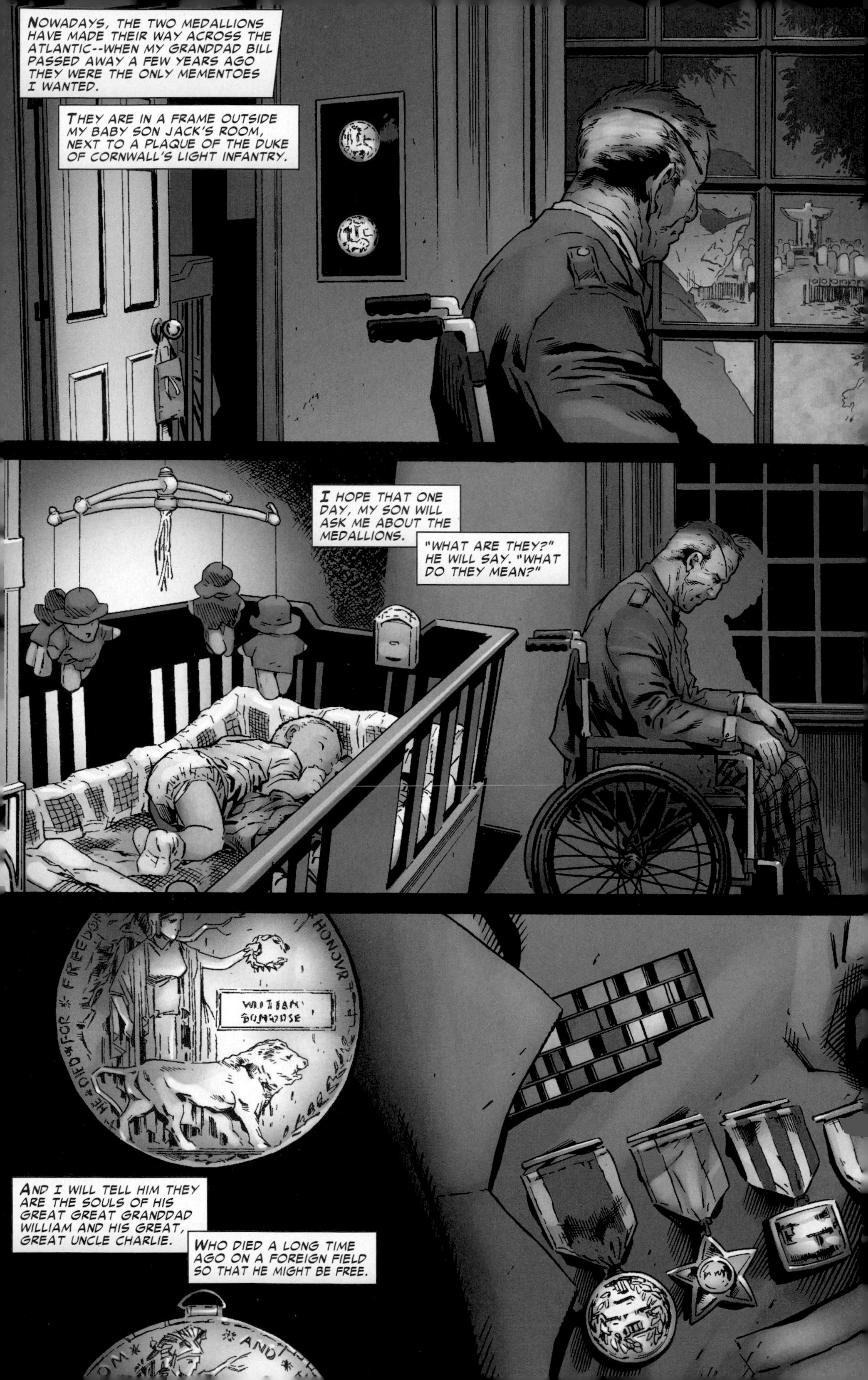
NOWADAYS, THE TWO MEDALLIONS HAVE MADE THEIR WAY ACROSS THE ATLANTIC--WHEN MY GRANDDAD BILL PASSED AWAY A FEW YEARS AGO THEY WERE THE ONLY MEMENTOES I WANTED.
THEY ARE IN A FRAME OUTSIDE MY BABY SON JACK'S ROOM, NEXT TO A PLAQUE OF THE DUKE OF CORNWALL'S LIGHT INFANTRY.
I HOPE THAT ONE DAY, MY SON WILL ASK ME ABOUT THE MEDALLIONS.
"WHAT ARE THEY?" HE WILL SAY. "WHAT DO THEY MEAN?"
AND I WILL TELL HIM THEY ARE THE SOULS OF HIS GREAT GREAT GRANDDAD WILLIAM AND HIS GREAT, GREAT UNCLE CHARLIE.
WHO DIED A LONG TIME AGO ON A FOREIGN FIELD SO THAT HE MIGHT BE FREE.

FRONT LINE
A MARVEL COMICS EVENT

CIVIL WAR

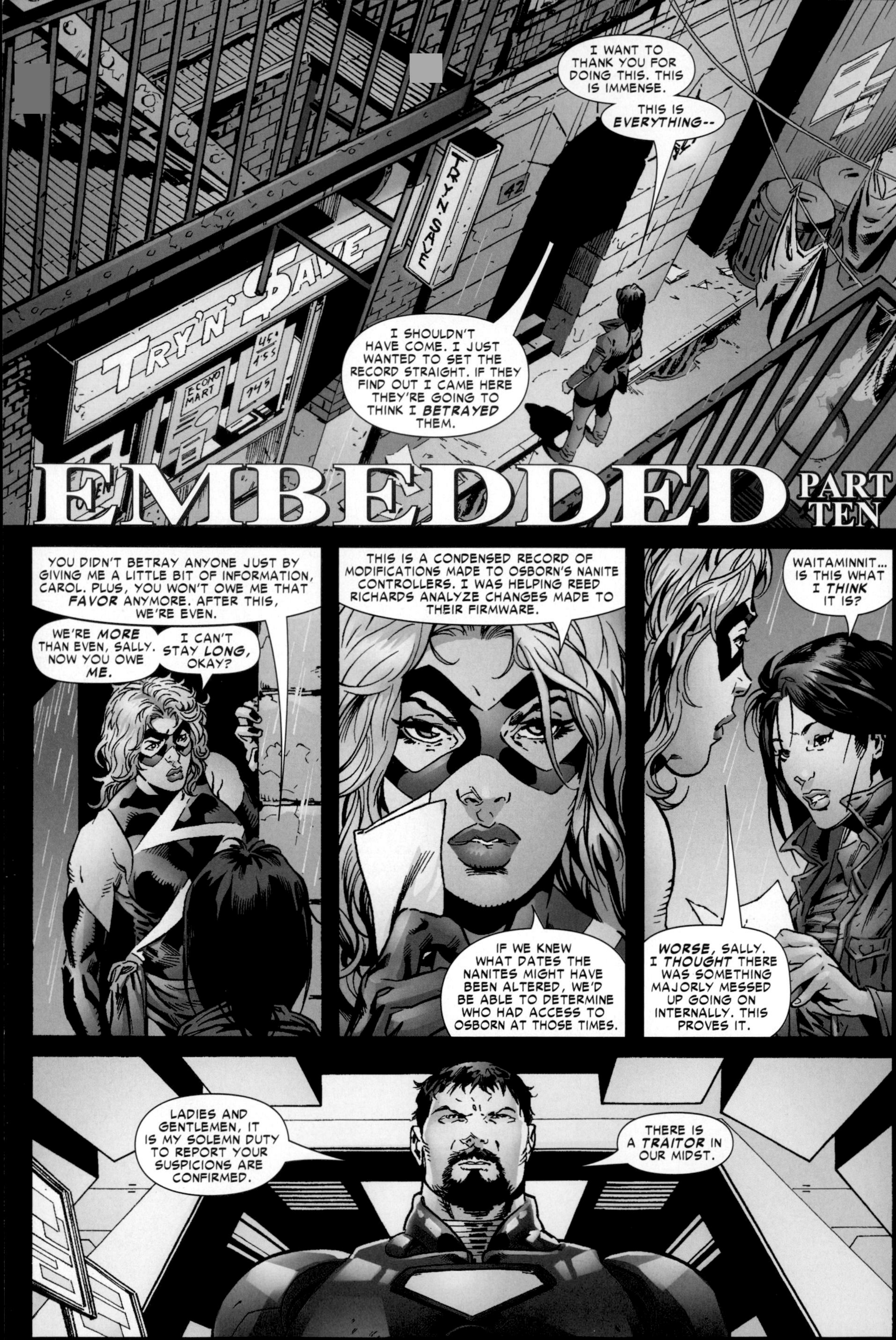
I WANT TO THANK YOU FOR DOING THIS. THIS IS IMMENSE.
THIS IS EVERYTHING--
I SHOULDN'T HAVE COME. I JUST WANTED TO SET THE RECORD STRAIGHT. IF THEY FIND OUT I CAME HERE THEY'RE GOING TO THINK I BETRAYED THEM.
TRY'N' SAVE
TRY'N' $AVE
ECONO MART
EMBEDDED PART TEN
YOU DIDN'T BETRAY ANYONE JUST BY GIVING ME A LITTLE BIT OF INFORMATION, CAROL. PLUS, YOU WON'T OWE ME THAT FAVOR ANYMORE. AFTER THIS, WE'RE EVEN.
WE'RE MORE THAN EVEN, SALLY. NOW YOU OWE ME.
I CAN'T STAY LONG, OKAY?
THIS IS A CONDENSED RECORD OF MODIFICATIONS MADE TO OSBORN'S NANITE CONTROLLERS. I WAS HELPING REED RICHARDS ANALYZE CHANGES MADE TO THEIR FIRMWARE.
IF WE KNEW WHAT DATES THE NANITES MIGHT HAVE BEEN ALTERED, WE'D BE ABLE TO DETERMINE WHO HAD ACCESS TO OSBORN AT THOSE TIMES.
WAITAMINNIT... IS THIS WHAT I THINK IT IS?
WORSE, SALLY. I THOUGHT THERE WAS SOMETHING MAJORLY MESSED UP GOING ON INTERNALLY. THIS PROVES IT.
LADIES AND GENTLEMEN, IT IS MY SOLEMN DUTY TO REPORT YOUR SUSPICIONS ARE CONFIRMED.
THERE IS A TRAITOR IN OUR MIDST.

PAUL JENKINS WRITER | RAMON BACHS PENCILER | JOHN LUCAS INKER | LAURA MARTIN COLORIST | VC'S RANDY GENTILE LETTERER | MOLLY LAZER & AUBREY SITTERSON ASSISTANT EDITORS | TOM BREVOORT EDITOR | JOE QUESADA EDITOR IN CHIEF | DAN BUCKLEY PUBLISHER

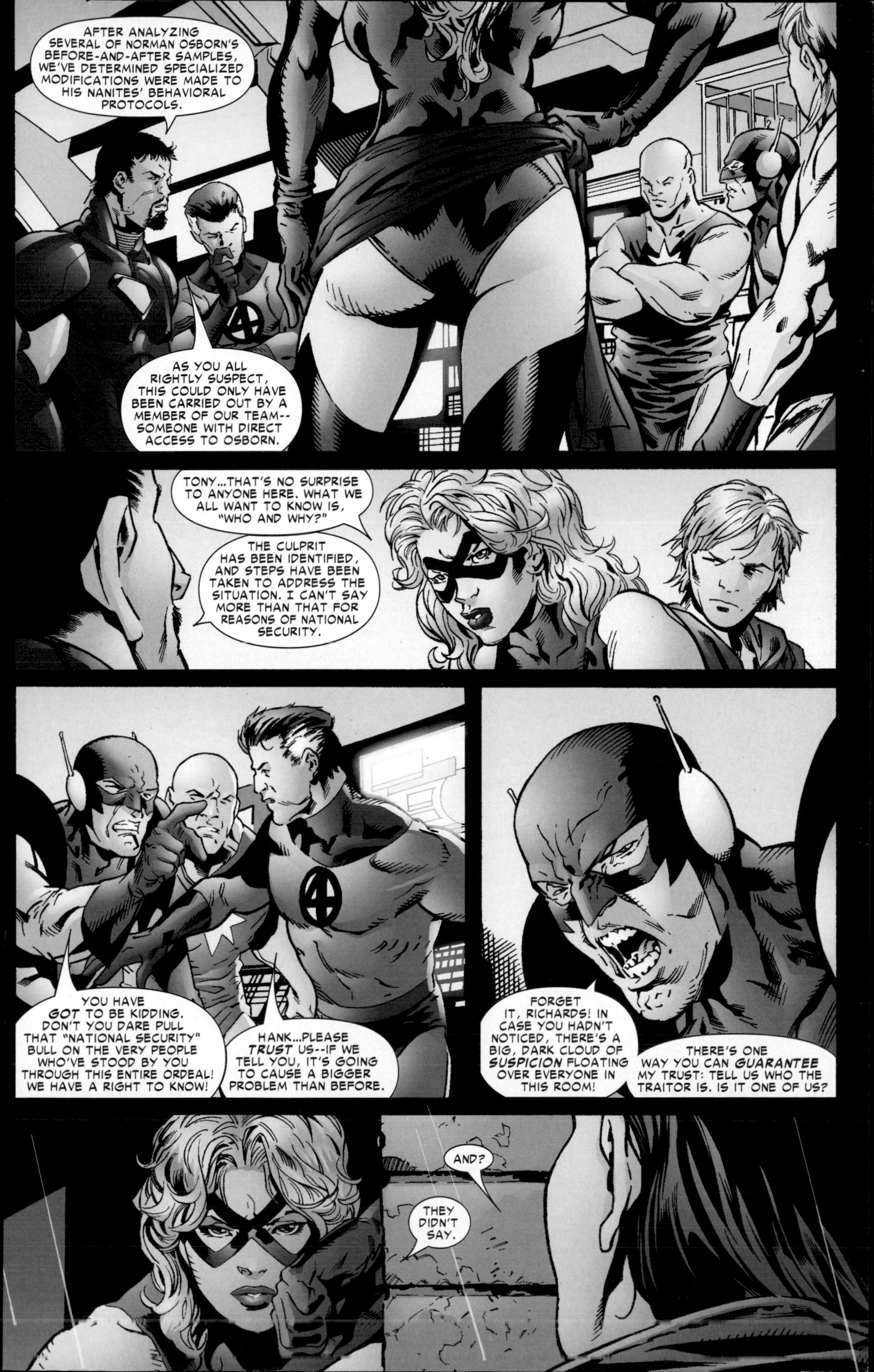
AFTER ANALYZING SEVERAL OF NORMAN OSBORN'S BEFORE-AND-AFTER SAMPLES, WE'VE DETERMINED SPECIALIZED MODIFICATIONS WERE MADE TO HIS NANITES' BEHAVIORAL PROTOCOLS.
AS YOU ALL RIGHTLY SUSPECT, THIS COULD ONLY HAVE BEEN CARRIED OUT BY A MEMBER OF OUR TEAM-- SOMEONE WITH DIRECT ACCESS TO OSBORN.
TONY...THAT'S NO SURPRISE TO ANYONE HERE. WHAT WE ALL WANT TO KNOW IS, "WHO AND WHY?"
THE CULPRIT HAS BEEN IDENTIFIED, AND STEPS HAVE BEEN TAKEN TO ADDRESS THE SITUATION. I CAN'T SAY MORE THAN THAT FOR REASONS OF NATIONAL SECURITY.
YOU HAVE GOT TO BE KIDDING. DON'T YOU DARE PULL THAT "NATIONAL SECURITY" BULL ON THE VERY PEOPLE WHO'VE STOOD BY YOU THROUGH THIS ENTIRE ORDEAL! WE HAVE A RIGHT TO KNOW!
HANK...PLEASE TRUST US--IF WE TELL YOU, IT'S GOING TO CAUSE A BIGGER PROBLEM THAN BEFORE.
FORGET IT, RICHARDS! IN CASE YOU HADN'T NOTICED, THERE'S A BIG, DARK CLOUD OF SUSPICION FLOATING OVER EVERYONE IN THIS ROOM!
THERE'S ONE WAY YOU CAN GUARANTEE MY TRUST: TELL US WHO THE TRAITOR IS. IS IT ONE OF US?
AND?
THEY DIDN'T SAY.

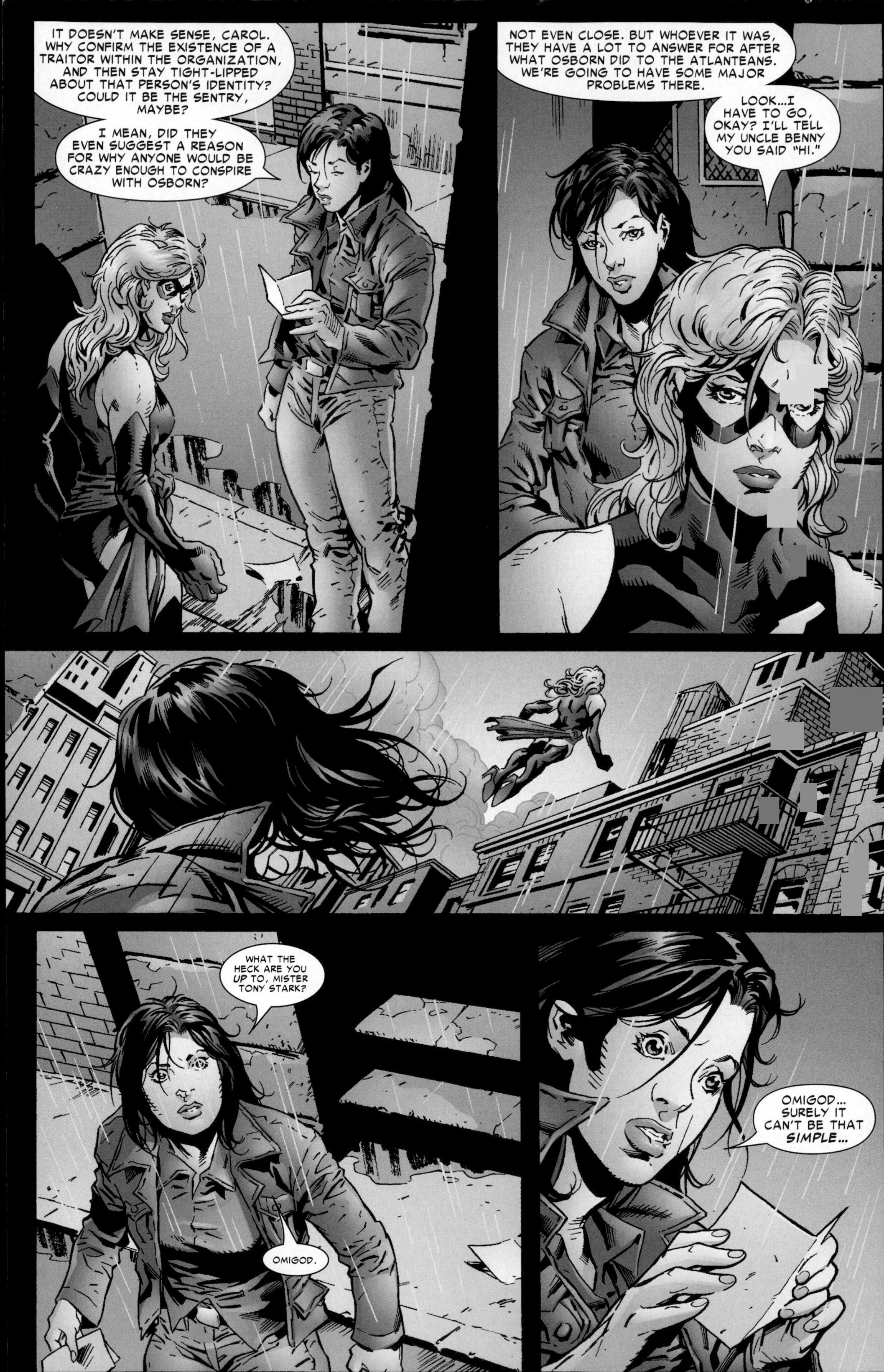
IT DOESN'T MAKE SENSE, CAROL. WHY CONFIRM THE EXISTENCE OF A TRAITOR WITHIN THE ORGANIZATION, AND THEN STAY TIGHT-LIPPED ABOUT THAT PERSON'S IDENTITY? COULD IT BE THE SENTRY, MAYBE?
I MEAN, DID THEY EVEN SUGGEST A REASON FOR WHY ANYONE WOULD BE CRAZY ENOUGH TO CONSPIRE WITH OSBORN?
NOT EVEN CLOSE. BUT WHOEVER IT WAS, THEY HAVE A LOT TO ANSWER FOR AFTER WHAT OSBORN DID TO THE ATLANTEANS. WE'RE GOING TO HAVE SOME MAJOR PROBLEMS THERE.
LOOK...I HAVE TO GO, OKAY? I'LL TELL MY UNCLE BENNY YOU SAID "HI."
WHAT THE HECK ARE YOU UP TO, MISTER TONY STARK?
OMIGOD.
OMIGOD... SURELY IT CAN'T BE THAT SIMPLE...

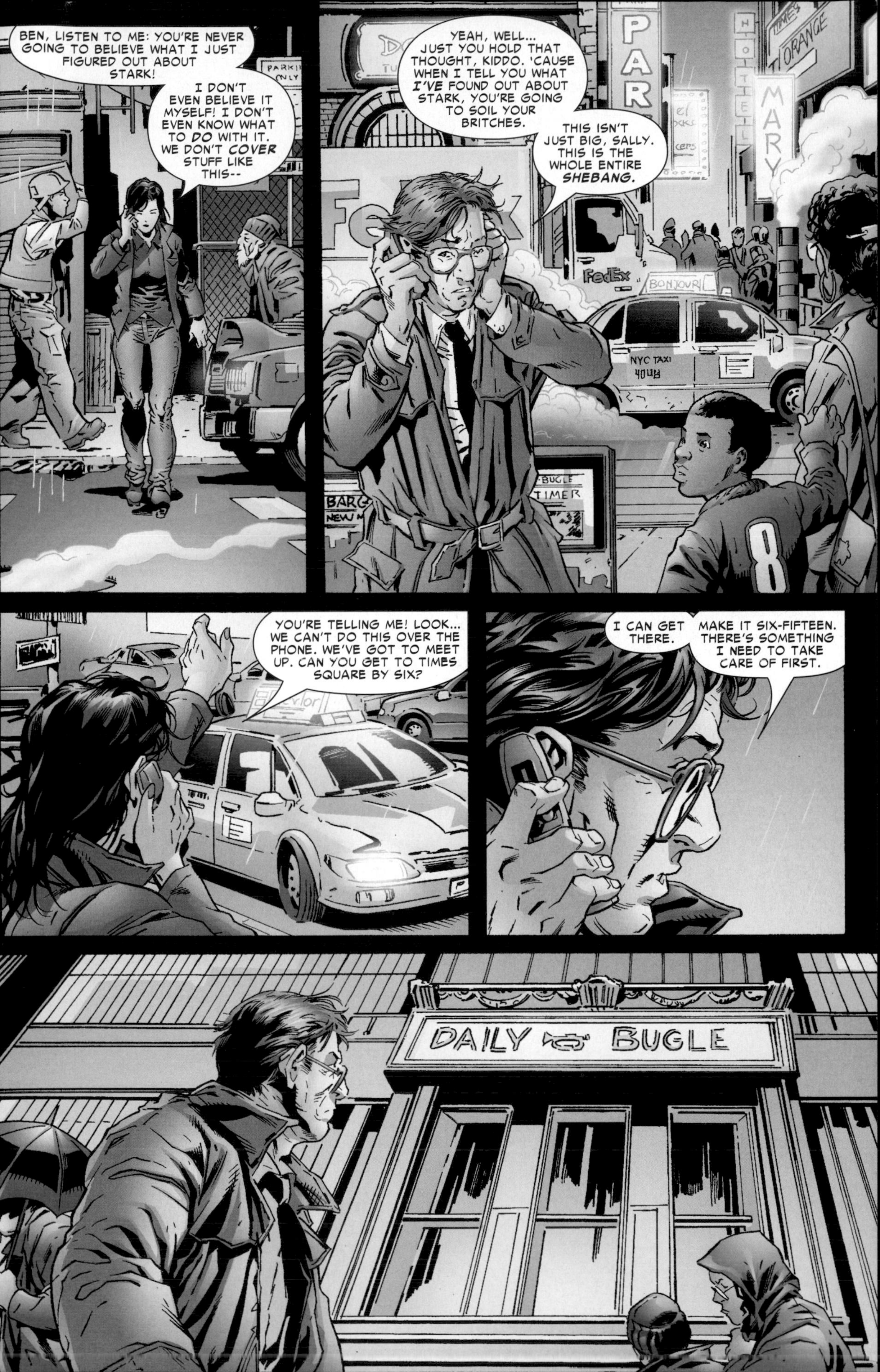

BEN, LISTEN TO ME: YOU'RE NEVER GOING TO BELIEVE WHAT I JUST FIGURED OUT ABOUT STARK!
I DON'T EVEN BELIEVE IT MYSELF! I DON'T EVEN KNOW WHAT TO DO WITH IT. WE DON'T COVER STUFF LIKE THIS--
YEAH, WELL... JUST YOU HOLD THAT THOUGHT, KIDDO. 'CAUSE WHEN I TELL YOU WHAT I'VE FOUND OUT ABOUT STARK, YOU'RE GOING TO SOIL YOUR BRITCHES.
THIS ISN'T JUST BIG, SALLY. THIS IS THE WHOLE ENTIRE SHEBANG.
YOU'RE TELLING ME! LOOK... WE CAN'T DO THIS OVER THE PHONE. WE'VE GOT TO MEET UP. CAN YOU GET TO TIMES SQUARE BY SIX?
I CAN GET THERE.
MAKE IT SIX-FIFTEEN. THERE'S SOMETHING I NEED TO TAKE CARE OF FIRST.
DAILY BUGLE

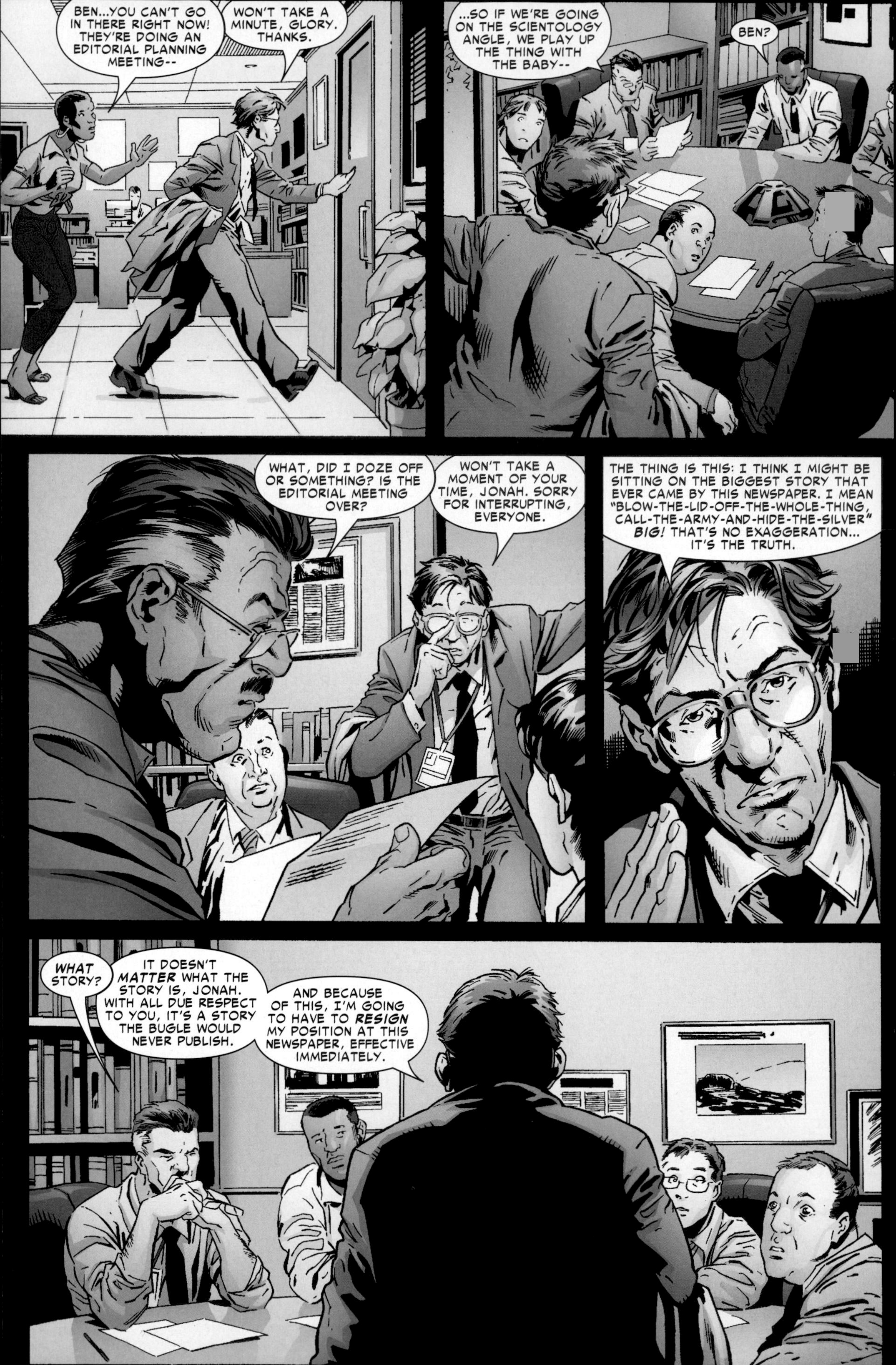

BEN...YOU CAN'T GO IN THERE RIGHT NOW! THEY'RE DOING AN EDITORIAL PLANNING MEETING--
WON'T TAKE A MINUTE, GLORY. THANKS.
...SO IF WE'RE GOING ON THE SCIENTOLOGY ANGLE, WE PLAY UP THE THING WITH THE BABY--
BEN?
WHAT, DID I DOZE OFF OR SOMETHING? IS THE EDITORIAL MEETING OVER?
WON'T TAKE A MOMENT OF YOUR TIME, JONAH. SORRY FOR INTERRUPTING, EVERYONE.
THE THING IS THIS: I THINK I MIGHT BE SITTING ON THE BIGGEST STORY THAT EVER CAME BY THIS NEWSPAPER. I MEAN "BLOW-THE-LID-OFF-THE-WHOLE-THING, CALL-THE-ARMY-AND-HIDE-THE-SILVER" BIG! THAT'S NO EXAGGERATION... IT'S THE TRUTH.
WHAT STORY?
IT DOESN'T MATTER WHAT THE STORY IS, JONAH. WITH ALL DUE RESPECT TO YOU, IT'S A STORY THE BUGLE WOULD NEVER PUBLISH.
AND BECAUSE OF THIS, I'M GOING TO HAVE TO RESIGN MY POSITION AT THIS NEWSPAPER, EFFECTIVE IMMEDIATELY.

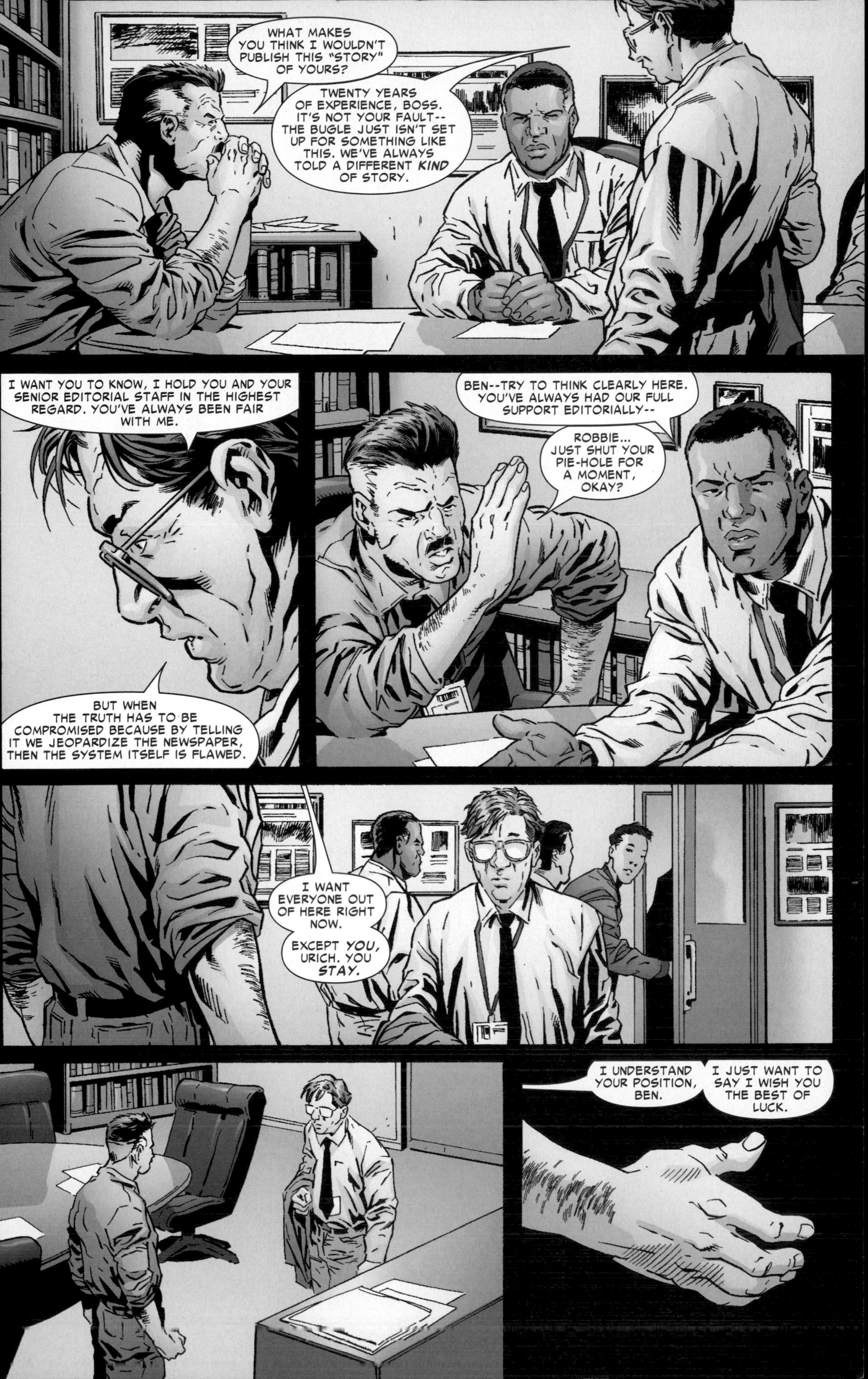
WHAT MAKES YOU THINK I WOULDN'T PUBLISH THIS "STORY" OF YOURS?
TWENTY YEARS OF EXPERIENCE, BOSS. IT'S NOT YOUR FAULT-- THE BUGLE JUST ISN'T SET UP FOR SOMETHING LIKE THIS. WE'VE ALWAYS TOLD A DIFFERENT KIND OF STORY.
I WANT YOU TO KNOW, I HOLD YOU AND YOUR SENIOR EDITORIAL STAFF IN THE HIGHEST REGARD. YOU'VE ALWAYS BEEN FAIR WITH ME.
BUT WHEN THE TRUTH HAS TO BE COMPROMISED BECAUSE BY TELLING IT WE JEOPARDIZE THE NEWSPAPER, THEN THE SYSTEM ITSELF IS FLAWED.
BEN--TRY TO THINK CLEARLY HERE. YOU'VE ALWAYS HAD OUR FULL SUPPORT EDITORIALLY--
ROBBIE... JUST SHUT YOUR PIE-HOLE FOR A MOMENT, OKAY?
I WANT EVERYONE OUT OF HERE RIGHT NOW.
EXCEPT YOU, URICH. YOU STAY.
I UNDERSTAND YOUR POSITION, BEN.
I JUST WANT TO SAY I WISH YOU THE BEST OF LUCK.

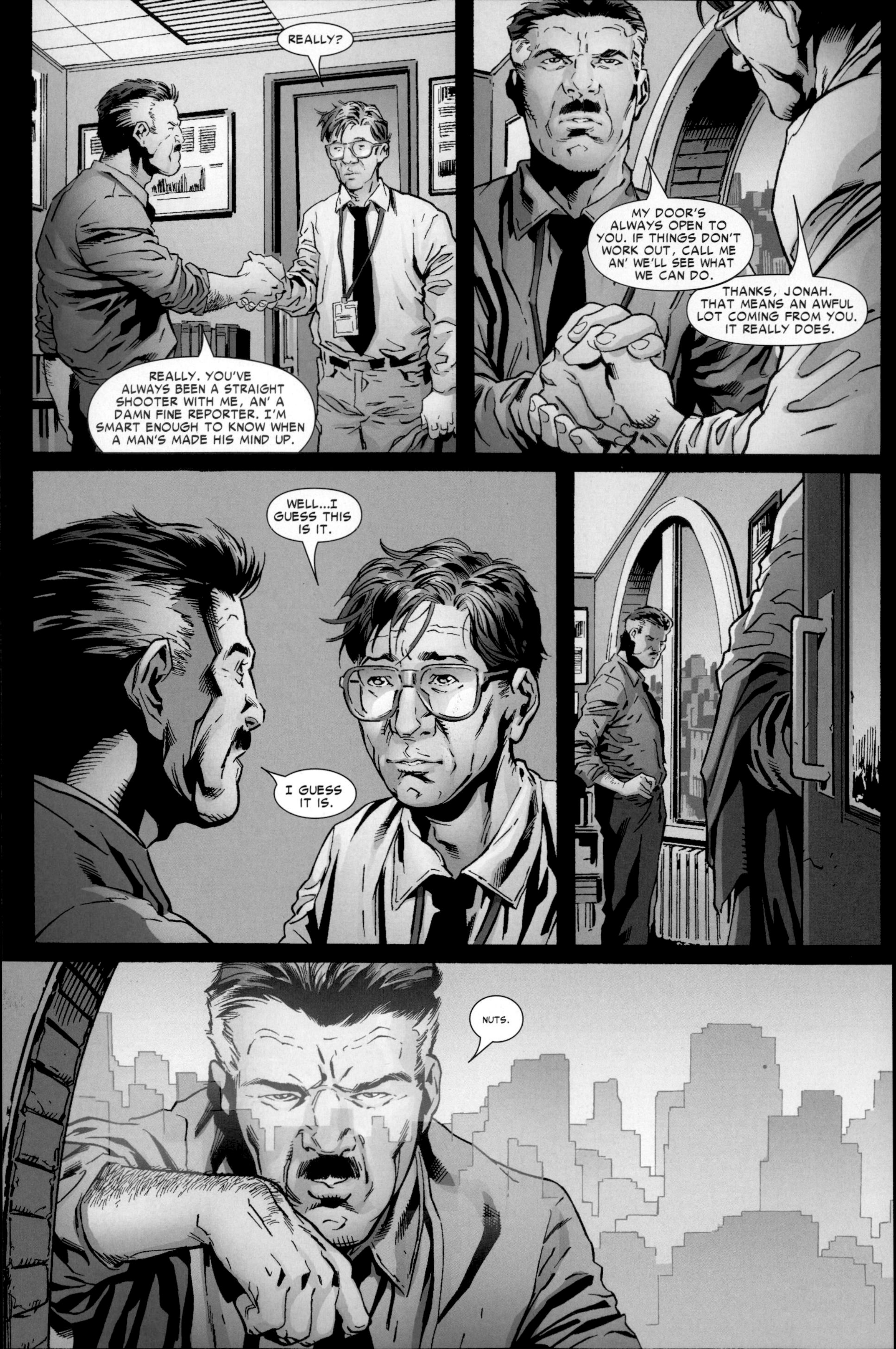
REALLY?
REALLY. YOU'VE ALWAYS BEEN A STRAIGHT SHOOTER WITH ME, AN' A DAMN FINE REPORTER. I'M SMART ENOUGH TO KNOW WHEN A MAN'S MADE HIS MIND UP.
MY DOOR'S ALWAYS OPEN TO YOU. IF THINGS DON'T WORK OUT, CALL ME AN' WE'LL SEE WHAT WE CAN DO.
THANKS, JONAH. THAT MEANS AN AWFUL LOT COMING FROM YOU. IT REALLY DOES.
WELL...I GUESS THIS IS IT.
I GUESS IT IS.
NUTS.

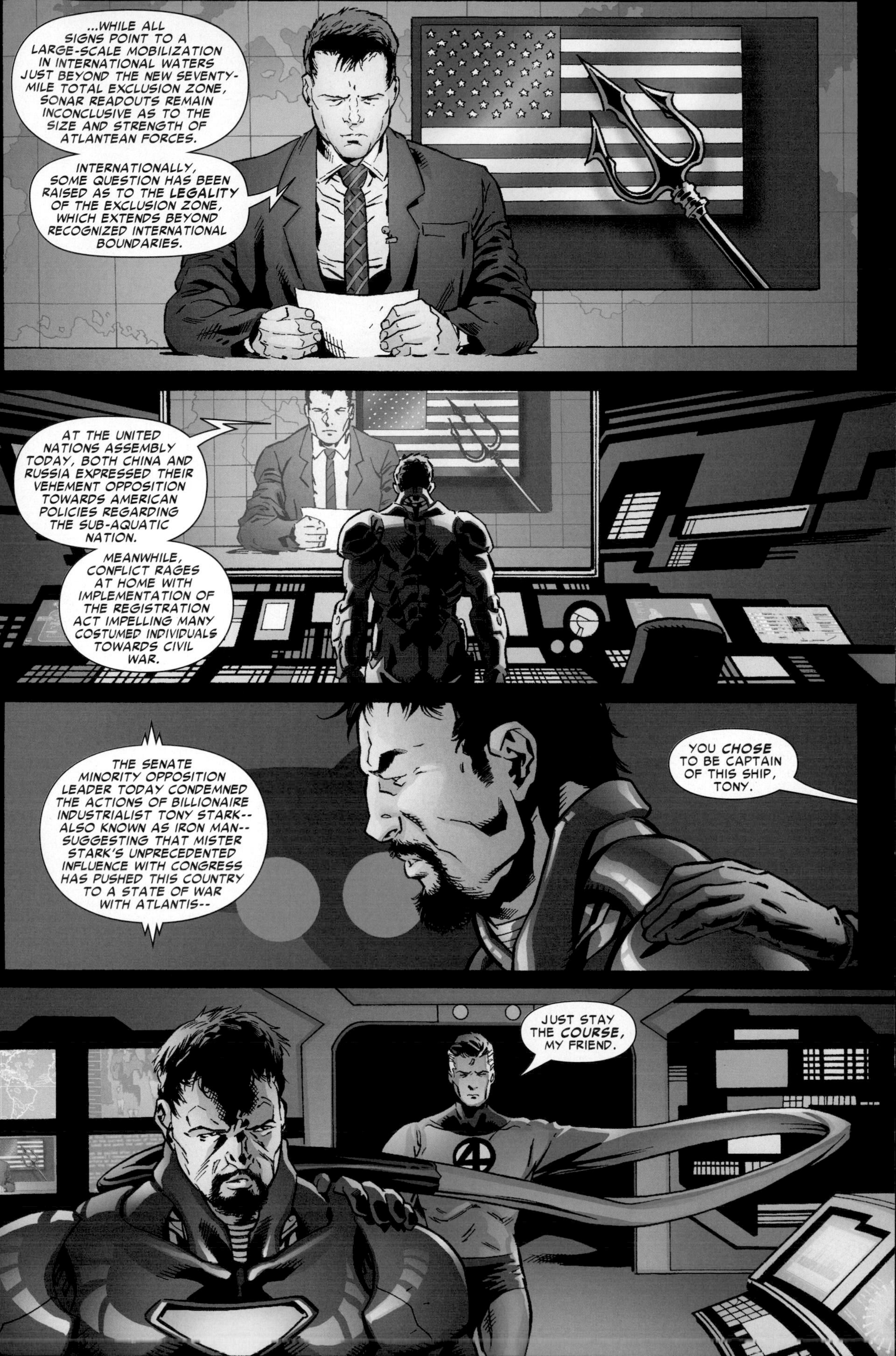
...WHILE ALL SIGNS POINT TO A LARGE-SCALE MOBILIZATION IN INTERNATIONAL WATERS JUST BEYOND THE NEW SEVENTY-MILE TOTAL EXCLUSION ZONE, SONAR READOUTS REMAIN INCONCLUSIVE AS TO THE SIZE AND STRENGTH OF ATLANTEAN FORCES.
INTERNATIONALLY, SOME QUESTION HAS BEEN RAISED AS TO THE LEGALITY OF THE EXCLUSION ZONE, WHICH EXTENDS BEYOND RECOGNIZED INTERNATIONAL BOUNDARIES.
AT THE UNITED NATIONS ASSEMBLY TODAY, BOTH CHINA AND RUSSIA EXPRESSED THEIR VEHEMENT OPPOSITION TOWARDS AMERICAN POLICIES REGARDING THE SUB-AQUATIC NATION.
MEANWHILE, CONFLICT RAGES AT HOME WITH IMPLEMENTATION OF THE REGISTRATION ACT IMPELLING MANY COSTUMED INDIVIDUALS TOWARDS CIVIL WAR.
THE SENATE MINORITY OPPOSITION LEADER TODAY CONDEMNED THE ACTIONS OF BILLIONAIRE INDUSTRIALIST TONY STARK--ALSO KNOWN AS IRON MAN--SUGGESTING THAT MISTER STARK'S UNPRECEDENTED INFLUENCE WITH CONGRESS HAS PUSHED THIS COUNTRY TO A STATE OF WAR WITH ATLANTIS--
YOU CHOSE TO BE CAPTAIN OF THIS SHIP, TONY.
JUST STAY THE COURSE, MY FRIEND.

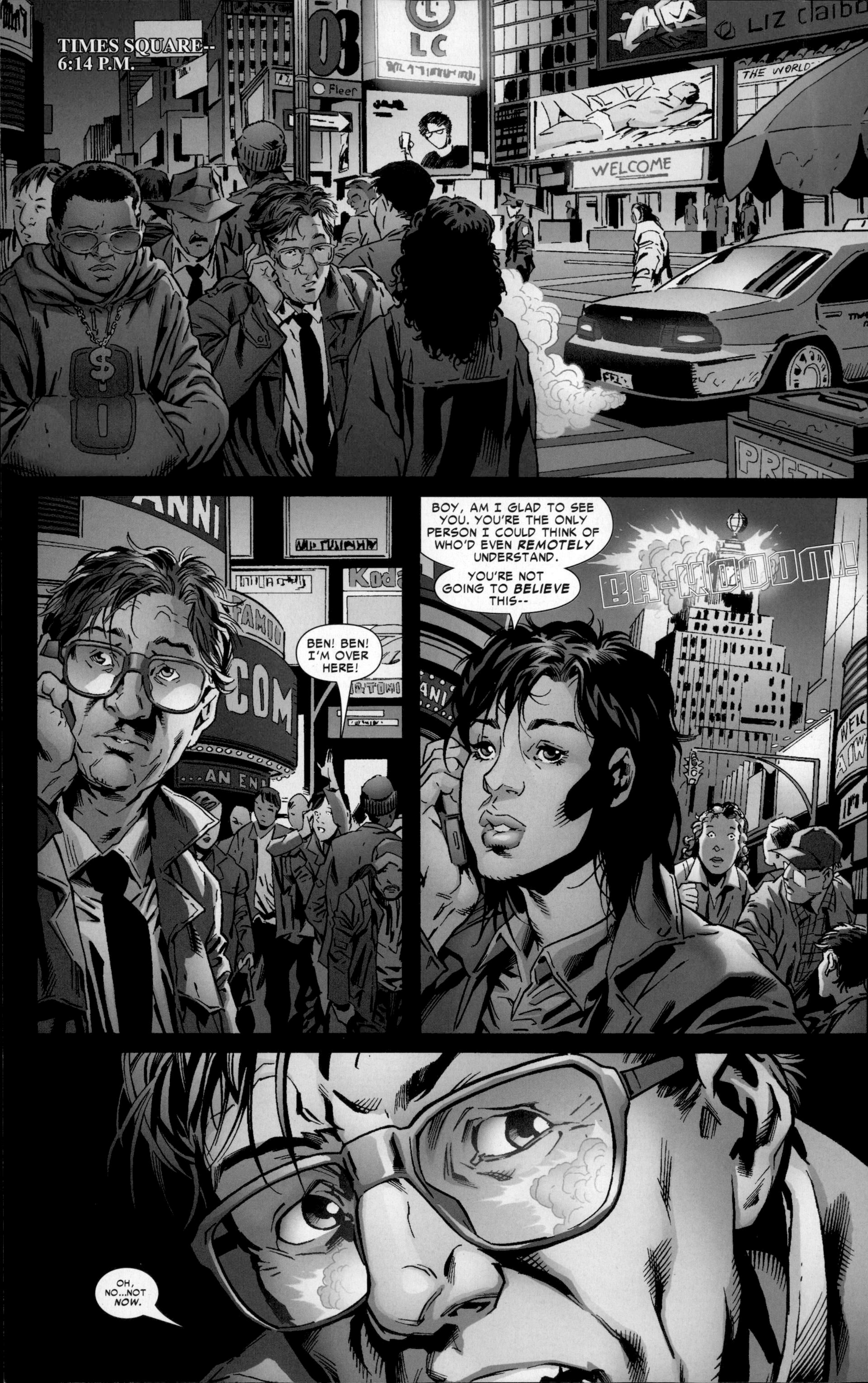
TIMES SQUARE--
6:14 P.M.
BEN! BEN! I'M OVER HERE!
BOY, AM I GLAD TO SEE YOU. YOU'RE THE ONLY PERSON I COULD THINK OF WHO'D EVEN *REMOTELY* UNDERSTAND.
YOU'RE NOT GOING TO *BELIEVE* THIS--
BA-KOOOM!
OH, NO...NOT *NOW*.

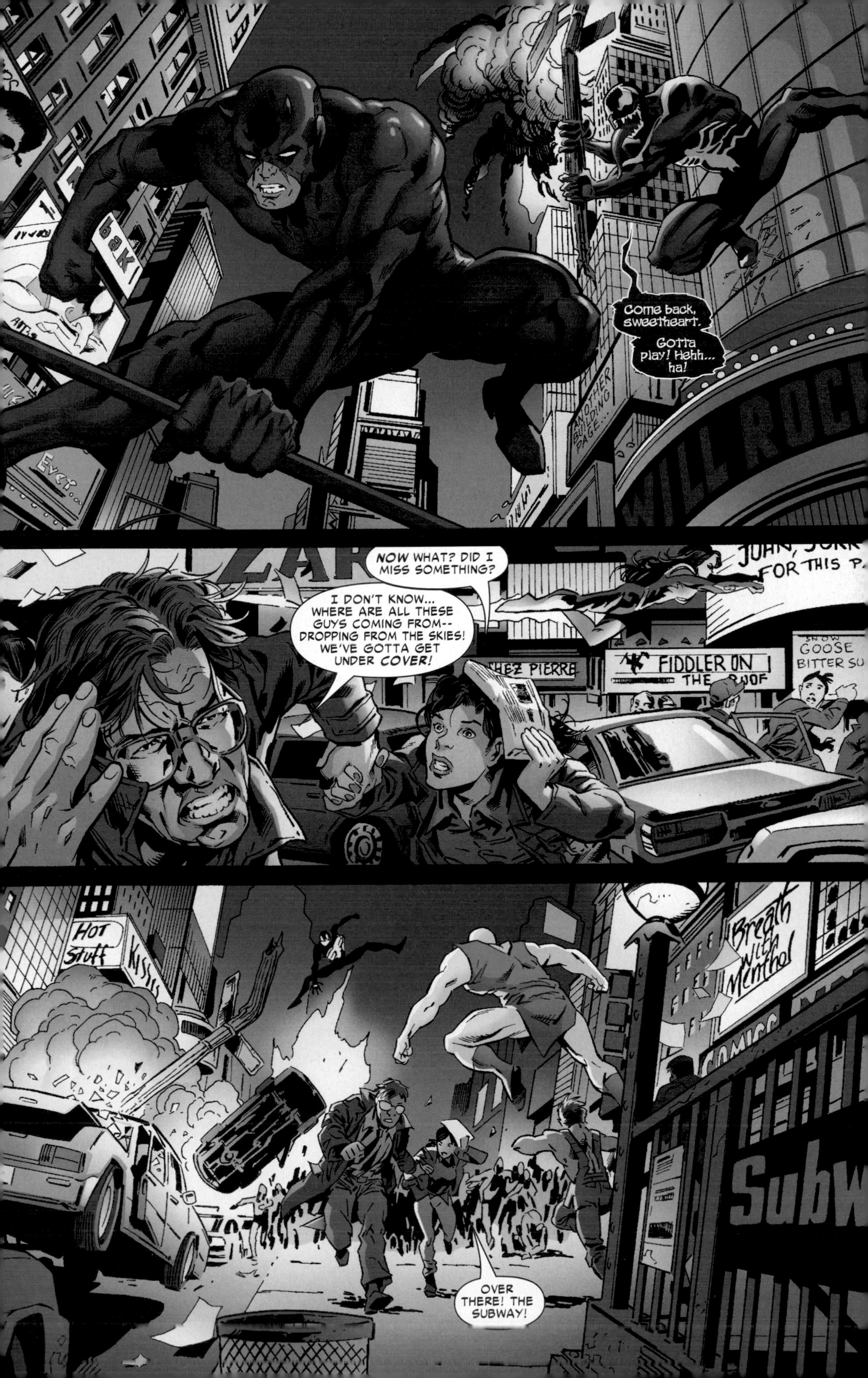
Come back, sweetheart.
Gotta play! Hehh... ha!
ANOTHER BUILDING PAGE...
WILL ROCK
NOW WHAT? DID I MISS SOMETHING?
I DON'T KNOW... WHERE ARE ALL THESE GUYS COMING FROM-- DROPPING FROM THE SKIES! WE'VE GOTTA GET UNDER COVER!
FOR THIS P
FIDDLER ON THE ROOF
GOOSE
HOT Stuff
Breath with Menthol
COMICS
OVER THERE! THE SUBWAY!

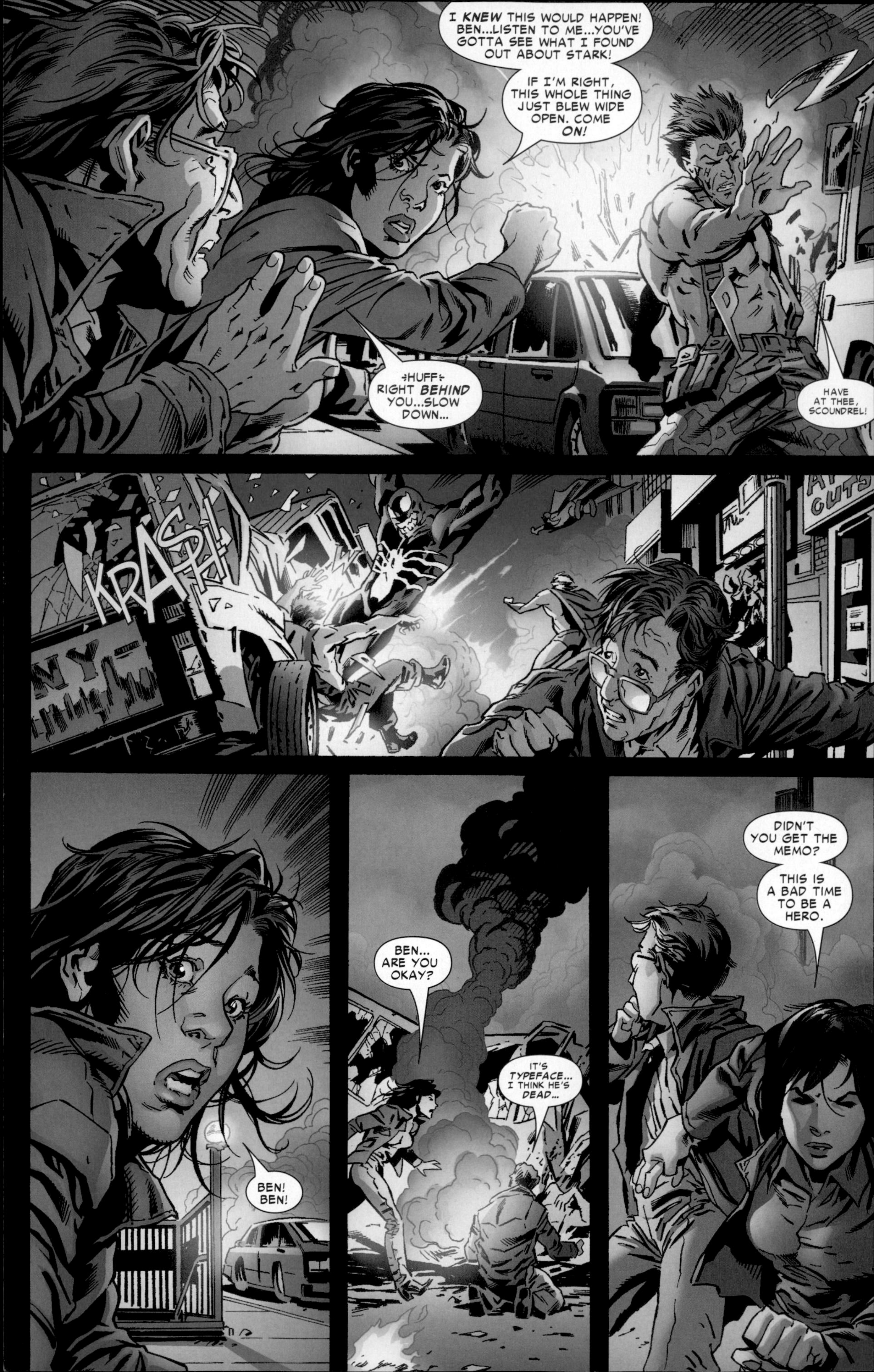
I KNEW THIS WOULD HAPPEN! BEN...LISTEN TO ME...YOU'VE GOTTA SEE WHAT I FOUND OUT ABOUT STARK!
IF I'M RIGHT, THIS WHOLE THING JUST BLEW WIDE OPEN. COME ON!
HUFF RIGHT BEHIND YOU...SLOW DOWN...
HAVE AT THEE, SCOUNDREL!
KRASH!
BEN! BEN!
BEN... ARE YOU OKAY?
IT'S TYPEFACE... I THINK HE'S DEAD...
DIDN'T YOU GET THE MEMO?
THIS IS A BAD TIME TO BE A HERO.

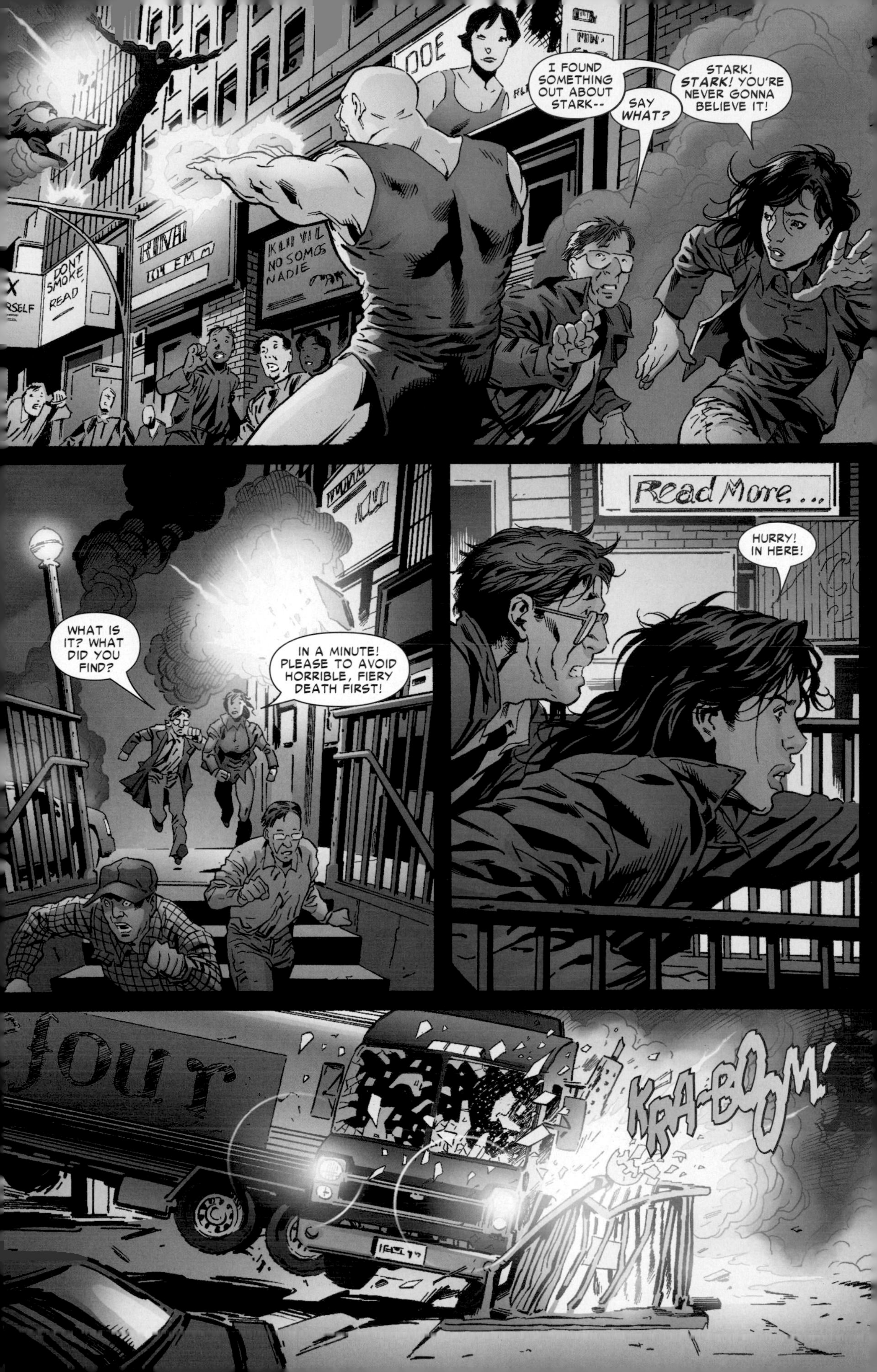
DOE
DONT SMOKE READ
NO SOMOS NADIE
I FOUND SOMETHING OUT ABOUT STARK--
SAY WHAT?
STARK! STARK! YOU'RE NEVER GONNA BELIEVE IT!
WHAT IS IT? WHAT DID YOU FIND?
IN A MINUTE! PLEASE TO AVOID HORRIBLE, FIERY DEATH FIRST!
Read More...
HURRY! IN HERE!
Jour
KRA-BOOM!

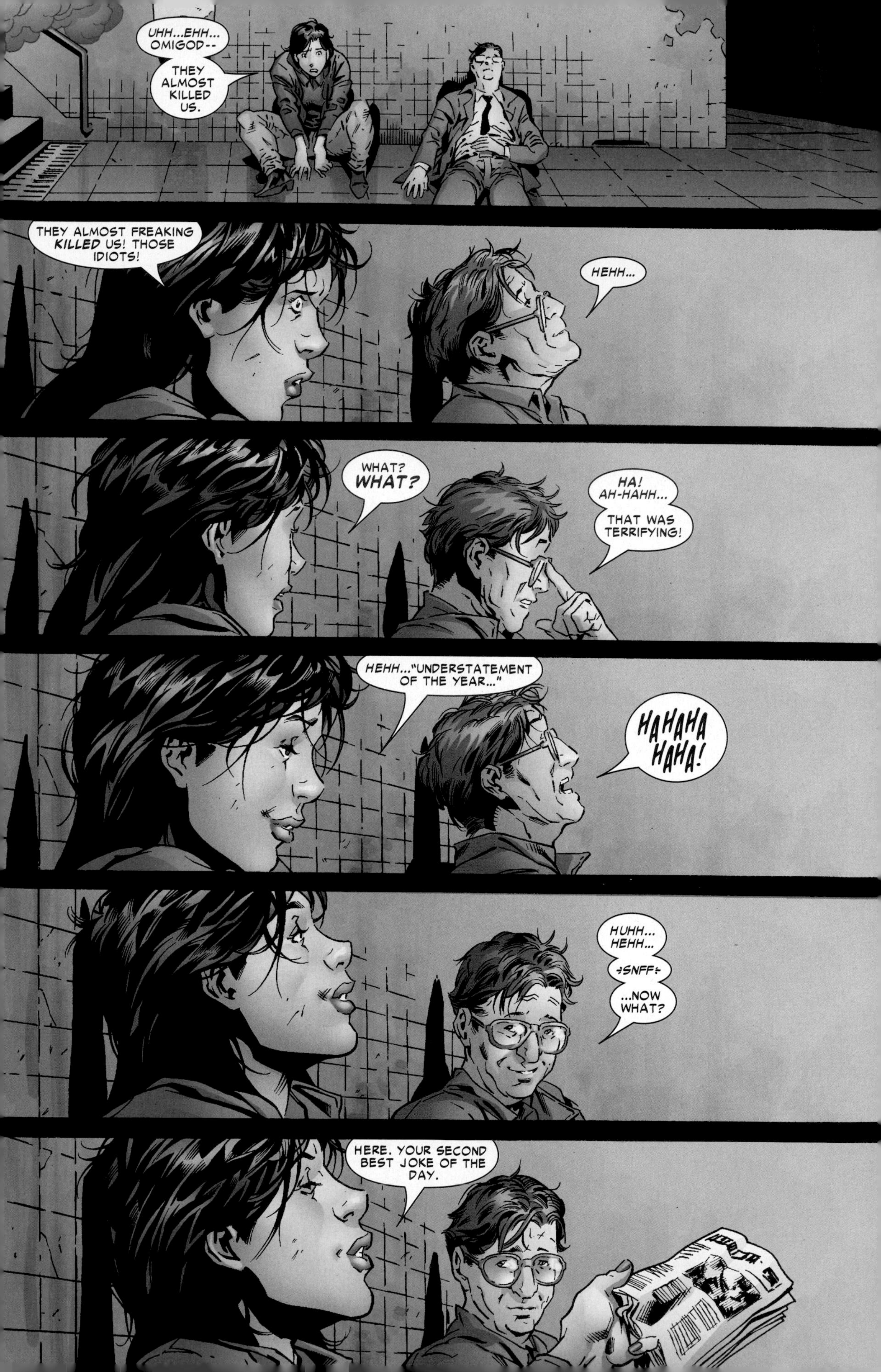
UHH...EHH... OMIGOD--
THEY ALMOST KILLED US.
THEY ALMOST FREAKING *KILLED* US! THOSE IDIOTS!
HEHH...
WHAT? *WHAT?*
HA! AH-HAHH...
THAT WAS TERRIFYING!
HEHH..."UNDERSTATEMENT OF THE YEAR..."
HAHAHA HAHA!
HUHH... HEHH...
SNFF
...NOW WHAT?
HERE. YOUR SECOND BEST JOKE OF THE DAY.

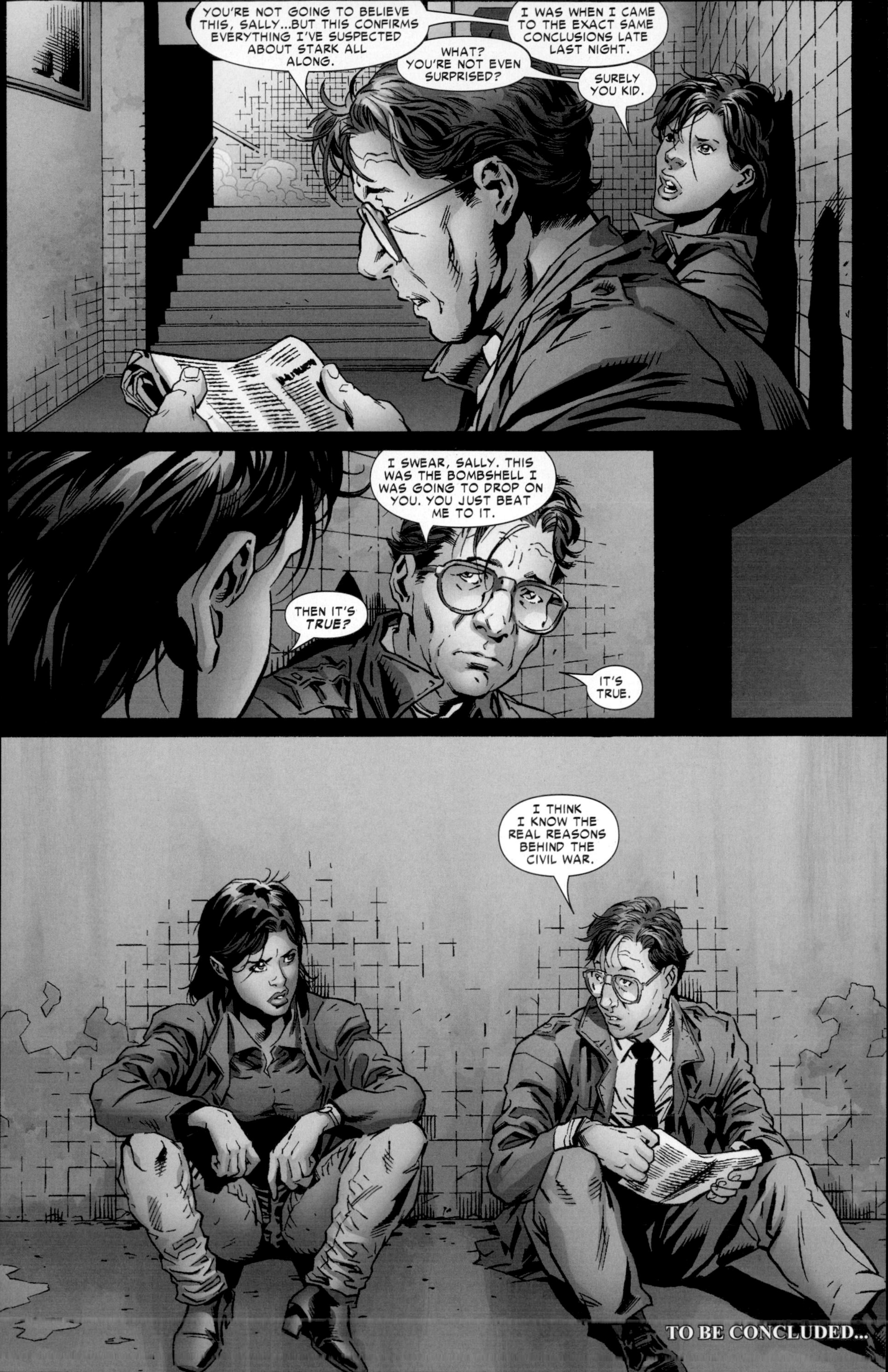
YOU'RE NOT GOING TO BELIEVE THIS, SALLY...BUT THIS CONFIRMS EVERYTHING I'VE SUSPECTED ABOUT STARK ALL ALONG.
I WAS WHEN I CAME TO THE EXACT SAME CONCLUSIONS LATE LAST NIGHT.
WHAT? YOU'RE NOT EVEN SURPRISED?
SURELY YOU KID.
I SWEAR, SALLY. THIS WAS THE BOMBSHELL I WAS GOING TO DROP ON YOU. YOU JUST BEAT ME TO IT.
THEN IT'S *TRUE?*
IT'S TRUE.
I THINK I KNOW THE REAL REASONS BEHIND THE CIVIL WAR.
TO BE CONCLUDED...

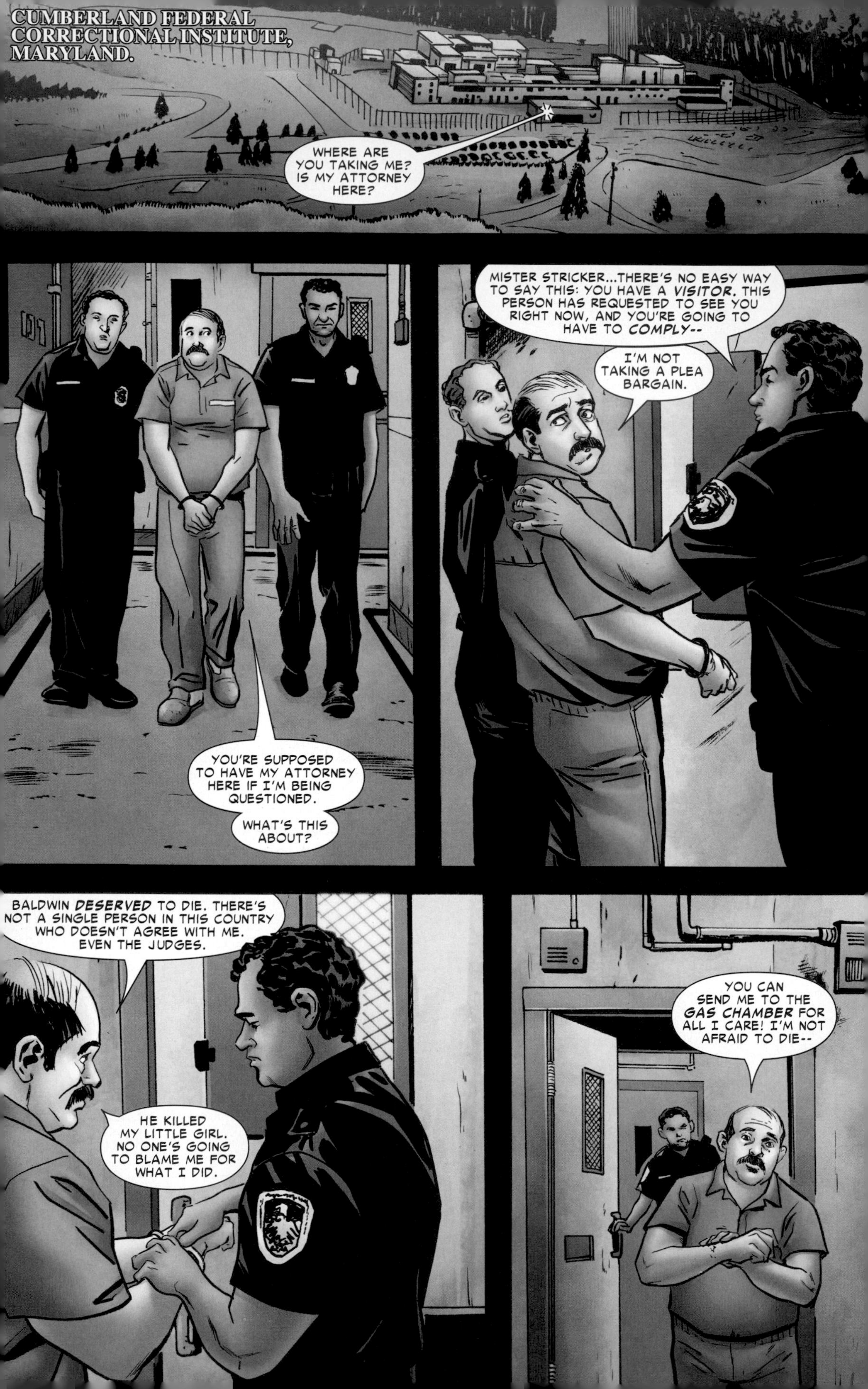
CUMBERLAND FEDERAL CORRECTIONAL INSTITUTE, MARYLAND.
WHERE ARE YOU TAKING ME? IS MY ATTORNEY HERE?
YOU'RE SUPPOSED TO HAVE MY ATTORNEY HERE IF I'M BEING QUESTIONED.
WHAT'S THIS ABOUT?
MISTER STRICKER...THERE'S NO EASY WAY TO SAY THIS: YOU HAVE A VISITOR. THIS PERSON HAS REQUESTED TO SEE YOU RIGHT NOW, AND YOU'RE GOING TO HAVE TO COMPLY--
I'M NOT TAKING A PLEA BARGAIN.
BALDWIN DESERVED TO DIE. THERE'S NOT A SINGLE PERSON IN THIS COUNTRY WHO DOESN'T AGREE WITH ME. EVEN THE JUDGES.
HE KILLED MY LITTLE GIRL. NO ONE'S GOING TO BLAME ME FOR WHAT I DID.
YOU CAN SEND ME TO THE GAS CHAMBER FOR ALL I CARE! I'M NOT AFRAID TO DIE--

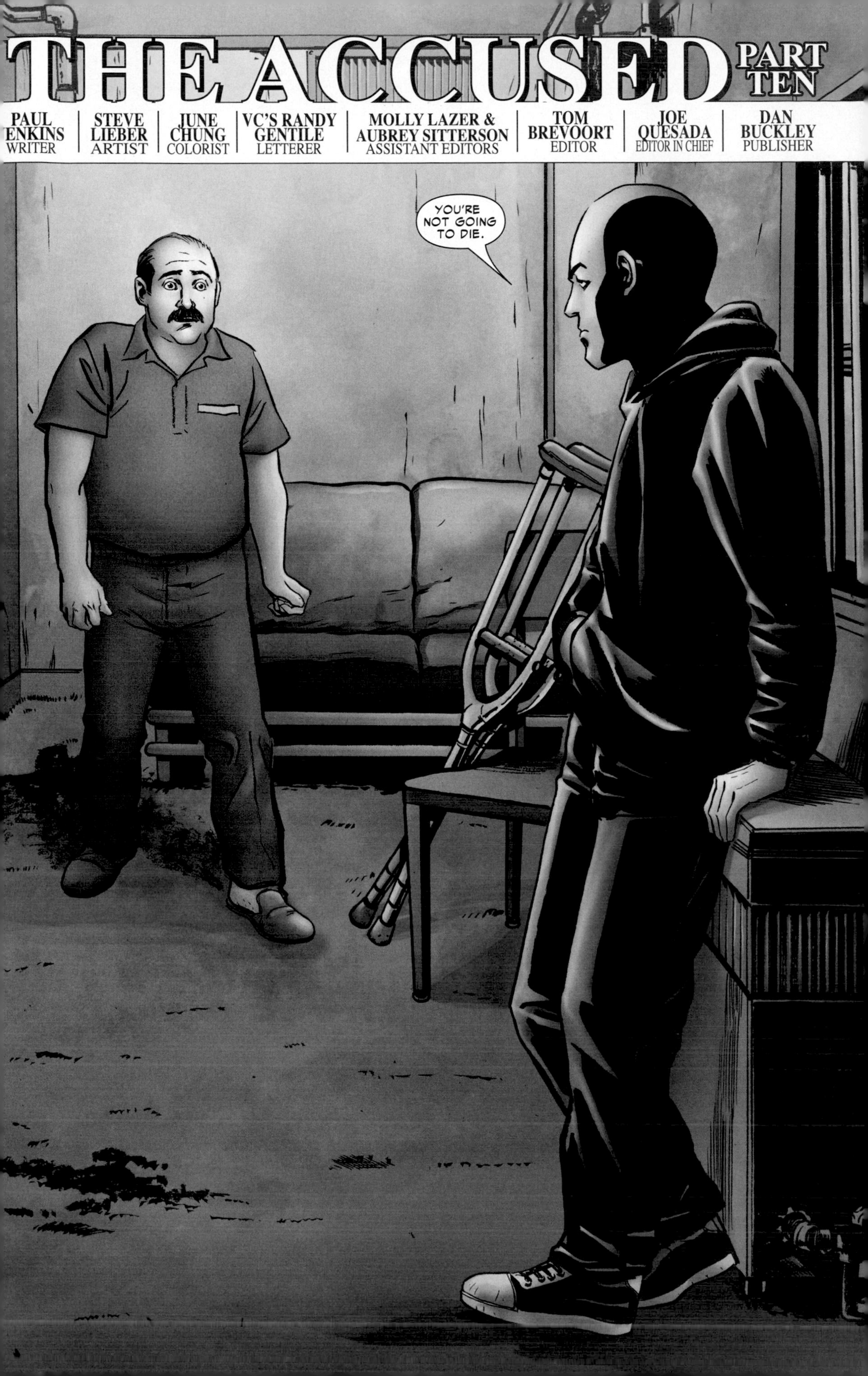
THE ACCUSED PART TEN
PAUL JENKINS WRITER
STEVE LIEBER ARTIST
JUNE CHUNG COLORIST
VC'S RANDY GENTILE LETTERER
MOLLY LAZER & AUBREY SITTERSON ASSISTANT EDITORS
TOM BREVOORT EDITOR
JOE QUESADA EDITOR IN CHIEF
DAN BUCKLEY PUBLISHER
YOU'RE NOT GOING TO DIE.

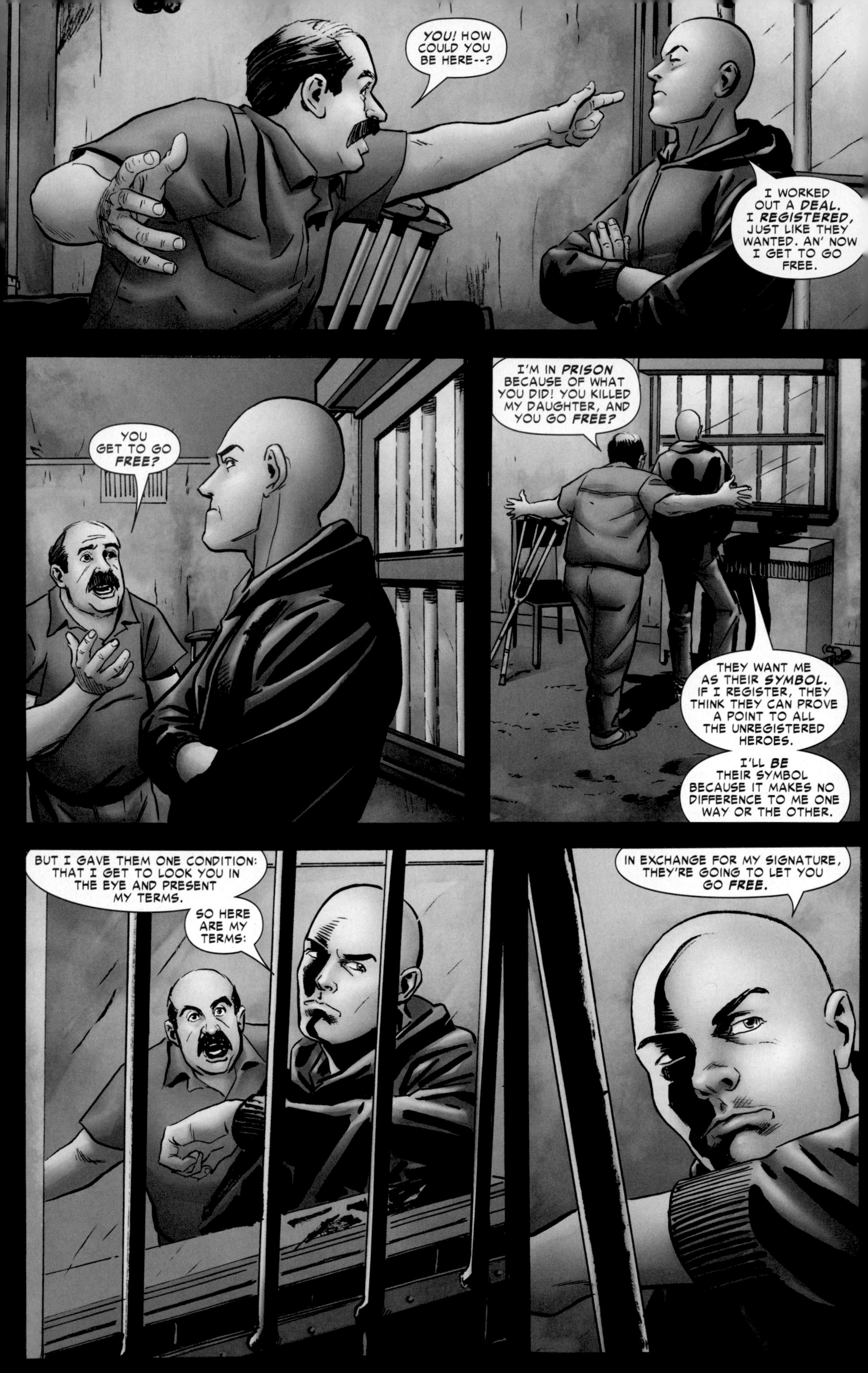
YOU! HOW COULD YOU BE HERE--?
I WORKED OUT A DEAL. I REGISTERED, JUST LIKE THEY WANTED. AN' NOW I GET TO GO FREE.
YOU GET TO GO FREE?
I'M IN PRISON BECAUSE OF WHAT YOU DID! YOU KILLED MY DAUGHTER, AND YOU GO FREE?
THEY WANT ME AS THEIR SYMBOL. IF I REGISTER, THEY THINK THEY CAN PROVE A POINT TO ALL THE UNREGISTERED HEROES.
I'LL BE THEIR SYMBOL BECAUSE IT MAKES NO DIFFERENCE TO ME ONE WAY OR THE OTHER.
BUT I GAVE THEM ONE CONDITION: THAT I GET TO LOOK YOU IN THE EYE AND PRESENT MY TERMS.
SO HERE ARE MY TERMS:
IN EXCHANGE FOR MY SIGNATURE, THEY'RE GOING TO LET YOU GO FREE.

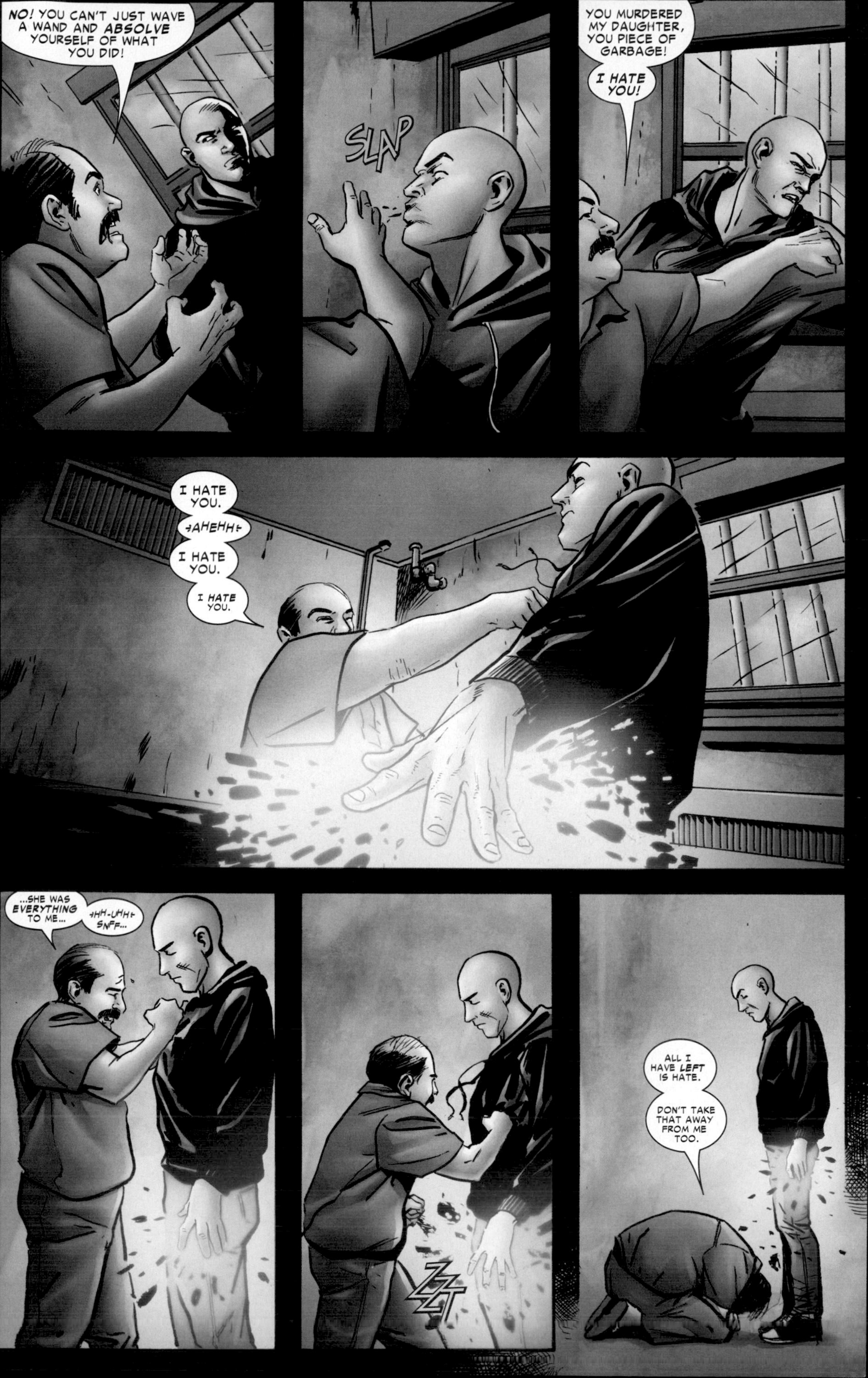
NO! YOU CAN'T JUST WAVE A WAND AND ABSOLVE YOURSELF OF WHAT YOU DID!
SLAP
YOU MURDERED MY DAUGHTER, YOU PIECE OF GARBAGE!
I HATE YOU!
I HATE YOU.
AHEHH
I HATE YOU.
I HATE YOU.
...SHE WAS EVERYTHING TO ME...
HH-UHH SNFF...
ZZT
ALL I HAVE LEFT IS HATE.
DON'T TAKE THAT AWAY FROM ME TOO.

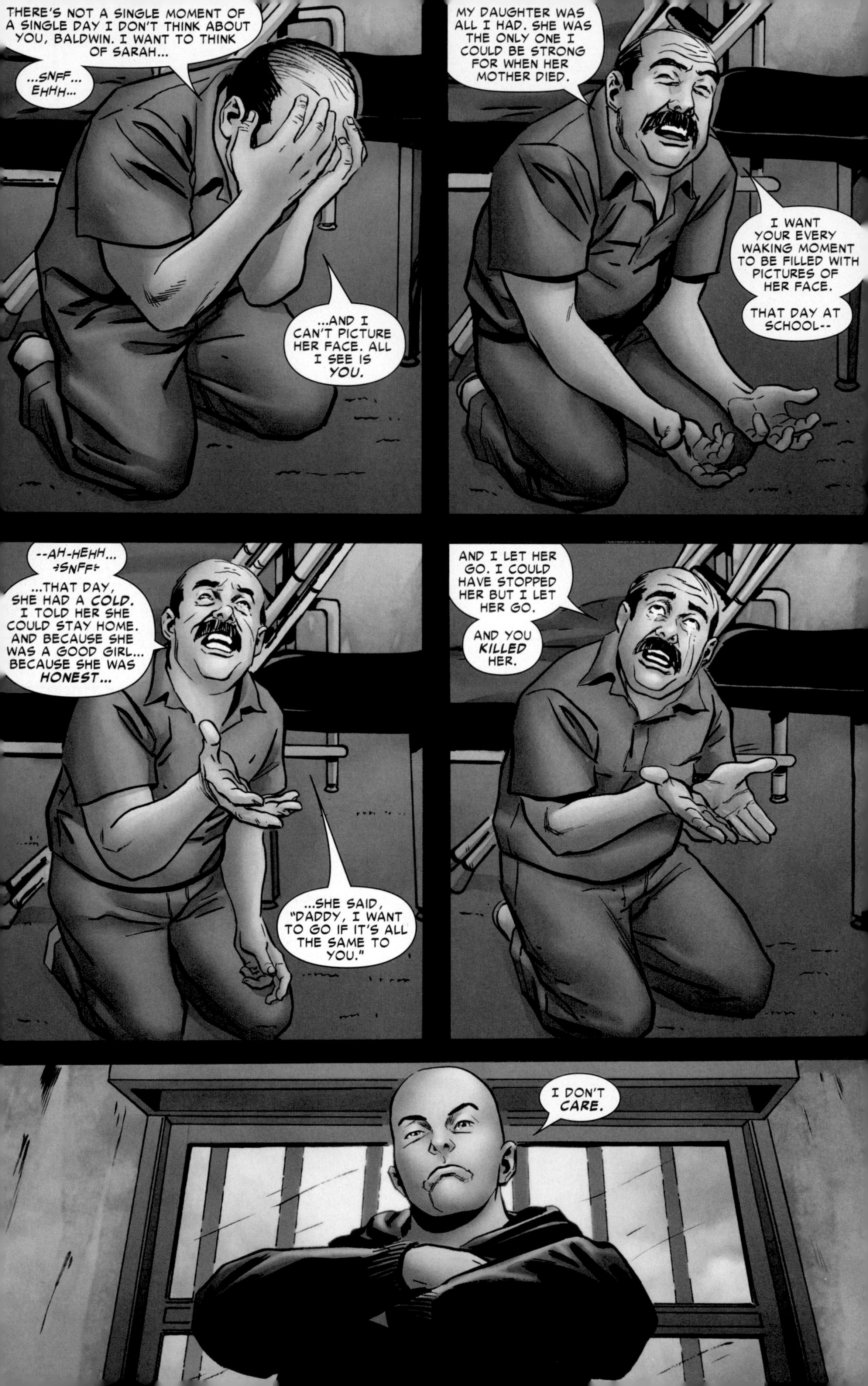
THERE'S NOT A SINGLE MOMENT OF A SINGLE DAY I DON'T THINK ABOUT YOU, BALDWIN. I WANT TO THINK OF SARAH...
...SNFF... EHHH...
...AND I CAN'T PICTURE HER FACE. ALL I SEE IS YOU.
MY DAUGHTER WAS ALL I HAD. SHE WAS THE ONLY ONE I COULD BE STRONG FOR WHEN HER MOTHER DIED.
I WANT YOUR EVERY WAKING MOMENT TO BE FILLED WITH PICTURES OF HER FACE.
THAT DAY AT SCHOOL--
--AH-HEHH... SNFF
...THAT DAY, SHE HAD A COLD. I TOLD HER SHE COULD STAY HOME. AND BECAUSE SHE WAS A GOOD GIRL... BECAUSE SHE WAS HONEST...
...SHE SAID, "DADDY, I WANT TO GO IF IT'S ALL THE SAME TO YOU."
AND I LET HER GO. I COULD HAVE STOPPED HER BUT I LET HER GO.
AND YOU KILLED HER.
I DON'T CARE.

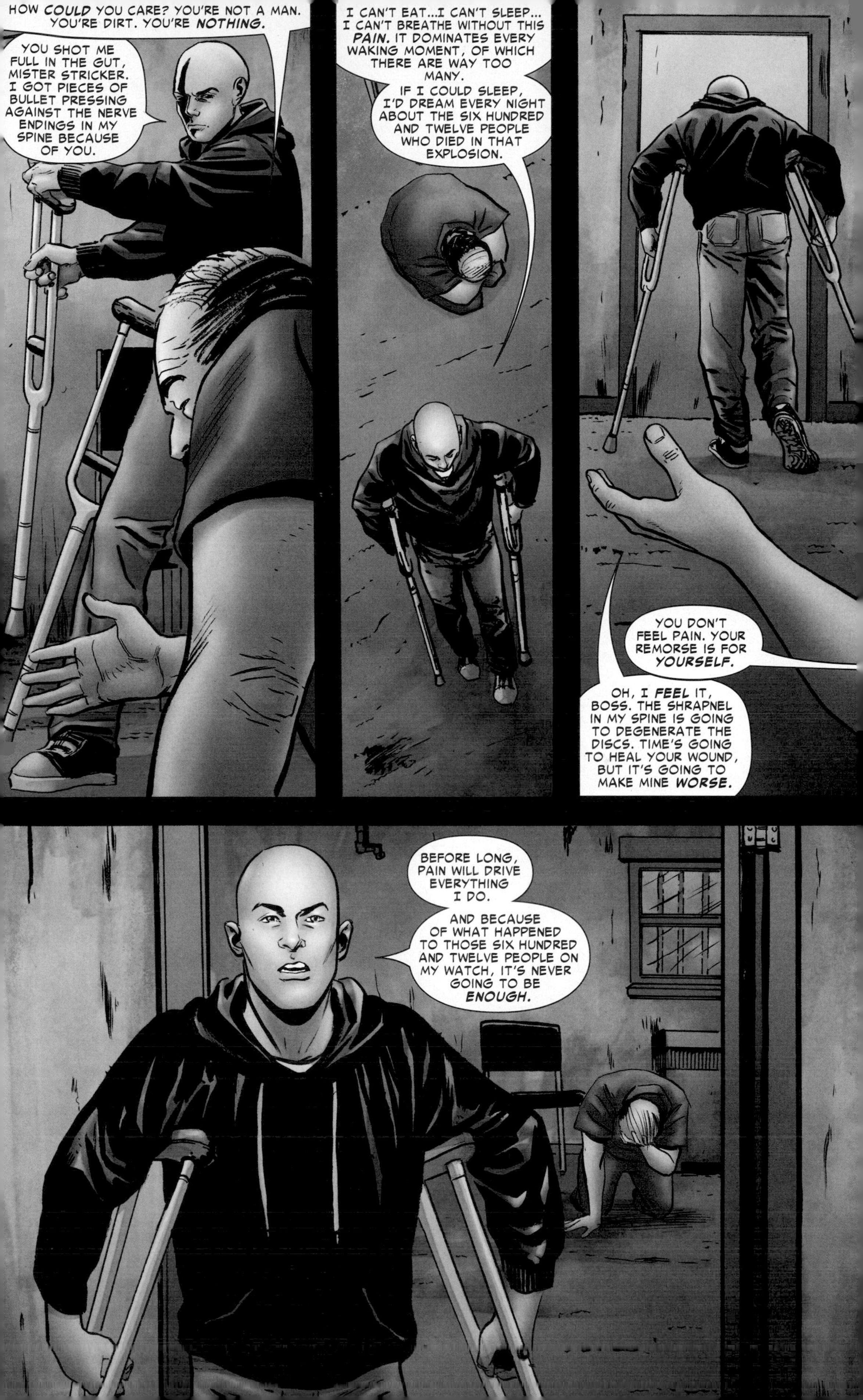
HOW *COULD* YOU CARE? YOU'RE NOT A MAN. YOU'RE DIRT. YOU'RE *NOTHING.*
YOU SHOT ME FULL IN THE GUT, MISTER STRICKER. I GOT PIECES OF BULLET PRESSING AGAINST THE NERVE ENDINGS IN MY SPINE BECAUSE OF YOU.
I CAN'T EAT...I CAN'T SLEEP... I CAN'T BREATHE WITHOUT THIS *PAIN.* IT DOMINATES EVERY WAKING MOMENT, OF WHICH THERE ARE WAY TOO MANY.
IF I COULD SLEEP, I'D DREAM EVERY NIGHT ABOUT THE SIX HUNDRED AND TWELVE PEOPLE WHO DIED IN THAT EXPLOSION.
YOU DON'T FEEL PAIN. YOUR REMORSE IS FOR *YOURSELF.*
OH, I *FEEL* IT, BOSS. THE SHRAPNEL IN MY SPINE IS GOING TO DEGENERATE THE DISCS. TIME'S GOING TO HEAL YOUR WOUND, BUT IT'S GOING TO MAKE MINE *WORSE.*
BEFORE LONG, PAIN WILL DRIVE EVERYTHING I DO.
AND BECAUSE OF WHAT HAPPENED TO THOSE SIX HUNDRED AND TWELVE PEOPLE ON MY WATCH, IT'S NEVER GOING TO BE *ENOUGH.*

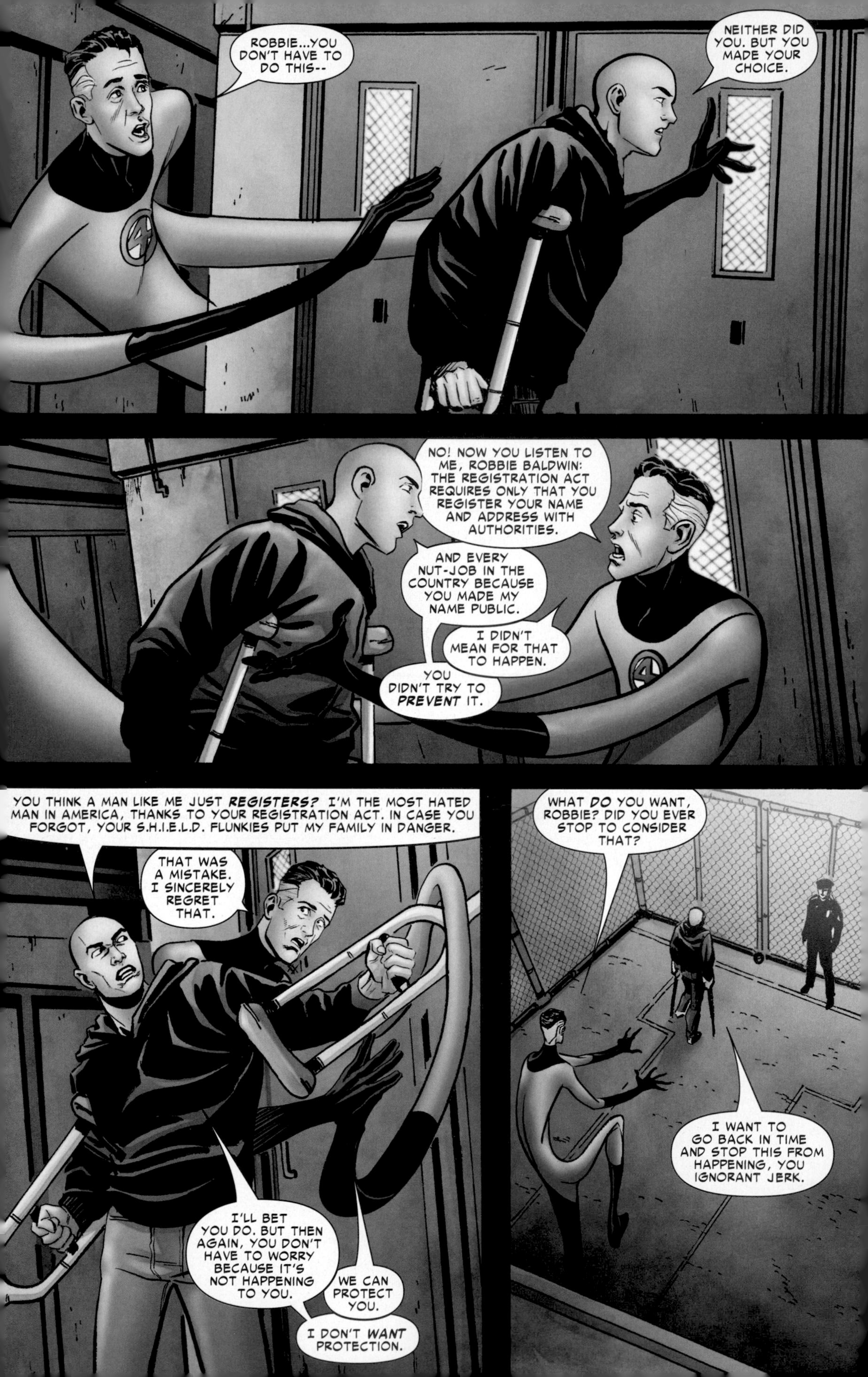

ROBBIE...YOU DON'T HAVE TO DO THIS--
NEITHER DID YOU. BUT YOU MADE YOUR CHOICE.
NO! NOW YOU LISTEN TO ME, ROBBIE BALDWIN: THE REGISTRATION ACT REQUIRES ONLY THAT YOU REGISTER YOUR NAME AND ADDRESS WITH AUTHORITIES.
AND EVERY NUT-JOB IN THE COUNTRY BECAUSE YOU MADE MY NAME PUBLIC.
I DIDN'T MEAN FOR THAT TO HAPPEN.
YOU DIDN'T TRY TO *PREVENT* IT.
YOU THINK A MAN LIKE ME JUST *REGISTERS?* I'M THE MOST HATED MAN IN AMERICA, THANKS TO YOUR REGISTRATION ACT. IN CASE YOU FORGOT, YOUR S.H.I.E.L.D. FLUNKIES PUT MY FAMILY IN DANGER.
THAT WAS A MISTAKE. I SINCERELY REGRET THAT.
I'LL BET YOU DO. BUT THEN AGAIN, YOU DON'T HAVE TO WORRY BECAUSE IT'S NOT HAPPENING TO YOU.
WE CAN PROTECT YOU.
I DON'T *WANT* PROTECTION.
WHAT *DO* YOU WANT, ROBBIE? DID YOU EVER STOP TO CONSIDER THAT?
I WANT TO GO BACK IN TIME AND STOP THIS FROM HAPPENING, YOU IGNORANT JERK.

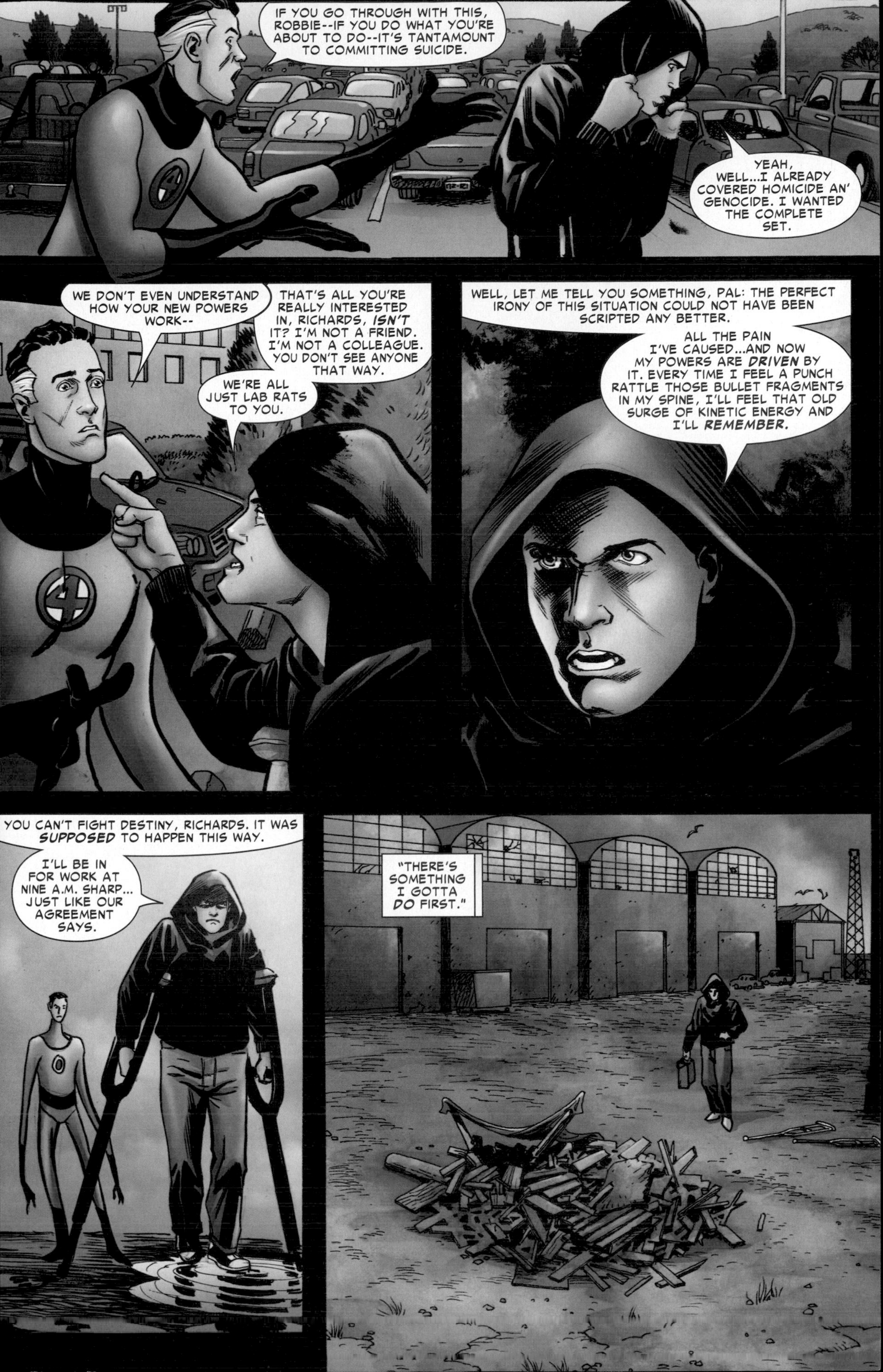
IF YOU GO THROUGH WITH THIS, ROBBIE--IF YOU DO WHAT YOU'RE ABOUT TO DO--IT'S TANTAMOUNT TO COMMITTING SUICIDE.
YEAH, WELL...I ALREADY COVERED HOMICIDE AN' GENOCIDE. I WANTED THE COMPLETE SET.
WE DON'T EVEN UNDERSTAND HOW YOUR NEW POWERS WORK--
THAT'S ALL YOU'RE REALLY INTERESTED IN, RICHARDS, *ISN'T* IT? I'M NOT A FRIEND. I'M NOT A COLLEAGUE. YOU DON'T SEE ANYONE THAT WAY.
WE'RE ALL JUST LAB RATS TO YOU.
WELL, LET ME TELL YOU SOMETHING, PAL: THE PERFECT IRONY OF THIS SITUATION COULD NOT HAVE BEEN SCRIPTED ANY BETTER.
ALL THE PAIN I'VE CAUSED...AND NOW MY POWERS ARE *DRIVEN* BY IT. EVERY TIME I FEEL A PUNCH RATTLE THOSE BULLET FRAGMENTS IN MY SPINE, I'LL FEEL THAT OLD SURGE OF KINETIC ENERGY AND I'LL *REMEMBER.*
YOU CAN'T FIGHT DESTINY, RICHARDS. IT WAS *SUPPOSED* TO HAPPEN THIS WAY.
I'LL BE IN FOR WORK AT NINE A.M. SHARP... JUST LIKE OUR AGREEMENT SAYS.
"THERE'S SOMETHING I GOTTA *DO* FIRST."

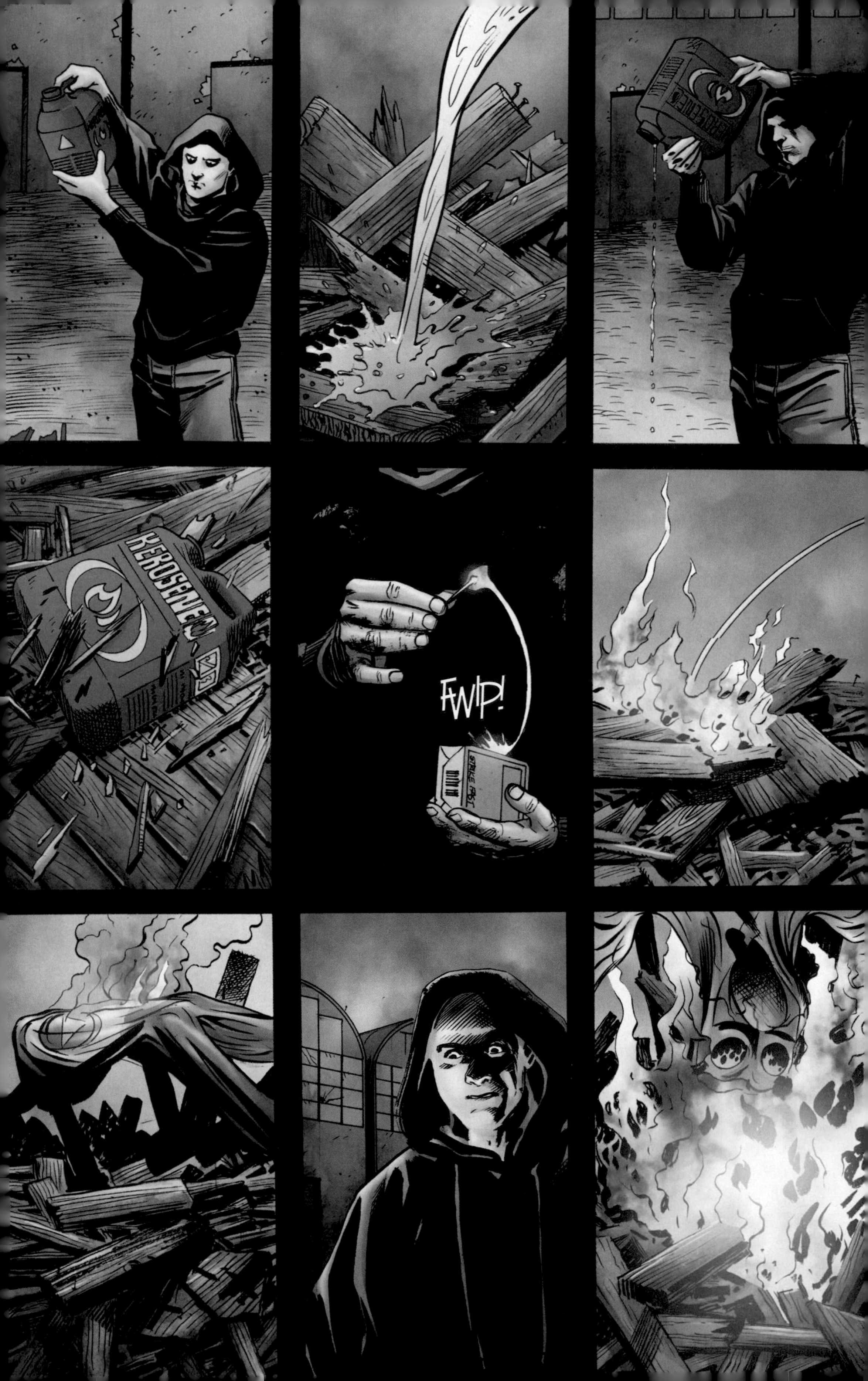
KEROSENE
FWIP!

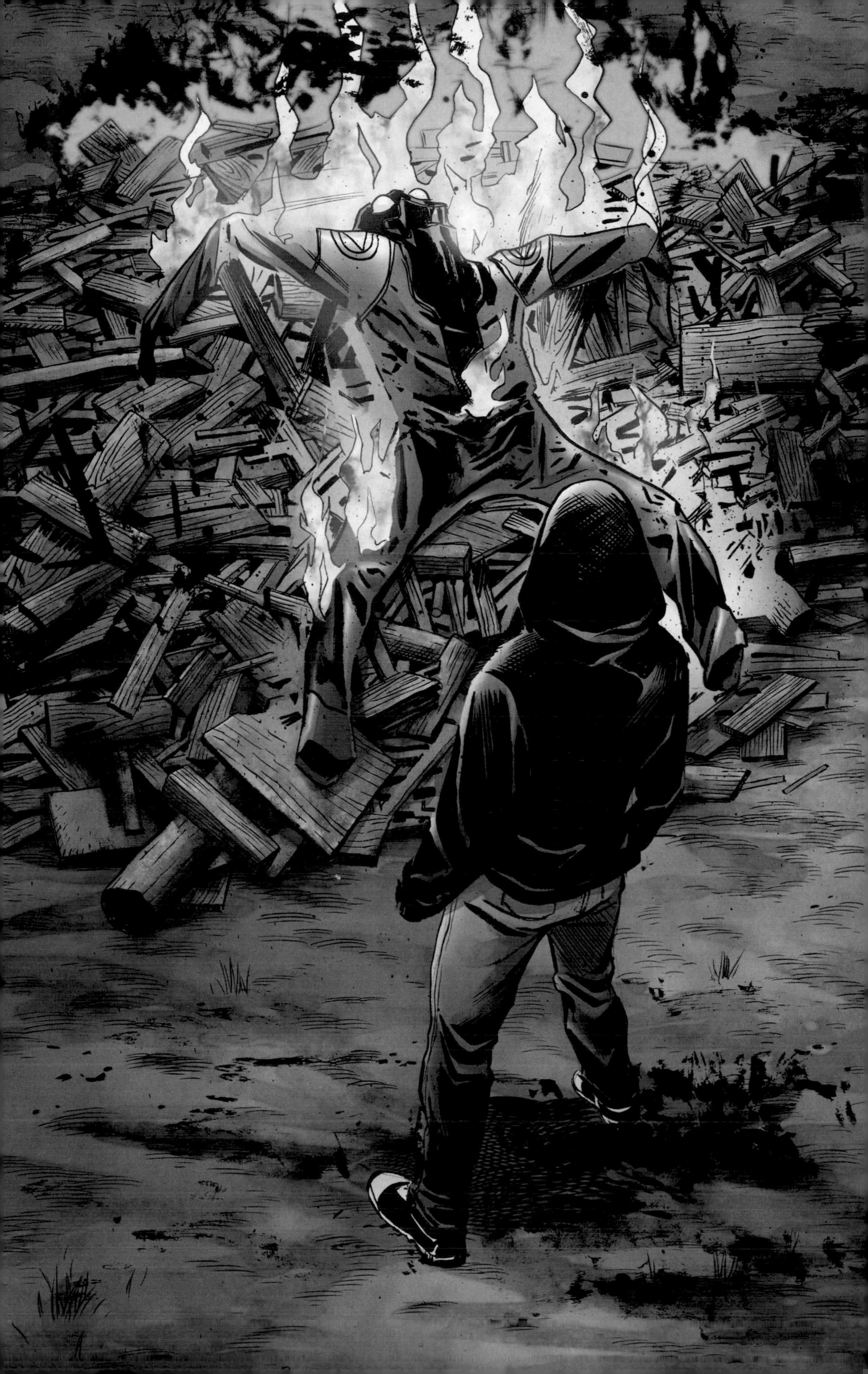

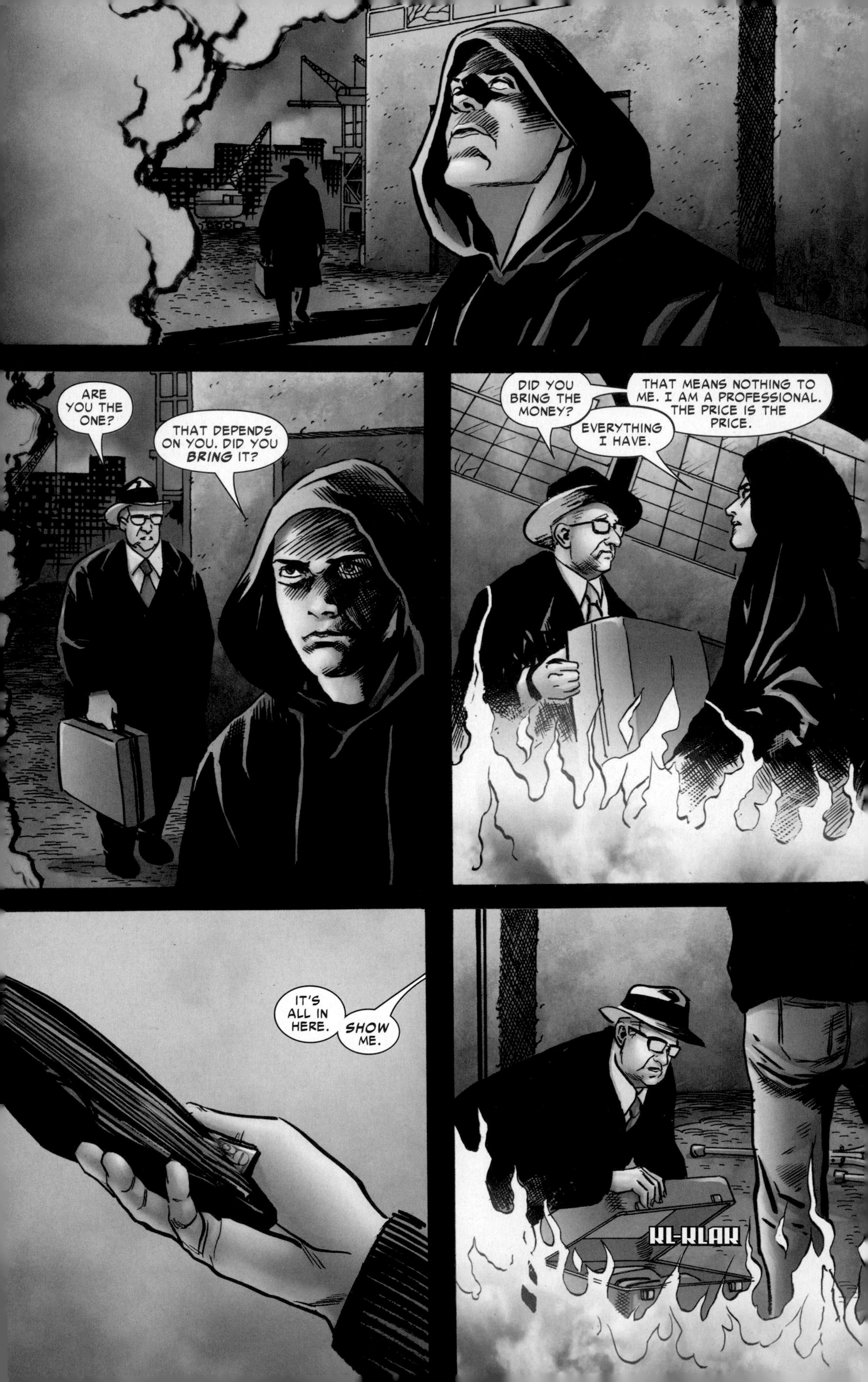
ARE YOU THE ONE?
THAT DEPENDS ON YOU. DID YOU BRING IT?
DID YOU BRING THE MONEY?
EVERYTHING I HAVE.
THAT MEANS NOTHING TO ME. I AM A PROFESSIONAL. THE PRICE IS THE PRICE.
IT'S ALL IN HERE.
SHOW ME.
KL-KLAK

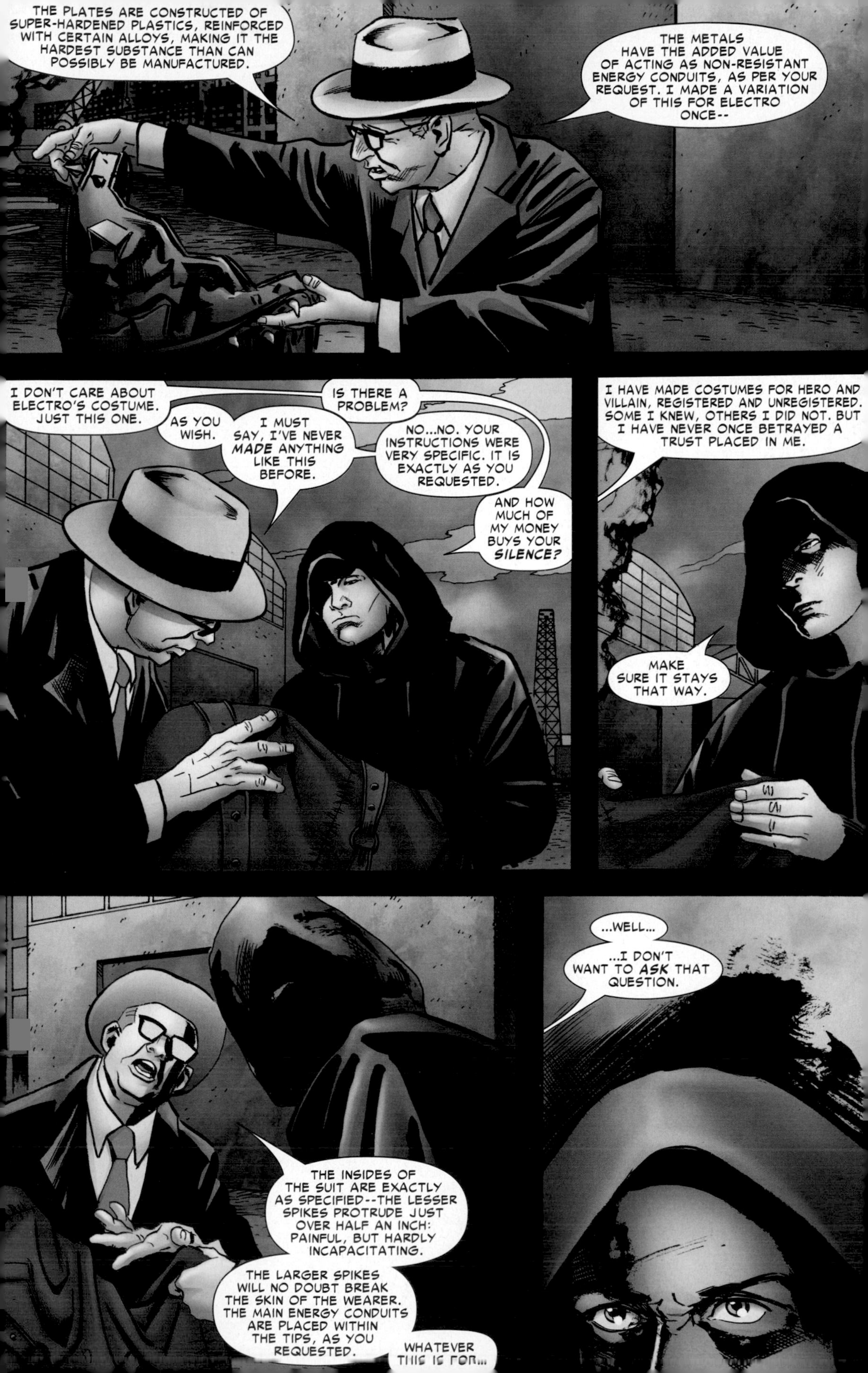
THE PLATES ARE CONSTRUCTED OF SUPER-HARDENED PLASTICS, REINFORCED WITH CERTAIN ALLOYS, MAKING IT THE HARDEST SUBSTANCE THAN CAN POSSIBLY BE MANUFACTURED.
THE METALS HAVE THE ADDED VALUE OF ACTING AS NON-RESISTANT ENERGY CONDUITS, AS PER YOUR REQUEST. I MADE A VARIATION OF THIS FOR ELECTRO ONCE--
I DON'T CARE ABOUT ELECTRO'S COSTUME. JUST THIS ONE.
AS YOU WISH.
I MUST SAY, I'VE NEVER MADE ANYTHING LIKE THIS BEFORE.
IS THERE A PROBLEM?
NO...NO. YOUR INSTRUCTIONS WERE VERY SPECIFIC. IT IS EXACTLY AS YOU REQUESTED.
AND HOW MUCH OF MY MONEY BUYS YOUR SILENCE?
I HAVE MADE COSTUMES FOR HERO AND VILLAIN, REGISTERED AND UNREGISTERED. SOME I KNEW, OTHERS I DID NOT. BUT I HAVE NEVER ONCE BETRAYED A TRUST PLACED IN ME.
MAKE SURE IT STAYS THAT WAY.
THE INSIDES OF THE SUIT ARE EXACTLY AS SPECIFIED--THE LESSER SPIKES PROTRUDE JUST OVER HALF AN INCH: PAINFUL, BUT HARDLY INCAPACITATING.
THE LARGER SPIKES WILL NO DOUBT BREAK THE SKIN OF THE WEARER. THE MAIN ENERGY CONDUITS ARE PLACED WITHIN THE TIPS, AS YOU REQUESTED.
WHATEVER THIS IS FOR...
...WELL...
...I DON'T WANT TO ASK THAT QUESTION.

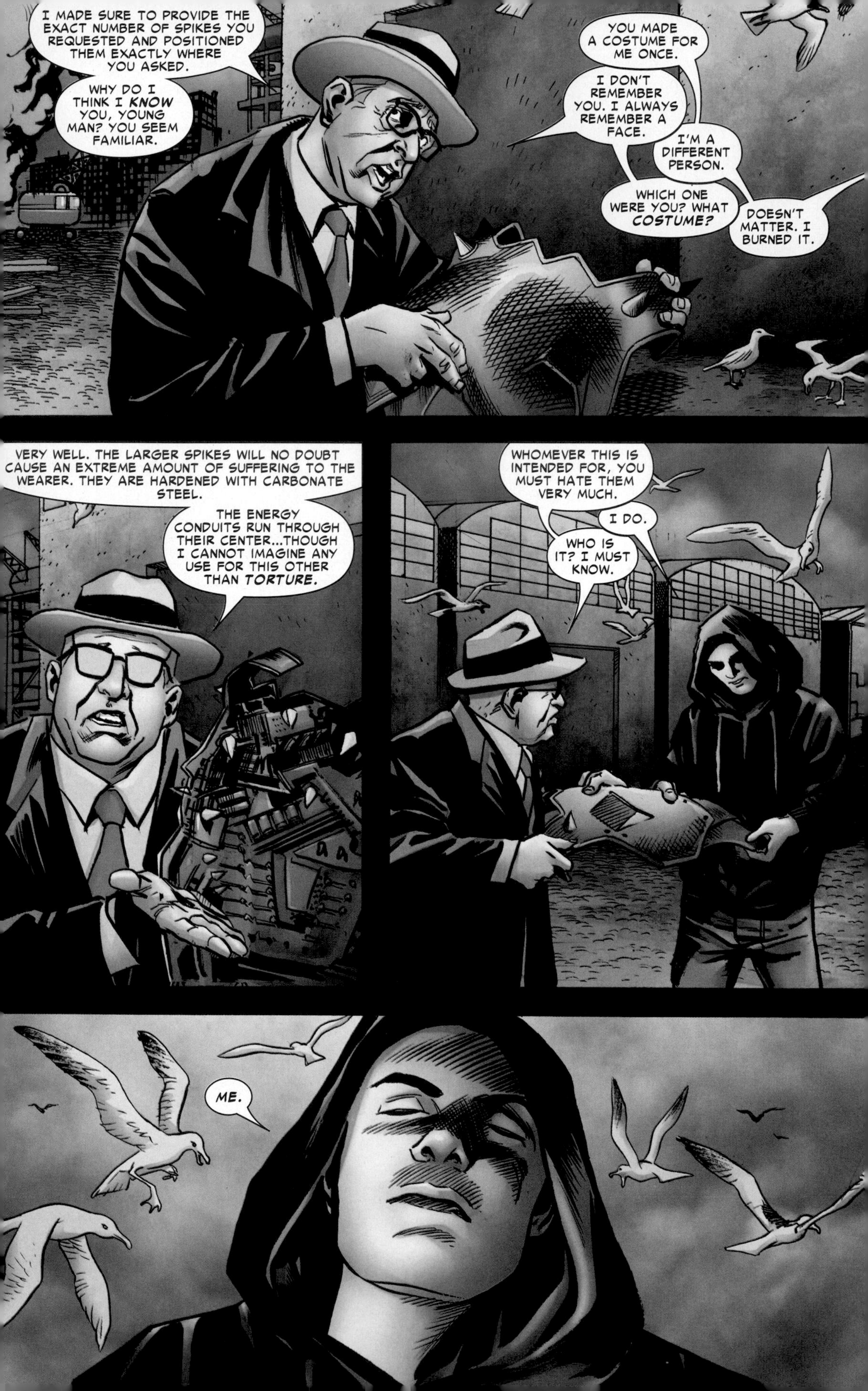
I MADE SURE TO PROVIDE THE EXACT NUMBER OF SPIKES YOU REQUESTED AND POSITIONED THEM EXACTLY WHERE YOU ASKED.
WHY DO I THINK I *KNOW* YOU, YOUNG MAN? YOU SEEM FAMILIAR.
YOU MADE A COSTUME FOR ME ONCE.
I DON'T REMEMBER YOU. I ALWAYS REMEMBER A FACE.
I'M A DIFFERENT PERSON.
WHICH ONE WERE YOU? WHAT *COSTUME?*
DOESN'T MATTER. I BURNED IT.
VERY WELL. THE LARGER SPIKES WILL NO DOUBT CAUSE AN EXTREME AMOUNT OF SUFFERING TO THE WEARER. THEY ARE HARDENED WITH CARBONATE STEEL.
THE ENERGY CONDUITS RUN THROUGH THEIR CENTER...THOUGH I CANNOT IMAGINE ANY USE FOR THIS OTHER THAN *TORTURE.*
WHOMEVER THIS IS INTENDED FOR, YOU MUST HATE THEM VERY MUCH.
I DO.
WHO IS IT? I MUST KNOW.
ME.

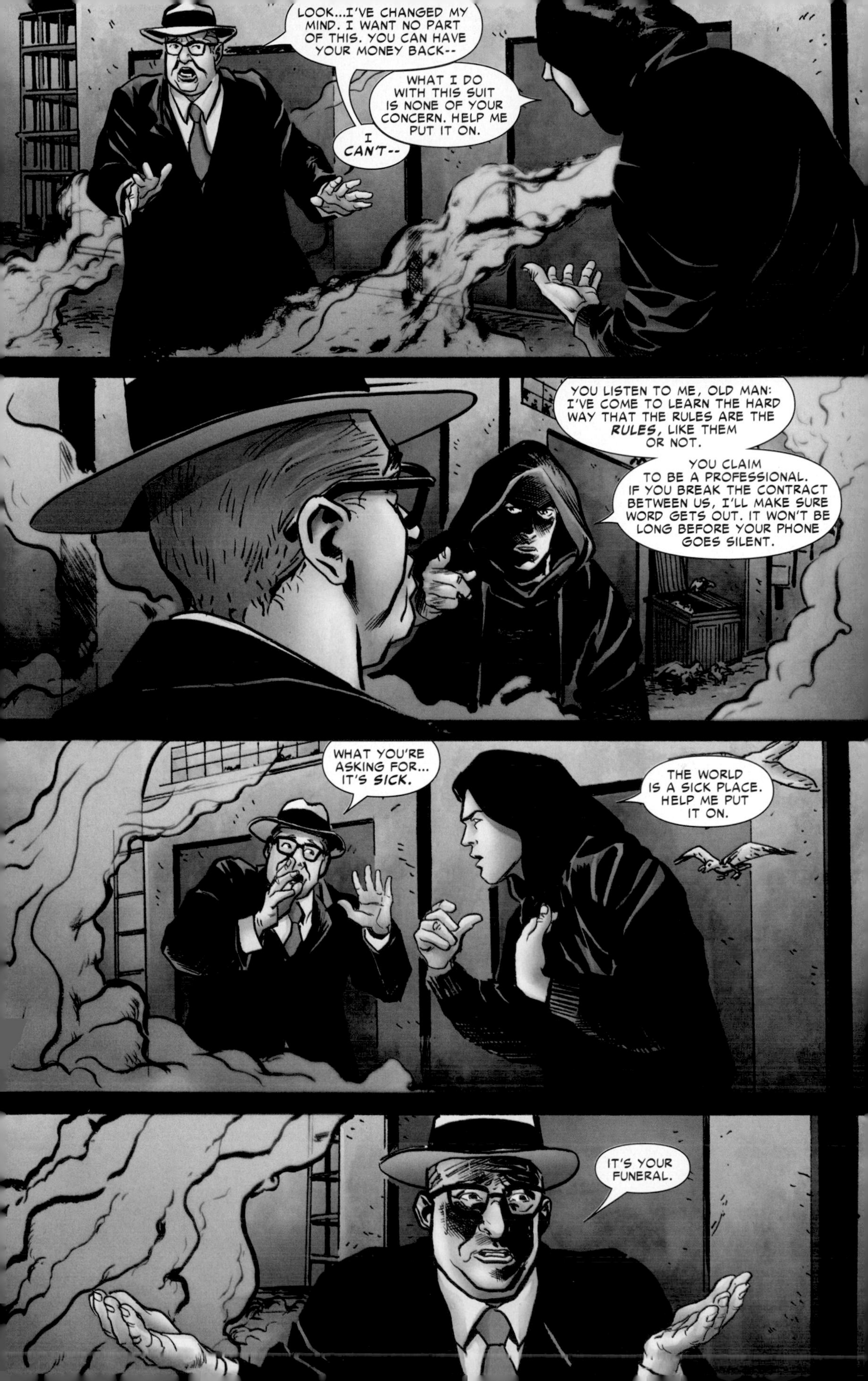

LOOK...I'VE CHANGED MY MIND. I WANT NO PART OF THIS. YOU CAN HAVE YOUR MONEY BACK--
WHAT I DO WITH THIS SUIT IS NONE OF YOUR CONCERN. HELP ME PUT IT ON.
I CAN'T--
YOU LISTEN TO ME, OLD MAN: I'VE COME TO LEARN THE HARD WAY THAT THE RULES ARE THE RULES, LIKE THEM OR NOT.
YOU CLAIM TO BE A PROFESSIONAL. IF YOU BREAK THE CONTRACT BETWEEN US, I'LL MAKE SURE WORD GETS OUT. IT WON'T BE LONG BEFORE YOUR PHONE GOES SILENT.
WHAT YOU'RE ASKING FOR... IT'S SICK.
THE WORLD IS A SICK PLACE. HELP ME PUT IT ON.
IT'S YOUR FUNERAL.

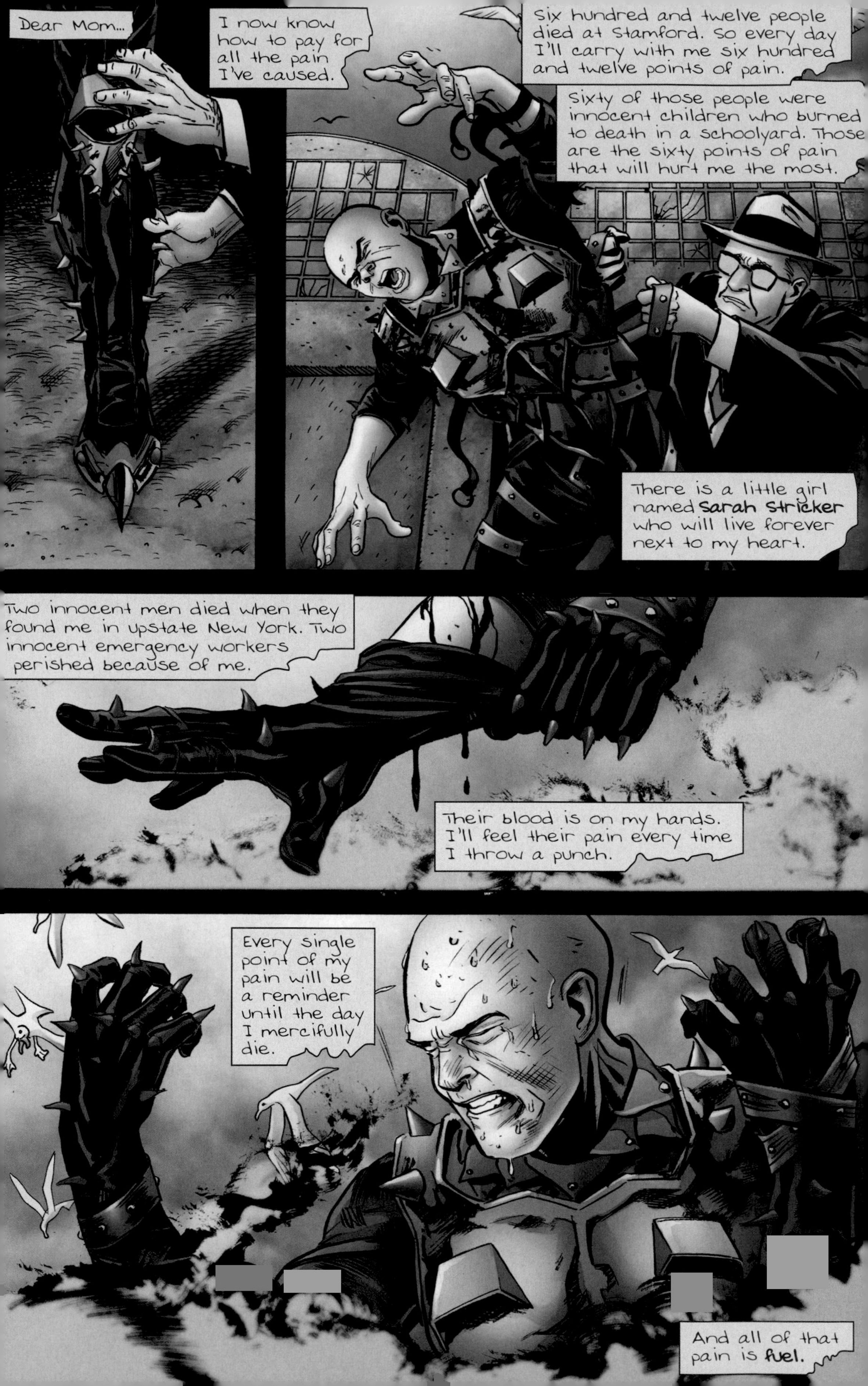
Dear Mom...
I now know how to pay for all the pain I've caused.
Six hundred and twelve people died at Stamford. So every day I'll carry with me six hundred and twelve points of pain.
Sixty of those people were innocent children who burned to death in a schoolyard. Those are the sixty points of pain that will hurt me the most.
There is a little girl named **Sarah Stricker** who will live forever next to my heart.
Two innocent men died when they found me in upstate New York. Two innocent emergency workers perished because of me.
Their blood is on my hands. I'll feel their pain every time I throw a punch.
Every single point of my pain will be a reminder until the day I mercifully die.
And all of that pain is **fuel.**

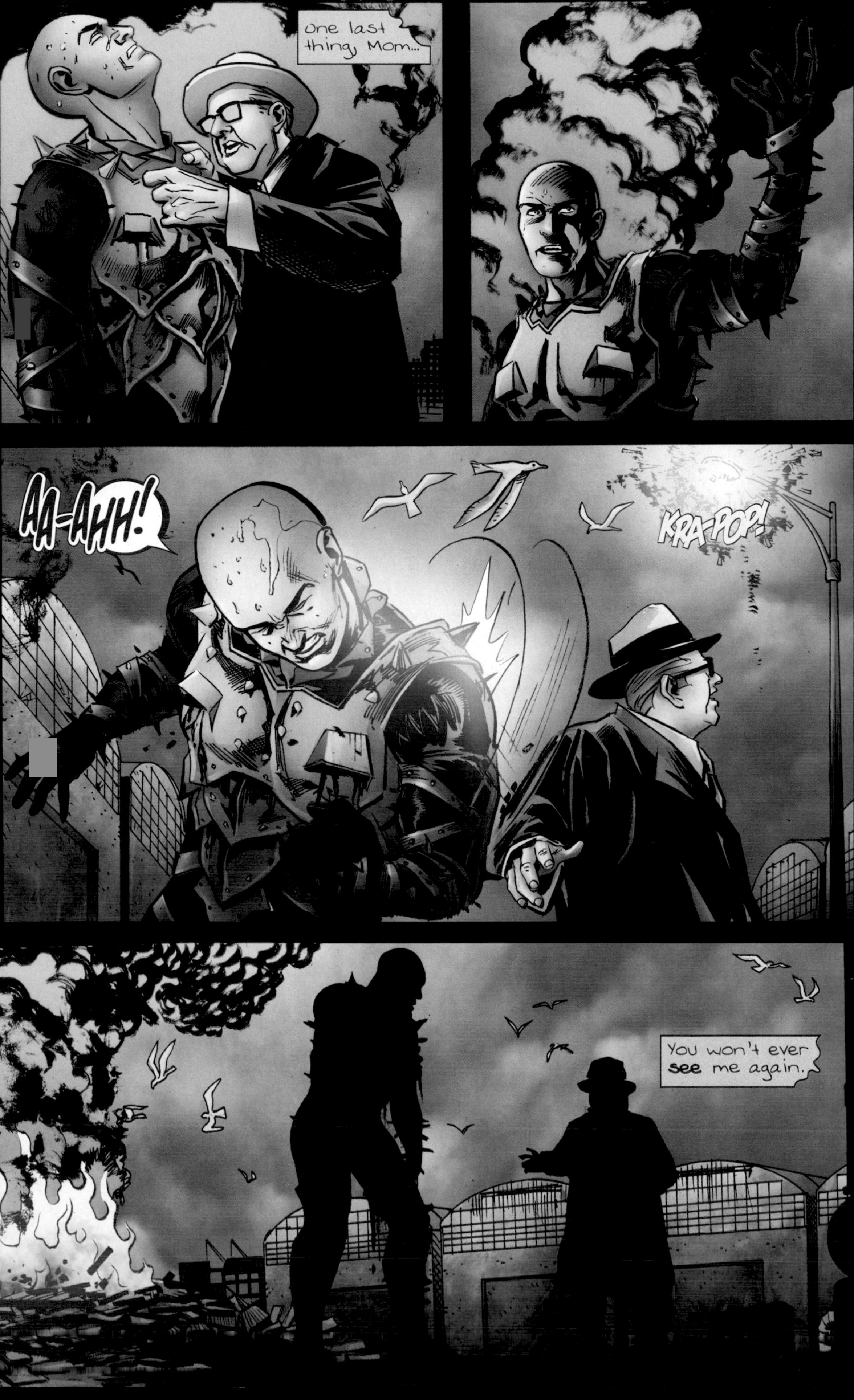
One last thing, Mom...
AA-AHH!
KRA-POP!
You won't ever **see** me again.

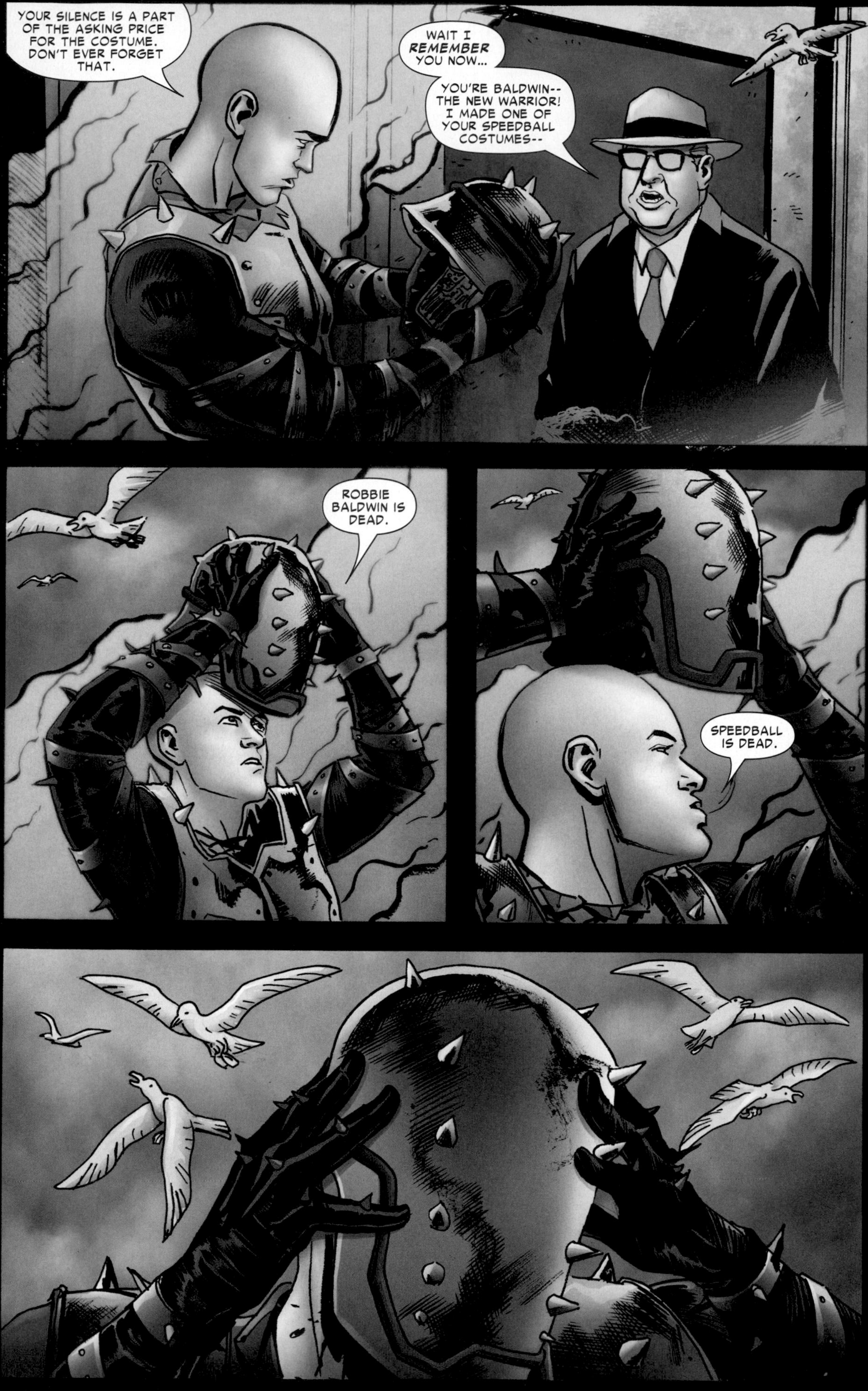

YOUR SILENCE IS A PART OF THE ASKING PRICE FOR THE COSTUME. DON'T EVER FORGET THAT.
WAIT I *REMEMBER* YOU NOW...
YOU'RE BALDWIN-- THE NEW WARRIOR! I MADE ONE OF YOUR SPEEDBALL COSTUMES--
ROBBIE BALDWIN IS DEAD.
SPEEDBALL IS DEAD.

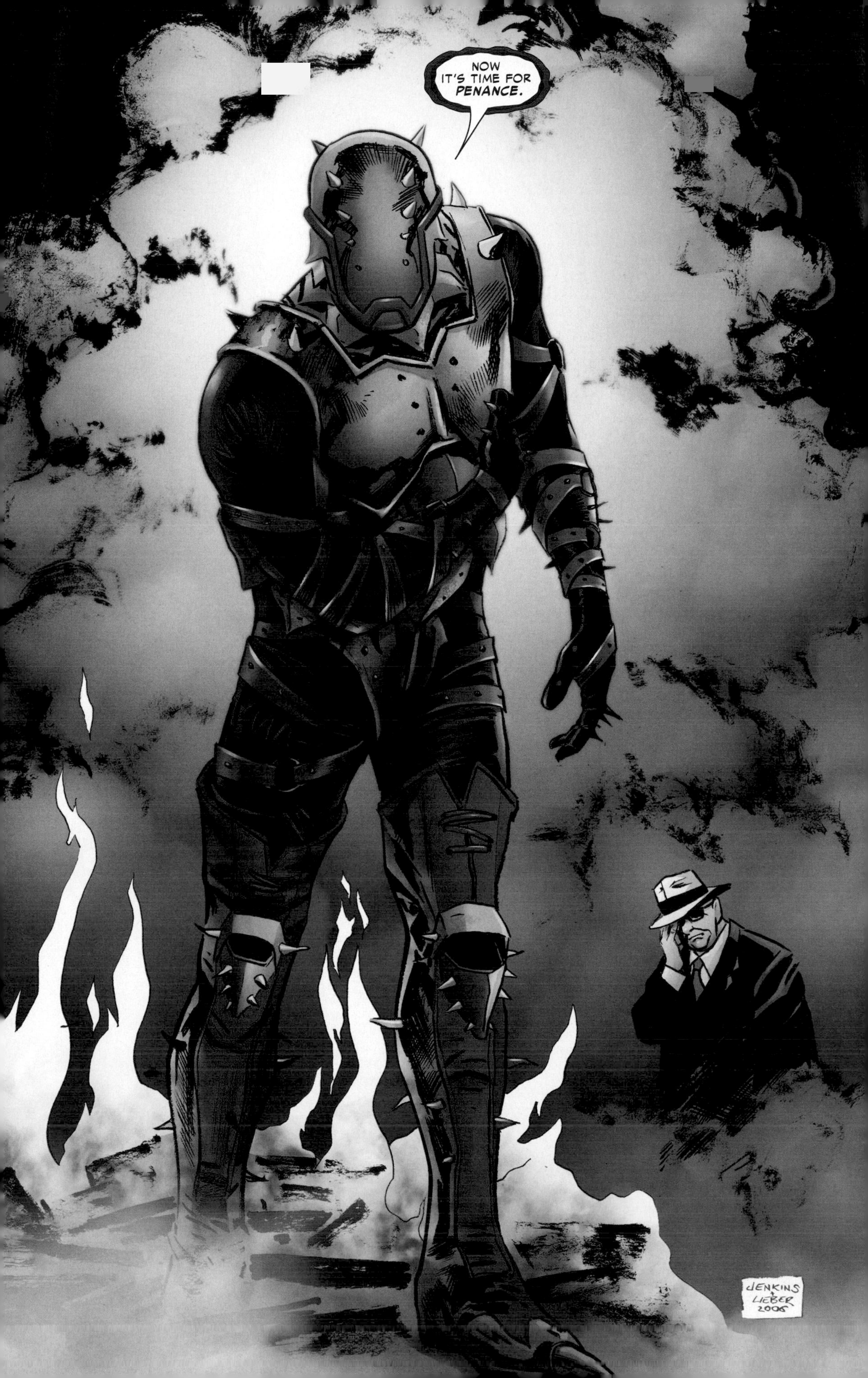
NOW IT'S TIME FOR PENANCE.
JENKINS + LIEBER 2006

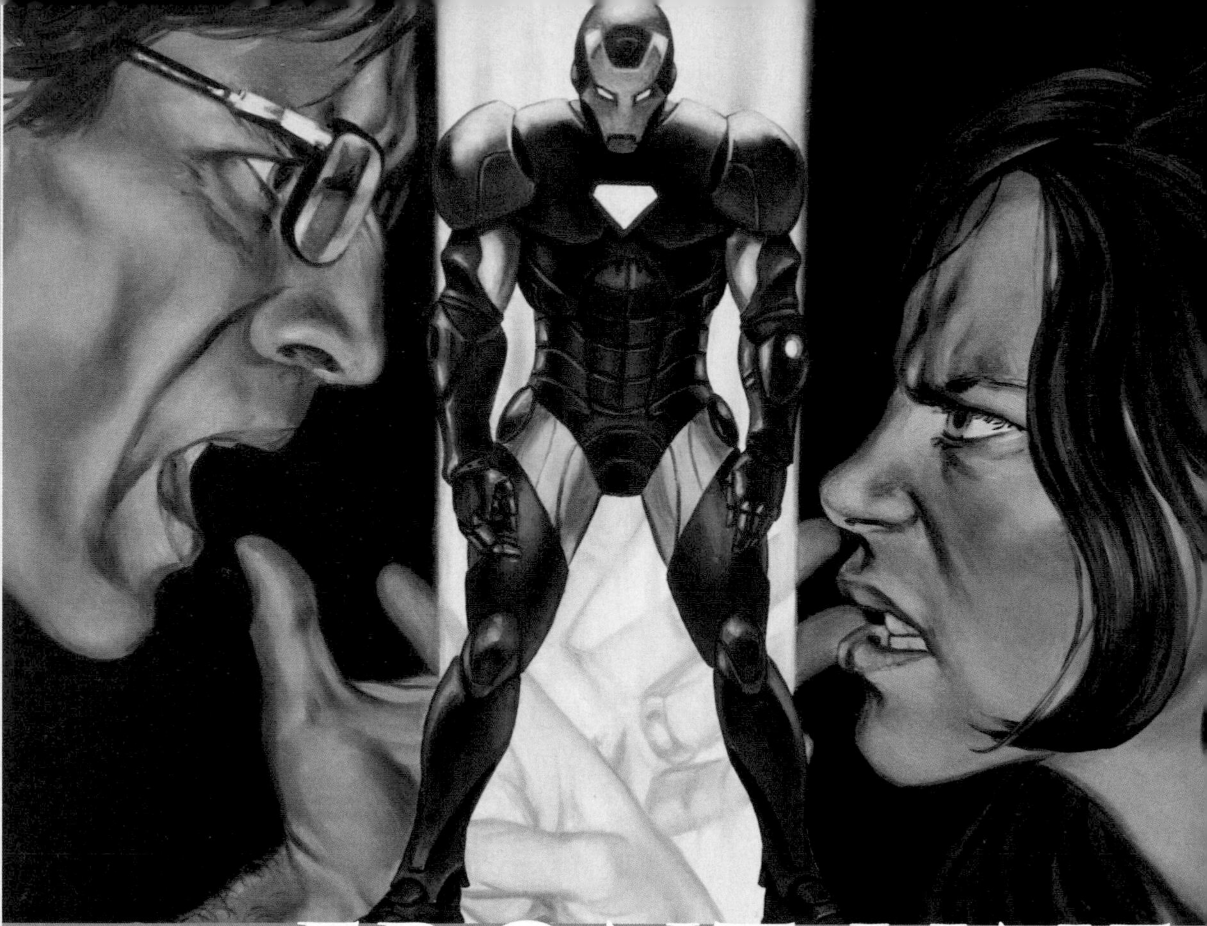

FRONT LINE

A MARVEL COMICS EVENT

CIVIL WAR

CIVIL WAR: FRONT LINE #11

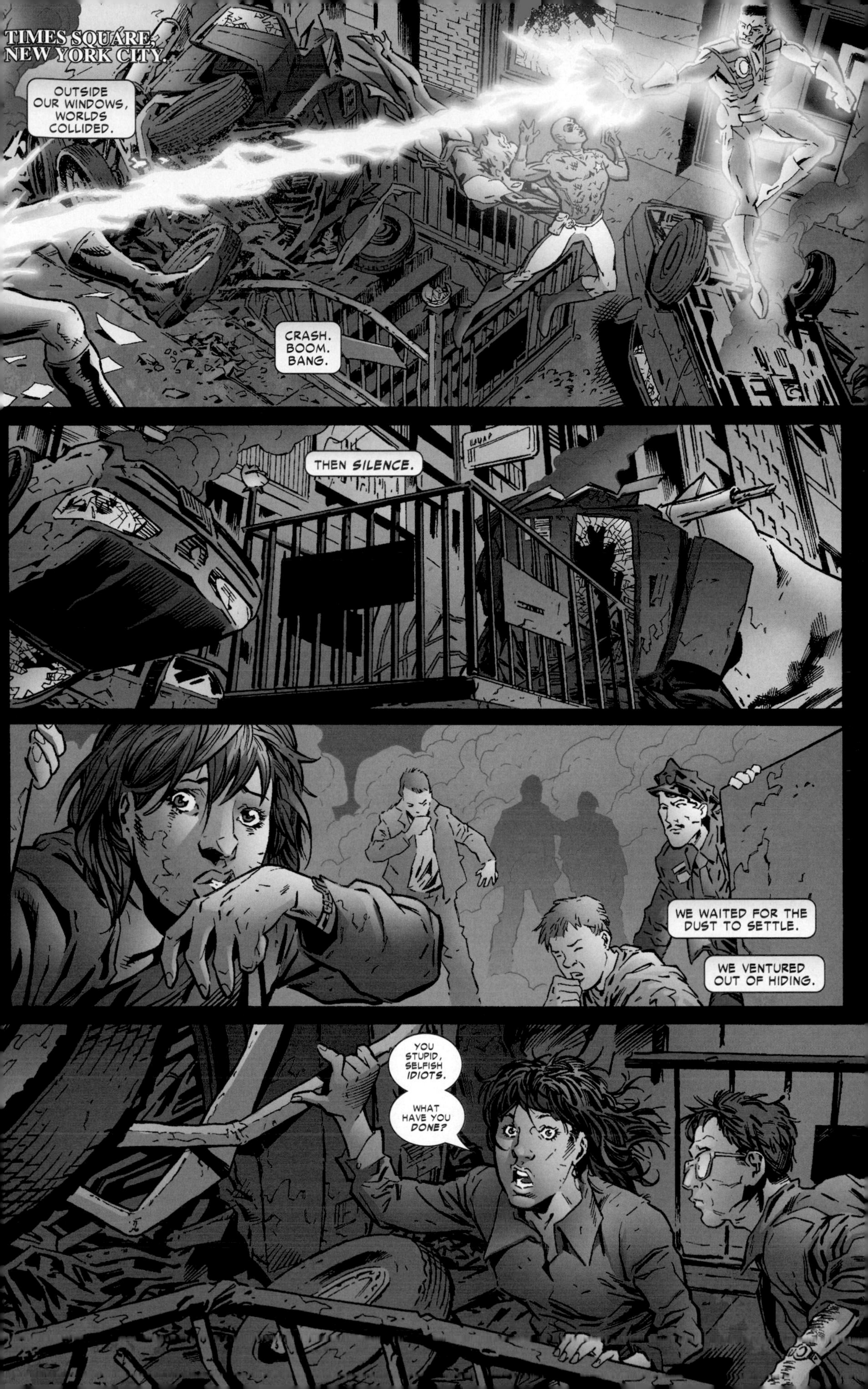
TIMES SQUARE, NEW YORK CITY.
OUTSIDE OUR WINDOWS, WORLDS COLLIDED.
CRASH. BOOM. BANG.
THEN SILENCE.
WE WAITED FOR THE DUST TO SETTLE.
WE VENTURED OUT OF HIDING.
YOU STUPID, SELFISH IDIOTS.
WHAT HAVE YOU DONE?

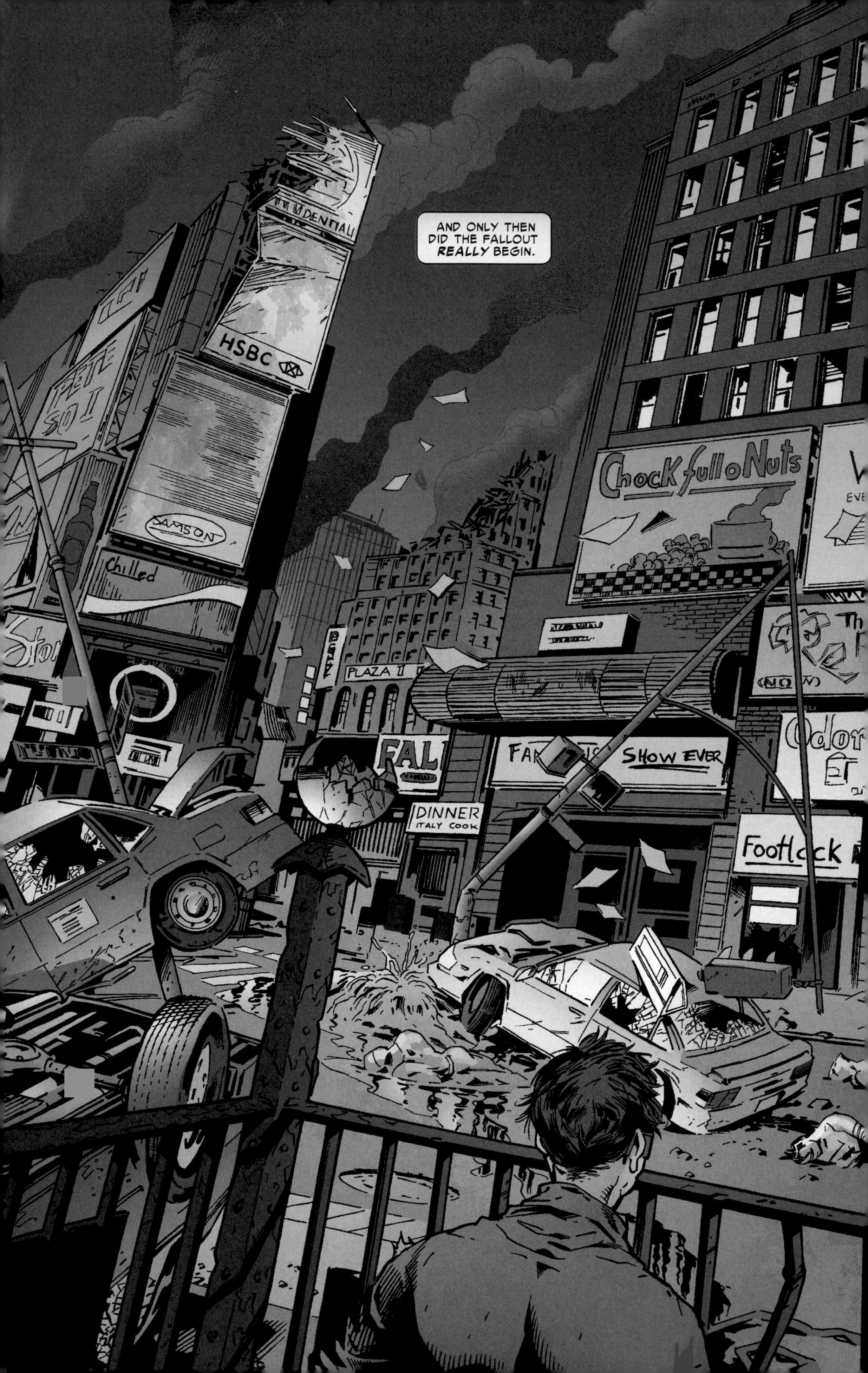
AND ONLY THEN DID THE FALLOUT *REALLY* BEGIN.
HSBC
SAMSON
Chilled
Chock full o Nuts
PLAZA II
DINNER
ITALY COOK
SHOW EVER

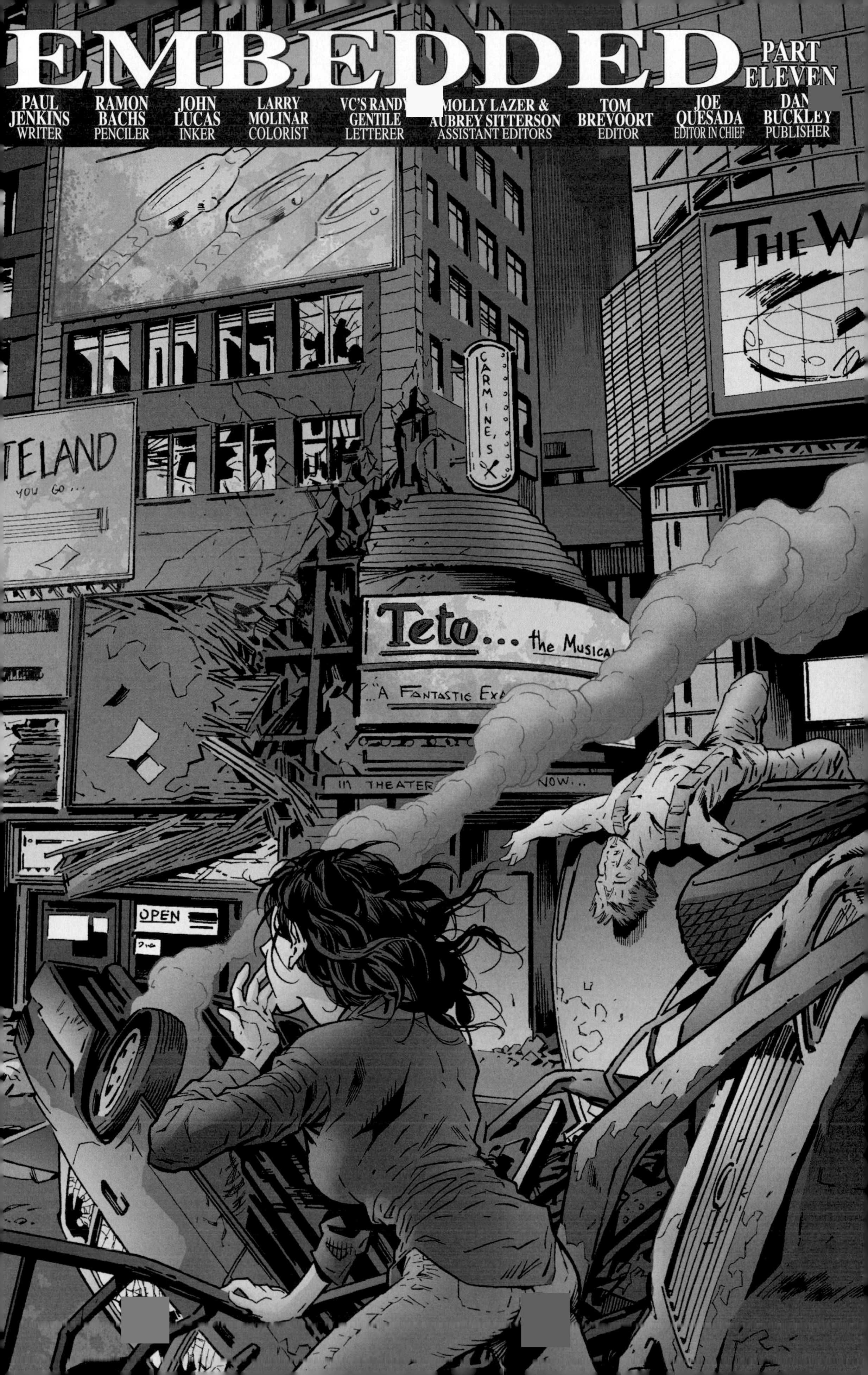
EMBEDDED PART ELEVEN
PAUL JENKINS WRITER
RAMON BACHS PENCILER
JOHN LUCAS INKER
LARRY MOLINAR COLORIST
VC'S RANDY GENTILE LETTERER
MOLLY LAZER & AUBREY SITTERSON ASSISTANT EDITORS
TOM BREVOORT EDITOR
JOE QUESADA EDITOR IN CHIEF
DAN BUCKLEY PUBLISHER
CARMINE'S
TELAND
YOU GO...
Teto... the Musical
...A Fantastic Exa
IN THEATER NOW...
OPEN

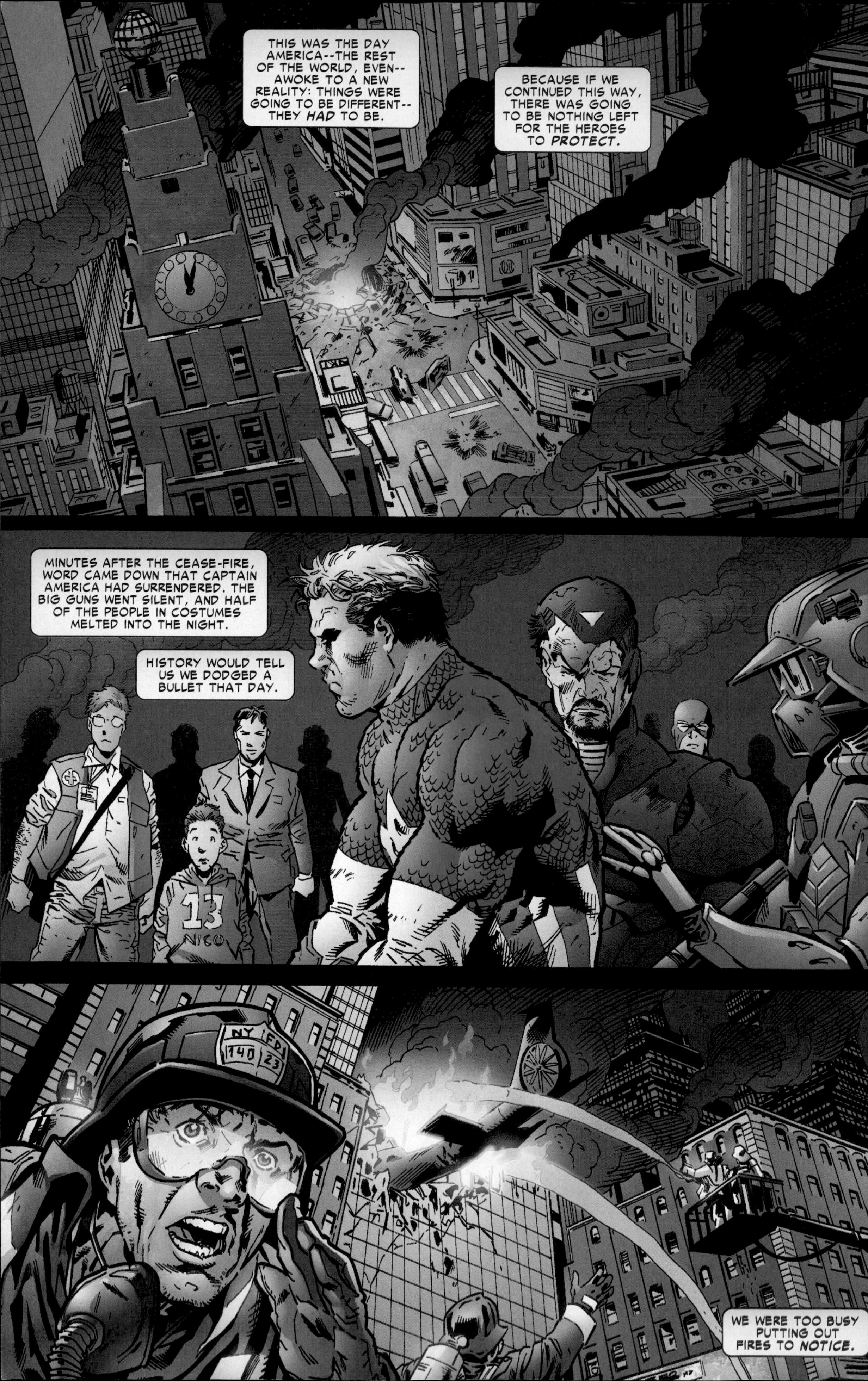
THIS WAS THE DAY AMERICA--THE REST OF THE WORLD, EVEN--AWOKE TO A NEW REALITY: THINGS WERE GOING TO BE DIFFERENT--THEY *HAD* TO BE.
BECAUSE IF WE CONTINUED THIS WAY, THERE WAS GOING TO BE NOTHING LEFT FOR THE HEROES TO *PROTECT*.
MINUTES AFTER THE CEASE-FIRE, WORD CAME DOWN THAT CAPTAIN AMERICA HAD SURRENDERED. THE BIG GUNS WENT SILENT, AND HALF OF THE PEOPLE IN COSTUMES MELTED INTO THE NIGHT.
HISTORY WOULD TELL US WE DODGED A BULLET THAT DAY.
13
NICO
NY FD 140 23
WE WERE TOO BUSY PUTTING OUT FIRES TO *NOTICE*.

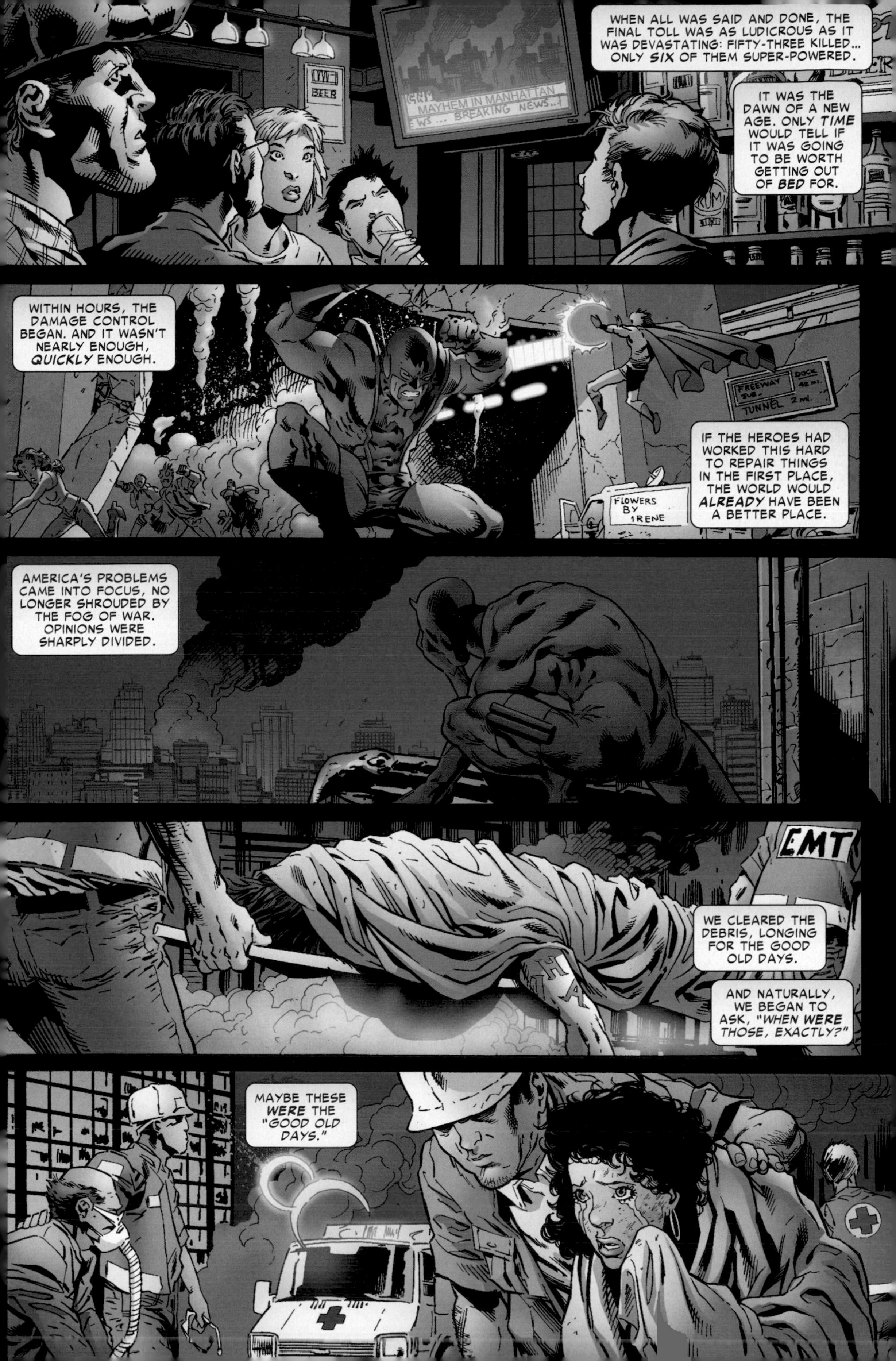

WHEN ALL WAS SAID AND DONE, THE FINAL TOLL WAS AS LUDICROUS AS IT WAS DEVASTATING: FIFTY-THREE KILLED... ONLY SIX OF THEM SUPER-POWERED.
IT WAS THE DAWN OF A NEW AGE. ONLY TIME WOULD TELL IF IT WAS GOING TO BE WORTH GETTING OUT OF BED FOR.
MAYHEM IN MANHATTAN
BREAKING NEWS...
BEER
WITHIN HOURS, THE DAMAGE CONTROL BEGAN. AND IT WASN'T NEARLY ENOUGH, QUICKLY ENOUGH.
IF THE HEROES HAD WORKED THIS HARD TO REPAIR THINGS IN THE FIRST PLACE, THE WORLD WOULD ALREADY HAVE BEEN A BETTER PLACE.
FREEWAY
DOCK
TUNNEL 2 mi.
FLOWERS BY IRENE
AMERICA'S PROBLEMS CAME INTO FOCUS, NO LONGER SHROUDED BY THE FOG OF WAR. OPINIONS WERE SHARPLY DIVIDED.
EMT
WE CLEARED THE DEBRIS, LONGING FOR THE GOOD OLD DAYS.
AND NATURALLY, WE BEGAN TO ASK, "WHEN WERE THOSE, EXACTLY?"
MAYBE THESE WERE THE "GOOD OLD DAYS."

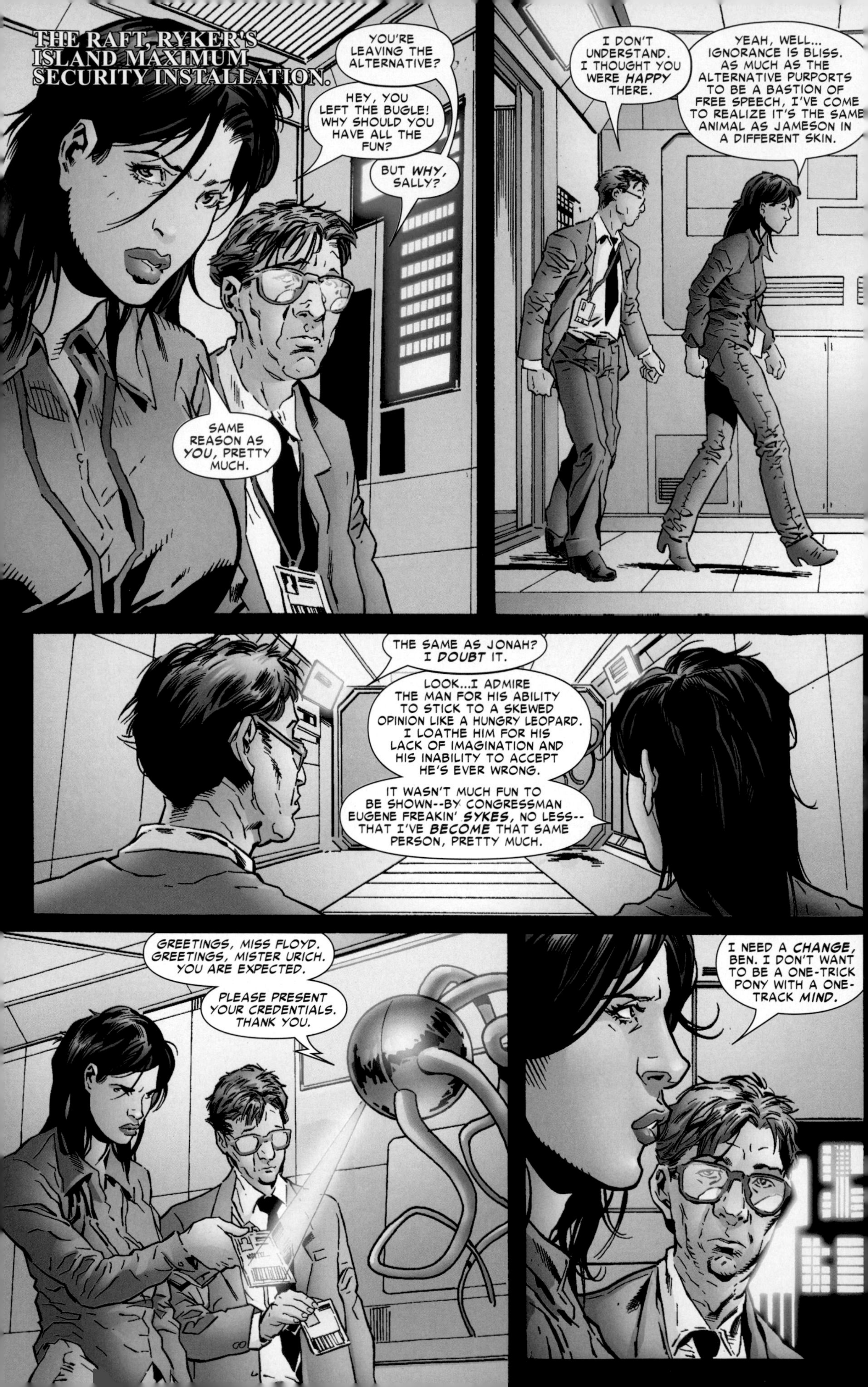
THE RAFT, RYKER'S ISLAND MAXIMUM SECURITY INSTALLATION.
YOU'RE LEAVING THE ALTERNATIVE?
HEY, YOU LEFT THE BUGLE! WHY SHOULD YOU HAVE ALL THE FUN?
BUT WHY, SALLY?
SAME REASON AS YOU, PRETTY MUCH.
I DON'T UNDERSTAND. I THOUGHT YOU WERE HAPPY THERE.
YEAH, WELL... IGNORANCE IS BLISS. AS MUCH AS THE ALTERNATIVE PURPORTS TO BE A BASTION OF FREE SPEECH, I'VE COME TO REALIZE IT'S THE SAME ANIMAL AS JAMESON IN A DIFFERENT SKIN.
THE SAME AS JONAH? I DOUBT IT.
LOOK...I ADMIRE THE MAN FOR HIS ABILITY TO STICK TO A SKEWED OPINION LIKE A HUNGRY LEOPARD. I LOATHE HIM FOR HIS LACK OF IMAGINATION AND HIS INABILITY TO ACCEPT HE'S EVER WRONG.
IT WASN'T MUCH FUN TO BE SHOWN--BY CONGRESSMAN EUGENE FREAKIN' SYKES, NO LESS--THAT I'VE BECOME THAT SAME PERSON, PRETTY MUCH.
GREETINGS, MISS FLOYD. GREETINGS, MISTER URICH. YOU ARE EXPECTED.
PLEASE PRESENT YOUR CREDENTIALS. THANK YOU.
I NEED A CHANGE, BEN. I DON'T WANT TO BE A ONE-TRICK PONY WITH A ONE-TRACK MIND.

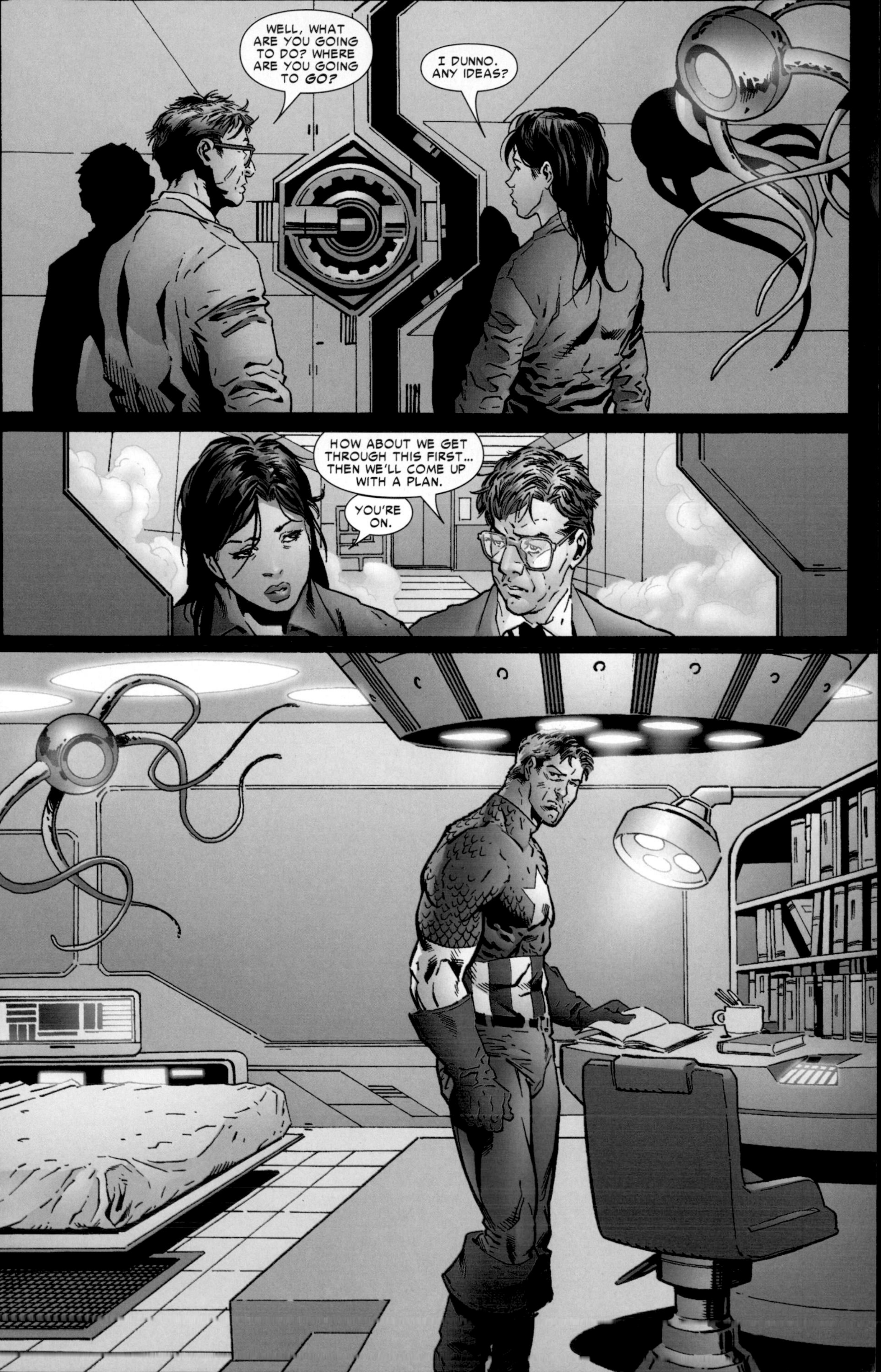
WELL, WHAT ARE YOU GOING TO DO? WHERE ARE YOU GOING TO GO?
I DUNNO. ANY IDEAS?
HOW ABOUT WE GET THROUGH THIS FIRST... THEN WE'LL COME UP WITH A PLAN.
YOU'RE ON.

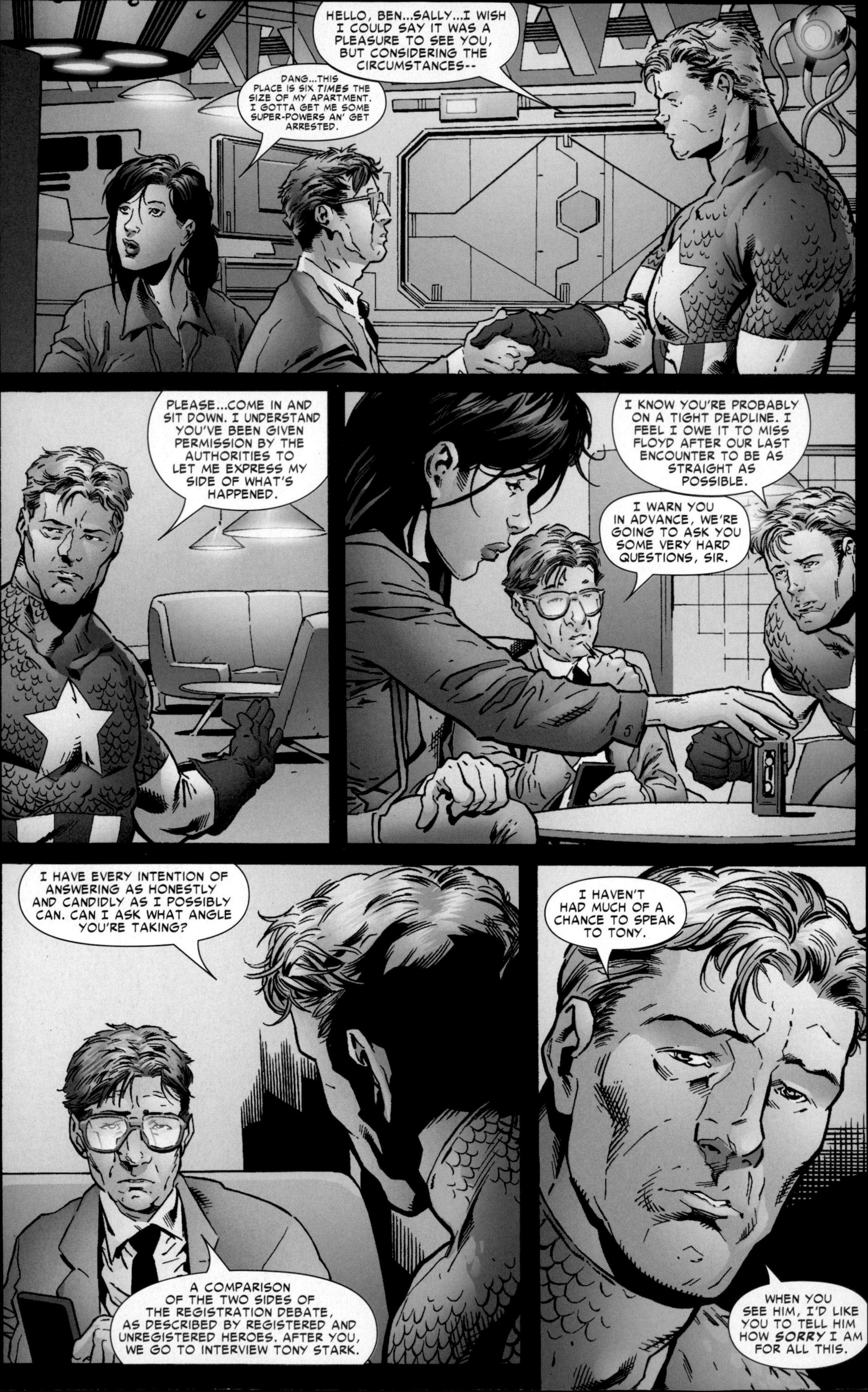
HELLO, BEN...SALLY...I WISH I COULD SAY IT WAS A PLEASURE TO SEE YOU, BUT CONSIDERING THE CIRCUMSTANCES--
DANG...THIS PLACE IS SIX *TIMES* THE SIZE OF MY APARTMENT. I GOTTA GET ME SOME SUPER-POWERS AN' GET ARRESTED.
PLEASE...COME IN AND SIT DOWN. I UNDERSTAND YOU'VE BEEN GIVEN PERMISSION BY THE AUTHORITIES TO LET ME EXPRESS MY SIDE OF WHAT'S HAPPENED.
I KNOW YOU'RE PROBABLY ON A TIGHT DEADLINE. I FEEL I OWE IT TO MISS FLOYD AFTER OUR LAST ENCOUNTER TO BE AS STRAIGHT AS POSSIBLE.
I WARN YOU IN ADVANCE, WE'RE GOING TO ASK YOU SOME VERY HARD QUESTIONS, SIR.
I HAVE EVERY INTENTION OF ANSWERING AS HONESTLY AND CANDIDLY AS I POSSIBLY CAN. CAN I ASK WHAT ANGLE YOU'RE TAKING?
A COMPARISON OF THE TWO SIDES OF THE REGISTRATION DEBATE, AS DESCRIBED BY REGISTERED AND UNREGISTERED HEROES. AFTER YOU, WE GO TO INTERVIEW TONY STARK.
I HAVEN'T HAD MUCH OF A CHANCE TO SPEAK TO TONY.
WHEN YOU SEE HIM, I'D LIKE YOU TO TELL HIM HOW *SORRY* I AM FOR ALL THIS.

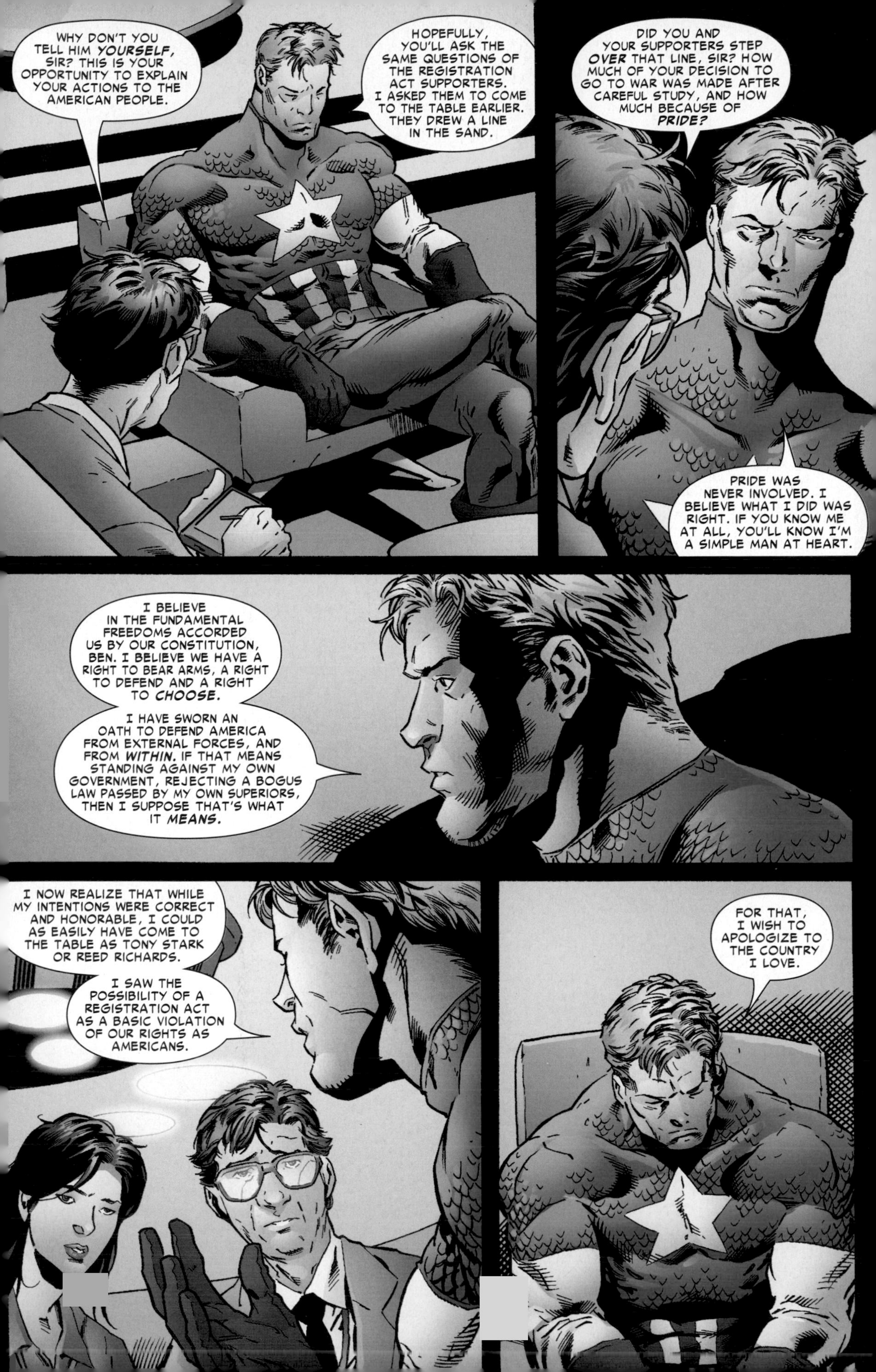
WHY DON'T YOU TELL HIM *YOURSELF*, SIR? THIS IS YOUR OPPORTUNITY TO EXPLAIN YOUR ACTIONS TO THE AMERICAN PEOPLE.
HOPEFULLY, YOU'LL ASK THE SAME QUESTIONS OF THE REGISTRATION ACT SUPPORTERS. I ASKED THEM TO COME TO THE TABLE EARLIER. THEY DREW A LINE IN THE SAND.
DID YOU AND YOUR SUPPORTERS STEP *OVER* THAT LINE, SIR? HOW MUCH OF YOUR DECISION TO GO TO WAR WAS MADE AFTER CAREFUL STUDY, AND HOW MUCH BECAUSE OF *PRIDE?*
PRIDE WAS NEVER INVOLVED. I BELIEVE WHAT I DID WAS RIGHT. IF YOU KNOW ME AT ALL, YOU'LL KNOW I'M A SIMPLE MAN AT HEART.
I BELIEVE IN THE FUNDAMENTAL FREEDOMS ACCORDED US BY OUR CONSTITUTION, BEN. I BELIEVE WE HAVE A RIGHT TO BEAR ARMS, A RIGHT TO DEFEND AND A RIGHT TO *CHOOSE.*
I HAVE SWORN AN OATH TO DEFEND AMERICA FROM EXTERNAL FORCES, AND FROM *WITHIN.* IF THAT MEANS STANDING AGAINST MY OWN GOVERNMENT, REJECTING A BOGUS LAW PASSED BY MY OWN SUPERIORS, THEN I SUPPOSE THAT'S WHAT IT *MEANS.*
I NOW REALIZE THAT WHILE MY INTENTIONS WERE CORRECT AND HONORABLE, I COULD AS EASILY HAVE COME TO THE TABLE AS TONY STARK OR REED RICHARDS.
I SAW THE POSSIBILITY OF A REGISTRATION ACT AS A BASIC VIOLATION OF OUR RIGHTS AS AMERICANS.
FOR THAT, I WISH TO APOLOGIZE TO THE COUNTRY I LOVE.

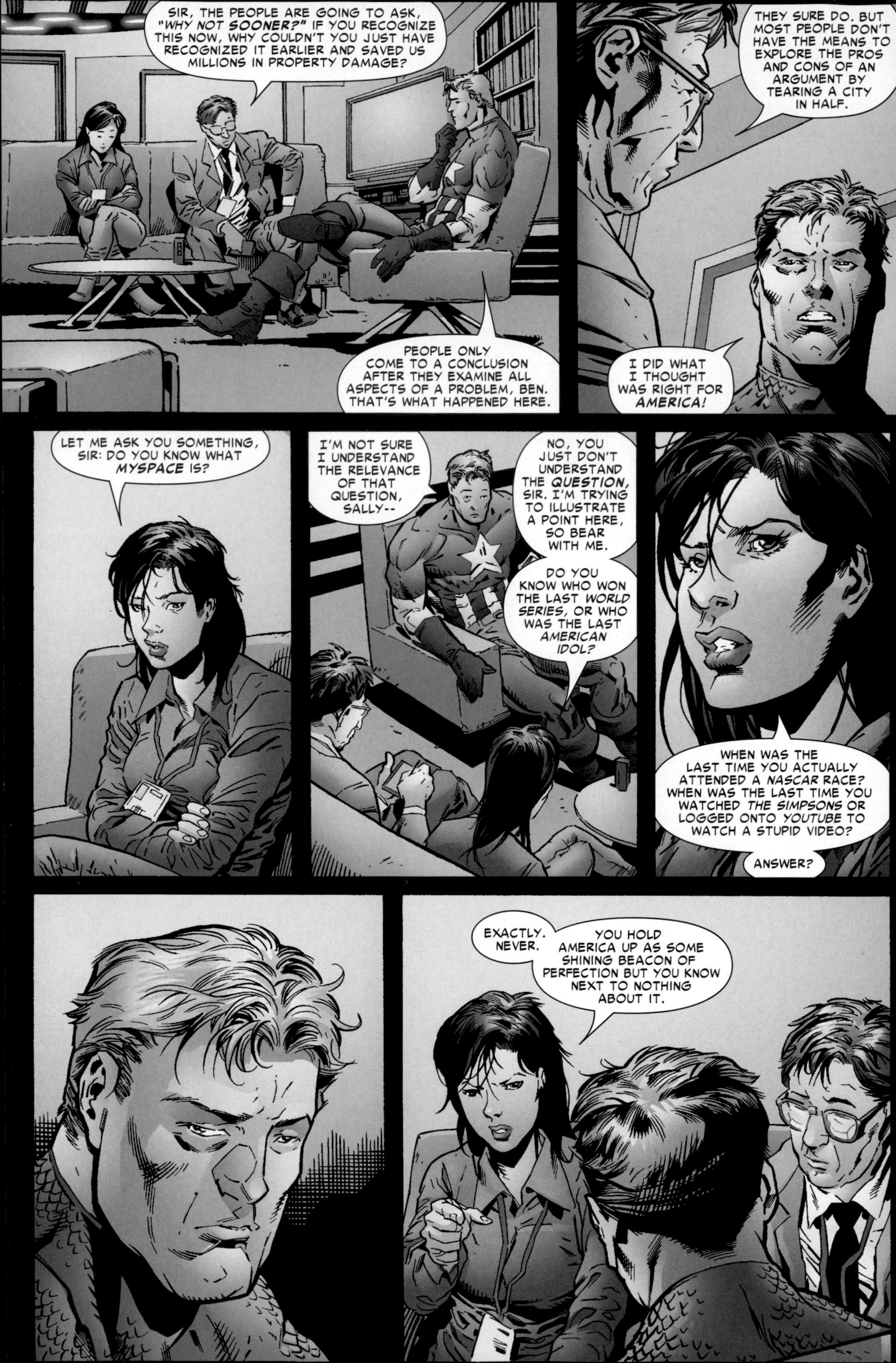
SIR, THE PEOPLE ARE GOING TO ASK, "WHY NOT SOONER?" IF YOU RECOGNIZE THIS NOW, WHY COULDN'T YOU JUST HAVE RECOGNIZED IT EARLIER AND SAVED US MILLIONS IN PROPERTY DAMAGE?
PEOPLE ONLY COME TO A CONCLUSION AFTER THEY EXAMINE ALL ASPECTS OF A PROBLEM, BEN. THAT'S WHAT HAPPENED HERE.
THEY SURE DO. BUT MOST PEOPLE DON'T HAVE THE MEANS TO EXPLORE THE PROS AND CONS OF AN ARGUMENT BY TEARING A CITY IN HALF.
I DID WHAT I THOUGHT WAS RIGHT FOR AMERICA!
LET ME ASK YOU SOMETHING, SIR: DO YOU KNOW WHAT MYSPACE IS?
I'M NOT SURE I UNDERSTAND THE RELEVANCE OF THAT QUESTION, SALLY--
NO, YOU JUST DON'T UNDERSTAND THE QUESTION, SIR. I'M TRYING TO ILLUSTRATE A POINT HERE, SO BEAR WITH ME.
DO YOU KNOW WHO WON THE LAST WORLD SERIES, OR WHO WAS THE LAST AMERICAN IDOL?
WHEN WAS THE LAST TIME YOU ACTUALLY ATTENDED A NASCAR RACE? WHEN WAS THE LAST TIME YOU WATCHED THE SIMPSONS OR LOGGED ONTO YOUTUBE TO WATCH A STUPID VIDEO?
ANSWER?
EXACTLY. NEVER.
YOU HOLD AMERICA UP AS SOME SHINING BEACON OF PERFECTION BUT YOU KNOW NEXT TO NOTHING ABOUT IT.

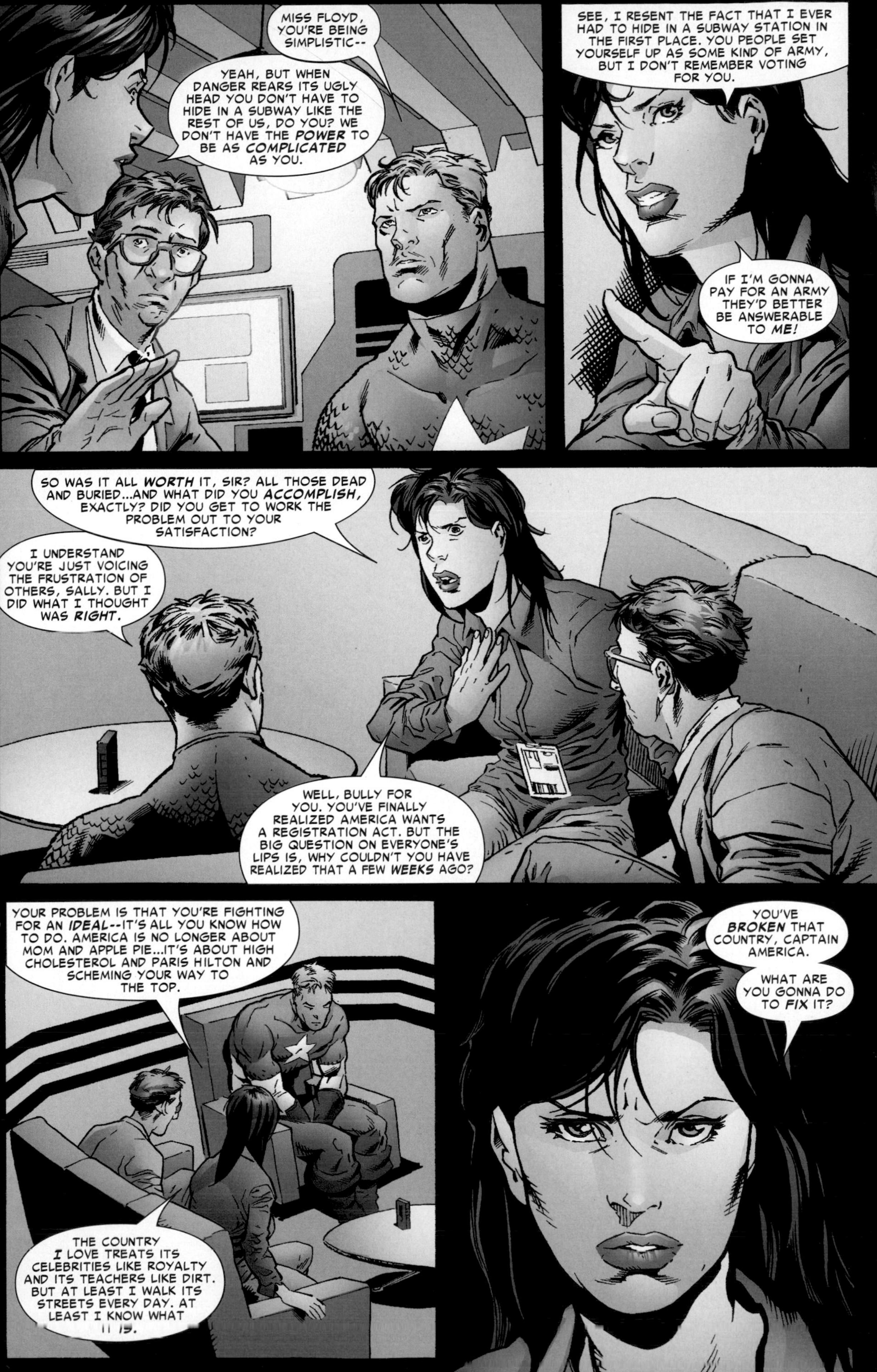

MISS FLOYD, YOU'RE BEING SIMPLISTIC--
YEAH, BUT WHEN DANGER REARS ITS UGLY HEAD YOU DON'T HAVE TO HIDE IN A SUBWAY LIKE THE REST OF US, DO YOU? WE DON'T HAVE THE *POWER* TO BE AS *COMPLICATED* AS YOU.
SEE, I RESENT THE FACT THAT I EVER HAD TO HIDE IN A SUBWAY STATION IN THE FIRST PLACE. YOU PEOPLE SET YOURSELF UP AS SOME KIND OF ARMY, BUT I DON'T REMEMBER VOTING FOR YOU.
IF I'M GONNA PAY FOR AN ARMY THEY'D BETTER BE ANSWERABLE TO *ME!*
SO WAS IT ALL *WORTH* IT, SIR? ALL THOSE DEAD AND BURIED...AND WHAT DID YOU *ACCOMPLISH,* EXACTLY? DID YOU GET TO WORK THE PROBLEM OUT TO YOUR SATISFACTION?
I UNDERSTAND YOU'RE JUST VOICING THE FRUSTRATION OF OTHERS, SALLY. BUT I DID WHAT I THOUGHT WAS *RIGHT.*
WELL, BULLY FOR YOU. YOU'VE FINALLY REALIZED AMERICA WANTS A REGISTRATION ACT. BUT THE BIG QUESTION ON EVERYONE'S LIPS IS, WHY COULDN'T YOU HAVE REALIZED THAT A FEW *WEEKS* AGO?
YOUR PROBLEM IS THAT YOU'RE FIGHTING FOR AN *IDEAL*--IT'S ALL YOU KNOW HOW TO DO. AMERICA IS NO LONGER ABOUT MOM AND APPLE PIE...IT'S ABOUT HIGH CHOLESTEROL AND PARIS HILTON AND SCHEMING YOUR WAY TO THE TOP.
THE COUNTRY *I* LOVE TREATS ITS CELEBRITIES LIKE ROYALTY AND ITS TEACHERS LIKE DIRT. BUT AT LEAST I WALK ITS STREETS EVERY DAY. AT LEAST I KNOW WHAT IT IS.
YOU'VE *BROKEN* THAT COUNTRY, CAPTAIN AMERICA.
WHAT ARE YOU GONNA DO TO *FIX* IT?

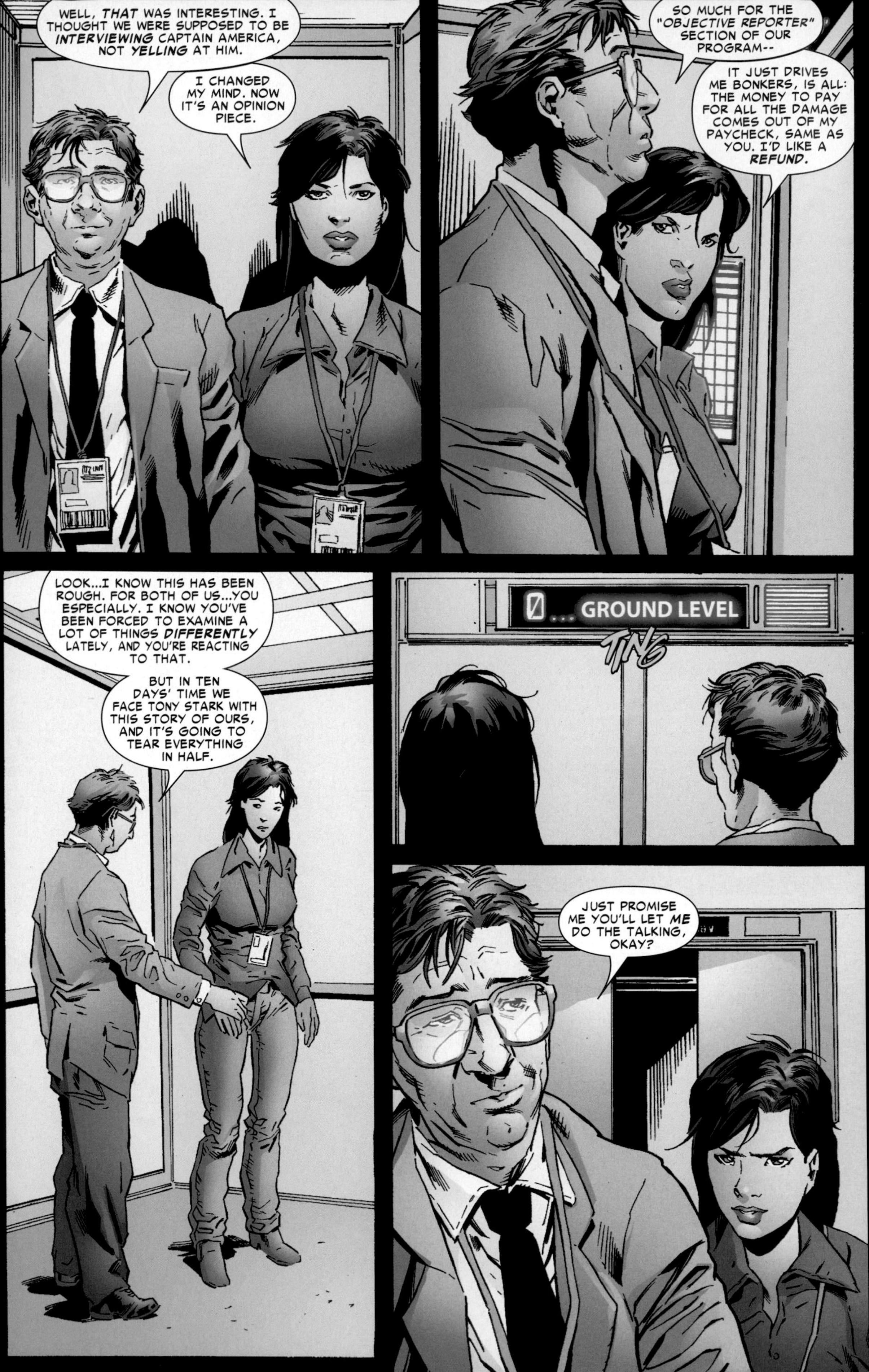
WELL, *THAT* WAS INTERESTING. I THOUGHT WE WERE SUPPOSED TO BE *INTERVIEWING* CAPTAIN AMERICA, NOT *YELLING* AT HIM.
I CHANGED MY MIND. NOW IT'S AN OPINION PIECE.
SO MUCH FOR THE "*OBJECTIVE REPORTER*" SECTION OF OUR PROGRAM--
IT JUST DRIVES ME BONKERS, IS ALL: THE MONEY TO PAY FOR ALL THE DAMAGE COMES OUT OF MY PAYCHECK, SAME AS YOU. I'D LIKE A *REFUND*.
LOOK...I KNOW THIS HAS BEEN ROUGH. FOR BOTH OF US...YOU ESPECIALLY. I KNOW YOU'VE BEEN FORCED TO EXAMINE A LOT OF THINGS *DIFFERENTLY* LATELY, AND YOU'RE REACTING TO THAT.
BUT IN TEN DAYS' TIME WE FACE TONY STARK WITH THIS STORY OF OURS, AND IT'S GOING TO TEAR EVERYTHING IN HALF.
0 ... GROUND LEVEL
TING
JUST PROMISE ME YOU'LL LET *ME* DO THE TALKING, OKAY?

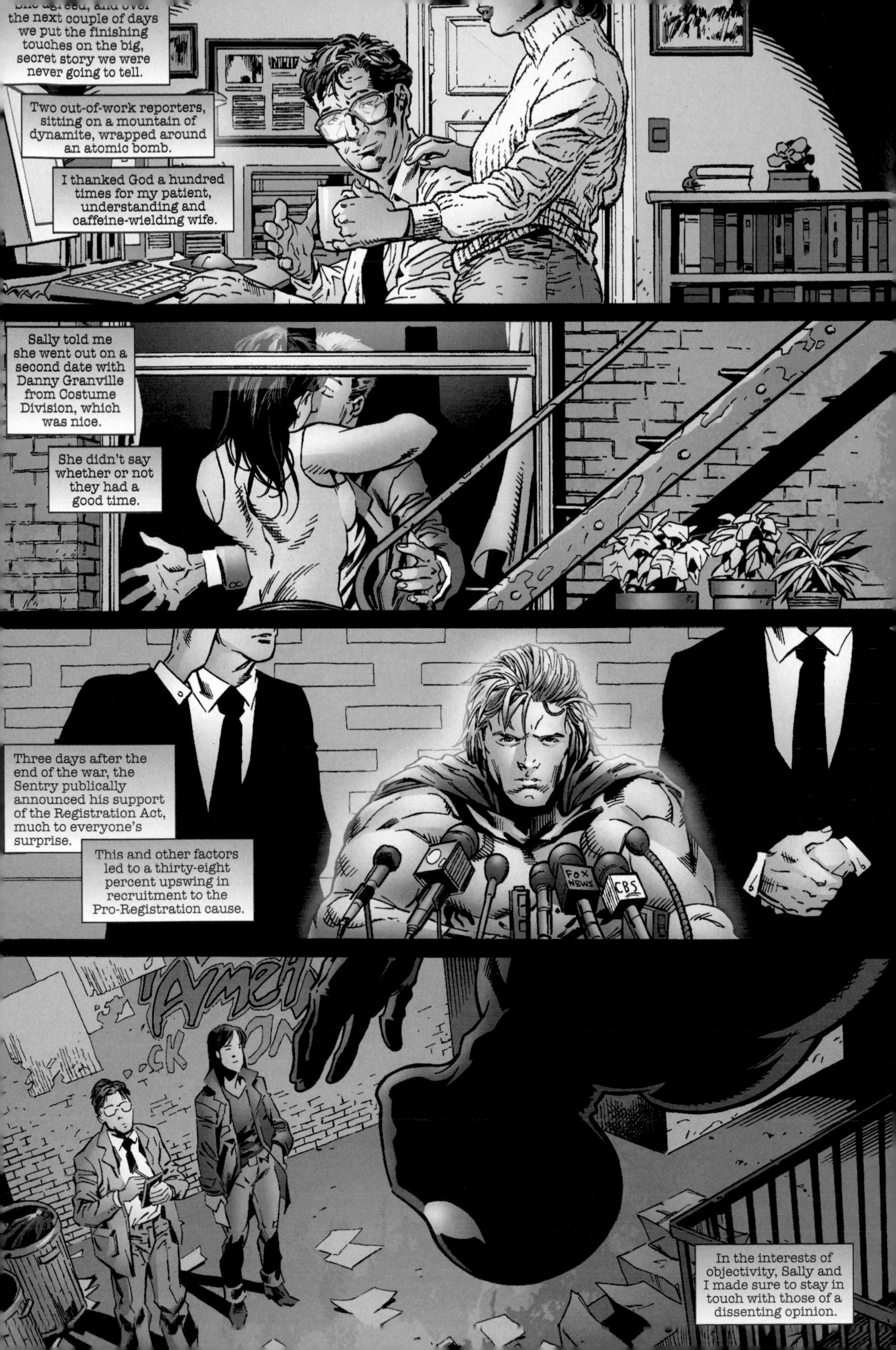

She agreed, and over the next couple of days we put the finishing touches on the big, secret story we were never going to tell.
Two out-of-work reporters, sitting on a mountain of dynamite, wrapped around an atomic bomb.
I thanked God a hundred times for my patient, understanding and caffeine-wielding wife.
Sally told me she went out on a second date with Danny Granville from Costume Division, which was nice.
She didn't say whether or not they had a good time.
Three days after the end of the war, the Sentry publically announced his support of the Registration Act, much to everyone's surprise.
This and other factors led to a thirty-eight percent upswing in recruitment to the Pro-Registration cause.
FOX NEWS
CBS
In the interests of objectivity, Sally and I made sure to stay in touch with those of a dissenting opinion.

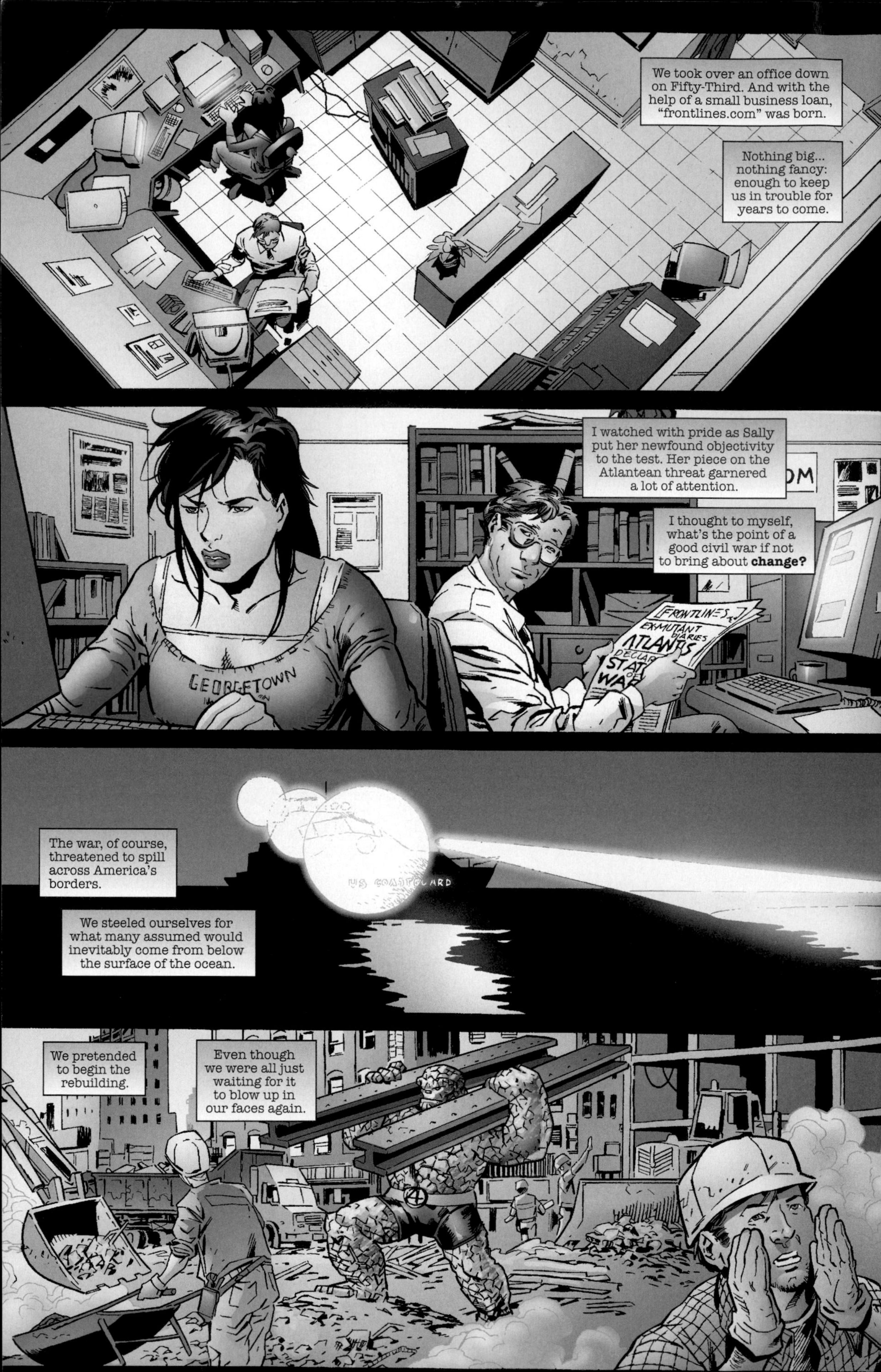
We took over an office down on Fifty-Third. And with the help of a small business loan, "frontlines.com" was born.
Nothing big... nothing fancy: enough to keep us in trouble for years to come.
I watched with pride as Sally put her newfound objectivity to the test. Her piece on the Atlantean threat garnered a lot of attention.
I thought to myself, what's the point of a good civil war if not to bring about **change?**
GEORGETOWN
FRONTLINES
EX-MUTANT DIARIES
ATLANTIS
STAT
WAR
The war, of course, threatened to spill across America's borders.
US COASTGUARD
We steeled ourselves for what many assumed would inevitably come from below the surface of the ocean.
We pretended to begin the rebuilding.
Even though we were all just waiting for it to blow up in our faces again.

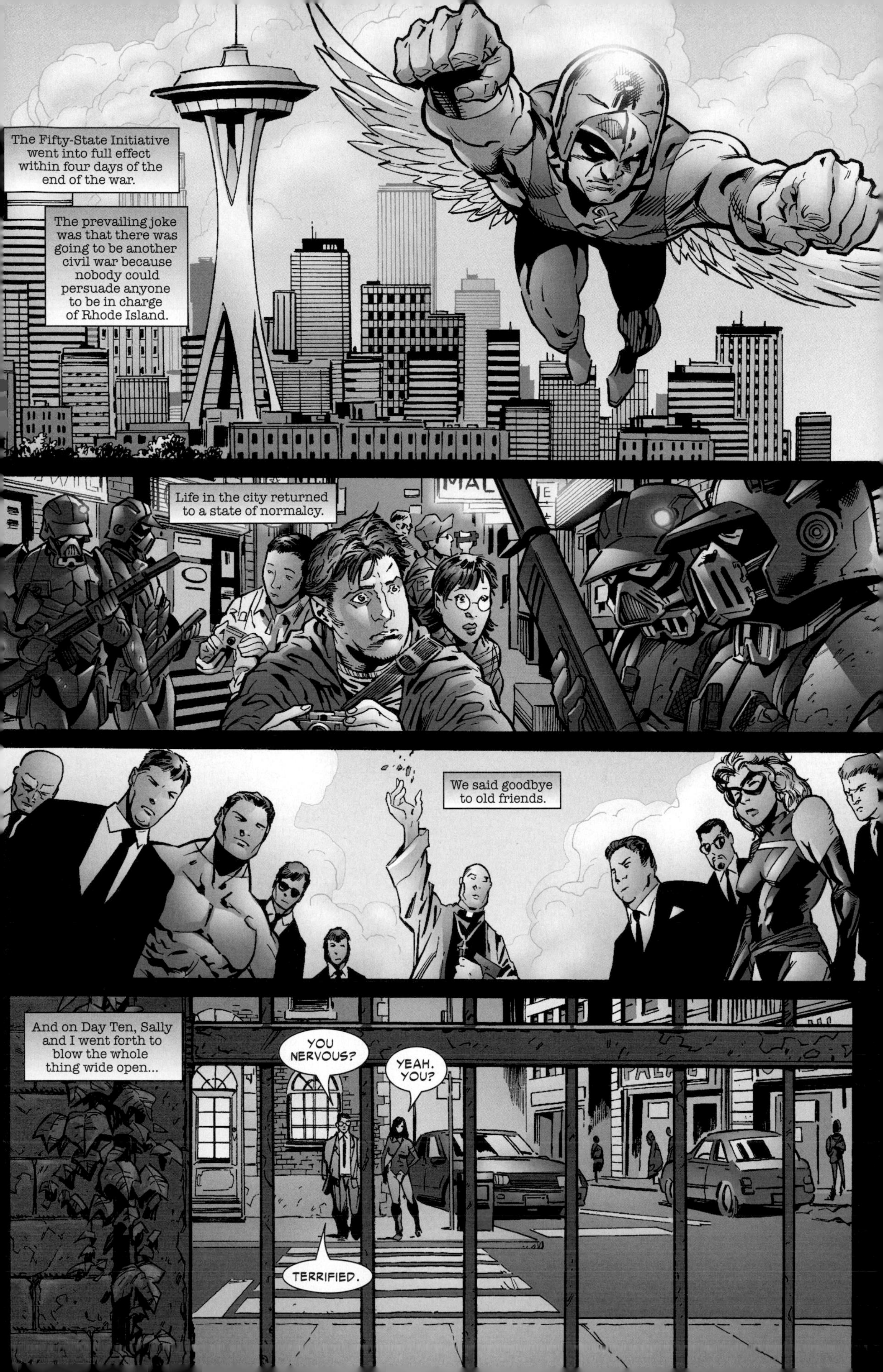
The Fifty-State Initiative went into full effect within four days of the end of the war.
The prevailing joke was that there was going to be another civil war because nobody could persuade anyone to be in charge of Rhode Island.
Life in the city returned to a state of normalcy.
We said goodbye to old friends.
And on Day Ten, Sally and I went forth to blow the whole thing wide open...
YOU NERVOUS?
YEAH. YOU?
TERRIFIED.

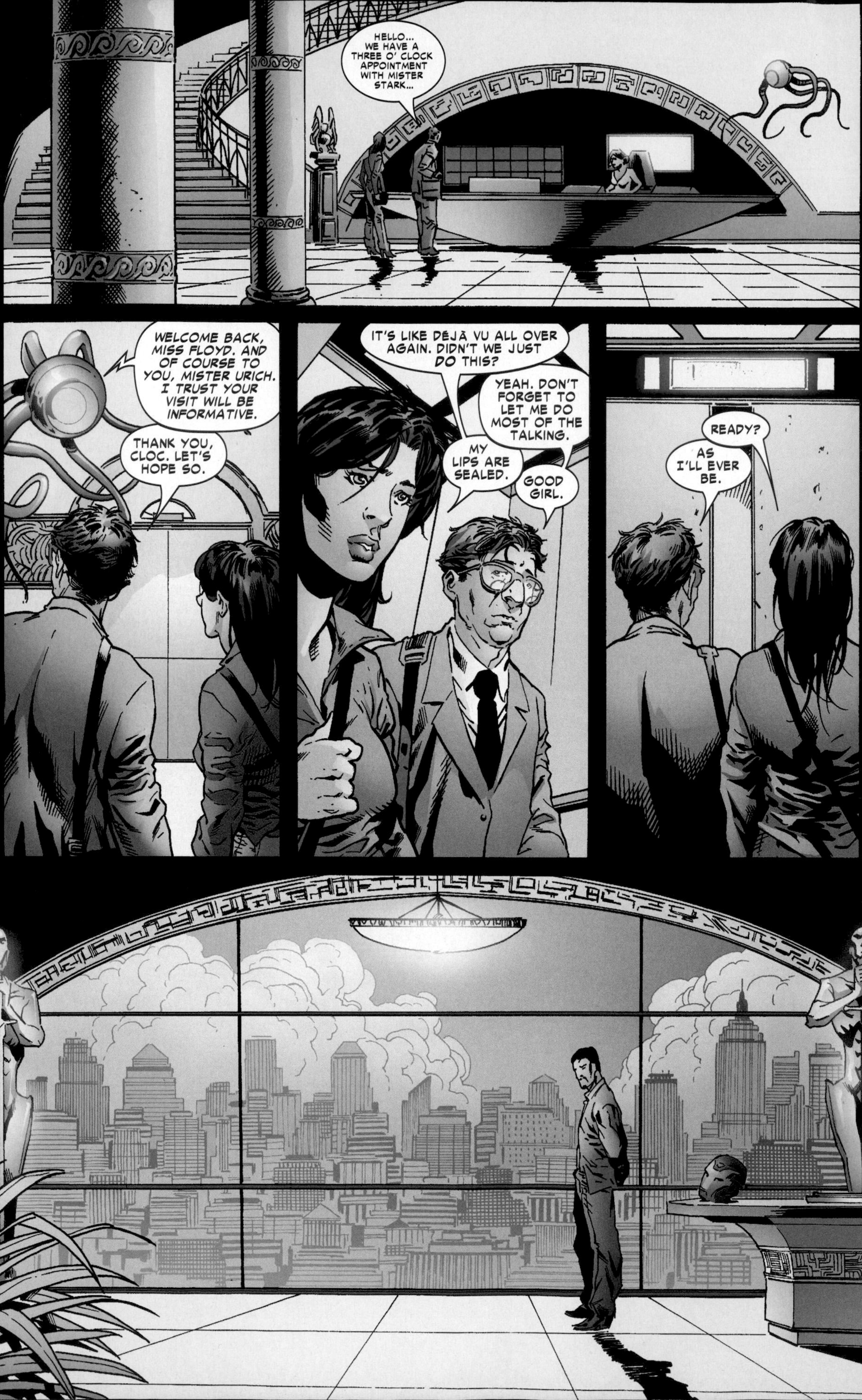
HELLO... WE HAVE A THREE O' CLOCK APPOINTMENT WITH MISTER STARK...
WELCOME BACK, MISS FLOYD. AND OF COURSE TO YOU, MISTER URICH. I TRUST YOUR VISIT WILL BE INFORMATIVE.
THANK YOU, CLOC. LET'S HOPE SO.
IT'S LIKE DÉJÀ VU ALL OVER AGAIN. DIDN'T WE JUST DO THIS?
YEAH. DON'T FORGET TO LET ME DO MOST OF THE TALKING.
MY LIPS ARE SEALED.
GOOD GIRL.
READY?
AS I'LL EVER BE.

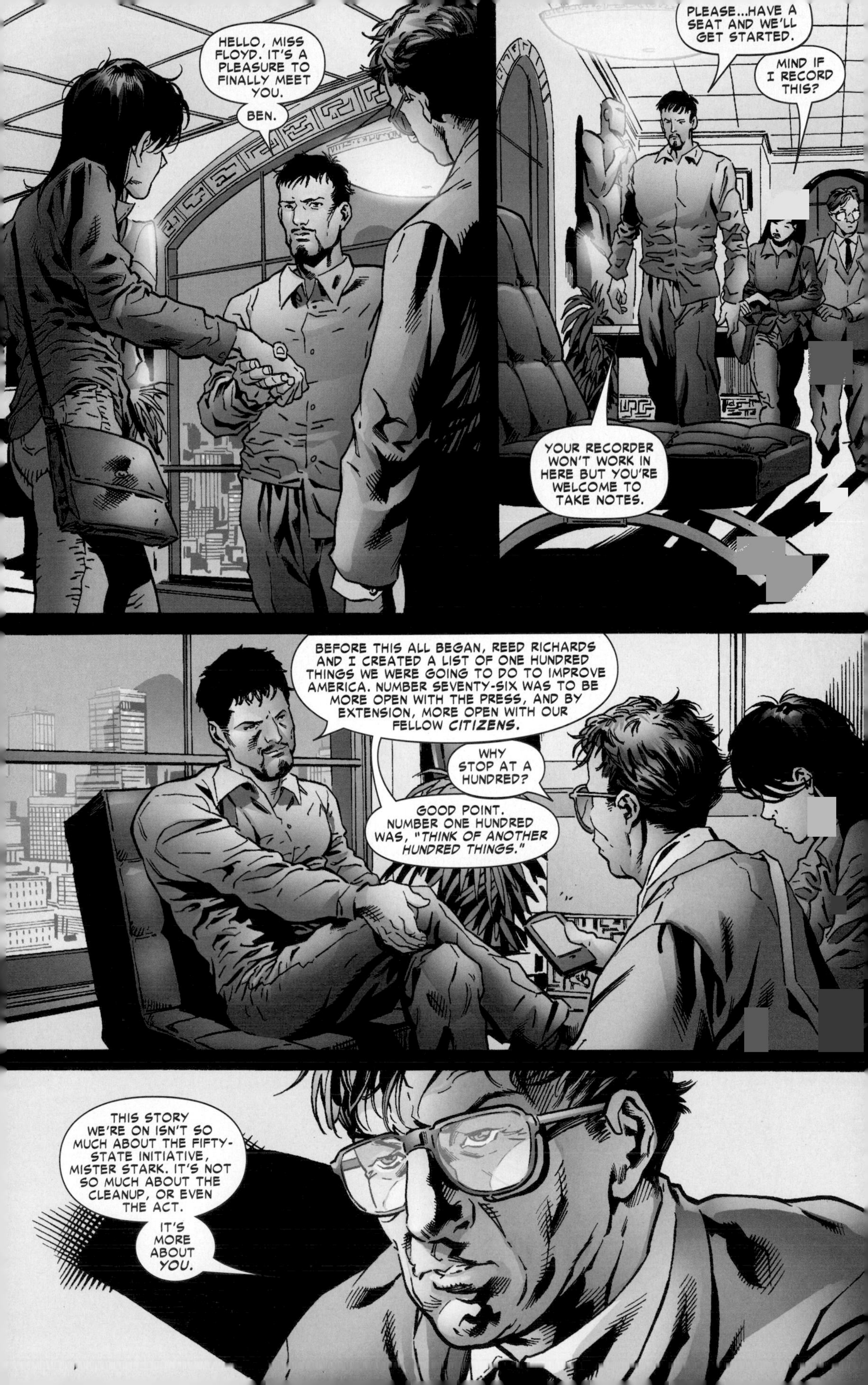
HELLO, MISS FLOYD. IT'S A PLEASURE TO FINALLY MEET YOU.
BEN.
PLEASE...HAVE A SEAT AND WE'LL GET STARTED.
MIND IF I RECORD THIS?
YOUR RECORDER WON'T WORK IN HERE BUT YOU'RE WELCOME TO TAKE NOTES.
BEFORE THIS ALL BEGAN, REED RICHARDS AND I CREATED A LIST OF ONE HUNDRED THINGS WE WERE GOING TO DO TO IMPROVE AMERICA. NUMBER SEVENTY-SIX WAS TO BE MORE OPEN WITH THE PRESS, AND BY EXTENSION, MORE OPEN WITH OUR FELLOW CITIZENS.
WHY STOP AT A HUNDRED?
GOOD POINT. NUMBER ONE HUNDRED WAS, "THINK OF ANOTHER HUNDRED THINGS."
THIS STORY WE'RE ON ISN'T SO MUCH ABOUT THE FIFTY-STATE INITIATIVE, MISTER STARK. IT'S NOT SO MUCH ABOUT THE CLEANUP, OR EVEN THE ACT.
IT'S MORE ABOUT YOU.

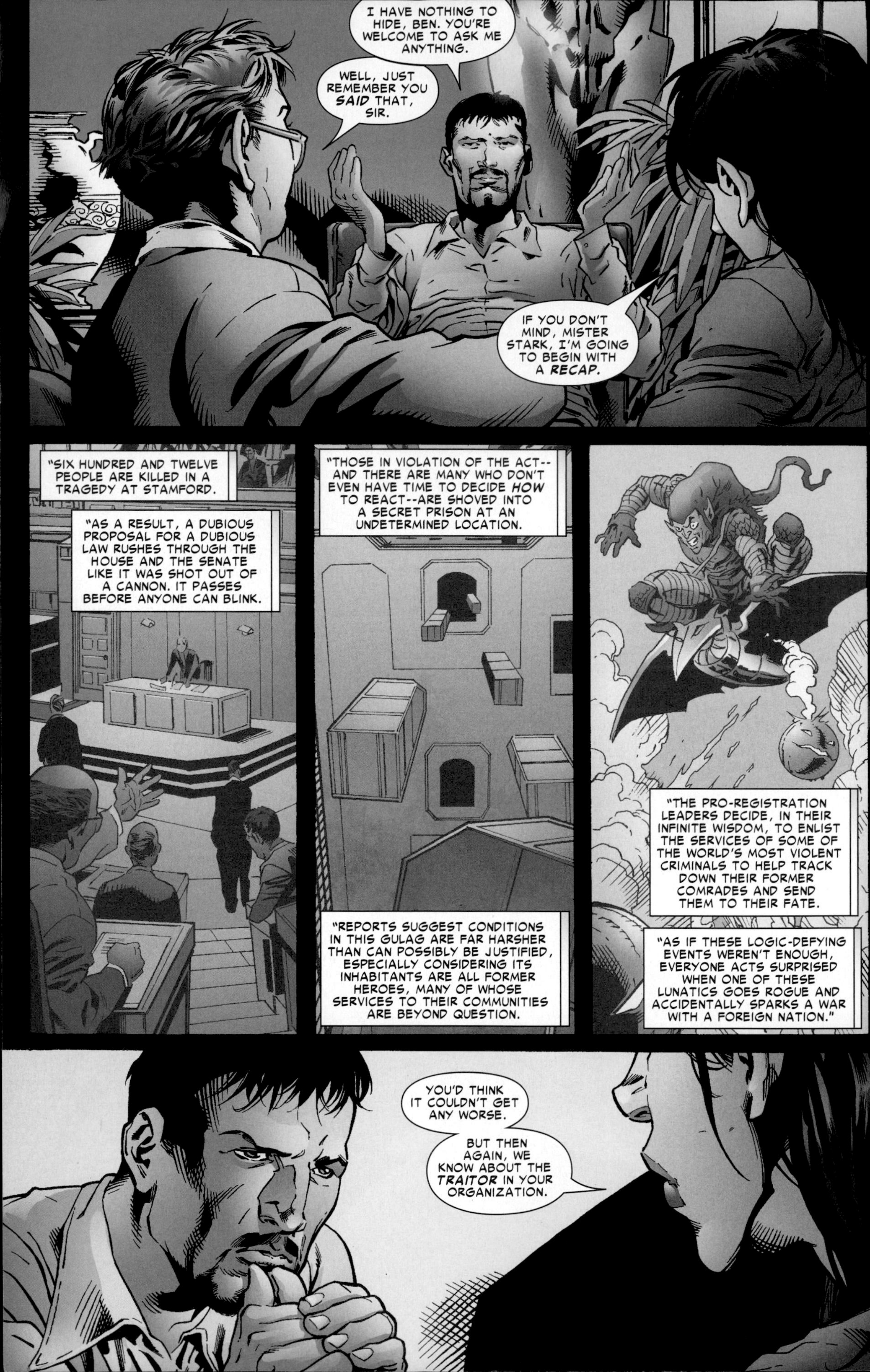
I HAVE NOTHING TO HIDE, BEN. YOU'RE WELCOME TO ASK ME ANYTHING.
WELL, JUST REMEMBER YOU SAID THAT, SIR.
IF YOU DON'T MIND, MISTER STARK, I'M GOING TO BEGIN WITH A RECAP.
"SIX HUNDRED AND TWELVE PEOPLE ARE KILLED IN A TRAGEDY AT STAMFORD.
"AS A RESULT, A DUBIOUS PROPOSAL FOR A DUBIOUS LAW RUSHES THROUGH THE HOUSE AND THE SENATE LIKE IT WAS SHOT OUT OF A CANNON. IT PASSES BEFORE ANYONE CAN BLINK.
"THOSE IN VIOLATION OF THE ACT--AND THERE ARE MANY WHO DON'T EVEN HAVE TIME TO DECIDE HOW TO REACT--ARE SHOVED INTO A SECRET PRISON AT AN UNDETERMINED LOCATION.
"REPORTS SUGGEST CONDITIONS IN THIS GULAG ARE FAR HARSHER THAN CAN POSSIBLY BE JUSTIFIED, ESPECIALLY CONSIDERING ITS INHABITANTS ARE ALL FORMER HEROES, MANY OF WHOSE SERVICES TO THEIR COMMUNITIES ARE BEYOND QUESTION.
"THE PRO-REGISTRATION LEADERS DECIDE, IN THEIR INFINITE WISDOM, TO ENLIST THE SERVICES OF SOME OF THE WORLD'S MOST VIOLENT CRIMINALS TO HELP TRACK DOWN THEIR FORMER COMRADES AND SEND THEM TO THEIR FATE.
"AS IF THESE LOGIC-DEFYING EVENTS WEREN'T ENOUGH, EVERYONE ACTS SURPRISED WHEN ONE OF THESE LUNATICS GOES ROGUE AND ACCIDENTALLY SPARKS A WAR WITH A FOREIGN NATION."
YOU'D THINK IT COULDN'T GET ANY WORSE.
BUT THEN AGAIN, WE KNOW ABOUT THE TRAITOR IN YOUR ORGANIZATION.

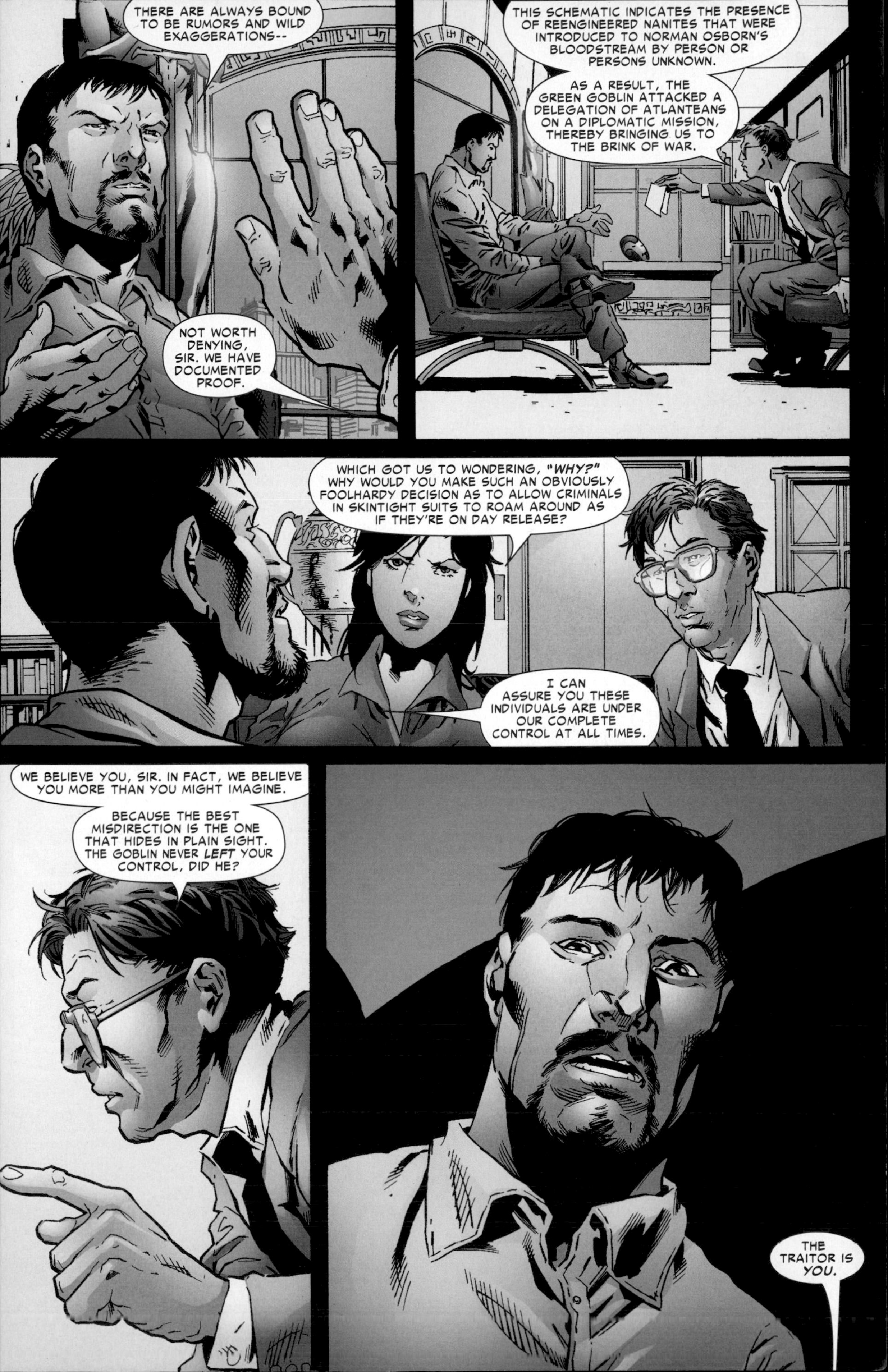
THERE ARE ALWAYS BOUND TO BE RUMORS AND WILD EXAGGERATIONS--
NOT WORTH DENYING, SIR. WE HAVE DOCUMENTED PROOF.
THIS SCHEMATIC INDICATES THE PRESENCE OF REENGINEERED NANITES THAT WERE INTRODUCED TO NORMAN OSBORN'S BLOODSTREAM BY PERSON OR PERSONS UNKNOWN.
AS A RESULT, THE GREEN GOBLIN ATTACKED A DELEGATION OF ATLANTEANS ON A DIPLOMATIC MISSION, THEREBY BRINGING US TO THE BRINK OF WAR.
WHICH GOT US TO WONDERING, "WHY?" WHY WOULD YOU MAKE SUCH AN OBVIOUSLY FOOLHARDY DECISION AS TO ALLOW CRIMINALS IN SKINTIGHT SUITS TO ROAM AROUND AS IF THEY'RE ON DAY RELEASE?
I CAN ASSURE YOU THESE INDIVIDUALS ARE UNDER OUR COMPLETE CONTROL AT ALL TIMES.
WE BELIEVE YOU, SIR. IN FACT, WE BELIEVE YOU MORE THAN YOU MIGHT IMAGINE.
BECAUSE THE BEST MISDIRECTION IS THE ONE THAT HIDES IN PLAIN SIGHT. THE GOBLIN NEVER LEFT YOUR CONTROL, DID HE?
THE TRAITOR IS YOU.

THAT'S PREPOSTEROUS, BEN. YOU'RE GRASPING AT STRAWS--

NOT TRUE, SIR. A COUPLE OF ROUTINE BACKGROUND CHECKS REVEALED YOUR KNOWLEDGE OF CERTAIN EVENTS--SUCH AS OSBORN'S ATTACK ON THE ATLANTEAN DELEGATION--WAS USED TO MANIPULATE THE STOCK MARKET TO THE TUNE OF OVER NINETY MILLION DOLLARS.

BUT NOW HERE'S WHERE IT GETS *INTERESTING*: FURTHER INVESTIGATION REVEALED THE MONEY WAS REROUTED THROUGH A SWISS BANK ACCOUNT AND PLACED INTO A NEW CHARITABLE ORGANIZATION PROVIDING PENSIONS FOR FIREFIGHTERS, POLICE--AND NOW, REGISTERED HEROES AND THEIR FAMILIES.

WE KEPT THINKING TO OURSELVES, "*WHY WOULD HE INTENTIONALLY TRY TO MAKE IT LOOK THIS BAD?*" WHAT WOULD WE DO IF WE WERE EVER IN THE UNENVIABLE POSITION OF HAVING TO PERSUADE A BUNCH OF HIGH-POWERED PEOPLE TO REGISTER THEIR IDENTITIES?

I KNOW WHAT *I'D* DO: I'D BUILD A BIG, NASTY PRISON IN AN UNDISCLOSED LOCATION THAT'D REALLY PUT A SCARE INTO THE UNREGISTERED HEROES. MOST LIKELY, THEY'D WONDER HOW COME WE NEVER MADE ANYTHING LIKE IT FOR THE VILLAINS.

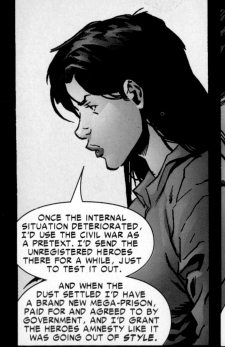

ONCE THE INTERNAL SITUATION DETERIORATED, I'D USE THE CIVIL WAR AS A PRETEXT. I'D SEND THE UNREGISTERED HEROES THERE FOR A WHILE, JUST TO TEST IT OUT.

AND WHEN THE DUST SETTLED I'D HAVE A BRAND NEW MEGA-PRISON, PAID FOR AND AGREED TO BY GOVERNMENT, AND I'D GRANT THE HEROES AMNESTY LIKE IT WAS GOING OUT OF *STYLE*.

IT'S A VERY EXOTIC STORY, BUT IT DOESN'T EXACTLY MAKE SENSE.

WE THOUGHT THAT TOO, SIR. WHY WOULD ANYONE BE CRAZY ENOUGH TO COERCE THE GREEN GOBLIN INTO ATTACKING A FOREIGN DELEGATION ON A DIPLOMATIC MISSION? WHY PUSH US TO THE BRINK OF YET ANOTHER WAR?

UNLESS YOU WERE SO SMART THAT YOU'D ALREADY WEIGHED THE PROS AND CONS, AND CALCULATED WHAT THE *OUTCOME* WAS GOING TO BE?

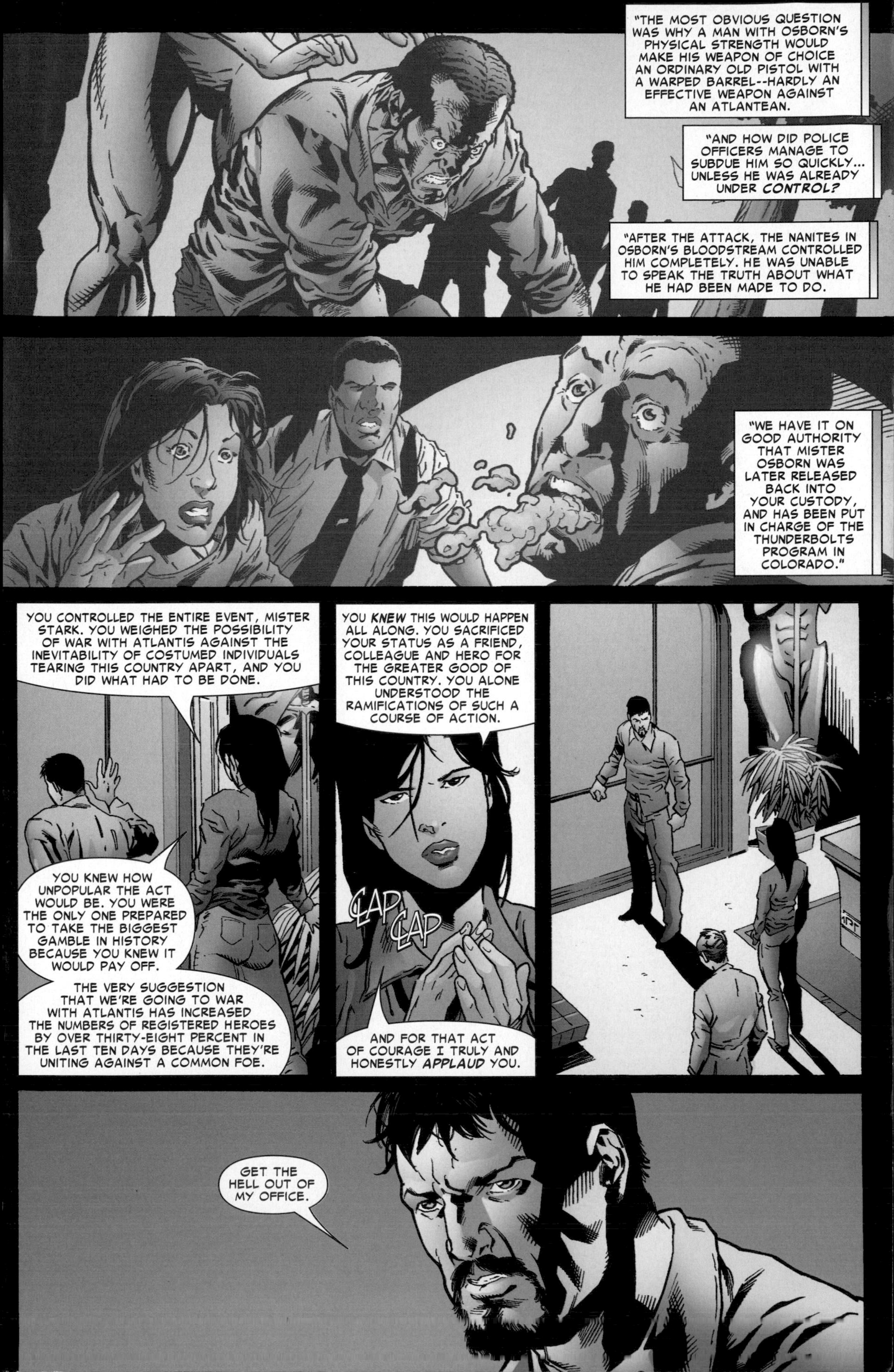
"THE MOST OBVIOUS QUESTION WAS WHY A MAN WITH OSBORN'S PHYSICAL STRENGTH WOULD MAKE HIS WEAPON OF CHOICE AN ORDINARY OLD PISTOL WITH A WARPED BARREL--HARDLY AN EFFECTIVE WEAPON AGAINST AN ATLANTEAN.
"AND HOW DID POLICE OFFICERS MANAGE TO SUBDUE HIM SO QUICKLY... UNLESS HE WAS ALREADY UNDER *CONTROL?*
"AFTER THE ATTACK, THE NANITES IN OSBORN'S BLOODSTREAM CONTROLLED HIM COMPLETELY. HE WAS UNABLE TO SPEAK THE TRUTH ABOUT WHAT HE HAD BEEN MADE TO DO.
"WE HAVE IT ON GOOD AUTHORITY THAT MISTER OSBORN WAS LATER RELEASED BACK INTO YOUR CUSTODY, AND HAS BEEN PUT IN CHARGE OF THE THUNDERBOLTS PROGRAM IN COLORADO."
YOU CONTROLLED THE ENTIRE EVENT, MISTER STARK. YOU WEIGHED THE POSSIBILITY OF WAR WITH ATLANTIS AGAINST THE INEVITABILITY OF COSTUMED INDIVIDUALS TEARING THIS COUNTRY APART, AND YOU DID WHAT HAD TO BE DONE.
YOU KNEW HOW UNPOPULAR THE ACT WOULD BE. YOU WERE THE ONLY ONE PREPARED TO TAKE THE BIGGEST GAMBLE IN HISTORY BECAUSE YOU KNEW IT WOULD PAY OFF.
THE VERY SUGGESTION THAT WE'RE GOING TO WAR WITH ATLANTIS HAS INCREASED THE NUMBERS OF REGISTERED HEROES BY OVER THIRTY-EIGHT PERCENT IN THE LAST TEN DAYS BECAUSE THEY'RE UNITING AGAINST A COMMON FOE.
YOU *KNEW* THIS WOULD HAPPEN ALL ALONG. YOU SACRIFICED YOUR STATUS AS A FRIEND, COLLEAGUE AND HERO FOR THE GREATER GOOD OF THIS COUNTRY. YOU ALONE UNDERSTOOD THE RAMIFICATIONS OF SUCH A COURSE OF ACTION.
CLAP CLAP
AND FOR THAT ACT OF COURAGE I TRULY AND HONESTLY *APPLAUD* YOU.
GET THE HELL OUT OF MY OFFICE.

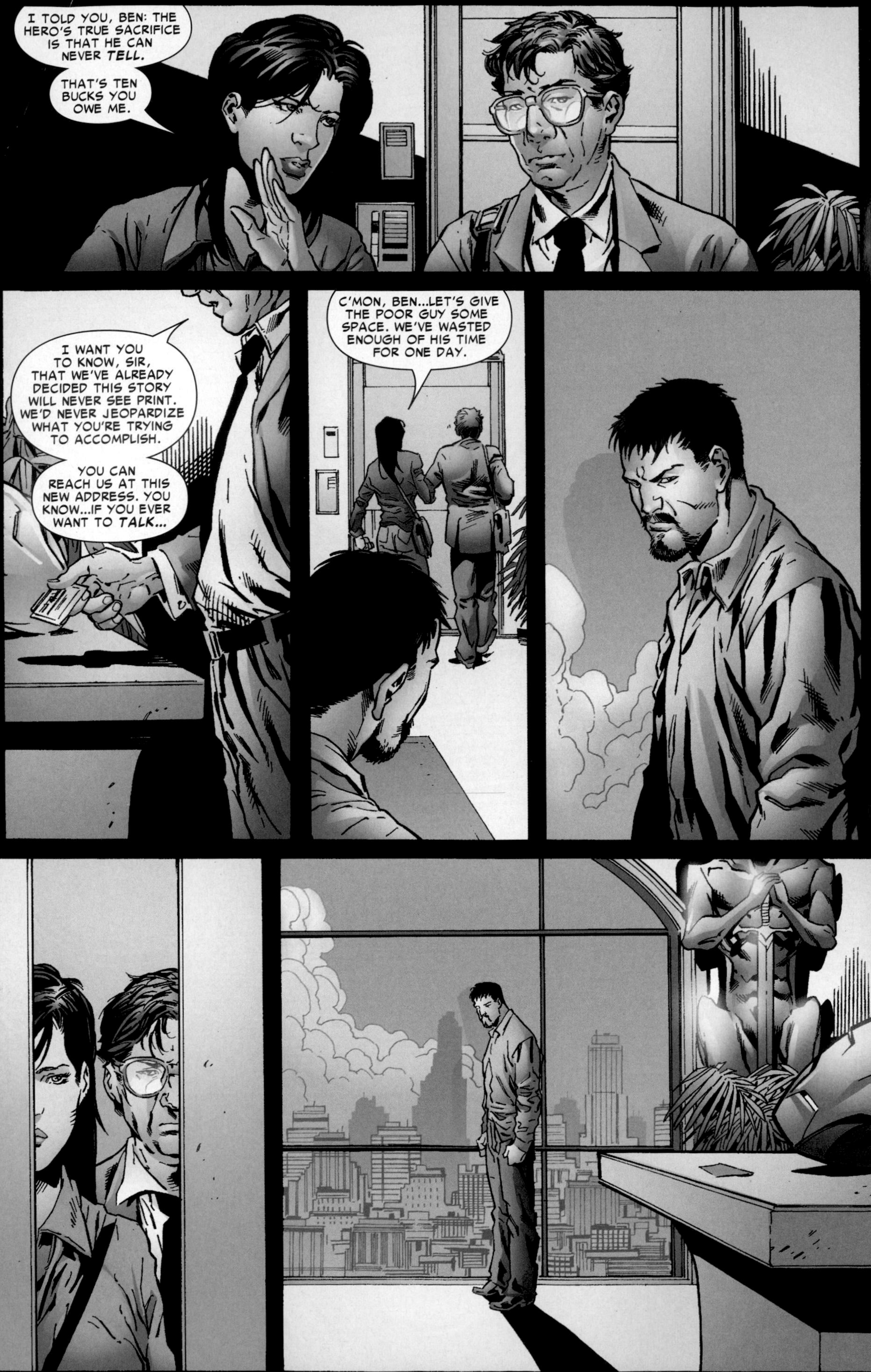
I TOLD YOU, BEN: THE HERO'S TRUE SACRIFICE IS THAT HE CAN NEVER TELL.
THAT'S TEN BUCKS YOU OWE ME.
I WANT YOU TO KNOW, SIR, THAT WE'VE ALREADY DECIDED THIS STORY WILL NEVER SEE PRINT. WE'D NEVER JEOPARDIZE WHAT YOU'RE TRYING TO ACCOMPLISH.
YOU CAN REACH US AT THIS NEW ADDRESS. YOU KNOW...IF YOU EVER WANT TO TALK...
C'MON, BEN...LET'S GIVE THE POOR GUY SOME SPACE. WE'VE WASTED ENOUGH OF HIS TIME FOR ONE DAY.

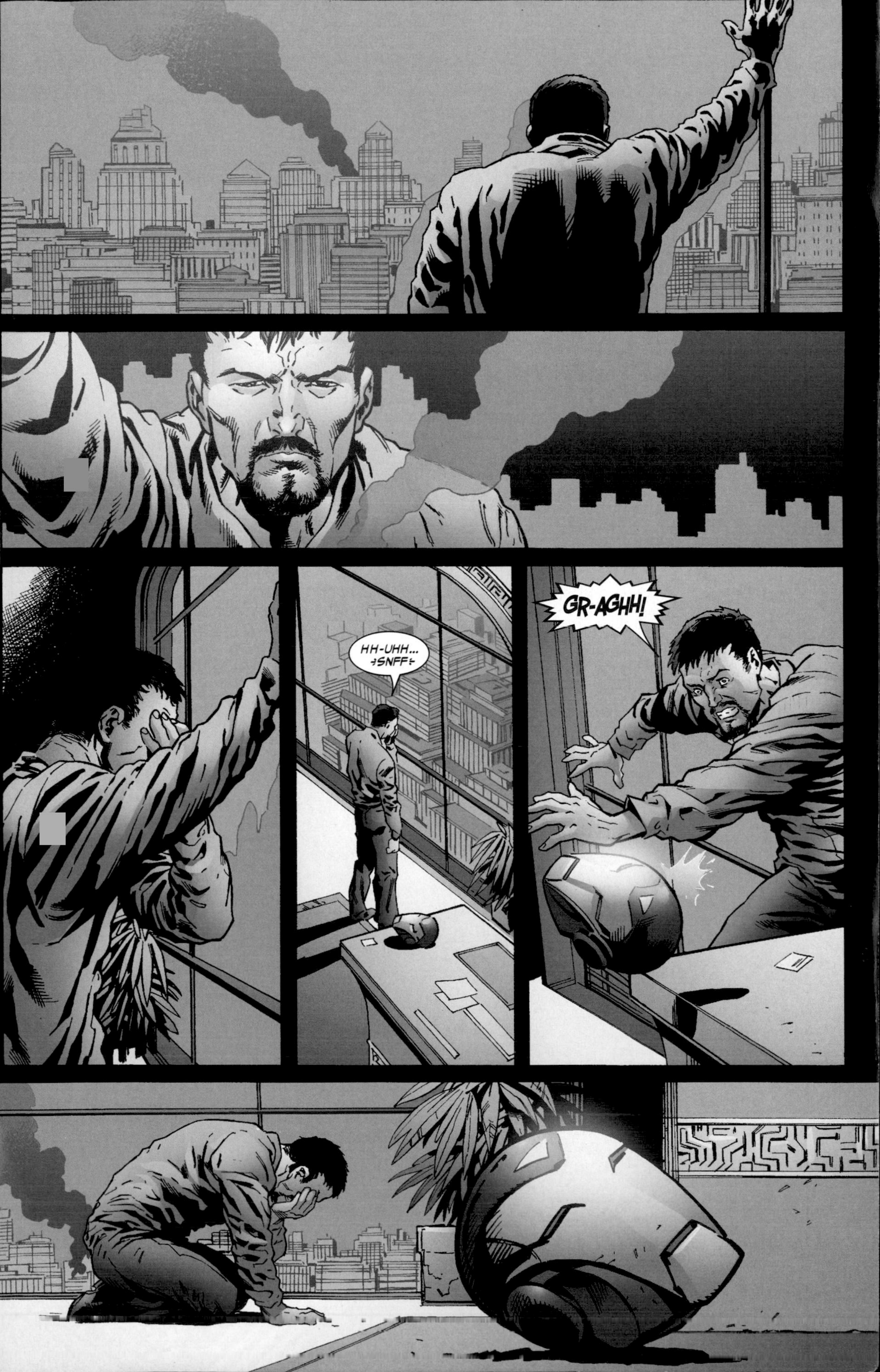
HH-UHH... ✧SNFF✧
GR-AGHH!

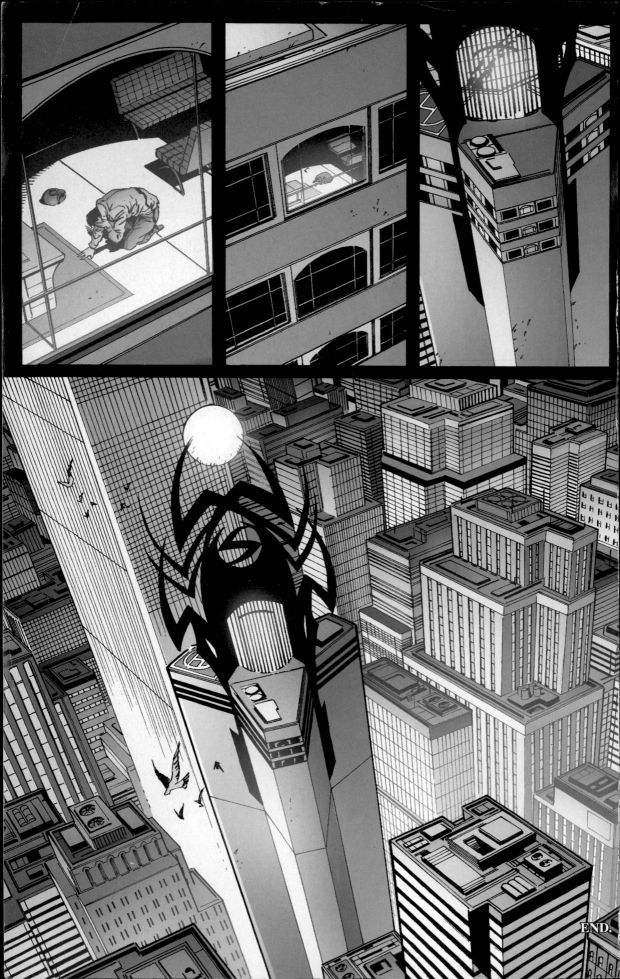

END.